"This interdisciplinary volume interrogates Western complicity in the ongoing genocide in Gaza—complicity manifested in political institutions, media discourse, and Christian theology. What does it mean to be Christian in the wake of Gaza's devastation and Israel's colonization of Palestinian land and people? Grappling with systemic violence and settler colonialism, this book models Christian responsibility, prophetic witness, and a hunger for justice in an age of global indifference."

—**Mitri Raheb**
President, Dar al-Kalima University

"This timely book confronts readers with truths that are suppressed by the narrative of unconditional support for Israel. It contests the simplistic thinking that casts the conflict as a war between good and evil. It sets the devastation of Gaza within historical and contemporary contexts. It humanizes the Palestinian people and presents unflinching accounts of their suffering. It exposes the twisted use of Christian Scripture and theology that justifies the massive violence Israel inflicts. Each essay is written with acuity and compassion. Together, the writers call us to reject Christian complicity with Israel's campaign of bombing, starvation, and destruction and to pursue a just peace."

—**L. Daniel Hawk**
Professor of Old Testament and Hebrew, Ashland Theological Seminary, and author of *Undoing Manifest Destiny: Settler America, Christian Colonists, and the Pursuit of Justice* (2026)

"At once disturbing and eye-opening, *Being Christian After the Desolation of Gaza* unpacks the deadly error of uncritical Christian support for Israel's war on Gaza and destruction of the Palestinian people. Thankfully, it offers us not just critique but also a vision for the future. It is one of the most important books for Christians of every tradition to read at this time."

—**Michael J. Gorman**
Raymond E. Brown Professor of Biblical and Theological Studies,
St. Mary's Seminary and University

"I despair as Christian Zionists continue to dehumanize Palestinians and cheer on Gaza's obliteration. Should we identify any longer with the 'Christian' brand? Whether these essays serve as prophetic indictment or final epitaph for the Christian faith remains to be seen. But I am grateful for this text and will be assigning it to prospective peacebuilders."

—Brad Jersak
Principal, St. Stephen's University

"To be Christian does not entail the embrace of an aberrant eschatology used to justify war crimes; to be Christian is to walk this world in a deliberate attempt to imitate the Prince of Peace. And thus *Being Christian After the Desolation of Gaza* could not be more timely."

—Brian Zahnd
Pastor of Word of Life Church, St. Joseph, Missouri,
and author of *A Farewell To Mars*

"A bold, clear-eyed, and timely intervention at a moment of catastrophe for the Palestinian people. Exploring the theological props and political narratives that uphold genocide, ethnic cleansing, and occupation, the authors of *Being Christian After the Desolation of Gaza* convict the church to declare 'no more.'"

—Melissa Florer-Bixler
Pastor of Raleigh Mennonite Church, North Carolina,
and author of *How to Have an Enemy: Righteous Anger and the Work of Peace*

"*Being Christian After the Desolation of Gaza* gathers sixteen courageous Christian voices that expose Israel's overwhelming violence against Palestinians and trace today's conflict to seventy-five years of settler-colonial injustice, echoing Indigenous North American histories. I urge Jesus-followers to respond with open hearts and courageous action to this clarion call for a just and non-violent peace."

—Terry M. Wildman
Lead Translator and Project Manager for the *First Nations Version New Testament and Psalms and Proverbs*

"This book challenges evangelical Christians' relentless support for the state of Israel's war against Palestinians. These pages testify to God's love for all, while protesting the terror of bombs and tanks, and the weaponization of food and water. In these chapters we hear God's call for peace and mercy."

—Isaac Villegas

Author of *Migrant God: A Christian Vision for Immigrant Justice*

"Never has a book been so devastating, so painful, and so needed. Packed with Christian prophets, exemplifying the courage and conviction of Jeremiah, this book challenges any would-be-follower of Jesus with a moral reckoning that seeks to rescue a people in crisis, bring needed peace to a region, and save our warmongering, complicit souls."

—Jon Lemmond

Lead Pastor, Trinity Covenant Church, Salem, Oregon

"Through personal stories and analysis of the Bible and popular American Christian discourse, these authors powerfully demonstrate that once again how Western Christians interpret the Bible and who we regard as not fully human is leading to death and destruction. They join the Christian leaders of the past in pointing the way to conviction, repentance, and change."

—Heather Keaney

Associate Professor, Department of History, Westmont College

"Concerned for all peoples of the land, committed to Christ-centered ethics, free of Christian Zionist distortion, rooted in the authors' lived experience in Israel/Palestine, this book critiques Israel's morally disastrous devastation of Gaza since October 7 but doesn't minimize Hamas's morally disastrous attacks on October 7."

—David Gushee

Distinguished University Professor of Christian Ethics, Mercer University

Being Christian
After the Desolation of Gaza

Being Christian
After the Desolation of Gaza

Edited by
BRUCE N. FISK
and J. ROSS WAGNER

CASCADE *Books* · Eugene, Oregon

BEING CHRISTIAN AFTER THE DESOLATION OF GAZA

Copyright © 2025 Wipf and Stock Publishers. All rights reserved. Except for brief quotations in critical publications or reviews, no part of this book may be reproduced in any manner without prior written permission from the publisher. Write: Permissions, Wipf and Stock Publishers, 199 W. 8th Ave., Suite 3, Eugene, OR 97401.

Cascade Books
An Imprint of Wipf and Stock Publishers
199 W. 8th Ave., Suite 3
Eugene, OR 97401

www.wipfandstock.com

PAPERBACK ISBN: 979-8-3852-5485-9
HARDCOVER ISBN: 979-8-3852-5486-6
EBOOK ISBN: 979-8-3852-5487-3

Cataloguing-in-Publication data:

Names: Fisk, Bruce N., editor | Wagner, J. Ross, editor.

Title: Being Christian after the desolation of Gaza / edited by Bruce N. Fisk and J. Ross Wagner.

Description: Eugene, OR : Cascade Books, 2025 | Includes bibliographical references.

Identifiers: ISBN 979-8-3852-5485-9 (paperback) | ISBN 979-8-3852-5486-6 (hardcover) | ISBN 979-8-3852-5487-3 (ebook)

Subjects: LCSH: Palestine—In Christianity. | Arab-Israeli conflict—Religious aspects—Christianity. | Arab-Israeli conflict—History—21st century. | Israel-Hamas War, 2023–. | Israel—Foreign relations—Palestine. | Race relations—Religious aspects—Christianity.

Classification: BT93.8 .B45 2025 (paperback) | BT93.8 (ebook)

VERSION NUMBER 08/07/25

All author royalties from the sale of this book will support the heroic labors of Médecins Sans Frontières (Doctors Without Borders).

Readers wishing to make their own donations to MSF may do so here: https://www.msf.org/donate.

Contents

Permissions | vii
Contributors | ix
A Poem, a Painting, and a Psalm | xi

Introduction—The Wrong Sort of Christians | 1
—Bruce N. Fisk

PART I—War on the Land: Witnessing Israel's Desolation of Gaza

Chapter One—Gaza Undone | 23
—Bruce N. Fisk

Chapter Two—Israel's Christian Armada Sets Sail | 49
—Bruce N. Fisk

Chapter Three—Bombing in the Name of the Gospel | 88
—Gary M. Burge

Chapter Four—Prisoner Abuse and Evangelical Indifference | 100
—David M. Crump

Chapter Five—Hamas and Violence: Ideology, Militarism, and the Quest for Liberation | 116
—Daniel Bannoura

Chapter Six—Palestinian Citizens of Israel in the Shadow of the War on Gaza | 142
—Lamma Mansour

Chapter Seven—The Political Perils of Biblical Archaeology in the Holy Land | 155
—Donald D. Binder

PART II—The Bible and the Land: Listening for God's Voice in the Tempest

Chapter Eight—How Can We Sing the Lord's Song? | 177
—Lisa Loden

Chapter Nine—Theologizing and De-theologizing Genocide | 191
—Yousef Kamal AlKhouri

Chapter Ten—Doing Justice: The Unequivocal Calling of God's People | 207
—Ruth Padilla DeBorst

Chapter Eleven—Missiology After Gaza: Christian Zionism, God's Character, and the Gospel | 214
—Anton Deik

Chapter Twelve—October 7 and Armageddon: Misreading Revelation, Justifying Genocide | 235
—Rob Dalrymple

PART III—The Peoples of the Land: Taking Our Stand with the Vulnerable

Chapter Thirteen—Living the Future We Hope For: Christians, Jews, and Muslims at the Gaza Border | 249
—Mercy Aiken

Chapter Fourteen—Passing By on the Other Side: *Christianity Today* Since October 7 | 261
—Benjamin Norquist

Chapter Fifteen—A Tale of Two Trips | 273
—Suzanne Watts Henderson

Chapter Sixteen—Worshiping Jerusalem: Christian Colonizers and Colonized Christians | 290
—David M. Crump

Chapter Seventeen—A Great Awakening: Mennonite Action and Palestinian Liberation | 302
—Amy Yoder McGloughlin

Chapter Eighteen—Being Christian After the Desolation of Gaza | 314
—J. Ross Wagner

Appendix—A Gaza Timeline | 349
—Bruce N. Fisk

Permissions

Scripture quotations marked (NRSV) are from the New Revised Standard Version Bible, copyright © 1989 National Council of the Churches of Christ in the United States of America. Used by permission. All rights reserved worldwide.

Scripture quotations marked (NASB) are from the New American Standard Bible, copyright © 1995 The Lockman Foundation. Used by permission. All rights reserved worldwide.

Scripture quotations marked (ESV) are from The ESV® Bible (The Holy Bible, English Standard Version®), © 2001 by Crossway, a publishing ministry of Good News Publishers. Used by permission. All rights reserved.

Scripture quotations marked (NIV) are from The Holy Bible, New International Version® NIV® Copyright © 1973, 1978, 1984, 2011 by Biblica, Inc. Used with permission. All rights reserved worldwide.

Lyrics from Bruce Cockburn, "The Trouble with Normal" (Track 1 on *The Trouble with Normal*; True North Productions, 1983). Used by permission.

Photo Credits:

Figure 1: Saffuriya, 1931: Courtesy of the Institute for Palestine Studies.

Figure 2: Hurva Synagogue:
https://commons.wikimedia.org/wiki/File:Hurva_sideview.jpg
Public domain.

Figure 3, Upper: Mughrabi Quarter:
https://commons.wikimedia.org/wiki/File:Jerusalem,_1917.JPG
Public domain.

Figure 3, Lower: Western Wall Plaza:
יהודה גרינברג Pikiwiki Israel
https://commons.wikimedia.org/wiki/File:PikiWiki_Israel_47231_Revealing_of_the_Western_Wall_.jpg.
Creative Commons Attribution 2.5 Generic license.

Contributors

Mercy Aiken (MA, Saint Stephen's University, New Brunswick), Area Manager, Peace Catalyst International

Yousef Kamal AlKhouri (PhD, Free University of Amsterdam), Assistant Professor of Biblical Studies and Academic Dean, Bethlehem Bible College, Palestine

Daniel Bannoura (PhD, University of Notre Dame), Adjunct Professor at the University of Notre Dame, host of *Across the Divide Podcast*, and advocacy officer at the Bethlehem Institute for Peace and Justice

Donald D. Binder (PhD, Southern Methodist University), Chaplain to the Anglican Archbishop in Jerusalem, Canon Pastor at St. George's Cathedral, Jerusalem, and Undersecretary to the Council of the Patriarchs and Heads of the Churches in Jerusalem

Gary M. Burge (PhD, University of Aberdeen), Professor of New Testament Emeritus (Wheaton College) and Professor of New Testament and Dean, Calvin Theological Seminary (retired)

David M. Crump (PhD, University of Aberdeen), Professor of New Testament, Calvin University (retired); former pastor, Christian Reformed Church

Rob Dalrymple (PhD, Westminster Theological Seminary), Executive Director of Determinetruth Ministries; Adjunct Professor of New Testament, Grand Canyon University; Instructor of New Testament and Biblical Interpretation, Flourish Institute of Theology

Contributors

Anton Deik (PhD Candidate, University of Aberdeen with Trinity College, Bristol, UK); Lecturer in Biblical Studies, Bethlehem Bible College, Palestine; networking team and board member, the International Fellowship for Mission as Transformation (INFEMIT)

Bruce N. Fisk (PhD, Duke University), Senior Research Fellow, Network of Evangelicals for the Middle East; Professor of New Testament, Westmont College (retired)

Suzanne Watts Henderson (PhD, Duke University), Senior Director, Interfaith America, Chicago, Illinois

Lisa Loden (MTh, South African Theological Seminary), International Advisory Board, Bethlehem Institute of Peace and Justice and former Head of Leadership Development Program; Lecturer in Leadership Studies and Christian Spirituality, Nazareth Evangelical Theological Seminary (NETS); Lecturer in Reconciliation Studies and the Spirituality of Peace Building

Lamma Mansour (DPhil, University of Oxford; Rhodes Scholar), Lecturer and researcher in the Social Sciences

Amy Yoder McGloughlin (MDiv, Lutheran Theological Seminary at Philadelphia), Conference Minister, Allegheny Mennonite Conference of Mennonite Church USA

Benjamin Norquist (PhD, Azusa Pacific University), Director, Network of Evangelicals for the Middle East; former Ambassador Warren Clark Fellow at Churches for Middle East Peace; former Assistant Director, Opus Center at Wheaton College

Ruth Padilla DeBorst (PhD, Boston University), Professor of World Christianity, Western Theological Seminary; Coordinator of the International Fellowship for Mission as Transformation (INFEMIT); Dean of Certificates at Comunidad de Estudios Teológicos Interdisciplinarios (CETI)

J. Ross Wagner (PhD, Duke University), Associate Professor of New Testament, Duke Divinity School; Director of Graduate Studies, The Graduate Program in Religion, Duke University

A Poem, a Painting, and a Psalm

Rachel Still Weeps: A Lament For Gaza's Children

His mother's gone, his father's lost, they cannot kiss their child's tear.
The death that rained upon their heads left him to languish in his fear.
They cannot see his desperate state, how blast has carved his neck and face.
In bed nearby their daughter whom, now burned to black, they can't embrace.

Wait, from the grave a woman cries, refusing every consolation.
Neath veiled head, with darkened eyes, she offers up loud ululation.
This one who mourned the slaughters dealt by Rome, Assyria, Babylon
weeps now for Gaza's innocents extinguished south of Ashkelon.

Yet on the wind a whisper's heard, a prophet's oracle sounds forth.
Our tears will cease, our burden lift, lament will turn to joy henceforth.
When Justice flows at last to finally overturn this circumstance,
these children singing will arrive on gladness borne to join the dance.

B.N.F. 2024

This poem's first stanza recalls the testimony of Dr. Tanya Haj-Hassan, pediatric intensive care surgeon and volunteer in Gaza with Doctors Without Borders. See below, pages 89–90. Stanza two imagines Rachel, the Israelite matriarch who weeps for Israel's exiles in Jer 31:15 and for Bethlehem's innocents in Matt 2:17. Here she weeps over the children of Gaza. Stanza three finds the hope we need in Jeremiah's oracles of restoration.

A Poem, a Painting, and a Psalm

Cover Art: This Is My Body

This Is My Body, by Ramone Romero, an American artist living in Osaka, Japan, is inspired by Caravaggio's *The Incredulity of Saint Thomas* (1603; cf. John 20:27), and by a photograph taken in 2024 by Ezzedine Al Muasher of seven-year-old Sidra Hassouna who died when an Israeli bomb shredded her legs and hurled her body onto a wall where it hung from debris.

The three figures on the right are Christian ministers who appear unmoved by the atrocity. As Ramone explains, "Many of us who claim to be his disciples can't see Jesus in the 'least of these' in Gaza (cf. Matt 25:31–46), believing their lives are not as valuable to him as ours or the lives of Israeli Jews. Christ confronts us today as He did Thomas, bearing Gaza's little ones in His arms: 'Look and see! Touch My wounds, and believe.'"

Psalm 82 (NRSV)

> God has taken his place in the divine council;
> > in the midst of the gods he holds judgment:
>
> "How long will you judge unjustly
> > and show partiality to the wicked?
>
> Give justice to the weak and the orphan;
> > maintain the right of the lowly and the destitute.
>
> Rescue the weak and the needy;
> > deliver them from the hand of the wicked."
>
> They have neither knowledge nor understanding,
> > they walk around in darkness;
> > all the foundations of the earth are shaken. . . .
>
> Rise up, O God, judge the earth;
> > for all the nations belong to you!

Introduction
The Wrong Sort of Christians

BRUCE N. FISK

Two Kinds of Victims

IT WAS EARLY IN February 2025 when the first foreign leader to visit Donald Trump during his second term as president arrived in Washington. That visitor was Benjamin Netanyahu. On the night before his visit to the West Wing, Israel's longest-serving head of state met with fourteen influential Americans in the historic Blair House nearby.

The American group included not a single Jew. Nor were moguls and military industrialists in the room. Every one of the fourteen attendees was an evangelical Christian, among them Franklin Graham, John Hagee, Robert Jeffress, Ralph Reed, Paula White, Mike Evans, Mario Bramnick, and Tony Perkins—all of them invited by fellow evangelical Mike Huckabee, the next US ambassador to Israel.

Having witnessed Israel extinguish thousands of innocent lives—women and men, young and old—and purposely destroy homes, schools, hospitals, churches, mosques, power stations, and anything else that might sustain life, these evangelical leaders gathered to profess their unwavering zeal for Israel.

Having watched American leaders defend mass killing—and having watched American industries supply, American taxes fund, American technologies streamline, and American weapons accomplish it—these public figures chose not to confront the American-Israeli war machine. They hastened instead to celebrate the choreographer of Gaza's decimation.

Having witnessed Gaza become the world's deadliest place to be a child, they requested no reprieve for the sake of the little ones. Presented no petition. Delivered no ultimatum. They simply pledged more evangelical support and promised soon to resume Holy Land bus tours.[1]

Five days before this assembly of evangelicals would reassert their support for Netanyahu and their love for the Jewish people, Peter Beinart's latest book hit the shelves: *Being Jewish After the Destruction of Gaza: A Reckoning*.[2] I'm guessing few in the group had brought a copy in their carry-on en route to DC.

A professor, editor, political commentator, and notable public figure, Beinart is also an observant Jew who worships in a Modern Orthodox New York synagogue. His slim volume, already a *New York Times* bestseller, recounts tragedies from October 7, introduces us to some of the hostages, and describes the collective trauma experienced by Jews in Israel and across the world. It also provides trenchant critique of, and historical context for, what Israel has been up to in Gaza: "the flattening of universities, the people forced to make bread from hay, the children freezing to death under buildings turned to rubble by a state that speaks in our name."[3]

In what one reviewer calls "a spiritual manifesto for the future of Judaism,"[4] Beinart writes to summon his fellow Jews to a moral reckoning, calling them audaciously to embrace "equality rather than supremacy."[5] He seeks to persuade his extended family to "tell a new story," an unvarnished recitation in which:

> We are not history's permanent virtuous victims. We are not hardwired to forever endure evil but never commit it. That false innocence, which pervades contemporary Jewish life, camouflages domination as self-defense. It exempts Jews from external judgment. It offers infinite license to fallible human beings.[6]

Nor is Beinart's the only voice crying out in the Judean wilderness. The Iranian-Israeli human rights activist Orly Noy, after beholding the intense

---

1. Rosenberg, "Huckabee Takes ALL ISRAEL NEWS 'Inside the Room'"; Wagenheim, "Evangelicals Encourage Netanyahu"; Abraham, "Why Younger Evangelical Christians Are Losing Their Faith in Israel."
2. Knopf, 2025.
3. Beinart, *Being Jewish*, 9.
4. Rosen, "Peter Beinart's 'Being Jewish After the Destruction of Gaza.'"
5. Beinart, *Being Jewish*, 10.
6. Beinart, *Being Jewish*, 10.

response in Israel to the release of Jewish hostages, sounded a warning before her compatriots:

> The war will not end with a ceasefire, the return of all the hostages, or even a full military withdrawal from Gaza. The war will end only when Israeli society realizes that it is not only immoral but also impossible to secure our existence through the oppression and subjugation of another people—and that the people we imprison, bomb, starve, and rob of their freedom and land are entitled to the exact same rights as we are, down to the last note.[7]

This book does not presume to tell Jews how to rewrite their story after Gaza. That burden belongs on the shoulders of Peter Beinart, Orly Noy, and other brave Jewish sages who sense first-hand the existential fear embedded in Jewish identity,[8] and who are witnesses not only to their people's trauma but also to Israel's doomed quest for permanent security. It takes courage for a Jew to testify that the Jewish state has succumbed to rage, that its military has fused enemy combatant with civilian, that the foot soldiers conducting its slaughter are darkening their own souls.[9] It takes audacity in this moment for Jews publicly to model empathy toward Palestinians and to pursue justice for all, not just survival for some.[10]

This book summons a different community—our own—to its own moral reckoning. We are responding to Gaza's destruction as would-be followers of Jesus. We write from different cultural contexts, lived experiences, and professional disciplines, but we are united in our desire to see Christians in the West tell a new story. That story must begin with pledges of political allegiance not to the State of Israel but to God's just and peaceable kingdom; it must be willing to echo Jesus's "inflammatory critique of those in power,"[11] and it must be marked by a collective lament for Christian complicity in a massacre.

---

7. Noy, "War Will Only End."
8. Matar, "Grappling with Jewish Fears."
9. On the perils of moral injury see Meagher, *Killing from the Inside Out*.
10. This cloud of Jewish witnesses within Israel includes Arik Ascherman, Gershon Baskin, Jeff Halper, Amira Haas, Maoz Inon, Haggai Matar, Yuli Novak, Mairav Zonszein, Ori Hanan Weisberg, and others. From beyond Israel's borders, our list could begin with Omer Bartov, Norman Finkelstein, Lara Friedman, Neve Gordon, Antony Loewenstein, Gabor Maté, Ilan Pappé, Raz Segal, Eyal Weizman, and Simone Zimmerman. Compare the catalog of Jewish voices and organizations in Crump, *Like Birds in a Cage*, 234–35.
11. Hays, *Reading with the Grain of Scripture*, 141.

Western Christians shed tears for Jewish hostages and celebrate their release. But rarely do our hearts break for Palestinians. We have muffled, not amplified, calls for ceasefire. Some of us have made the crisis in Gaza a plot point in our End Times bestsellers or an applause line in our Sunday sermons.[12] We have provided biblical justification, political support, and financial backing for discrimination, displacement and, now, genocide. We have ignored the cries of some 40,000 children left without one or both parents.[13] We have abandoned hapless hostages subjected to unlawful detention and abuse in Israeli prisons.[14] We have demonized non-Jews the way our ancestors demonized Jews.

Mistaking good intentions for good theology, we have conflated Zionism with Judaism and treated the State of Israel as trustworthy and righteous by definition, and thus virtually incapable of criminal behavior. Not only have we credulously amplified false claims of burned and beheaded babies.[15] We have uncritically repeated memes about human shields and self-defense and Israel's "unprecedented" efforts to avoid civilian casualties.[16]

---

12. Greg Laurie on October 9 and 19, 2023; Wayne J. Edwards on October 11, 2023; John Hagee, quoted in Lehmann, "American Evangelicals Await the Final Battle"; Robert Jeffress, quoted in André, "American Evangelicals Interpret Israel-Hamas War."

13. "Over 14,500 children have been killed since October 2023, according to the health ministry. Of the 1.9 million people—9 out of 10 residents in Gaza—who have been internally displaced, half of them are children, according to UNICEF" (Jalal, "Nearly 40,000 Palestinian Children Orphaned"). See also Yee and Shbair, "War in Gaza Is Making Thousands of Orphans"; *Middle East Monitor*, "Gaza Coins a New Acronym." Reporting in October 2024, Save the Children said that "about 30% of the 11,300 identified children killed in Gaza between last October and 31 August were *younger than five*, according to a newly published breakdown of the ages of about 34,000 people whose deaths have been verified by Gaza's Ministry of Health. Of those about *710 were babies aged under 12 months*. Another 2,800 children killed have yet to be identified" ("Gaza: At Least 3,100 Children"; emphasis added).

14. See David Crump, "Prisoner Abuse and Evangelical Indifference," ch. 4 in this volume; see also B'Tselem's August 2024 report, "Welcome to Hell."

15. Fabricated (and quickly debunked) reports that Hamas militants decapitated babies on October 7 helped to dehumanize the people of Gaza and thus justify violence against them. See Ismail, "What Dehumanization Has Wrought"; Jones, "Evidencing Alethocide: Israel's War on Truth in Gaza," 8–12; Speri, "'Beheaded Babies' Report Spread Wide and Fast"; Scahill, "Joe Biden Keeps Repeating His False Claim." The killings that day included one infant, nine months old, shot dead in her mother's arms at Kibbutz Be'eri.

16. Many are rallying behind the IDF by appealing to opinion pieces by John W. Spencer, who teaches urban warfare studies at West Point's Modern War Institute. Mike Cosper, for example, in *Christianity Today*'s *Promised Land* podcast (The Bulletin, "Part Six"), claims that Spencer's "very, very important" work shows that Israel's efforts to limit collateral damage are "kind of extraordinary." Spencer has written thirteen articles on Israel and Gaza since October 7, 2023: five for *Newsweek*, five for *Modern*

We have narrated low-tech mass killing as barbaric terrorism while writing off high-tech mass killing as mere collateral damage. We have distinguished two kinds of victims, worthy and unworthy: "those we are allowed to pity" and "those whose suffering is minimized, dismissed, or ignored."[17]

In his 2002 book *A Moral Reckoning*, Daniel Jonah Goldhagen summoned the Roman Catholic church and its clergy to confront their complicity in the Holocaust. "What must a religion of love and goodness do," he asks, "to confront its history of hatred and harm, and to perform restitution?" To followers of Jesus, Goldhagen poses several stark questions:

> Would Jesus, a man who spoke truth to power, have said that his Church should have shouted protest, have spoken moral truth to evil, instead of being virtually silent, as the Jews were being hounded, tortured, and exterminated? Would Jesus himself, in the face of such evil, have publicly condemned the evildoers?[18]

Goldhagen could imagine three possible replies. Christians could remain silent; they could say that Jesus would *not* have called for protest; or . . . they could say

> that Jesus would have told his Church that it must not be a silent witness, complicit in the evil of the slaughtering of his people or, for that matter, of any people, that Jesus himself, this forthright man of goodness, would, of course, have publicly, repeatedly decried the evil in explicit, unambiguous, powerful, and ringing language.[19]

Allow me to rephrase Goldhagen's question for us today:

> Would Jesus say "that his Church should have shouted protest, have spoken moral truth to evil, instead of being virtually silent," as Gazans were bombed, arrested, "tortured, and exterminated?

War Institute, and one each for *Time*, *CNN*, and *Soldier of Fortune Magazine*, all linked on his West Point faculty page (https://mwi.westpoint.edu/staff/john-spencer/). See, for example, "Israel Implemented More Measures to Prevent Civilian Casualties." A number of Spencer's claims derive directly or indirectly from Israeli military sources. For robust challenges to Spencer's defense of the IDF, however, see Lewis, "Israeli Civilian Harm Mitigation in Gaza"; Bryant, "We Must Face the Hard Truth in Gaza"; and Spagat, "Netanyahu Got It Wrong Before the US Congress."

17. Hedges, *Greatest Evil Is War*, 21. Hedges borrows this distinction from Noam Chomsky. On Palestinian babies deemed *worthy* of killing, see Jones, "Evidencing Alethocide," 10–11.

18. Goldhagen, *Moral Reckoning*, 97.

19. Goldhagen, *Moral Reckoning*, 97.

Would Jesus himself, in the face of such evil, have publicly condemned the evildoers?"[20]

Why, in other words, do our theologians and clergy "whisper when they should scream"?[21]

How Many? How Long?

In the final chapter of *Being Jewish After the Destruction of Gaza*, Beinart also pictures himself asking questions to his people:

> How many Palestinians would Israel have to kill in Gaza before you urged the United States to stop sending it weapons? How many Palestinian prisoners would Israel have to torture and sexually abuse with impunity before you acknowledged the right of international courts to put Israeli leaders on trial? How long must West Bank Palestinians live under military law before you stop calling Israel a democracy? How many human rights groups have to accuse it of apartheid before you question the principle that Jews alone must rule?[22]

Beinart thinks he knows how his Jewish kinfolk would reply.

> They'd likely include references to Hamas, human shields, Iran, and antisemitism, coupled with expressions of regret that the cruel realities of the Middle East require Israel to protect itself in such painful ways. But the essential answer would be clear: There is no limit. No matter how many Palestinians die, they do

---

20. It is not lost on me that "the evildoers" in Goldhagen's original question are Nazis, and "the evildoers" in my formulation are Israeli Jews (albeit enabled by Americans and Europeans). My aim here is to challenge American Christians to speak out against injustice rather than repeat the egregious error European Christians made two generations ago. My aim here is *not* to equate Nazi and Israeli behavior, though it seems obvious to me that we might learn much by comparing *and contrasting* various episodes of mass killing. For its part, Jewish Voice for Peace is not shy to call Israel's "deliberate mass slaughter of Palestinian people" a holocaust: "The photos and videos coming out of North Gaza are a terrifying echo of all-too-familiar images of European ghettos and Nazi concentration camps in the 2nd World War. The Nazi camps were hidden from the world, but . . . Israel is committing the holocaust of our time, and it is doing it in full view of a seemingly indifferent world" (JVP Rabbinical Council, "Speak Truth"). Rejecting such comparisons is the ADL's "Backgrounder: Allegation."
21. Echoing Palestinian poet Mohammed El-Kurd, *Perfect Victims*, 16.
22. Beinart, *Being Jewish*, 101.

not tip the scales, because the value of a Palestinian is finite and the value of a Jewish state is infinite.[23]

Some respondents, it is safe to say, would go beyond handwringing, Jewish solidarity, and Realpolitik to openly advocate collective punishment, mass killing, and wholesale displacement of Palestinians. New York–based Israeli journalist Liel Leibovitz sees Israel "fighting millions of little Hamans, murderous marauders who will grow emboldened the more we offer them mercy."[24] His problem is not simply with Hamas militants but with *all* of "Israel's neighbors to the south," who are collectively possessed by "the singular idea that gives them life and meaning: Kill the Jews, all of them, gleefully."[25] Leibovitz's cartoonish depiction of the Palestinian collective would be funny if it were not toxic and deadly. Rabbi Eliyahu Mali of the Shirat Moshe Yeshiva in Jaffa, in an address to IDF soldiers on March 7, 2024, invoked Scripture to justify killing all Gazans, including women, children, and the elderly.[26] Randy Fine, the right-wing Zionist US senator from Florida, didn't require an essay or a homily to slate all Gazans for annihilation. A breezy three-word tweet would do, which he posted to X on February 20, 2025: *"Palestinian" = Hamas. #BombsAway.*[27]

What about *our* people? How might *our* tribe of predominantly pro-Israel North American Christians reply to Beinart's questions: How many?

---

23. Beinart, *Being Jewish*, 101.

24. See our discussion of the weaponization of Amalek (and Haman) in ch. 2.

25. Leibovitz, "Their Time Is Up." Donald Trump's inclination to "relocate" Gaza's population is, says Leibovitz, "more merciful than any Gazan deserves." (Trump possesses "uncommon moral clarity," by the way.) In addition to advocating the crime of ethnic cleansing, Leibovitz bolsters his argument by distorting the findings of a January 2025 Oxford survey of Gaza public opinion. The *Foreign Affairs* study (Atran and Gómez, "What Gazans Want") reported that 27 percent of those surveyed preferred "a single state under sharia law that would tolerate a Jewish presence but allow Jews less than full rights." In Leibovitz's retelling, "47% said they wanted to see Israel destroyed and replaced with a strict Islamic state governed by Sharia law." Leibovitz claims, further, that the survey shows that popular support for Hamas "began to decline" from "well over half in March 2024." In fact, the study notes a "steep decline" from "more than 50 percent" to "only a fifth of Gaza's population."

26. *Middle East Monitor*, "Yaffa Rabbi." In June, the Israel police recommended the case brought against him be shelved.

27. The tweet was flagged with a warning: "Visibility limited: this Post may violate X's rules against Violent Speech." The word "may" is telling. One wonders if X would be as tolerant if a US politician openly called for the massacre of Israeli Jews. At the time of writing Fine's tweet had 4,100 likes. This is the same Randy Fine who cheerily signed a 155-mm artillery shell bound for Israel that kills on impact anyone within a 160-foot radius. See Kane, "Book of Randy." Many Israeli public figures have made genocidal statements.

How long? With American evangelicals consistently proving themselves more reliably pro-Israel than American Jews,[28] it is not hard to predict some of the responses. They might begin by opening their Bibles, turning to Ezekiel, say, or Revelation to explain that the apocalypse is dawning. Or they'd look up that verse in Romans where God ordains governments to bear the sword against evil actors. Some of our theologians would invoke Just War theory or speak of Judeo-Christian solidarity. Others would identify Palestinians with the biblical Philistines, or with the Canaanites whom Joshua displaced at God's command. Some would read Genesis as reason to bless and support the State of Israel no matter what.[29] More than a few would simply hold their tongues and scan the clouds for signs of Jesus's return.

All members of the tribe, I suspect, would lament the deaths of Palestinian women and children (though probably not men). I can hear us supplementing our prayers for Israel's protection with something generic about suffering Gazans.[30] But most would hasten to clarify that blame for the body count rests entirely on Hamas,[31] who, it is maintained, uses civilians as human shields[32] and hospitals as staging areas. Israel, by contrast, would be celebrated as a "rare example of democracy in a region dominated by authoritarian regimes,"[33] whose army is doing "all it can" to avoid civilian casualties.[34]

---

28. Spoken by Ron Dermer, Israel's former ambassador to the US. See Magid, "Dermer Suggests Israel Should Prioritize." For Dermer, currently Israel's Minister of Strategic Affairs, evangelicals are the "backbone of Israel's support in the United States." Benjamin Netanyahu, likewise, speaking at a Christians United for Israel conference, once said, "We have no greater friends than Christian supporters of Israel" (Kristof, "Why Palestinian Christians Feel Betrayed by American Christians").

29. On the problems with this understanding of the blessing of Abraham, see Fisk, "Genesis 12:3, Christian Zionism, and Blessing Israel."

30. Howard, "5 Ways to Pray for Israel in Church."

31. E.g., in the "Open Letter" from the Union of Messianic Jewish Congregations. Included among the thirty-four signatories are David Brickner, David Rudolph, Richard Harvey, Mitch Glaser, Russ Resnik, Michael Brown, Daniel Juster, and Mark Kinzer.

32. On "human shields," see Erakat, *Justice for Some*, 203–5; Sherwood, "In Gaza, Hamas Fighters Are Among Civilians." In their 2009 report "White Flag Deaths," Human Rights Watch "found no evidence that the civilian victims were used by Palestinian fighters as human shields or were shot in the crossfire between opposing forces." The UN Human Rights Council, "Report of the United Nations Fact-Finding Mission on the Gaza Conflict," by contrast, documented multiple cases of the IDF using Palestinian detainees as human shields.

33. Ethics and Religious Liberty Commission of the Southern Baptist Convention, "Evangelical Statement in Support of Israel."

34. Such talking points in Christian discourse are indistinguishable from statements by Israeli government ministers. At the January 2025 World Economic Forum in Davos, for example, Israel's Minister of Economy Nir Barkat insisted: "We used

Like Beinart's imagined Jewish community, my imagined Christian one would draw no red lines. Our beloved Israel must do what it needs to do. Gaza may have become uninhabitable, but we could never admit that Israel has gone too far. The logic, albeit unacknowledged, seems to be that "any violence committed by Palestinians justifies all violence by Israel, and no violence committed by Israel justifies any by Palestinians."[35] To think otherwise would be for Christians to succumb once again to the sin of antisemitism.

The contributors to this book refuse to defend the indefensible. Egregious criminal behavior on one side does not justify mass killing, brutality, and displacement on the other. Neither Islamist militancy nor surging global antisemitism nor the fog of war can excuse the scale of collective punishment we have witnessed over more than 500 days. Gaza's wreckage is more than the detritus of exploded homes and bombed hospitals. The smoldering pyramids of concrete are more than monumental tombs for trapped and crushed civilians. The fetid refuse, the mass graves, the toxic rubble are something else: forensic evidence of the collective moral failure and silent complicity of millions of American Christians.

The Wrong Sort of Christians

In one of Winnie-the-Pooh's early adventures, the beloved bear, clutching a balloon, floats upward toward a beehive on a tree branch where, he reasons, there *must* be honey. Alas, the bees begin to buzz suspiciously, one landing on Pooh's nose, prompting him to announce soberly to Christopher Robin that the threatening swarm must be "the wrong sort of bees." Which means, he calculates, they would make "the wrong sort of honey."

Many of Israel's evangelical defenders, including the fourteen who pledged loyalty to Netanyahu in February 2025, are likely to conclude that the contributors to this book are "the wrong sort of Christians." Why haven't we given equal billing to Jewish fear and generational trauma? Why are there only passing references to the Israeli civilians massacred and captured by Hamas? Why so little on the despotism of Israel's neighbors, and so much about Israel's rage and revenge?

---

everything not to hurt innocent civilians and it's very unfortunate but it's Hamas's fault. They have to take all the responsibility for what they've done. They hide behind their own civilians and when there are casualties they cry about it." See *CNBC International*, "Ceasefire with Hamas."

35. Stevenson, "Illusions of Containment."

Introduction

As we see it, evangelicals don't need encouragement to recoil from the horrors of October 7 and condemn the perpetrators. Our tribe is eager to stand with bereaved Jewish and Israeli friends, and to repudiate Hamas for attacking civilians. Where evangelicals *do* need help is in cherishing the full humanity of Palestinians alongside that of their Jewish neighbors; in acknowledging what should now be obvious: that Israel aims to empty Gaza (and large parts of the West Bank) of Palestinians; in decrying the injustice of dispossession; and in recognizing our own complicity in Gaza's incineration.

The contributors to this book are an improbable collective. One is a Jewish Israeli advocate for reconciliation. Four are Palestinian academics, one of whom grew up in Gaza and is the new academic dean at Bethlehem Bible College. One of us serves with distinction an Anglican church in East Jerusalem. One is a renowned Latin American theologian.

We hail from a variety of Christian communities: Anglican, Christian Church, Christian Reformed, Evangelical Covenant, Greek Orthodox, Mennonite, Messianic, Pentecostal, Presbyterian, and non-denominational. We are activists, advocates, organizers, professors, priests, pastors, theologians, and graduate students. We have taught courses; written books, articles, and blog posts; preached sermons; composed poems; produced films; hosted interviews; offered seminars; and organized conferences, all while praying for justice and peace to prevail in the Land. We have led study programs across the region for undergraduates, seminarians and adults, and we've watched how the same Bible can inspire peacemakers and stir up warmongers.

We have waited hours at checkpoints, graffitied the Wall, witnessed brutality, choked on tear gas, shielded children, tended the wounded, enjoyed Arab and Jewish hospitality, camped with Bedouin, marched for justice, battled despair, and clung to hope.

We have raised candles in the churches of Bethlehem, danced in the alleys of Jerusalem, prayed at the Western Wall, watched the sun set on the Sea of Galilee, and ascended Masada at dawn. We have spent sabbaths with Jewish friends, shared Iftar with Muslim friends, and broken bread with followers of Jesus Orthodox, Protestant, and Catholic. We have pursued Jesus to Capernaum, sipped water from Jacob's Well, harvested olives in the West Bank hills, and savored apricots in the Makrour valley.

Declare us "the wrong sort of Christians" if you must. But don't say we haven't spent years listening, learning, laboring, yearning, and praying for a durable, just peace between Palestinians and their Jewish neighbors whose Messiah we follow. Our impressions have formed slowly over many years in the land, through lingering encounters, hard conversations, and troubling experiences. Disagree with us if you must, but first hear us out.

Jews and Palestinians both have ancient and authentic ties to the Land we call Holy. A lasting resolution must recognize these twin realities. The State of Israel, born of European Zionist aspirations for self-determination and need for refuge, welcomed and empowered Jews from around the world. It also displaced and evicted Palestinians, hundreds of thousands of whom were driven out or forced to flee when the state was founded. Those who remained saw their lives and lands come under Israeli occupation and control.

Palestinian reactions to this catastrophe have run the gamut: from resignation and collaboration to political advocacy and international diplomacy, to peaceful demonstration and boycott, to civil unrest, exasperation and emigration, to religious zealotry, violence and terrorism. None of these tactics has met with much success. Some have brought disaster.

The "conflict" between Jews and Palestinians is not one thing. It is a battle for land and water and holy sites. It is a war of demographics and religions and dueling nationalisms. Complicating the matter are false binaries, weaponized ideologies, tribal rivalries, delusional power games, assassinations, corruption, American duplicity, international collusion, and climate change. Nor should we discount the influence of "violent fundamentalism and messianic prejudices, fantasies and symbols, and deep-rooted anxieties."[36]

To this dire list of formidable obstacles we must add one more: Western Christian complicity. Israel's Christian partisans in North America and Europe perpetuate injustice and further entrench the conflict when they imagine that love for the Jewish people means defending the apocalypse Israel has unleashed on Palestinians; when they equate "blessing" Abraham with abetting Israel's military; when they let Israel respond to a perceived demographic threat with mass expulsion; when they broadcast palpable falsehoods about Israel's treatment of Palestinians;[37] when they embrace the toxic fiction that sympathy for Palestinians promotes "deranged and

---

36. Segev, "Israel's Forever War."

37. In a recent "groundbreaking resolution" ("Reaffirming the Jewish People's Right to the Biblical Heartland"), American Christian Leaders for Israel "reject[ed] all efforts—both from the United States and the international community—to pressure the Jewish people to relinquish their ancestral homeland in Judea and Samaria," a rejection grounded in part in the claim that "the modern Jewish presence and sovereignty over Jerusalem, Judea, and Samaria . . . [is] improving the standard of living . . . and enhancing the lives of all its inhabitants." ACLI forwarded the resolution to Donald Trump on February 27, 2025. Among the 205 signatories are Michele Bachmann (Regent University), Gary Bauer (American Values), James Dobson, Justin Kron (Kesher Project), Troy Miller (NRB), Gordon Robertson (CBN), and Joel Rosenberg (*All Israel News*).

murderous Jew-hatred"[38] or, to flip it around, when they behave as if standing with the Jews means supporting their efforts to banish others.

I hold out little hope that the fourteen evangelicals who sat down with Benjamin Netanyahu in February 2025 will read this book, "come to Jesus," and rethink what it means to *be Christian* after the desolation of Gaza. But Jesus rose from the dead, so you never know. For the rest of us who are asking how things got so bad and wondering where to go from here, perhaps these essays will cast a few shards of light on a darkened path.

What Lies Ahead

How to describe the chapters that follow? They are personal testimony and travel narrative, journalistic reporting and historical review, theological argument, prophetic indictment, and biblical inquiry: some of it American, some global, all of it asking fellow Christians where they were when Gaza's starving needed food, thirsty needed water, homeless needed shelter, orphans needed embrace, captives needed liberation, wounded needed care, and innocents needed protection during Israel's relentless assault. Each of us must answer that question for ourselves.

Part 1 of the book, War on the Land: Witnessing Israel's Desolation of Gaza, has seven chapters. In chapter 1 ("Gaza Undone"), I (**Bruce Fisk**) provide historical context: Hamas's rise to power in Gaza; Israel's blockade; Gaza's tunnel economy; previous clashes and attacks (2008–2009, 2012, 2014, 2018); the brutality of Israel's pre-October 7 grip on Gaza; daily life in the West Bank (pogroms, demolitions, annexation, abuse); and Israel's push for normalization in the Arab world. I aim to show that the disproportionate and collective punishment Israel has unleashed on Gaza, far from incidental, are established policy.

Chapter 2 ("Israel's Christian Armada Sets Sail") is about how Christians, especially evangelicals, have responded in the aftermath of October 7. Some claim to have "moral clarity." Some see Israel engaging only in self-defense and dismiss charges of genocide as outrageous. For others, Hamas is the new Amalek. I (**Bruce**) conclude by naming six factors to explain why so many Christians continue to provide relentless support for the Jewish state.

In chapter 3 ("Bombing in the Name of the Gospel"), **Gary M. Burge** assesses the grim scale of Israel's bombing campaign and their use of

---

38. Phillips, "Truth of the Palestinian Cause." Phillips's article equating Palestinian solidarity with antisemitism was originally titled "If You Support the Palestinian Cause in Any Form, You're Facilitating Jew-Hate."

massive American weapons in urban settings, all with impunity. He quotes Dr. Tanya Haj-Hassan from Doctors Without Borders who describes how this looks in the Emergency department. After surveying Israel's new AI targeting systems, Gary explains why they have caused stunning numbers of civilian casualties, and why IDF claims to be following international law are implausible when, for example, they bomb an elementary school where thousands were sheltering in a "safe zone." Incredibly, Israel names one of its weapons systems *The Gospel*.

The stories **David M. Crump** tells in chapter 4 ("Prisoner Abuse and Evangelical Indifference") are not easy reading. Hamas's imprisonment of several hundred Israeli hostages has rightly provoked global outrage. Barely noticed, meanwhile, have been the thousands of Palestinians held in Israeli prisons without charge, under "administrative detention." After describing the harrowing five-month ordeal of his Palestinian friend, a peace activist from Aida refugee camp, and his encounters with others recently released from prison, David asks (and explains) why evangelicals are reluctant to condemn such injustice and urges all followers of Jesus to speak out.

In chapter 5 ("Hamas and Violence: Ideology, Militarism, and the Quest for Liberation"), **Daniel Bannoura** explores the ideology and aspirations of the Islamic Resistance Movement, including its Palestinian nationalism, critique of Zionism, and defense of armed struggle as a tactic for liberation. Few realize that the group's 2017 charter (replacing the 1988 precursor) implicitly accepts coexistence and a two-state solution. Bannoura investigates Hamas as a "terrorist" organization and compares the movement to other liberationist struggles, to help explain—not defend— the October 7 attack. Concluding the chapter is a challenge, expressed in the form of an "open letter," from Palestinian Christians.

In chapter 6 ("Palestinian Citizens of Israel in the Shadow of the War on Gaza"), **Lamma Mansour** describes daily realities inside Israel where Palestinian citizens make up a fifth of Israel's population. From life under military rule prior to 1966, to the "infrastructure of repression" that has prevailed since, including police brutality in 2000 and 2001, to systematic retaliation for any show of empathy for Gazans since October 7, Lamma offers a Nazarene insider's view.

In chapter 7 ("The Political Perils of Biblical Archaeology in the Holy Land"), **Donald D. Binder** takes us on a journey into the politics of archaeology. Excavations, especially in the Holy Land, are "neither neutral nor objective." They can be exploited for religious and nationalistic purposes. Such is the case, for example, with a hilltop near Nazareth where Jewish layers are on display while centuries of Arab/Palestinian presence have been erased. Israel likewise bulldozed a 700-year-old neighborhood in Jerusalem's Old

City to create the Western Wall Plaza. If biblical archaeology can be "warfare by other means," Donald invites us to see "heritage sites as resources for . . . strengthening bonds between peoples and cultures."

Part 2, The Bible and the Land: Listening for God's Voice in the Tempest, has five chapters. In chapter 8 ("How Can We Sing the Lord's Song?"), **Lisa Loden** teaches us to lament. A messianic Jew living in Israel, she describes her land as "lacerated by war, covered in loss, grief, and trauma." The Lord's song, she says, "has become a requiem for the dead." Lisa grieves with the mothers of Jewish hostages and, remarkably, also with Gazan mothers fleeing with their children. She feels no less morally responsible to orphaned Palestinians than to Israeli hostages. Drawing on the psalms, prophets, and New Testament epistles, Lisa shows us that lament is incomplete if it only decries evil. Biblical lament must end with a declaration of resurrection hope without which, she says, she would be shipwrecked.

In chapter 9 ("Theologizing and De-theologizing Genocide"), **Yousef Kamal AlKhouri**, whose family lives in Gaza, poses a stark question: "How have Zionism and the Christian Zionist lobby turned biblical stories into a blueprint for genocide and made God its mastermind?" Long before the Gaza massacre, AlKhouri contends, a genocidal ideology "began in the minds of the proto-Zionist Christians, Jewish Zionists, and Orientalists who claimed that Palestine was a land without people." In other words, Palestinians were perceived as non-existent. The problem is that "stories can kill," especially when they incorporate biblical themes like chosenness and demonic hostility; sacred texts become pretexts for genocide. AlKhouri's remedy? "Prophetic courage, nonviolent resistance, and faithful resilience in the face of settler-colonial oppression."

In chapter 10 ("Doing Justice: The Unequivocal Calling of God's People"), **Ruth Padilla DeBorst** draws parallels between the Judea of the prophet Micah, the Argentina of her youth, and the fractured Holy Land of today. In each setting religious rituals and symbols can blind us to injustice swirling round about. Ruth is troubled by the growing number of Latin American Christians who, by embracing the trappings of Zionism, are unknowingly abetting the unjust treatment of Palestinians. Micah offers the remedy: God's love, not religiosity, is what empowers us to pursue justice and engage in political action for the common good.

In chapter 11 ("Missiology After Gaza: Christian Zionism, God's Character, and the Gospel"), **Anton Deik** argues that associating God's name with the Zionist colonization of Palestine has dire consequences for Christian witness. Christian Zionism portrays God as a racist, tribal deity, and uses biblical terms like *chosen people* and *promised land* to legitimize settler-colonialism, a term that applies when "colonizers immigrate to a territory not to live among and integrate with the local population, but *to replace them*." Deik argues that when theologians describe modern Israel's founding as a sign of God's covenant faithfulness, they implicate God in the ethnic cleansing of Palestine, as One who "sanctions the slaughter and displacement of an indigenous people." The alternative Deik proposes entails three steps: proclaiming God's goodness and justice, calling Christian Zionist theologians to repentance, and working for justice by embracing Jesus's ethic of love.

In chapter 12 ("October 7 and Armageddon: Misreading Revelation, Justifying Genocide"), **Rob Dalrymple** confronts claims that Israel's assault on Gaza is a divinely ordained prelude to Armageddon. In light of the way "Armageddon" is used in the book of Revelation, Rob shows it to be Satan's attack upon God's people, aimed at rendering impotent our missional call to embody Christ's sacrificial love to the nations. It turns out that end times speculation is not only a direct capitulation to the Enemy's plans; it is also providing a profoundly flawed biblical warrant for mass killing in Gaza.

Finally, Part 3, The Peoples of the Land: Taking Our Stand with the Vulnerable, has six chapters. In chapter 13 ("Living the Future We Hope For: Christians, Jews, and Muslims at the Gaza Border)," **Mercy Aiken** takes us along on her recent journey across the West Bank and down to Gaza. She writes of a depopulated Bedouin village, a prayer vigil outside Ofer Prison, and botanic evidence of a Palestinian village emptied in 1948. We meet a rabbi who survived October 7, observe a closed checkpoint, and watch Mercy package food bound for Gaza's hungry. In the darkest of times, Mercy calls us to persevere in hope.

In chapter 14 ("Passing By on the Other Side: *Christianity Today* Since October 7)," **Benjamin Norquist** reviews the coverage of a venerable evangelical institution whose editors, articles, and podcasts, sadly, have amplified pro-Israel talking points, neglected historical context, idealized Israel, and dehumanized Palestinians. The stories and interviews included in Mike Cosper's *Promised Land* series showcase *CT*'s reluctance to attach weight to Palestinians grievances. What editor Russell Moore presents as "moral clarity" strikes Ben as culpable partisanship. Christian media should be helping us amplify victims' voices and recover their humanity. The question remains: will *Christianity Today* help us in that quest?

In chapter 15 ("A Tale of Two Trips"), **Suzanne Watts Henderson** demonstrates the power of personal encounter. Her first visit to the Holy Land "underscored and normalized Zionist assumptions" about modern Israel's biblical right to the land, and about the "vaguely sinister" and "violent" Palestinians. Her second visit six years later "jarringly disrupted" her Christian and American assumptions. Suzanne introduces us to a Palestinian shopkeeper, a taxi driver, a Muslim tour guide, and Father Elias Chacour. We visit Palestinian Hebron and Israel's Holocaust memorial, and hear stories of land confiscation, settlements, and roadblocks. Finally, we encounter a Jesus who stood with those who mourned and hungered for justice. It was this way of vulnerable solidarity that marked Jesus's life and death.

In chapter 16 ("Worshiping Jerusalem: Christian Colonizers and Colonized Christians"), **David Crump** contributes a second piece in which he provides evidence that Jewish-Christian Zionists in Israel are perpetuating, not challenging, European colonialism. After interviewing numerous Christian leaders from local churches on both sides of the barrier and attending a messianic Jewish service in Jerusalem, Crump critiques the near-worship of Jerusalem, laments the moribund state of Jewish–Palestinian Christians relations, and points to evidence that the minds of some Palestinian Christians have been colonized.

In chapter 17 ("A Great Awakening: Mennonite Action and Palestinian Liberation"), **Amy Yoder McGloughlin** recounts her scramble to get a delegation of pilgrims safely out of the Holy Land in the days after October 7 and tells how the ongoing Gaza crisis led to the founding of Mennonite Action, an organization anchored in God's liberating love that mobilizes publicly for peace across the US and Canada. Actions may differ, but the cry is the same: for "aid, not bombs," for ceasefire, for freedom for all. Mennonite Action, says Amy, is a sign of another Great Awakening, this one demonstrating faith through communal performance and spiritual practices in the public square. Jesus' provocation in Nazareth (Luke 4) shows the way, as does the holy commotion of Pentecost (Acts 2) and the justice theology of the Anabaptist tradition.

Chapter 18 ("Being Christian After the Desolation of Gaza") draws inspiration from Peter Beinart's reflections in *Being Jewish After the Destruction of Gaza*. In this final chapter, **Ross Wagner** asks why so many American Christians uncritically champion the State of Israel as it wages total war on the population of Gaza. Like Beinart, Wagner finds his faith community held captive to false narratives: in this case, to deeply entangled stories of American and Israeli exceptionalism. In response, he turns to the Scriptures to recover "the story of the God who liberates us from our misplaced loyalties and empowers us to live the gospel of Jesus Christ, who is our peace." This is a *kairos* moment, Wagner contends—a moment of truth—in which we must heed the call to deep and lasting repentance, "a radical reorientation of mind that will bring our lives into alignment with the truth of the gospel." In this moment of crisis and opportunity, Jesus summons us to walk with our Palestinian brothers and sisters in creative, nonviolent resistance to injustice through practices of solidarity such as prayer, prophetic witness, and presence.

Bibliography

Abraham, Fares. "Why Younger Evangelical Christians Are Losing Their Faith in Israel." *Religion News Service*, February 11, 2025. https://religionnews.com/2025/02/11/why-younger-evangelical-christians-are-losing-their-faith-in-israel/.

ADL. "Backgrounder: Allegation: Israel's Actions Against the Palestinians Can Be Compared to the Nazis." November 18, 2021. https://www.adl.org/resources/backgrounder/allegation-israels-actions-against-palestinians-can-be-compared-nazis.

American Christian Leaders for Israel. "Reaffirming the Jewish People's Right to the Biblical Heartland." https://aclforisrael.com/reaffirming-the-jewish-peoples-right-to-the-biblical-heartland/.

André, Fiona. "American Evangelicals Interpret Israel-Hamas War as a Prelude to End Times." *Word and Way*, November 20, 2023. https://wordandway.org/2023/11/20/american-evangelicals-interpret-israel-hamas-war-as-a-prelude-to-end-times/.

Atran, Scott, and Ángel Gómez. "What Gazans Want." *Foreign Affairs*, February 14, 2025. https://www.foreignaffairs.com/israel/what-gazans-want.

Beinart, Peter. *Being Jewish After the Destruction of Gaza: A Reckoning*. New York: Knopf, 2025.

Bryant, Wes J. "We Must Face the Hard Truth in Gaza: Israel Has Lost Its Moral Authority." *The Hill*, July 18, 2024. https://thehill.com/opinion/international/4777940-idf-gaza-civilian-harm/.

B'Tselem. "Welcome to Hell: The Israeli Prison System as a Network of Torture Camps." August 2024. https://www.btselem.org/publications/202408_welcome_to_hell.

The Bulletin. "Part Six: Vote for Peace in a Time of War." *Promised Land. Christianity Today*, June 19, 2024. https://www.christianitytoday.com/podcasts/promised-land/vote-for-peace-in-time-of-war/.

CNBC International. "Ceasefire with Hamas Is Not a Strategic Victory for Israel: Minister." January 22, 2025. https://www.youtube.com/watch?v=EpMv1-BoRoI.

Crump, David. *Like Birds in a Cage: Christian Zionism's Collusion in Israel's Oppression of the Palestinian People*. Eugene, OR: Cascade, 2021.

Edwards, Wayne J. "'Israel: God's Timepiece' Matthew 24:32–34." Sermon preached on October 11, 2023. https://theheritagechurch.org/sermon/israel-gods-timepiece-matthew-2432-34/.

El-Kurd, Mohammed. *Perfect Victims and the Politics of Appeal*. Chicago: Haymarket, 2025.

Erakat, Noura. *Justice for Some: Law and the Question of Palestine*. Stanford, CA: Stanford University Press, 2019.

Ethics and Religious Liberty Commission of the Southern Baptist Convention. "Evangelical Statement in Support of Israel." October 11, 2023. https://erlc.com/policy-content/israel/.

Fisk, Bruce N. "Genesis 12:3, Christian Zionism, and Blessing Israel." *Bibliotheca Sacra* 180 (2023) 144–63.

Goldhagen, Daniel Jonah. *A Moral Reckoning: The Role of the Church in the Holocaust and Its Unfulfilled Duty of Repair.* New York: Knopf Doubleday, 2003.

Hays, Richard B. *Reading with the Grain of Scripture.* Grand Rapids: Eerdmans, 2020.

Hedges, Chris. *The Greatest Evil Is War.* New York: Seven Stories, 2022.

Howard, Bernard. "5 Ways to Pray for Israel in Church." *The Gospel Coalition*, October 5, 2024. https://www.thegospelcoalition.org/article/5-ways-pray-israel/.

Human Rights Watch. "White Flag Deaths: Killing of Palestinian Civilians During Operation Cast Lead." August 13, 2009. https://www.hrw.org/report/2009/08/13/white-flag-deaths/killings-palestinian-civilians-during-operation-cast-lead.

Ismail, Aymann. "What Dehumanization Has Wrought." *Slate*, October 13, 2023. https://slate.com/news-and-politics/2023/10/decapitated-babies-claim-intent-dehumanization.html.

Jalal, Rasha Abou. "Nearly 40,000 Palestinian Children Orphaned by War in Gaza." *Drop Site*, January 22, 2025. https://www.dropsitenews.com/p/20000-palestinian-children-orphaned-by-gaza-war.

Jones, Marc Owen. "Evidencing Alethocide: Israel's War on Truth in Gaza." *Third World Quarterly*, March 1, 2025.

JVP Rabbinical Council. "Speak Truth: These Atrocities Are Crimes Against Humanity." October 2024. https://www.jewishvoiceforpeace.org/2024/10/22/rabcab-speak-truth/.

Kane, Alex. "The Book of Randy." *Jewish Currents*, August 12, 2024. https://jewishcurrents.org/the-book-of-randy.

Kristof, Nicholas. "Why Palestinian Christians Feel Betrayed by American Christians." *The New York Times*, April 9, 2025. https://www.nytimes.com/2025/04/09/opinion/palestinian-christian-us-evangelicals-gaza.html?unlocked_article_code=1.-k4.qtO4.mrOkA3jUTa1e&smid=nytcore-android-share.

Laurie, Greg. "What the Terror Attacks on Israel Mean for End Times Prophecy." Sermon preached on October 9, 2023. https://www.youtube.com/watch?v=5495g3NT4VA.

———. "Wipe Israel Off the Map: Israel, Apartheid, Hamas and the Bible." Sermon preached on October 19, 2023. https://www.youtube.com/watch?v=7bGk7KQmCos.

Lehmann, Chris. "American Evangelicals Await the Final Battle in Gaza." *The Nation*, November 2, 2023. https://www.thenation.com/article/world/american-evangelicals-israel-gaza/.

Leibovitz, Liel. "Their Time Is Up." *Tablet*, February 20, 2025. https://www.tabletmag.com/sections/israel-middle-east/articles/bibas-children-israel-gaza.

Lewis, Larry. "Israeli Civilian Harm Mitigation in Gaza: Gold Standard or Fool's Gold?" *Just Security*, March 12, 2024. https://www.justsecurity.org/93105/israeli-civilian-harm-mitigation-in-gaza-gold-standard-or-fools-gold/.

Magid, Jacob. "Dermer Suggests Israel Should Prioritize Support of Evangelicals over US Jews." *The Times of Israel*, May 10, 2021. https://www.timesofisrael.com/dermer-suggests-israel-should-prioritize-support-of-evangelicals-over-us-jews/.

Matar, Haggai. "Grappling with Jewish Fears in a Just Palestinian Struggle." *+972 Magazine*, November 26, 2024. https://www.972mag.com/jewish-fears-just-palestinian-struggle/.

Meagher, Robert Emmet. *Killing from the Inside Out: Moral Injury and Just War.* Eugene, OR: Cascade, 2014.

Middle East Monitor. "Gaza Coins a New Acronym: WCNSF—Wounded Child No Surviving Family." November 7, 2023. https://www.middleeastmonitor.com/20231107-gaza-coins-a-new-acronym-wcnsf-wounded-child-no-surviving-family/.

———. "Yaffa Rabbi: 'According to Jewish Law, All Gaza Residents Must Be Killed.'" March 9, 2024. https://www.middleeastmonitor.com/20240309-yaffa-rabbi-according-to-jewish-law-all-gaza-residents-must-be-killed/.

Noy, Orly. "The War Will Only End When Israelis Understand This Simple Truth." *+972 Magazine*, January 24, 2025. https://www.972mag.com/israelis-end-war/.

Phillips, Melanie. "The Truth of the Palestinian Cause." *The Jewish Chronicle*, February 20, 2025. https://www.thejc.com/opinion/if-you-support-the-palestinian-cause-in-any-form-youre-facilitating-jew-hate-shyhqyo5.

Rosen, Brant. "Peter Beinart's 'Being Jewish After the Destruction of Gaza' Expertly Dismantles Pro-Israel Propaganda—But Does It Adequately Reckon with the Genocide?" *Religion Dispatches*, February 19, 2025. https://religiondispatches.org/peter-beinarts-being-jewish-after-the-destruction-of-gaza-expertly-dismantles-pro-israel-propaganda-but-does-it-adequately-reckon-with-the-genocide/.

Rosenberg, Joel C. "Huckabee Takes ALL ISRAEL NEWS 'Inside the Room' as Netanyahu Met with 14 Evangelical Leaders Before Trump Meeting." *All Israel News*, February 5, 2025. https://allisrael.com/huckabee-takes-all-israel-news-inside-the-room-as-netanyahu-met-with-14-evangelical-leaders-before-his-meetings-with-trump.

Save the Children. "Gaza: At Least 3,100 Children Aged Under Five Killed with Others at Risk as Famine Looms." October 10, 2024. https://www.savethechildren.net/news/gaza-least-3100-children-aged-under-five-killed-others-risk-famine-looms.

Scahill, Jeremy. "Joe Biden Keeps Repeating His False Claim That He Saw Pictures of Beheaded Babies." *The Intercept*, December 14, 2023. https://theintercept.com/2023/12/14/israel-biden-beheaded-babies-false/.

Segev, Tom. "Israel's Forever War." *Foreign Affairs*, May/June 2024. https://www.foreignaffairs.com/israel/israels-forever-war-gaza-tom-segev.

Sherwood, Harriet. "In Gaza, Hamas Fighters Are Among Civilians. There Is Nowhere Else for Them to Go." *The Guardian*, July 24, 2014. https://www.theguardian.com/world/2014/jul/24/gaza-hamas-fighters-military-bases-guerrilla-war-civilians-israel-idf.

Spagat, Mike. "Netanyahu Got It Wrong Before the US Congress: IDF's Clean Performance in Gaza Is a Lie." *Action on Armed Violence*, August 2, 2024. https://aoav.org.uk/2024/netanyahu-got-it-wrong-before-the-us-congress-idfs-clean-performance-in-gaza-is-a-lie/.

Spencer, John W. "Israel Implemented More Measures to Prevent Civilian Casualties Than Any Other Nation in History." *Newsweek*, January 31, 2024. https://www.newsweek.com/israel-implemented-more-measures-prevent-civilian-casualties-any-other-nation-history-opinion-1865613.

Speri, Alice. "'Beheaded Babies' Report Spread Wide and Fast—but Israel Military Won't Confirm It." *The Intercept*, October 11, 2023. https://theintercept.com/2023/10/11/israel-hamas-disinformation/.

Stevenson, Tom. "Illusions of Containment." *London Review of Books* 47 (February 6, 2025). https://www.lrb.co.uk/the-paper/v47/n02/tom-stevenson/illusions-of-containment.

Union of Messianic Jewish Congregations. "Open Letter." December 20, 2023. https://www.umjc.org/latestnews/2023/12/20/messianic-leaders-post-open-letter-of-support-for-israel.

United Nations Human Rights Council. "Report of the United Nations Fact-Finding Mission on the Gaza Conflict." September 25, 2009. https://digitallibrary.un.org/record/666096/?v=pdf.

Wagenheim, Mike. "Evangelicals Encourage Netanyahu Ahead of Oval Office Visit." *Jewish News Syndicate*, February 4, 2025. https://www.jns.org/evangelicals-encourage-netanyahu-ahead-of-oval-office-visit/.

Yee, Vivian, and Bilal Shbair. "The War in Gaza Is Making Thousands of Orphans." *The New York Times*, August 22, 2024. https://www.nytimes.com/2024/08/22/world/middleeast/gaza-orphans.html.

PART I

War on the Land
Witnessing Israel's Desolation of Gaza

CHAPTER ONE

Gaza Undone

Bruce N. Fisk

If only I had known to plan for a genocide, I would have cherished those last moments at home, my last night in a bed, my last morning coffee, my last kibbe dipped in hummus, my last day at work, my last laugh, my last birthday celebration, my last everything. If only I had known, I would have packed up a few of those memories with me. —Heba Almaqadma, Gaza[1]

Didn't Palestinians *Vote* for Violence?

It was 2 a.m. on the last day of July 2024 when an explosion rocked a guest house in Tehran, a building thought to be secured by Iran's Islamic Revolutionary Guards Corps. Weeks earlier, Mossad agents had planted a device they could detonate remotely. One victim of the bombing was a bodyguard. The other was the Palestinian leader of Hamas, Ismail Haniyeh.[2]

---

1. Almaqadma, "If Only I Had Known," 15.
2. Two months before the assassination, the International Criminal Court had charged Haniyeh with war crimes and crimes against humanity and issued an arrest warrant. On the details of the operation, see Bergman et al., "Bomb Smuggled into Tehran Guesthouse." Bergman is the author of *Rise and Kill First*, an account of

Then-President Biden remarked obliquely that the assassination "doesn't help." Meaning it would disrupt progress toward a ceasefire and hostage release, which Haniyeh himself had been negotiating at the time of his death. But with US elections approaching, disruption and delay were precisely what Israel had in mind.

Eighteen years earlier, it was this Haniyeh who led Hamas, the *Islamic Resistance Movement* (under the banner of "Change and Reform"), to a surprise victory in the January 2006 Palestinian parliamentary elections.[3] Voter turnout was an impressive 77 percent, and international observers found the results trustworthy. Out of 132 seats in the Legislative Council, Hamas wound up with 74.

A few months after that election I found myself living in the West Bank, volunteering for the Israeli Committee Against House Demolitions and experiencing up close what life was like under Israel's military occupation: long lines at checkpoints, restrictions on movement, the Wall, vandalized olive groves, land confiscation, streets "sterilized" of Arabs, settler violence, and demolished houses.[4] While I was encountering these "facts on the ground," Hezbollah was launching rockets at northern Israel, Israel was conducting airstrikes on Lebanon, and both sides were committing war crimes against civilian populations.

In Ramallah I met with the Director General of the Palestinian Authority Negotiations Affairs Department, Maen Areichat. The director pinned his party's embarrassing electoral defeat on three factors:

- Fatah had failed to make headway in negotiations with Israel to end the Occupation.
- Fatah party leadership was widely seen as plagued by corruption.
- Hamas was better organized and socially active in Palestinian society.

Mr. Areichat put words to the impressions I had gleaned from my time in places like Dheisheh refugee camp, Anata, and Nablus. Hamas was winning Palestinian hearts and minds by opening clinics, running children's camps, and sponsoring a network of social programs, all seemingly without succumbing to corruption.

---

extra-judicial killings by Israel's Mossad, Shin Bet, and IDF. In the years since World War II, writes Bergman, "Israel has assassinated more people than any other country in the Western world" (xxii).

3. On Hamas's ideological and political agenda, see ch. 5 in this volume by Daniel Bannoura, "Hamas and Violence."

4. On house demolitions as Israeli policy in the West Bank, see Israeli Committee Against House Demolitions, "Statistics on House/Structure Demolitions."

Hamas was steeled at this point to establish a sovereign Palestine in the West Bank and Gaza, with an East Jerusalem capital, if not through diplomacy, then through violence. Contrary to reporting in the West, however, Hamas's electoral victory testified less to a collective Palestinian zeal for violent resistance and more to grassroots frustration. Palestinians voted for Hamas, concludes British Middle East correspondent Robert Fisk, "more out of disgust at Palestinian Authority corruption than any new-found love for a holy struggle against Israel and the West."[5] Palestinian support for violence, Peter Beinart observes, "'responds to threat perception, to the level of pain and suffering imposed by the policies and actions of Israel.' . . . [It] goes up when Palestinian hopes of freedom go down."[6]

The infuriated West responded to the election by issuing ultimatums: Hamas must commit to nonviolence, recognize Israel, and respect existing agreements. Having pushed for the election—and wrongly predicted its outcome—the Bush administration had other cards to play. Robert Fisk, looking back, recalls "deep suspicions that the Western powers conspired to overthrow the results of the Hamas victory in 2007 by supporting a clumsily organised coup—to be staged by Abbas and his electorally defeated Fatah movement." But, Fisk continues,

> If a coup was being planned, Hamas forestalled it. The wholesale massacre and dispossession of Abbas supporters—and innocent civilians—that began on 10 June 2007 was a frightful moment in Palestinian history; men who had fought together in Beirut against Israel's 1982 siege now killed each other with equal venom. Abbas' fighters were gunned down outside their homes, thrown from rooftops or executed in the streets. At least 350 Palestinians were killed.[7]

At the time of this bloodbath I was leading a study-abroad program nearby. We heard reports and rumors but, like Israelis on the beaches of Tel Aviv and in the cafés of West Jerusalem, the students felt no qualms and faced no threats. So close and yet worlds apart.

With Hamas in control of the Gaza Strip, the "Quartet" (US, UN, EU, Russia) cut off aid to the Palestinian Authority. Civil servants and security forces—roughly a quarter of the Palestinian population—paid the price

---

5. R. Fisk, *Night of Power*, 265.

6. Beinart, *Being Jewish*, 43, quoting Shikaki, "Willing to Compromise." As Beinart later comments: "if people in Gaza aren't safe, they will sooner or later ensure that Israelis aren't either" (*Being Jewish*, 68). See also Stevenson, "Illusions of Containment."

7. R. Fisk, *Night of Power*, 266.

when their salaries disappeared.[8] Meanwhile, Israel tightened its land, sea, and air blockade of Gaza—a blockade Egypt and the West helped to enforce, ostensibly to prevent Hamas from smuggling arms but also to punish an entire population for picking the wrong side at the polls. According to a US diplomatic cable dispatched in March 2008 (and made public on Wikileaks), Israel's official plan was "to keep the Gazan economy on the brink of collapse without quite pushing it over the edge." This is textbook collective punishment.

Operation *Cast Lead* and the Trouble with Normal

The ceasefire Egypt brokered in June 2008 lasted into November, when Israeli forces launched a raid allegedly to destroy a tunnel and killed six Hamas fighters. Things deteriorated from there, until Israel launched a full assault on Gaza on December 27, 2008, in the waning hours of George Bush's presidency. Beyond retaliation, Israel's goal was regime change and even "*politicide*," the attempt to "deny the Palestinians any independent existence in Palestine."[9]

In the course of operation *Cast Lead*,[10] Hamas and other armed groups fired hundreds of rockets and mortar shells—homemade, cheap, and inaccurate—reaching as far as forty kilometers away and forcing thousands of Israeli families to flee. Casualties in Israel would amount to ten combatants and three non-combatants.

Flight was not an option for Gazans, however. Over twenty-two days, Israel killed some 1,400 Palestinians using both high-precision and imprecise weapons. The war dead included more than 300 children "and hundreds of other unarmed civilians, including more than 115 women and some 85 men aged over 50."[11] The operation destroyed or damaged 6,400 public buildings (hospitals, clinics, schools, places of worship) and 46,000 private residences.[12] With his inauguration around the corner, Obama pres-

---

8. Rose, "Gaza Bombshell."

9. Shlaim, "Israel and the Arrogance of Power," 156.

10. Israel's terminology. Arab media called it *The War on Gaza*. Hamas called it *The Battle Between Right and Wrong*.

11. Amnesty International, "Israel/Gaza: Operation 'Cast Lead.'" See also Finkelstein, *Gaza: An Inquest*, ch. 4; Filiu, *Gaza: A History*, 317; Interactive Encyclopedia of the Palestine Question, "War on Gaza, 2008–2009." According to Israel, the number killed was less than 1,200. See *The Jerusalem Post*, "IDF: 709 of 1166 Killed in Cast Lead."

12. Numbers from Filiu, *Gaza: A History*, 318: "The number of public buildings that had been destroyed or very seriously damaged was 6,400, including thirty-four

sured Israel to stop its bombing campaign and withdraw ground troops.[13] Israel announced a ceasefire on January 17, 2009, and Hamas followed on January 18. By war's end, dust had settled upon 600,000 tons of rubble.

Operation *Cast Lead* drew heavy criticism, both at the time and thereafter. The kill ratio of Palestinians to Israelis was more than 100:1, and that of Palestinian to Israeli civilians about 400:1.[14] Amnesty International, calling it "22 days of death and destruction," documented Israel's use of white phosphorus in populated areas in violation of international humanitarian law. So too, Human Rights Watch.[15] Breaking the Silence published damning soldier testimonies.[16] By June 2009, US voter support for Israel had dropped from 69 percent to 49 percent.[17]

On September 15, 2009, the UN Human Rights Council released a 452-page report, finding evidence of:

> grave breaches of the Fourth Geneva Convention in respect of wilful killings and wilfully causing great suffering to protected persons [that] as such give rise to individual criminal responsibility.[18]

In the estimation of the UN,

> What occurred in just over three weeks at the end of 2008 and the beginning of 2009 was a deliberately disproportionate attack designed to punish, humiliate and terrorize a civilian

hospitals and clinics, 214 schools and fifty-two places of worship. In addition, 46,000 private residences had been hit, leaving 100,000 people homeless, and there was 600,000 tons of rubble and mess to remove; 80 percent of the harvest and of the agricultural infrastructure had also been destroyed. The overall estimate of the damage was between 1.6 and 1.9 billion dollars."

13. Hersh, "Syria Calling." Many have compared this to President-Elect Donald Trump's equivalent demand in 2025.

14. Finkelstein, *Gaza: An Inquest*, ch. 4.

15. Amnesty International, "Israel/Gaza: Operation 'Cast Lead,'" e.g., section 1.3.1; Human Rights Watch, "Rain of Fire: Israel's Unlawful Use of White Phosphorus in Gaza." In response to criticism, Israel's Ministry of Foreign Affairs ("Operation in Gaza: Factual and Legal Aspects") claimed the IDF used white phosphorus solely to create smokescreens to protect IDF troops, and that, given the operational advantage, the number of incidental human casualties was reasonable. On the laws of armed conflict applicable to white phosphorus, see Coble and Tramazzo, "Israel—Hamas 2023 Symposium."

16. Breaking the Silence, "Soldiers' Testimonies."

17. Finkelstein, *"This Time We Went Too Far,"* 103, citing the Jewish Telegraphic Agency, "Poll Shows Dip in American Voters' Supporting Israel" (June 16, 2009).

18. UN Human Rights Council, "Report" (commonly called the Goldstone Report), para. 815; cf. para. 1921.

population, radically diminish its local economic capacity both to work and to provide for itself, and to force upon it an ever increasing sense of dependency and vulnerability.[19]

Israeli journalist Gideon Levy summed up the operation in six words: "this time we went too far."[20]

Those three weeks of war seventeen years ago demand our attention today for several reasons. Operation *Cast Lead* marked the moment when Israel resolved to protect its troops *at almost any cost*, even when fighting in densely populated areas, and thus relaxed the rules of engagement. A near-zero risk, shoot-first strategy has governed IDF behavior ever since.[21]

At the time, the ferocity of Israel's assault was thought to be unprecedented—in terms of firepower, civilians killed, and structures demolished. But it was not accidental. Ever since Israel's 2006 war with Hezbollah, the IDF's "deliberate policy" has included "disproportionate destruction and violence against civilians."[22] Nor was this policy of disproportionality a secret. Well before *Cast Lead* began, General Gadi Eizenkot, head of the Israeli army's Northern Command, was candid and explicit about Israel's military intentions:

> What happened in the Dahiyah quarter of Beirut . . . will happen in every village from which Israel is fired on . . . . We will apply disproportionate force on it and cause great damage and destruction there. From our standpoint, these are no civilian villages, they are military bases. This is not a recommendation. This is a plan. And it has been approved.[23]

In describing Israel's intentional disproportionality, Eizenkot was saying the quiet part out loud. This was no innovation of policy. Witness the mass expulsion of Palestinian civilians in 1948–1949. Witness Yitzhak Rabin's "Iron Fist" policy of collective and indiscriminate punishment in the 1980s.[24]

---

19. UN Human Rights Council, "Report," para. 1893.

20. Levy, "Goldstone's Gaza Probe Did Israel a Favor." The phrase became the title of a book by Norman Finkelstein that documented extensively Israel's 2008–2009 assault on Gaza.

21. Stollar, "10 Years Since 'Cast Lead.'"

22. Katz, "Dahiya Doctrine"; Horowitz, "Goldstone Found"; IMEU, "Dahiya Doctrine."

23. Quoted in the Israeli newspaper *Yedioth Ahronoth*; cited by R. Fisk, *Night of Power*, 277.

24. The misery Rabin inflicted included house demolitions, deportation, imprisonment without trial, torture, the use of live ammunition against unarmed demonstrators, assassinations, long curfews, and confiscation of property. See Sosebee, "Passing of Yitzhak Rabin."

Witness the rampant destruction of Jenin during operation *Defensive Shield* in 2002.[25]

Today, having watched the world tolerate a far more massive assault—one that has lasted more than twenty-one times longer than *Cast Lead* with a death toll at least thirty-three times greater, we can only conclude that what was once unthinkable has become acceptable, unremarkable, normalized. The media mostly look the other way, as correspondent Robert Fisk laments: "the more normal a crime, the less you need to report it."[26] Alas, history teaches us that "the trouble with *normal* is it always gets worse."[27]

Obama's New Beginning That Wasn't

Five months after pressuring Israel to end the operation, the new US president was in Cairo, where he delivered a speech to the Muslim world on June 4, 2009. I was teaching students in Jerusalem at the time. We printed out Obama's transcript and took turns reading sections aloud to each other. One of us recited Obama's call for mutual respect and tolerance; someone else read his words about civilization's debt to Islam. When we rehearsed his line that the Palestinian people "have endured the pain of dislocation" for too long, tears flowed.

> Many wait in refugee camps in the West Bank, Gaza, and neighboring lands for a life of peace and security that they have never been able to lead. They endure the daily humiliations—large and small—that come with occupation.[28]

Not only did Obama declare the plight of Palestinians "intolerable." He pledged that we Americans would "not turn our backs on the legitimate Palestinian aspiration for dignity, opportunity, and a state of their own." Reiterating the official US position, he said "the only resolution is for the aspirations of both sides to be met through two states, where Israelis and Palestinians each live in peace and security." While he challenged Hamas to "put an end to violence, recognize past agreements, and recognize Israel's right to exist," he also rejected the "legitimacy of continued Israeli settlements" and warned that "the continuing humanitarian crisis in Gaza

---

25. Baroud, *Second Palestinian Intifada*. Palestinian militants are likewise criminally guilty for their practice of targeting and killing civilians. A major difference is the scale and asymmetry of the atrocities committed.

26. R. Fisk, *Night of Power*, 255.

27. Cockburn, "Trouble with Normal."

28. White House, "Remarks by the President."

does not serve Israel's security."[29] Unlike Palestinians who had learned to be skeptical of American rhetoric, I felt a surge of hope. Could this be "a new beginning"?

As it turned out, no.

Already in September 2009, Obama was retracting his demand that Israel freeze settlement construction. By February 2011, less than two years later, his administration would be vetoing a draft UN Security Council resolution that declared the illegality of Israeli settlements. Three months after that, in May 2011, Benjamin Netanyahu publicly rejected Obama's peace framework; and it was Netanyahu, not Obama, who received twenty-nine standing ovations during his address before a joint meeting of Congress—one every 104 seconds. So too in March 2015, in the same setting, Netanyahu's full-frontal assault on Obama's Iran strategy was interrupted by applause thirty-nine times, twenty-three of which were ovations.[30] By the time Obama turned over the White House keys to Donald Trump, his plan to pressure Israel into making concessions with the Palestinians had been thwarted.

Sipping Tea Underneath Egypt

I first visited the Gaza Strip in May 2010. Invited and sponsored by the Palestinian Bible Society, I arrived at the Erez Crossing and entered the massive terminal where border police, though finding me on their pre-approved list, inquired at length about my intentions. After navigating corridors, metal detectors, and turnstiles, I exited into a caged walkway that traversed Gaza's broad, bleak buffer zone. At the other end, Hamas officials recorded my arrival and confirmed I wasn't importing alcohol. After that, a taxi waited to take me to Gaza City.

Inside the enclave, the devastation inflicted by Israel's blockade, global sanctions, and operation *Cast Lead* was painfully evident. Bombed out buildings threatened to collapse. Electricity was intermittent. Diesel generators grumbled. Donkey carts rolled past abandoned cars. In the gritty refugee camp I visited, food insecurity plagued families. Touring Al-Shifa hospital—the same one Israel besieged in November 2023 and obliterated in March 2024—I asked about some brand new, shrink-wrapped medical technology standing in a corridor. It turned out Israel wasn't allowing into

---

29. *New York Times*, "Text: Obama's Speech in Cairo."

30. Elliott, "Netanyahu Gets More Standing Ovations"; Norton, "Over One Quarter of Netanyahu's Speech."

Gaza the graph paper that the machine needed for its printouts. Expensive, life-saving technology donated from who-knows-where was collecting dust.

I returned to Gaza in 2012 during the "Arab Spring," not long after the ouster of Egypt's Hosni Mubarak in nearby Egypt. With a friend I traveled south from Gaza City along the shoreline to Rafah on the Egyptian border. Rafah was briefly in the spotlight during Israel's deadly operation there in May 2024.[31] To our surprise, Hamas police at a flying checkpoint welcomed us with smiles. No one prevented our driver from entering the so-called Philadelphi corridor and proceeding past a long row of tents and Quonset huts, each one marking the egress of a smuggling tunnel: Gaza's solution to Israel's blockade. The scale of the tunnel economy at the time was impressive; by the time of operation *Cast Lead* (2008–2009) tunnels accounted for 90 percent of Gaza's imports.[32]

Rafah's tunnel zone was new to our young driver. At our request, he pulled up to one of the huts, where we were greeted by a few curious teenagers whose job was to run the winch and cable used to extract contraband from a two-meter-diameter hole. After a few minutes of banter, they invited us to tour their tunnel. Impulsively we agreed.

My colleague went first, the cable lowering him and a youngster into the abyss. I followed. Fifteen meters below ground level, maybe twenty, we dismounted. Our guides led us, hunched and squinting, along the gloomy shaft carved out of packed sand, avoiding electrical wires, grateful for the rare dangling bulb. This was nothing like the reinforced concrete and steel tunnels Hamas is famous for.

I was mildly distressed by how long the tunnel was, at the end of which we must have been "in" Egypt. Three surprised boys welcomed us to their lair beneath the Sinai desert. They smoked, smiled, and shared tea until loose gravel began to rattle through the pipe that protruded from the low ceiling. Once the row of sledges was loaded, each of us straddled a sledge and rode "horseback" on the gravel as the winch pulled our train back to Gaza.

The UN calculated at one point that 3,000 tons of gravel were entering by tunnel daily. We couldn't know which Egyptian clan or Palestinian co-op our operation was enriching, nor how much tax per truckload Hamas would collect, nor whether the gravel was destined for a UN school, a Hamas hideout, or a bombed-out apartment complex. What we did know is that Israel's economic siege on Gaza had reduced these Palestinian kids to

---

31. *Al Jazeera* Staff, "What Happened When Israel Attacked Rafah?"
32. Pelham, "Gaza's Tunnel Complex."

day laborers in a death trap. By November 2011, according to a *Ma'an News* report, at least 160 children had died in the tunnels.[33]

Mowing the Grass

In the years since, waves of violence have continued to deluge Gaza's shores. These periodic, large-scale, deadly incursions are designed to deter militancy and win for Israel periods of quiet along its border. This cyclical program of deterrence, this update of Ze'ev Jabotinsky's "Iron Wall," is not so much a policy as it is "an inappropriate military response to what is essentially a political problem." It has a name in Israel: "mowing the grass."[34]

In 2012, with Israel and Hamas having engaged in mutual provocations for some time, Israel launched eight days of airstrikes. Operation *Pillar of Defense*—named in Hebrew after the cloud that guided the Israelites in the wilderness (Exod 13:21)—left 168 dead, among them 101 civilians, including 33 children and 13 women, according to a UN report. Both sides committed war crimes.[35]

On the evening of June 12, 2014, two Palestinian militants kidnapped and killed three yeshiva students from a settlement in the West Bank, about fifteen minutes from where I was staying at the time. Israel's forces quickly learned, but did not acknowledge, that the teens were already dead when it launched operation *Brother's Keeper*, a sustained assault on Hamas operations that saw at least 350 Palestinians arrested, 11 killed, and many wounded, and new rounds of collective punishment, including sweeping travel restrictions and punishment of Palestinian prisoners.[36]

A few weeks later Israel launched operation *Protective Edge* against Gaza: fifty days of airstrikes, military incursions, and naval blockades. The intention was ostensibly to protect terrified Israeli civilians from rockets being launched from the enclave to draw attention to the Palestinian plight, most of which were intercepted by Israel's Iron Dome defense system.[37] When the guns fell silent on August 26, 2014, more than 2,200 Gazans were dead, 559 of whom were under eighteen and 247 of whom were women. Many more were injured and displaced. Seventeen thousand homes were

---

33. Pelham, "Gaza's Tunnel Phenomenon," 23.

34. Shlaim, "Israel's War on Gaza." See also Inbar and Shamir, "Mowing the Grass in Gaza."

35. Relief Web, "Human Rights Violations During Operation Pillar of Defense."

36. Goldberg, "How Politics and Lies Triggered an Unintended War"; B'Tselem, "Human Rights Organizations."

37. Gorzewski, "No Sign of a Ceasefire."

destroyed. On the Israeli side, the dead numbered sixty-three soldiers and six civilians.[38]

Two things that happened in 2018 should be mentioned. Beginning on March 30 and stretching over eighteen months, Gaza's Palestinians, inspired by civil society as well as Hamas, conducted *The Great March of Return*, a gutsy visualization of the right that they claimed to return to the homes and lands inside Israel from which their parents and grandparents had been expelled seventy years earlier, in 1948.

Tens of thousands participated each week, gathering after Friday prayers at five encampments along the eastern edge of the Gaza Strip. The story Israel told was that its forces shot only those who got too close to the fence and thus posed a security risk. Some demonstrators were indeed armed—with rocks, Molotov cocktails, burning tires, flaming kites, and more. Some sought to breach the barrier. But most of those who were maimed or killed by Israeli snipers were unarmed and posed no threat. Palestinian fatalities added up to 223, with another 35,450 injured by sniper fire, "rubber" bullets, and gas inhalation. Many of the wounded would have limbs amputated.

In a 2021 report, the Israeli Human Rights organization B'Tselem complained that "well-armored security forces continued to use lethal fire against protestors on the other side of the fence who posed no real danger, over the course of the protests." Six human rights organizations jointly filed petitions in April, "asking the High Court to disqualify the open-fire policy permitting live fire against demonstrators where there is no clear and immediate danger to human life." The court dismissed the petition, one justice finding that "the fire was used in pursuit of a lawful purpose—protecting the citizens of the State of Israel and IDF soldiers."[39]

While these weekly protests continued, the Israeli Knesset in July passed *Basic Law: Israel—The Nation-State of the Jewish People*, which declared the land of Israel to be "the historical homeland of the Jewish people" and the State of Israel "the national home of the Jewish people." Lest there be any confusion, it added that "the right to exercise national self-determination in the State of Israel is unique to the Jewish people" and that "the state will be open for Jewish immigration and the ingathering of exiles."[40]

So, two concurrent performances in 2018: one mounted on the dunes of Gaza, one staged in the halls of parliament. In the former were Palestinian

---

38. B'Tselem, "50 Days: More Than 500 Children"; *The Jerusalem Post*, "Scale of Gaza Destruction Unprecedented."

39. B'Tselem, "Unwilling and Unable," 15, 21, 22.

40. Lamma Mansour considers the nation-state law from the perspective of Palestinian citizens of Israel in ch. 6 of this volume.

PART I: War on the Land

civilians and militants demanding an end to blockades and free passage to their ancestral lands. In the latter, Israeli lawmakers ascribing national rights and freedom of entry to Jews and Jews alone.

Statistics have their limitations. Figures are inevitably disputed. Some casualties are wrongly left out or wrongly included. That said, here are two bar graphs that track the number of deaths: the first compares four episodes between 2008 and 2019; the second extends the comparison to include the crisis of 2023–2025 in order to underscore the breathtaking spike in deadly violence.[41]

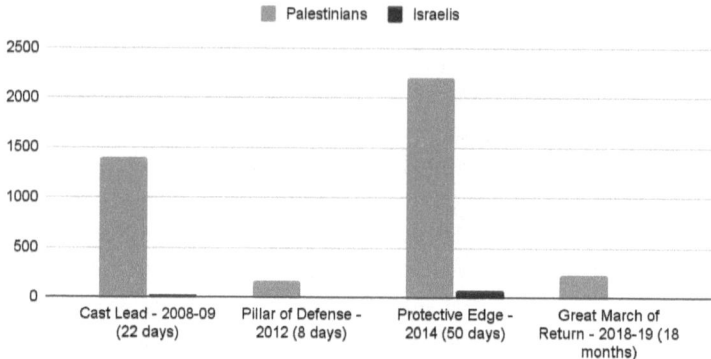

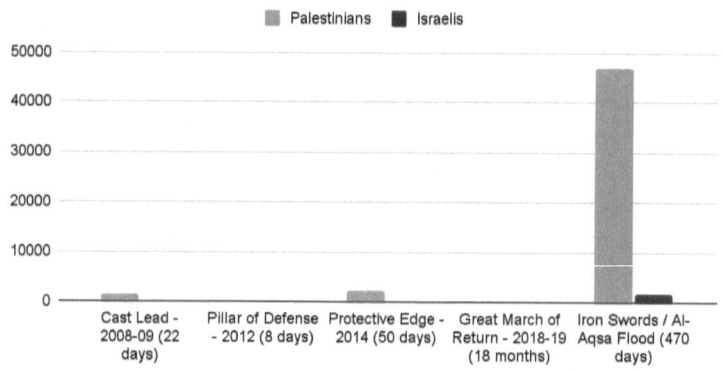

---

41. These figures do not distinguish combatants from non-combatants (nor adults from children, men from women, etc.). Nor do we include estimates of the number unaccounted for, nor "indirect deaths," nor casualty figures from the West Bank, nor data about injuries. For greater detail, see UN Office for the Coordination of Humanitarian Affairs, "Reported Impact Snapshot"; Nolen, "Estimated Gaza Toll"; *Al Jazeera* Labs, "Israel-Gaza War in Maps and Charts."

Israel's Darkest Day

The twenty-second day of the Hebrew month of Tishrei, year 5784 of the Jewish calendar, was the joyful holiday of *Simchat Torah* (*Rejoicing of the Torah*) when synagogue chanters reach the final portion of Deuteronomy and renew the reading cycle with the first chapter of Genesis.

On that day, also known as October 7, 2023, at 6:39 in the morning, Hamas, Palestinian Islamic Jihad, and other paramilitaries set operation *Al-Aqsa Flood* into motion by launching thousands of rockets while simultaneously breaching Israel's "unbreachable" barrier with explosives and bulldozers. Riding motorcycles and pickup trucks, paragliders and boats, several thousand fighters moved into Israel and within minutes had reached dozens of sites: six army bases along the length of Gaza, several kibbutzim, and a nearby music festival where some 3,000 young people had congregated. So began the brutal crime spree: shooting soldiers, slaughtering civilians door-to-door, detonating grenades, burning houses, wounding thousands, mutilating and dismembering corpses, and abducting hostages who were swiftly removed to Gaza.

There was also sexual violation, though initial reports of widespread and systematic rape have been undermined. In March 2024, Pramila Patten, UN Special Representative, produced an unofficial report that spoke of "reasonable grounds to believe that conflict-related sexual violence occurred in multiple locations." In her press briefing, however, Patten distanced herself from Israeli claims of "hundreds if not thousands of cases of brutal sexual violence." Nor did she find credible evidence of systematic, top-down directives from Hamas.[42] Top down or not, widespread or not, one rape is horrific.

Terrified families hid in safe rooms listening to mortars and gunfire. They whispered for rescue until their phone batteries died. Or they valiantly tried to resist. At some locations army reinforcements—distracted, underinformed—didn't arrive for hours. And this in a country ostensibly founded to keep Jews safe. By the end of the bloodbath attackers had killed as many

---

42. United Nations, "'Clear and Convincing Information.'" For the full twenty-three-page report, see the "Mission Report" by the UN Office of the Special Representative of the Secretary-General on Sexual Violence in Conflict. See also Rozovsky et al., "Sexual Violence Evidence." Journalist Ryan Grim ("How a Well-Connected Israeli Legal Expert") has shown, however, that the UN statement has been over- and misinterpreted. Patten "lacked the legal mandate to conduct a formal investigation," and her unofficial report relied entirely on Israeli sources; Israel chose not to cooperate with the UN Human Rights Council's Independent Commission of Inquiry. Notably, Patten's report "does not ascribe any act to particular groups, including Hamas."

as 1,139 people and abducted 251 (men, women, and children; alive and dead), including 44 from the festival and 74 from kibbutz Nir Oz.[43]

That Palestinian militants committed untold atrocities on October 7 is undeniable. Less clear, however, is the number of Israelis killed by the "friendly fire" of disoriented Israeli forces. Or the number of houses and occupants incinerated by Israeli shelling.[44] Or the number of Gaza-bound hostages—soldiers and civilians—that the IDF killed in accord with their Hannibal Directive.[45] Or how many hostages held inside Gaza were later killed by Israeli airstrikes. This is not to diminish the staggering cruelty inflicted by Hamas and other militants who, it appears, were responsible for the overwhelming majority of deaths that day. But it is to insist that Israel's response accounts for an unknown percentage of Israeli fatalities.

As always in war, truth is the first casualty, and "disinformation is the bullet that kills it."[46] Propaganda and speculation compete with facts for our attention. Fabricated reports of babies beheaded or incinerated in ovens were quickly debunked,[47] but not before they stirred up waves of revulsion—churned by President Biden and Secretary Blinken—that served nicely to dehumanize Gazans and legitimize Israel's decision to release the IDF from all restraints (to borrow then-Minister of Defense Yoav Gallant's diction) in its war of revenge. In this vexed context, we now know, intelligence personnel who were tracking a single militant *without knowing his precise whereabouts* would approve carpet-bombing operations that flattened entire blocks and anticipated triple-digit civilian casualties.[48]

---

43. For a graphic timeline with images, maps, and videos, see *Haaretz*, "October 7: How Hamas Attacked." For a harrowing, first-hand account of survival at Nahal Oz, a kibbutz that lost thirteen members (out of four hundred fifty) plus two foreigners and saw seven taken captive, see Tibon, *Gates of Gaza*, by a *Haaretz* correspondent.

44. Winstanley, "We Blew Up Israeli Houses on October 7"; Blumenthal, "October 7 Testimonies Reveal."

45. This directive is an Israeli military policy that calls for the use of maximum force to prevent a soldier from being captured, even at the risk of killing the soldier. It appears that the scope of this directive was expanded on October 7 to include captured Israeli civilians. See Winstanley, "How Israel Killed Hundreds"; Kubovich, "IDF Ordered Hannibal Directive on October 7."

46. Jones, "Evidencing Alethocide: Israel's War on Truth in Gaza." Jones applies the term "alethocide" to "a systematic strategy that not only erases truths around egregious acts of violence but also actively constructs false narratives that seek to reshape societal norms, manipulate public opinion, and dismantle solidarity movements seeking to end that violence."

47. Hasson and Rozovsky, "Hamas Committed Documented Atrocities."

48. Abraham, "Bomb the Area, Gas the Tunnels." See further ch. 3 of this volume by Gary Burge, "Bombing in the Name of the Gospel."

Within four hours, Israel began striking locations in Gaza. After five, Netanyahu was declaring war. Although military reservists were immediately called up, it was not until October 10 that the army confirmed they had extinguished the last sparks of resistance.

What they had not even begun to extinguish, of course, were the flames of collective anguish, grief, fear, and rage that now burned across Israel. An entire nation was experiencing a horror film. Millions of Israelis, not just the hundreds evacuated from villages bordering Gaza, were living with undiagnosed PTSD. This collective Jewish trauma captured the world's attention, evoked comparisons to the Holocaust (with Hamas as the new Nazis), and drew understandable sympathy.

Sadly, that pain would also be swiftly weaponized in the service of state propaganda. All but erased was the line between commemorating trauma and weaponizing it, between honoring the dead and recruiting them for the cause, as Naomi Klein would observe on the first anniversary of October 7. Like George W. Bush exploiting 9/11 anguish and fear to justify his War on Terror, Netanyahu lost little time turning the atrocities of 10/7 into grounds for launching (better: continuing) his war on Palestinians. Both stories follow the same plot.

> It's a simple fable of good and evil, in which Israel is unblemished in its innocence, deserving unquestioning support, while its enemies are all monsters, deserving of violence unbounded by laws or borders, whether in Gaza, Jenin, Beirut, Damascus or Tehran. It's a story in which Israel's very identity as a nation is forever fused with the terror it suffered on 7 October, an event that, in Netanyahu's telling, will be seamlessly merged both with the Nazi Holocaust and a battle for the soul of western civilization.[49]

Unfit for Human Habitation, as Promised

We condemn Hamas and PIJ for war crimes and crimes against humanity on October 7—there can be no equivocation on this point. What we must

---

49. Klein, "How Israel Has Made Trauma a Weapon of War." In the introduction to her book *The Shock Doctrine*, Klein described the exploitation of trauma in the aftermath of 9/11: "A new army of experts instantly materialized to write new and beautiful words on the receptive canvas of our posttrauma consciousness: 'clash of civilizations,' they inscribed. 'Axis of evil,' 'Islamo-fascism,' 'homeland security.' With everyone preoccupied by the deadly new culture wars, the Bush administration was able to pull off what it could only have dreamed of doing before 9/11."

also recall is that the situation in the Strip *before* that day was not sustainable. As Gaza journalist Mohammed Mhawish reminds us, Israel's longstanding plan to "manage," rather than solve, the occupation was doomed.

> Palestinians have been sounding the alarm, warning that the blockade, persistent impoverishment, repeated Israeli aggressions, and fragmentation of their communities would eventually lead to an explosion.[50]

In Jerusalem the precarious status quo on al-Aqsa had broken down. Settler pogroms, house demolitions, and West Bank annexation were advancing unchecked. Prisoner abuse was rampant and, under National Security minister Itamar Ben-Gvir, getting worse. Israel was pushing for normalization in the Arab world. Meanwhile, on the ground in Gaza,

> approximately 97% of the water in the strip is considered unsafe for drinking; over half of the population lives under the poverty line; 80% of the strip's population relies on foreign aid; and the future for most youth is uncertain, with 64% of them unemployed and their dreams and aspirations stifled by the limitations of the blockade.[51]

All of this is (essential, but incomplete) context for understanding—*not* excusing, *not* cheering, *not* defending—the resentment and rage that led Hamas to justify the atrocities they committed that dark day in October. And it is this context that many would largely ignore when Israel launched its retaliation and revenge. Parliament buildings, universities, police stations, hospitals, mosques, and homes—all quickly became indistinguishable folds of concrete and twisted rebar: fifty million tons of rubble, according to a recent UN estimate. Bombs, bullets, drones, and snipers targeted public spaces, institutions, and residential compounds.

And people.

When 1,000 displaced Gazans were sheltering in Al-Ahli Arab Hospital, Israel—after issuing several evacuation orders and firing artillery at the hospital's cancer ward—struck the compound and killed hundreds.[52] When

---

50. Mhawish, "Gaza Shatters the Facade of 'Calm.'"
51. Mhawish, "Gaza Shatters the Facade of 'Calm.'"
52. Israel initially attributed the explosion on October 17, 2023, to an errant Palestinian Islamic Jihad missile, a view quickly adopted by the US, France, the UK, Canada, and many media, but seriously undermined, if not debunked, by Forensic Architecture, Earshot, UK's Channel 4, and others. See Forensic Architecture, "Israeli Disinformation: Al-Ahli Hospital"; Forensic Architecture, "When It Stopped Being a War"; Baig, "Gaza Hospital Blast." For *Christianity Today's* treatment of this tragedy (The Bulletin, "Part Four"), see ch. 2 and especially ch. 14 in this volume.

throngs of starving Gazans rushed an aid convoy west of Gaza City on February 29, 2024, Israeli forces opened fire with live ammunition and killed 115 starving people and injured 750.[53] To flee a war-torn neighborhood was to escape neither danger nor death. Trudging under duress from one "safe" zone to another, homeless non-combatants, most of them women and children, were far from safe. As early as January 2024, Martin Griffiths, UN Under-Secretary-General for Humanitarian Affairs and Emergency Relief Coordinator, was reporting that:

> More and more people are being crammed into an ever-smaller sliver of land, only to find yet more violence and deprivation, inadequate shelter and a near absence of the most basic services .... There is no safe place in Gaza .... Even if people were able to return home, many no longer have homes to go to.[54]

There is no shortage of reporting about the death and destruction that has rained down upon Gaza. It is viewable on any smartphone or laptop. The UN and Gaza's Health Ministry track it.[55] Medical doctors testify to it.[56] Humanitarian organizations document it.[57] Satellite data map it.[58] Genocide scholars name it.[59] Palestinian journalists humanize it.[60] Soldiers on social media celebrate it.[61] Politicians quote the Bible to sanctify it.[62]

---

53. Hajjaj, "Flour Soaked in Blood."

54. United Nations, "As Israel's Aerial Bombardments Intensify."

55. Between October 12, 2023, and June 30, 2024, reports the UN, "there were at least 136 strikes on at least 27 hospitals and 12 other medical facilities, claiming significant casualties among doctors, nurses, medics and other civilians and causing significant damage, if not complete destruction of civilian infrastructure" (UN Office of the High Commissioner for Human Rights, "Pattern of Israeli Attacks on Gaza Hospitals").

56. *Democracy Now*, "'Worst of What Humanity Is Capable Of.'"

57. Amnesty International, "Amnesty International Investigation"; Samad et al., "Water War Crimes." See also reporting by Human Rights Watch, B'Tselem, Breaking the Silence, Al Haq, The Electronic Intifada, and the UN Office of the High Commissioner for Human Rights.

58. Holder, "Gaza After Nine Weeks of War."

59. E.g., Bartov, "'Total Moral, Ethical Failure.'"

60. Bisan Owda, who has millions of followers on YouTube, won an Emmy in 2024 for her documentary, "It's Bisan from Gaza and I'm Still Alive."

61. Toler et al., "What Israeli Soldiers' Videos Reveal."

62. Pfeffer, "Ethnic Cleansing in God's Name." NPR, "Netanyahu's References to Violent Biblical Passages." See also ch. 2 below on Netanyahu's weaponization of the biblical Amalek story (pp. 63–66).

Qualified observers have tracked Gaza's degradation from every angle. Forensic Architecture documents "ecocide."[63] Academic societies allege "scholasticide."[64] Others decry medicide, domicide, urbicide, econocide, memoricide—the various "sub-cides" of geno-cide, so to speak. "Reported Impact Snapshots" provided by the United Nations Office for the Coordination of Humanitarian Affairs and posted widely mean anyone with internet access can stay in the loop.[65] Here are excerpts for the period from November 13 to December 10, 2024:

> As of 3 December 2024, Israel's offensive in Gaza has killed 44,786 Palestinians and injured more than 106,000, while more than 10,000 are reported missing and likely buried under the rubble. Approximately 80% of Gaza's territory remains under forced displacement orders by Israeli forces, with 1.9 million people, or 90% of the total population, having been internally displaced multiple times during the past year.
>
> Palestinians in Gaza are facing the combined effects of a lack of critical resources, collapse of public order, and worsening weather conditions. Without adequate humanitarian assistance, Gaza has become "unfit for human survival," as Joyce Msuya, the acting UN Under-Secretary General for Humanitarian Affairs told the UN Security Council in November.
>
> An average of only 65 humanitarian trucks per day entered Gaza in November, well below the 500 humanitarian truckloads per working day allowed before October 7, 2023, which were already insufficient to meet the needs of the population. In the same period, commercial supplies have come to a near halt.
>
> Attacks on aid workers have continued: on November 30, alone, three separate Israeli airstrikes killed a Palestinian soup kitchen chef feeding hundreds of families in the besieged Beit Lahia, one Save the Children staff member and three staff from World Central Kitchen, pushing the latter to pause its operations altogether. The total confirmed death toll among humanitarian workers since October 7, 2023 now stands at 343.
>
> As acute food insecurity and desperation spread across Gaza, UN and humanitarian organizations continued to experience looting of aid convoys, including by armed gangs, in central and southern Gaza. In some cases, unarmed individuals

---

63. Forensic Architecture, "'No Trace of Life.'"

64. Quinn, "AAUP Joins Labor Union Call for Ceasefire"; Quinn, "Historians Condemn 'Scholasticide' in Gaza."

65. UN Office for the Coordination of Humanitarian Affairs: Occupied Palestinian Territory: www.ochaopt.org.

seized supplies during unloading or transit to distribution points. These incidents underscore the extreme desperation and suffering inflicted on Palestinians, who have been living in conditions that undermine their survival for over a year....

Meanwhile, heavy rains hit the Gaza Strip on 25 November, marking the start of the winter season. The worsening weather conditions are expected to affect more than 1.6 million people living in makeshift shelters, including half a million in flood-prone areas.[66]

Israel needed more than a by-the-book military operation to carve this apocalyptic hellscape. It needed media collusion and self-censorship,[67] government propaganda, dehumanization, and more—what Indian essayist Pankaj Mishra calls a "constellation of Israel's moral and legal infractions" that include

> the frank and routine resolves from Israeli leaders to eradicate Gaza; their implicit sanction by a public opinion deploring inadequate retribution by the IDF in Gaza; their identification of victims with irreconcilable evil; the fact that most victims were entirely innocent, many of them women and children; the scale of the devastation, proportionally greater than achieved by the Allied bombing of Germany in the Second World War; the pace of the killings, filling up mass graves across Gaza, and their modes, sinisterly impersonal (reliant on AI algorithms), and personal (snipers shooting children in the head, often twice); the denial of access to food and medicine; the hot metal sticks inserted into the rectum of naked prisoners; the destruction of schools, universities, museums, churches, mosques and even cemeteries; the puerility of evil embodied by Israel Defense Forces soldiers dancing around in the lingerie of dead or fleeing Palestinian women; the popularity of such TikTok infotainment in Israel; and the careful execution of the journalists in Gaza documenting the annihilation of their own people.[68]

With the precarious ceasefire that began on January 19, 2025, the world watched in amazement as more than half a million internally displaced Gazans began trekking north, asserting with their feet the "right of return," enacting a physical reversal of the Nakba. Alas, the jubilation of

---

66. Excerpts from Relief Web, "Gaza Humanitarian Access Snapshot #8."
67. Scheindlin, "Why There's No Excuse for Israelis Not Knowing."
68. Mishra, *World After Gaza*, 5–6.

reunion gave way to anguish as many found homes unrecognizable and began to dig for the remains of loved ones.

While Israel and Hamas exchanged prisoners and some aid trucks were allowed to enter Gaza, the IDF turned its fury toward the West Bank, starting with refugee camps in Jenin and Tul Karm. By February Donald Trump was pledging to rebuild a destroyed and ethnically cleansed Gaza as the Middle East's Riviera. With March came Ramadan and Israel's demand for changes in the negotiated ceasefire. Netanyahu blocked aid from reaching Gaza's wretched and, by mid-month, Israeli airstrikes were a daily horror that killed and wounded hundreds. Israel went public with its plans to displace all Gazans and permanently seize the Strip. By the end of March, the official death toll had surpassed fifty thousand. The desolation of Gaza became daily more visible, and the future of its people more bleak.

Bibliography

Abraham, Yuval. "Bomb the Area, Gas the Tunnels: Israel's Unbridled War on Gaza's Underground." *+972 Magazine* and *Local Call*, February 6, 2025. https://www.972mag.com/tunnels-hamas-lethal-gas-bombs-gaza/.

Al Jazeera Labs. "Israel-Gaza War in Maps and Charts: Live Tracker." Updated February 3, 2025. https://www.aljazeera.com/news/longform/2023/10/9/israel-hamas-war-in-maps-and-charts-live-tracker.

Al Jazeera Staff. "What Happened When Israel Attacked Rafah?" May 28, 2024. https://www.aljazeera.com/news/2024/5/28/what-happened-when-israel-attacked-rafah.

Almaqadma, Heba. "If Only I Had Known." In *Daybreak in Gaza: Stories of Palestinian Lives and Culture*, edited by Mahmoud Muna and Matthew Teller, 15–18. London: Saqi, 2024.

Amnesty International. "Amnesty International Investigation Concludes Israel Is Committing Genocide Against Palestinians in Gaza." December 5, 2024. https://www.amnesty.org/en/latest/news/2024/12/amnesty-international-concludes-israel-is-committing-genocide-against-palestinians-in-gaza/.

———. "Israel/Gaza: Operation 'Cast Lead'—22 Days of Death and Destruction." July 2, 2009. https://www.amnesty.org/en/wp-content/uploads/2021/07/mde150212009eng.pdf.

Baig, Rachel. "Gaza Hospital Blast: What Investigations Show So Far." *DW*, October 27, 2023. https://www.dw.com/en/gaza-hospital-blast-what-investigations-have-revealed-so-far/a-67237447.

Baroud, Ramzy. *The Second Palestinian Intifada: A Chronicle of a People's Struggle*. Ann Arbor: Pluto, 2006.

Bartov, Omer. "'Total Moral, Ethical Failure': Holocaust Scholar Omer Bartov on Israel's Genocide in Gaza." *Democracy Now*, December 30, 2024. https://www.youtube.com/watch?v=V5Bg-lKUeUo.

Beinart, Peter. *Being Jewish After the Destruction of Gaza: A Reckoning*. New York: Knopf, 2025.
Bergman, Ronen. *Rise and Kill First: The Secret History of Israel's Targeted Assassinations*. Translated by Ronnie Hope. New York: Random House, 2018.
Bergman, Ronen, et al. "Bomb Smuggled into Tehran Guesthouse Months Ago Killed Hamas Leader." *The New York Times*, August 1, 2024. https://www.nytimes.com/2024/08/01/world/middleeast/how-hamas-leader-haniyeh-killed-iran-bomb.html.
Blumenthal, Max. "October 7 Testimonies Reveal Israel's Military 'Shelling' Israeli Citizens with Tanks, Missiles." *The Grayzone*, October 27, 2023. https://thegrayzone.com/2023/10/27/israels-military-shelled-burning-tanks-helicopters/.
Breaking the Silence. "Soldiers' Testimonies from Operation Cast Lead, Gaza 2009." https://www.breakingthesilence.org.il/wp-content/uploads/2011/02/Operation_Cast_Lead_Gaza_2009_Eng.pdf.
B'Tselem. "50 Days: More Than 500 Children: Facts and Figures on Fatalities in Gaza, Summer 2014." https://www.btselem.org/2014_gaza_conflict/en/.
———. "Human Rights Organizations: 'Refrain from Collectively Punishing Palestinians.'" June 22, 2014. https://www.btselem.org/press_releases/20140622_joint_release.
———. "Unwilling and Unable: Israel's Whitewashed Investigations of the Great March of Return Protests." December 2021. https://www.btselem.org/publications/202112_unwilling_and_unable.
The Bulletin. "Part Four: Empire of Refugees: Victims, Villains, and Settler Colonialism." *Promised Land. Christianity Today*, March 21, 2024. https://www.christianitytoday.com/podcasts/promised-land/empire-of-refugees-victims-villains-and-settler-colonialism/.
Coble, Kevin S., and John C. Tramazzo. "Israel—Hamas 2023 Symposium—White Phosphorus and International Law." October 25, 2023. https://lieber.westpoint.edu/white-phosphorus-and-international-law/.
Cockburn, Bruce. "The Trouble with Normal." Track 1 on *The Trouble with Normal*. Waterdown, Ontario: True North Productions, 1983.
Democracy Now. "'The Worst of What Humanity Is Capable Of': Pediatrician Dr. Tanya Haj-Hassan on What She Saw in Gaza." March 28, 2024. https://www.democracynow.org/2024/3/28/gaza_msf.
Elliott, Justin. "Netanyahu Gets More Standing Ovations Than Obama." *Salon*, May 24, 2011. https://www.salon.com/2011/05/24/netanyahu_standing_ovations/.
Filiu, Jean-Pierre. *Gaza: A History*. New York: Oxford, 2014.
Finkelstein, Norman. *Gaza: An Inquest into Its Martyrdom*. Oakland: University of California Press, 2018.
———. *"This Time We Went Too Far": Truth and Consequences of the Gaza Invasion*. New York: OR Books, 2010.
Fisk, Robert. *Night of Power: The Betrayal of the Middle East*. London: 4th Estate, 2024.
Forensic Architecture. "Israeli Disinformation: Al-Ahli Hospital." February 14, 2024. https://forensic-architecture.org/investigation/israeli-disinformation-al-ahli-hospital.
———. "'No Trace of Life': Israel's Ecocide in Gaza 2023–2024." https://forensic-architecture.org/investigation/ecocide-in-gaza.

———. "'When It Stopped Being a War': The Situated Testimony of Dr. Ghassan Abu-Sittah." October 17, 2024. https://forensic-architecture.org/investigation/when-it-stopped-being-a-war.

Goldberg, J. J. "How Politics and Lies Triggered an Unintended War in Gaza." *Forward*, July 10, 2014. https://forward.com/opinion/201764/how-politics-and-lies-triggered-an-unintended-war/.

Gordon, Neve, and Nicola Perugini. *Human Shields: A History of People in the Line of Fire*. Berkeley: University of California Press, 2020.

Gorzewski, Andreas. "No Sign of a Ceasefire." *DW*, July 23, 2014. https://www.dw.com/en/hamas-and-israel-cling-to-their-war-aims/a-17801137.

Grim, Ryan. "How a Well-Connected Israeli Legal Expert Influenced the UN Investigation into Sexual Violence on October 7." *Drop Site News*, February 19, 2025. https://www.dropsitenews.com/p/un-report-sexual-violence-israel-hamas-influence.

Haaretz. "October 7: How Hamas Attacked Israel Minute-by-Minute." April 18, 2024. https://www.haaretz.com/israel-news/2024-4-18/ty-article-static/.premium/what-happened-on-oct-7/0000018e-c1b7-dc93-adce-eff753020000.

Hajjaj, Tareq S. "Flour Soaked in Blood: 'Flour Massacre' Survivors Tell Their Story." *Mondoweiss*, March 4, 2024. https://mondoweiss.net/2024/03/flour-soaked-in-blood/.

Hasson, Nir, and Liza Rozovsky. "Hamas Committed Documented Atrocities. But a Few False Stories Feed the Deniers." *Haaretz*, December 4, 2024. https://www.haaretz.com/israel-news/2023-12-04/ty-article-magazine/.premium/hamas-committed-documented-atrocities-but-a-few-false-stories-feed-the-deniers/0000018c-34f3-da74-afce-b5fbe24f0000.

Hersh, Seymour. "Syria Calling." *The New Yorker*, March 29, 2009. https://www.newyorker.com/magazine/2009/04/06/syria-calling.

Holder, Josh. "Gaza After Nine Weeks of War." *The New York Times*, December 12, 2023. https://www.nytimes.com/interactive/2023/12/12/world/middleeast/gaza-strip-satellite-images-israel-invasion.html.

Horowitz, Adam. "Goldstone Found That Israel's Collective Punishment Policy in Lebanon Served as a Model for Gaza." *Mondoweiss*, January 26, 2010. https://mondoweiss.net/2010/01/goldstone-found-that-israels-collective-punishment-policy-in-lebanon-served-as-a-model-for-gaza/.

Human Rights Watch. "Rain of Fire: Israel's Unlawful Use of White Phosphorus in Gaza." March 25, 2009. https://www.hrw.org/report/2009/03/25/rain-fire/israels-unlawful-use-white-phosphorus-gaza.

IMEU. "Explainer: The Dahiya Doctrine and Israel's Use of Disproportionate Force." July 21, 2024. https://imeu.org/article/the-dahiya-doctrine-and-israels-use-of-disproportionate-force.

Inbar, Efraim, and Eitan Shamir. "Mowing the Grass in Gaza." *The Jerusalem Post*, July 22, 2014. https://www.jpost.com/Opinion/Columnists/Mowing-the-grass-in-Gaza-368516.

Interactive Encyclopedia of the Palestine Question. "The War on Gaza, 2008–2009: Israel's Strategic Quandary." https://www.palquest.org/en/highlight/29896/war-gaza-2008%E2%80%932009.

Israeli Committee Against House Demolitions. "Statistics on House/Structure Demolitions—November 1947–December 2024." April 26, 2021. https://icahd.org/2021/04/26/statistics-on-house-structure-demolitions-november-1947/.

Israeli Ministry of Foreign Affairs. "The Operation in Gaza: Factual and Legal Aspects." July 29, 2009. https://www.gov.il/en/pages/the-operation-in-gaza-factual-and-legal-aspects-use-of-force-complaints-about-idf.

The Jerusalem Post. "IDF: 709 of 1166 Killed in Cast Lead Identified as Hamas Terror Operatives." March 26, 2009. https://www.jpost.com/Israel/IDF-709-of-1166-killed-in-Cast-Lead-identifed-as-Hamas-terror-operatives.

———. "Scale of Gaza Destruction Unprecedented, Rehabilitation Will Cost $7.8 Billion, PA Says." September 4, 2014. https://www.jpost.com/Arab-Israeli-Conflict/Scale-of-Gaza-destruction-unprecedented-rehabilitation-will-cost-78-billion-PA-says-374460.

Jones, Marc Owen. "Evidencing Alethocide: Israel's War on Truth in Gaza." *Third World Quarterly* (March 1, 2025) 1–18.

Katz, Yaakov. "The Dahiya Doctrine: Fighting Dirty or a Knock-Out Punch?" *The Jerusalem Post*, January 28, 2010. https://www.jpost.com/Features/Front-Lines/The-Dahiya-Doctrine-Fighting-dirty-or-a-knock-out-punch.

Kershner, Isabel. "Israel's Military Lays Out Its October 7 Failures." *The New York Times*, February 27, 2025. https://www.nytimes.com/2025/02/27/world/middleeast/israel-military-hamas-oct-7.html.

Klein, Naomi. "How Israel Has Made Trauma a Weapon of War." *The Guardian*, October 5, 2024. https://www.theguardian.com/us-news/ng-interactive/2024/oct/05/israel-gaza-october-7-memorials.

———. *The Shock Doctrine: The Rise of Disaster Capitalism.* New York: Metropolitan, 2007.

Kubovich, Yaniv. "IDF Ordered Hannibal Directive on October 7 to Prevent Hamas Taking Soldiers Captive." *Haaretz*, July 7, 2024. https://www.haaretz.com/israel-news/2024-7-07/ty-article-magazine/.premium/idf-ordered-hannibal-directive-on-october-7-to-prevent-hamas-taking-soldiers-captive/00000190-89a2-d776-a3b1-fdbe45520000.

Levy, Gideon. "Goldstone's Gaza Probe Did Israel a Favor." *Haaretz*, October 1, 2009. https://www.haaretz.com/2009-10-01/ty-article/goldstones-gaza-probe-did-israel-a-favor/0000017f-f879-ddde-abff-fc7d5fd80000.

Mhawish, Mohammed R. "Gaza Shatters the Facade of 'Calm.'" *+972 Magazine*, October 8, 2023. https://www.972mag.com/gaza-calm-facade-hamas/.

Mishra, Pankaj. *The World After Gaza: A History.* New York: Penguin, 2025.

The New York Times. "Text: Obama's Speech in Cairo." June 4, 2009. https://www.nytimes.com/2009/06/04/us/politics/04obama.text.html.

Nolen, Stephanie. "Estimated Gaza Toll May Have Missed 25,000 Deaths, Study Says." *The New York Times*, January 14, 2025. https://www.nytimes.com/2025/01/14/health/gaza-death-toll.html.

Norton, Ben. "Over One Quarter of Netanyahu's Speech to Congress Consisted of Applause and Standing Ovations." *Mondoweiss*, March 4, 2015. https://mondoweiss.net/2015/03/netanyahus-consisted-standing/.

NPR. "Netanyahu's References to Violent Biblical Passages Raise Alarm Among Critics." *Morning Edition*, November 7, 2023. https://www.npr.

org/2023/11/07/1211133201/netanyahus-references-to-violent-biblical-passages-raise-alarm-among-critics.

Owda, Bisan. "It's Bisan from Gaza and I'm Still Alive." November 3, 2023. https://www.youtube.com/watch?v=741knWh3hJo.

Pelham, Nicolas. "Gaza's Tunnel Complex." *Middle East Research and Information Project* (MERIP). Winter 2011.

———. "Gaza's Tunnel Phenomenon: The Unintended Dynamics of Israel's Siege." *Journal of Palestine Studies* 41 (2012) 6–31.

Pfeffer, Anshel. "Ethnic Cleansing in God's Name: The Only Israelis with a Plan for the 'Day After' in Gaza." *Haaretz*, January 29, 2024. https://www.haaretz.com/israel-news/2024-1-29/ty-article/.premium/ethnic-cleansing-in-gods-name-the-only-israelis-with-a-plan-for-the-day-after-in-gaza/0000018d-55e0-d997-adff-ddfa9b490000.

Quinn, Ryan. "AAUP Joins Labor Union Call for Ceasefire in Gaza." *Inside Higher Ed*, February 14, 2024. https://www.insidehighered.com/news/faculty-issues/academic-freedom/2024/02/14/aaup-joins-labor-unions-call-ceasefire-gaza/.

———. "Historians Condemn 'Scholasticide' in Gaza at Conference." *Inside Higher Ed*, January 5, 2025. https://www.insidehighered.com/news/faculty-issues/academic-freedom/2025/01/05/aha-convention-attendees-oppose-scholasticide-gaza.

Relief Web. "Gaza Humanitarian Access Snapshot #8 (13 November–10 December 2024)." December 13, 2024. https://reliefweb.int/report/occupied-palestinian-territory/gaza-humanitarian-access-snapshot-8-13-november-10-december-2024.

———. "Human Rights Violations During Operation Pillar of Defense 14–21 November 2012." May 13, 2013. https://reliefweb.int/report/occupied-palestinian-territory/human-rights-violations-during-operation-pillar-defense-14-21.

Rose, David. "The Gaza Bombshell." *Vanity Fair*, April 2008. https://archive.vanityfair.com/article/2008/04/01/the-gaza-bombshell.

Rozovsky, Liza, et al. "Sexual Violence Evidence Against Hamas Is Mounting, but the Road to Court Is Still Long." *Haaretz*, November 22, 2023. https://www.haaretz.com/israel-news/2023-11-22/ty-article-magazine/.premium/sexual-assault-evidence-against-hamas-is-mounting-but-the-road-to-court-is-still-long/0000018b-f6bb-dafe-a18f-f7fb0a570000.

Samad, Lama Abdul, et al. "Water War Crimes: How Israel Has Weaponised Water in Its Military Campaign in Gaza." *Oxfam International*, July 18, 2024. https://policy-practice.oxfam.org/resources/water-war-crimes-how-israel-has-weaponised-water-in-its-military-campaign-in-ga-621609/.

Scheindlin, Dahlia. "Why There's No Excuse for Israelis Not Knowing What's Happening in Gaza." *Haaretz*, December 4, 2024. https://www.haaretz.com/israel-news/2024-12-04/ty-article-magazine/.premium/why-theres-no-excuse-for-israelis-not-knowing-whats-happening-in-gaza/00000193-8de4-d3dc-a5bb-8dff5f8b0000.

Shikaki, Khalil. "Willing to Compromise: Palestinian Public Opinion and the Peace Process." Special Report No. 158. United States Institute of Peace. January 19, 2006. https://www.un.org/unispal/document/auto-insert-204121/.

Shlaim, Avi. "From the Historical Archive: Israel and the Arrogance of Power." *Irish Pages* 9 (2015) 133–80.

---. "Israel's War on Gaza." In *Deluge: Gaza and Israel from Crisis to Cataclysm*, edited by Jamie Stern-Weiner, 13–36. New York: OR Books, 2024.

Sosebee, Stephen J. "The Passing of Yitzhak Rabin, Whose 'Iron Fist' Fueled the Intifada." WRMEA. https://www.wrmea.org/1990-october/the-passing-of-yitzhak-rabin-whose-iron-fist-fueled-the-intifada.html.

Stevenson, Tom. "Illusions of Containment." *London Review of Books* 47 (February 6, 2025). https://www.lrb.co.uk/the-paper/v47/n02/tom-stevenson/illusions-of-containment.

Stollar, Avihai. "10 Years Since 'Cast Lead': How Israel First Declared Total War on Gaza." *+972 Magazine*, February 5, 2019. https://www.972mag.com/10-years-since-cast-lead/.

Thrall, Nathan. *The Only Language They Understand: Forcing Compromise in Israel and Palestine*. New York: Metropolitan, 2017.

Tibon, Amir. *The Gates of Gaza: A Story of Betrayal, Survival, and Hope in Israel's Borderlands*. New York: Little, Brown and Company, 2024.

Toler, Aric, et al. "What Israeli Soldiers' Videos Reveal: Cheering Destruction and Mocking Gazans." *The New York Times*, February 6, 2024. https://www.nytimes.com/2024/02/06/world/middleeast/israel-idf-soldiers-war-social-media-video.html.

United Nations. "As Israel's Aerial Bombardments Intensify, 'There Is No Safe Place in Gaza,' Humanitarian Affairs Chief Warns Security Council." January 12, 2024. https://press.un.org/en/2024/sc15564.doc.htm.

---. "'Clear and Convincing Information' That Hostages Held in Gaza Subjected to Sexual Violence, Says UN Special Representative." March 4, 2024. https://news.un.org/en/story/2024/03/1147217.

United Nations Human Rights Council. "Report of the United Nations Fact-Finding Mission on the Gaza Conflict." https://www.ohchr.org/en/hr-bodies/hrc/special-sessions/session9/fact-finding-mission.

United Nations Office for the Coordination of Humanitarian Affairs. "Reported Impact Snapshot: Gaza Strip (3 April 2025)." https://www.ochaopt.org/content/reported-impact-snapshot-gaza-strip-3-april-2025.

United Nations Office of the High Commissioner for Human Rights. "Pattern of Israeli Attacks on Gaza Hospitals Raises Grave Concerns—Report." December 31, 2024. https://www.ohchr.org/en/press-releases/2024/12/pattern-israeli-attacks-gaza-hospitals-raises-grave-concerns-report.

---. "UN Human Rights Chief Deplores Harrowing Killings of Children and Women in Rafah." April 23, 2024. https://www.ohchr.org/en/press-releases/2024/04/un-human-rights-chief-deplores-harrowing-killings-children-and-women-rafah.

United Nations Office of the Special Representative of the Secretary-General on Sexual Violence in Conflict. "Mission Report: Official Visit of the Office of the SRSG-SVC to Israel and the Occupied West Bank 29 January–14 February 2024." https://news.un.org/en/sites/news.un.org.en/files/atoms/files/Mission_report_of_SRSG_SVC_to_Israel-oWB_29Jan_14_feb_2024.pdf.

White House. "Remarks by the President at Cairo University, 6-04-09." https://obamawhitehouse.archives.gov/the-press-office/remarks-president-cairo-university-6-04-09.

Winstanley, Asa. "How Israel Killed Hundreds of Its Own People on 7 October." *The Electronic Intifada*, October 7, 2024. https://electronicintifada.net/content/how-israel-killed-hundreds-its-own-people-7-october/49216.

———. "We Blew Up Israeli Houses on October 7, Says Israeli Colonel." *Washington Report on Middle East Affairs*, December 20, 2023. https://www.wrmea.org/israel-palestine/we-blew-up-israeli-houses-on-oct.-7-says-israeli-colonel.html.

CHAPTER TWO

Israel's Christian Armada Sets Sail

BRUCE N. FISK

As we act, let us not become the evil we deplore.[1]

Moral Clarity or Moral Confusion?

IMMEDIATELY AFTER OCTOBER 7, 2023, Christians in America and around the world expressed outrage over Hamas's merciless slaughter and abduction of Jews. On the very day of the bloodbath, *Christianity Today*'s Russell Moore proclaimed the need for "moral clarity about this war" and called American Christians to "stand with Israel under attack."[2] A couple of months later, evangelicalism's flagship magazine aired its first episode of

---

1. Spoken by Congresswoman Barbara J. Lee, who cast the lone dissenting vote against a resolution that otherwise passed unanimously in the US Senate and House on September 14, 2001, authorizing the president to "use all necessary and appropriate force against those nations, organizations, or persons he determines planned, authorized, committed, or aided the terrorist attacks." Cited in Hedges, *War Is a Force That Gives Us Meaning*, 5. Barbara Lee's remarks are posted on Facebook: https://fb.watch/xnlVdiz47o/.

2. Moore, "American Christians Should Stand with Israel Under Attack." See Fisk, "Allure of Moral Clarity in a Time of War." Moore faces further criticism in David Crump's essay on "Prisoner Abuse and Evangelical Indifference" (ch. 4 in this volume).

Promised Land, a six-part podcast series hosted by Mike Cosper that ran from December 20, 2023, to June 19, 2024. Part One begins in the decimated community Cosper visited in November 2023, just two miles from Gaza. "There's an incredible amount of *moral clarity* to be found at Kfar Aza," he says about the Israeli kibbutz, one of several that encircle the blockaded Palestinian territory.

> When you stand in the shell of someone's home and smell the residual toxins from a fire that burned in their living room, when you see the bullet holes in the walls, blast marks from RPGs and grenades, when you hear about the abduction of women and children and friends and parents, spouses, *you find yourself suddenly allergic to the phrase "it's complicated."* Because when it comes to the attacks of October 7, it's actually not complicated. Evil wore no mask that day. It was not seductive. It was not subtle. And as Christians or otherwise, we don't need to qualify those statements when we make them. But that doesn't mean we can't interrogate why there isn't peace, why peace doesn't seem on the horizon, and why things have gone wrong so many times in the past.[3]

On the one hand, Cosper is right to condemn without qualification the brutal killing of 62 residents of Kfar Aza (out of some 950) and the abduction of 19 more. On the other hand, Cosper's "moral clarity" about October 7 translates in subsequent *Promised Land* episodes and essays into naive endorsements of Israeli propaganda, distortions of history, a preoccupation with antisemitism, a shameless dismissal of human rights agencies, caricatures of Palestinian grievances, and a consistent defense of Israel's behavior before and after October 7. Chapter 14 in this book will have more to say about this important podcast series. Here, we simply lament that Cosper and *Christianity Today* had an opportunity to challenge the popular, binary, Israelis=worthy/Palestinians=unworthy, evangelical worldview. Instead, they championed it. They could have looked Palestinians in the eye, the way they look at Israelis. Instead, they looked away.[4]

---

3. The Bulletin, "Part One: It's Complicated," emphasis added. In "Part Three: Rocks in Hard Places," when pressing Palestinian scholar Mitri Raheb on why we shouldn't simply condemn Hamas full stop, Cosper says, "There's something grotesque about saying 'let's look at the broader context' in the aftermath of 10/7." Elsewhere (Cosper, "Evil Ideas Behind October 7") the *Christianity Today* reporter insists that only those blinded by ideology cannot see the "moral asymmetry" between Israel and Hamas, between a humane nation that provides humanitarian corridors and minimizes civilian casualties and bestial Hamas who targets civilians and glorifies the murder of women and children.

4. Ben Norquist takes a close look at *Christianity Today's* problematic response to

The Gospel Coalition's Ivan Mesa and Bernard Howard likewise announced that the moral fog had lifted.[5] Equally clear-minded was Richard Land, executive editor of *The Christian Post* and former president of the Southern Baptists' Ethics and Religious Liberty Commission. "This is not a clash of civilizations," he wrote, echoing Samuel Huntingdon. "This is a clash between civilization and barbarism."[6]

Also trading in hard binaries was John Hagee, the megachurch pastor from San Antonio. Speaking at the *March for Israel* rally on the National Mall in Washington, DC, on November 14, 2023, he said: "Choose Israel or Hamas. There is no middle ground in this conflict. You're either for the Jewish people or you're not."[7]

Equally at home in this tidy moral universe was evangelical Mike Huckabee, who is openly pro-settlement, anti-Two States, and warm to Israel's annexation of "Judea and Samaria." During a December 2023 tour of Jewish communities attacked on October 7, Trump's future ambassador to Israel would say, "You either stand with Israel or you stand with hate and chaos. This is not a geographical or political conflict. It is not horizontal—left vs. right—but vertical—heaven and hell or good and evil."[8]

Reading from the same script before the Israeli Knesset on May 19, 2024, was Elise Stefanik, the Republican congresswoman nominated to UN ambassador. According to the fierce Trump supporter, "what we are witnessing today is a story of the forces of good versus evil. The forces of civilization against the forces of barbarism, of humanity versus depravity."[9]

The allure of this "Manichean dualism that masquerades as 'realism'"[10] is strong: darkness and light, tyranny and freedom, terrorist and soldier. Moral binaries were irresistible for Mike Cosper standing in that Hamas-ravaged kibbutz. They are similarly alluring and politically handy on the campaign trail or when mobilizing public support for the next war. And when the boys return from the front in body bags. Veteran war

---

the Gaza crisis in ch. 14 of this volume, "Passing By on the Other Side: *Christianity Today* Since October 7." On the West's dehumanization of Palestinians, see El-Kurd, *Perfect Victims*, 14–22.

5. Howard and Mesa, "Israel's 9/11: The Need for Moral Clarity."
6. Klett, "SBC Leaders Spearhead Evangelical Statement in Support of Israel."
7. *The Times of Israel*, "Pastor Hagee: 'There Is No Middle Ground in This Conflict.'"
8. Lefkovitz, "Huckabee Cites US Educational Fail During Gaza Border Tour."
9. Stefanik, "Stefanik Delivers Historic Address." On March 27, 2025, Donald Trump withdrew Stefanik's nomination to be US ambassador to the United Nations, fearing Republicans might lose their razor-thin majority in Congress.
10. Verhey, "Neither Devils nor Angels," 601. See also Daghrir, "Binary Discourse in U.S. Presidential Speeches."

correspondent Chris Hedges understands this "mythic reality" that the state constructs, that the media sells, and that we embrace:

> While we venerate and mourn our own dead we are curiously indifferent about those we kill.... Our dead. Their dead. They are not the same. Our dead matter, theirs do not.[11]

> We demonize the enemy so that our opponent is no longer human. We view ourselves, our people, as the embodiment of absolute goodness. Our enemies invert our view of the world to justify their own cruelty. In most mythic wars this is the case. Each side reduces the other to objects—eventually in the form of corpses.[12]

But wait, say evangelicals. Are not moral binaries *biblical*? Does not John's Gospel (1:5) describe Jesus as light shining in darkness? Is it not written that "people loved darkness rather than light because their deeds were evil" (3:19)? Did not Paul (in Col 1:13) say that God "rescued us from the power of darkness and transferred us into the kingdom"[13] of God's son? Did not Moses (in Deut 30:19) offer Israel a sum total of two options: "life and death, blessings and curses"?

Yes and No. The insight of Scripture (matched by every human's experience) is *not* that evil is *over there*. *Every* individual lingers in twilight between virtue and vice. *Every* nation is capable of reprehensible evil. *Each one* of us is a full-fledged moral agent ennobled or debased by the choices we make. "There is no one who is righteous," writes Paul in Romans chapter 3. "Hate what is evil, hold fast to what is good," he says in chapter 12 (cf. Rom 2:6–11; Eph 4:17–32).

Drop any mortal into a combat zone and watch the moral compass spin, as it did for the apostle Peter who, under duress in the High Priest's courtyard, betrayed not only Jesus but also his own moral code.[14] If there is a "clash of civilizations," confesses Martha Nussbaum, it is "not 'out there,' between admirable Westerners and Muslim zealots. It is here, within each person, as we oscillate uneasily between self-protective aggression and the ability to live in the world with others."[15]

Professing "moral clarity" in times of war provides theological justification for dehumanizing the Other. It pairs nicely with historical amnesia

---

11. Hedges, *War Is a Force That Gives Us Meaning*, 14.
12. Hedges, *War Is a Force That Gives Us Meaning*, 21.
13. All Scripture citations in this chapter are from the NRSV.
14. See Carter, "New Testament and Moral Injury," 165–66.
15. Nussbaum, *Clash Within*, 337, quoted by Brueggemann, "God of Joshua," 17.

and with enthusiasm for industrial slaughter. By demonizing one party, canonizing the other, and ignoring relevant historical context, we feel no pressure to investigate the political messiness and weigh antecedent grievances. Erased is the need to consider Hamas's atrocities in the context of Israeli brutality or Western duplicity. Indeed, we free ourselves to construct Hamas as "an example of primordial Middle Eastern savagery" and to declare war on this caricature, rather than deal with the real Hamas, a complex combination of militant ideology and violence, religious conviction, political pragmatism and historical trauma.[16]

Neither is there cause to inquire whether Israel's abuse of Palestinians over decades, abetted by America, might have kindled fires of resentment. Nor, for that matter, need we be troubled by the body count when the battle we wage has God on our side.[17]

In William Bennett's 2002 paean to patriotism, *Why We Fight: Moral Clarity and the War on Terrorism*, the former Education Secretary reminisced about how, in the wake of 9/11, "the doubts and questions... seemed to fade into insignificance. Good was distinguished from evil, truth from falsehood. We were firm, dedicated, unified. It was, in short, a moment of moral clarity."[18] It was this moral clarity about the righteousness of America's cause that accompanied US troops into Iraq on a misguided quest for regime change. Cheered on by *with-us-or-with-the-enemy* rhetoric, America's *war on terror*—"a warpath without end... which... had no finite aim, no foreseeable conclusion"[19]—left many thousands dead, wounded, and displaced, and sowed seeds of resentment and despotism across the region.

Hamas's October attack was Israel's 9/11. Indeed, per capita, the number of slain Israelis was more than ten times the number of Americans killed on that dark September day in 2001. Hamas perpetrated unspeakable evil and horrific war crimes. But to profess moral clarity in such moments *without providing historical context* is beyond irresponsible. It silences dissenting voices, trivializes Palestinian grievances, and dismisses out of hand the legal and moral case against Israel's occupation. Rather than *clarity*,

---

16. Stevenson, "Illusions of Containment." See also Daniel Bannoura, "Hamas and Violence," ch. 5 in this volume.

17. Echoing the Minnesota philosopher Bob Dylan, "With God on Our Side."

18. Bennett, *Why We Fight*.

19. R. Fisk, *Great War for Civilization*, 840. In George W. Bush's "Address to a Joint Session of Congress and the American People" (September 20, 2001), the president boldly declared to the world: "Either with us or with the terrorists." A few paragraphs later: "This is not, however, just America's fight.... This is the world's fight. This is civilization's fight. This is the fight of all who believe in progress and pluralism, tolerance and freedom.... The civilized world is rallying to America's side."

we promote *confusion* and all but guarantee that the cycle of tragedy will continue.

Word Wars: Ambiguity, Omission, Distortion

Those who want to tip-toe past wartime carnage or avoid ascribing moral responsibility often lace their narratives with euphemisms and convoluted diction. Particularly handy is the passive voice, as it was for Ronald Reagan describing the Iran-Contra scandal, when he famously told Congress that "mistakes were made."[20] "Correspondents kill us with passive voice," writes Palestinian poet Mohammed El-Kurd. "If we are lucky, diplomats say that our death concerns them, but they never mention the culprit, let alone condemn the culprit."[21] Newspapers excel at hiding responsibility and casting doubt using passives and byzantine expressions like "the pace of death," "lives ended" and "lifeless bodies." The *New York Times* is typically egregious when it informs us that an "Explosion leaves many casualties."[22]

On October 9, 2023, the World Evangelical Alliance stated that Hamas's attack on Israel "*has resulted in* escalating violence and *loss* of innocent civilian lives in Israel and in Palestine."[23] Unaccountably, violence *escalates*. Mysteriously, lives *are lost*. Out of sight are human agency and culpability. The WEA rightly singled out Hamas for killing Israeli civilians, but it left unspecified the agents killing innocents in Palestine. Violence was apparently an unintended outcome, one that would somehow "further spread" and require "de-escalation."

That same day, the National Association of Evangelicals referred to "actions by Israel that go beyond self-defense by taking revenge on those living in Gaza." The problem, we were told, was that these actions "risk inflicting further suffering on innocent civilians while undermining the

---

20. Reagan, "Address Before a Joint Session of Congress." This section includes material adapted from Fisk, "Praised by Faint Damnation."

21. El-Kurd, *Perfect Victims*, 14.

22. Rad, "I Fixed the *New York Times*' Pro-Israel Headlines on Gaza"; Rad, "How Western Media Has Manufactured Consent for Atrocities." Nor is obfuscation in headlines new. Reporting on the Israeli assassination of the prominent Palestinian journalist Shireen Abu Akleh, the *New York Times* headline (May 11, 2022) read "Trailblazing Palestinian Journalist Killed in West Bank." (Prior to emendation, it was worse: "A Trailblazing Palestinian Journalist Dies, Aged 51.") On July 10, 2014, the *Times* headline about an Israeli missile that killed eight on a Gaza beach the previous day: "In Rubble of Gaza Seaside Cafe, Hunt for Victims Who Had Come for Soccer." The original headline was: "Missile at Beachside Gaza Cafe Finds Patrons Poised for World Cup." See El-Kurd, *Perfect Victims*, 32.

23. World Evangelical Alliance, "WEA's Statement on the Holy Land Conflict."

long-term security of the Israeli people."[24] Stripped of clutter, the NAE worried that "actions . . . beyond self-defense . . . risk inflicting suffering." Had George Orwell been their editor, the statement would have read: "Israeli soldiers are needlessly killing Gazan civilians (at a rate unprecedented in modern warfare)."

In the first episode of *Christianity Today's Promised Land* podcast, host Mike Cosper deploys similarly opaque diction. "The war *came* to Gaza," he says. "Israel *intensified* an already-existing blockade in Gaza and began a *bombardment campaign* that had *devastating effects* on the ground."[25]

Wars don't *come*. Armies wage them. Israel *intensified* its blockade, but the *intensification* Defense Minister Yoav Gallant announced was a complete siege that would block the entry of all electricity, food, water, and gas. Cosper was right: the *effects* were *devastating on the ground*. But why use language so clinical and detached? Israel's *bombardment* killed, maimed, and buried human beings alive. From *the ground* of which Cosper speaks, their blood cries out.

Cosper claims to possess "moral clarity" about the unmasked evil of October 7, but when it comes to context and commentary, his language absolves Israel of wrongdoing and amplifies Israeli mythologies. Cosper's account of the October 17, 2023, explosion at the Al-Ahli hospital, for example, occupies a hefty four and a half minutes at the beginning of Part Four ("Empire of Refugees," posted March 21, 2024). Listeners learn that Israel's official version of events has proven correct: the deaths were caused by an errant Palestinian missile, not by an Israeli airstrike. What we do *not* hear about are the detailed, forensic investigations that undermined, if not debunked entirely, that Israeli narrative. Nor, remarkably, do we hear any expression of remorse for the hundreds of Palestinians who died that day, whatever the cause. The only "damage" Cosper laments was to Israel's global reputation.[26]

Cosper's discussion of the November 11, 2023, assault on Al-Shifa, Gaza's largest hospital, is similarly slanted. Israel's claim that the medical center was a "terrorist stronghold" initially faced "a great deal of skepticism

---

24. National Association of Evangelicals, "NAE Condemns Violence in Middle East." On the unprecedented pace of killing, see Leatherby, "Gaza Civilians, Under Israeli Barrage, Are Being Killed at Historic Pace."

25. The Bulletin, "Part One: It's Complicated," emphases added.

26. Cosper repeats Israel's account of the Al-Ahli incident at the end of the episode and suggests there that the deaths served Hamas's political calculations. Cosper exonerates Israel of blame for the Al-Ahli hospital explosion again in "Part Six," and then embraces Israel's account of the May 26, 2024, "tent massacre," blaming Hamas for the casualties and again expressing no remorse whatsoever for the loss of Palestinian life. We cite reports challenging Israel's Al-Ahli narrative in ch. 1, n52.

and derision," Cosper observes, before adding that subsequent "evidence confirmed, and continues to confirm" Israel's assessment, by which Cosper apparently means that the assault on the hospital was warranted. We hear not a whisper from Cosper about the propaganda Israel had manufactured (e.g., video footage, unsubstantiated statements) to advance its claims.[27]

Franklin Graham's affection for Israel, like his father's, is well known. Graham's Samaritan's Purse is among the largest US faith-based non-profits. Their November 9, 2023, press release lamented that "innocent families are suffering in Israel and Gaza as a result of the war, and many lives have been lost because they haven't been able to reach medical care fast enough." Not only is the phrase "lives have been lost" conveniently and suspiciously ambiguous, but the full statement implies that the folks who need urgent medical care are Israelis, which explains Samaritan Purse's plan to replace the *Magen David Adom* ambulances that Hamas destroyed.[28] On October 12, 2023, Graham explained the inaction of Samaritan's Purse on the other side of the fence with equally impressive ambiguity: "At this time, humanitarian access to Gaza is not possible, and the border is sealed." One wonders if the border sealed itself.[29]

Selective ambiguity and strategic omission were likewise deployed in the formal response to October 7 by Chosen People Ministries, which includes this statement: "We pray steps will be taken to eliminate the lethal presence of Hamas terrorists, the hostages be freed, Israel's borders be secured and noncombatant Palestinians in Gaza and other parts of Israel be spared from the evils of these and other Islamic terrorists." No prayers about securing *Gaza's* borders, no appeal that noncombatant Palestinians be spared from the carnage unleashed by the IDF, nor any lament for the thousands of Palestinians swept up and imprisoned without charge. Rather,

---

27. See Scahill, "Al-Shifa Hospital, Hamas's Tunnels, and Israeli Propaganda." The pro-Israel bias of *Promised Land* is not benign. The series distorts history. In "Part Two" ("The Zionist Story"), for example, we hear that the Palestinians who became refugees fled *during the 1948 war*. In fact, Zionist forces had already expelled about 250,000 Palestinians (a full third of the total) *before* the war began, including 60,000 each from Haifa and Jaffa, and 30,000 from West Jerusalem, a detail that undermines the Israeli fog-of-war narrative, and suggests that the Zionist project was as much about demography (i.e., displacement) as geography. (See, e.g., Khalidi, *Hundred Years' War on Palestine*, 74.) Elsewhere in the same episode, Cosper claims the Israelis were vastly outgunned and outmanned during the 1948 war, and that their army of "refugees, holocaust survivors and World War II veterans" won an improbable victory, when in fact by almost every metric, the Zionists had the advantage. On the popular, but misleading, claim of Zionist military inferiority in 1948, see below, pp. 70–71.

28. Samaritan's Purse, "Samaritan's Purse Responds in Israel."

29. Samaritan's Purse, "Important Message from Franklin Graham on Israel."

anodyne petitions ask God to bless "the steps taken" to "eliminate the lethal presence" of Hamas.[30]

Should Israel Not Defend Itself?

In the wake of October 7, many American Christians were quick to frame Israel's campaign as an exercise in legitimate self defense. It took only three days for Lindsey Graham, the Southern Baptist South Carolina senator, to wax genocidal on X and inform Fox News: "We're in a religious war here. I am with Israel. Do whatever the hell you have to do to defend yourself. Level the place."

The following day Graham's fellow Southern Baptists released an "Evangelical Statement in Support of Israel" which professed full support for "Israel's right and duty to defend itself against further attack."[31] The 358-word statement includes zero words about Palestinian grievances or aspirations; the only historical context it can recall is centuries of antisemitism:

> Jewish people . . . have been often targeted by their neighbors since God called them as His people in the days of Abraham (Gen. 12:1–3).
>
> Since . . . 1948, Israel has faced numerous attacks, incursions, and violations of its national sovereignty.
>
> The Jewish people have long endured genocidal attempts to eradicate them and to destroy the Jewish state. These antisemitic, deadly ideologies and terrorist actions must be opposed.

Southern Baptists were hardly alone in framing Israel's assault as justifiable self-defense. They stood shoulder to shoulder with President Biden, Vice President Harris, and countless others. "Israel is in a war of defense," Israeli lawyer Tal Becker told the International Court of Justice in January 2024.[32] Professors David Lyle Jeffrey and Jeff Levin would assert twice in

---

30. Chosen People Ministries, "Chosen People Ministries' Affirmation of Israel." Apart from the misleading inference that the West Bank lies within Israel, CPM prays about the threat Palestinians face from "these and other Islamic terrorists," while saying nothing about the larger threat of Israeli forces (who had killed 239 West Bank Palestinians in the first seven weeks after October 7).

31. The "Evangelical Statement in Support of Israel," produced by the Southern Baptist Ethics and Religious Liberty Commission, was signed by 2,000 evangelicals including Al Mohler, Greg Laurie, Darrell Bock, Mitch Glaser, and Mark Tooley. See B. N. Fisk, "Ever the Victim, Never the Aggressor," for critique.

32. Israeli Ministry of Foreign Affairs, "Opening Statement of MFA Legal Advisor Dr. Tal Becker."

Christian Scholar's Review that what students were protesting on American university campuses was Israel's right to defend itself.[33]

How compelling is Israel's "self-defense" defense?

Apart from the awkward problem that "self-defense" cannot seriously apply to obliterating hospitals, schools, apartment buildings, and churches or to killing medics, journalists, humanitarian workers, women, and children—apart from that, there is also a legal problem to consider, as human rights attorney Noura Erakat has observed. Erakat is among those who argue that Israel cannot legally declare war on territory it occupies. Even after "disengaging" from Gaza—removing settlers and relocating forces to Gaza's perimeter—Israel has remained in control:

> Israel reserved the right to use force against Palestinians living in the Gaza Strip *in the name of preventive and reactive self-defense*, and it has conducted several military operations in Gaza *in the name of such self-defense*. Israel has maintained control of [Gaza's] air space, its seaports, its telecommunications network, its electromagnetic sphere, its tax revenue distribution, and its population registry. Israel also has complete control of Palestinian movement as it controls four of its five border crossings with Gaza and therefore the ingress and egress of all the territory's goods and people. Upon announcing Israel's withdrawal, Israel's political elite made clear that Israel did not intend to relinquish control of the Gaza Strip. Dov Weisglass, senior adviser to Prime Minister Ariel Sharon, explained that the disengagement was meant to freeze the peace process by supplying "the amount of formaldehyde that is necessary so there will not be a political process with the Palestinians." Unilateral withdrawal sought to alter the balance of power by offering a veneer of Palestinian independence while retaining Israeli control.[34]

Israel insists that the "occupation" of Gaza ended in 2005. The rest of the world disagrees.

> The International Criminal Court, the Human Rights Council's Fact-Finding Mission to the Gaza Strip and multiple international human rights organizations have acknowledged that *Israel remains in effective control of the Gaza Strip. Accordingly, the laws of occupation should remain in force*, thus obligating

---

33. Jeffrey and Levin, "Anti-Semitism, Amalek, and the American University."
34. Erakat, *Justice for Some*, 195–96; emphasis added.

Israel to use its law enforcement authority to restore order and *prohibiting it from declaring war upon the territory it occupied.*[35]

Erakat is right, it seems to me. Israel cannot have it both ways:

> Israel insisted its occupation had ended, but it also recognized that Gaza was not sovereign. It declared Gaza a "hostile entity," which was neither a state wherein Palestinians have the right to police and protect themselves nor an occupied territory whose civilian population Israel had a duty to protect. This meant that it could deny Palestinians the right to fully govern themselves and simultaneously use military force to thwart their resistance to colonial domination.[36]

Since Israel effectively controls Gaza, it is legally obligated to protect Gaza's population and cannot legitimately define its operations against resistance forces as self-defense—so goes Erakat's argument. While international lawyers sort this out, we must grant that what seems obvious to many observers—that Israel's bombardment of Gaza is *defensive*—turns out not to be so straightforward. Indeed, there are good reasons to conclude that Israel is exploiting the opportunity afforded by Hamas's attack to wage an *offensive* battle, not just to dislodge Hamas but to cleanse Gaza of Palestinians, precisely what Donald Trump began advocating in early February 2025.

Worse Than Genocide?

On January 26, 2024, the International Court of Justice ruled, by fifteen votes to two, that:

> the State of Israel shall, in accordance with its obligations under the Convention on the Prevention and Punishment of the Crime of Genocide, in relation to Palestinians in Gaza, take all measures within its power to prevent the commission of all acts within the scope of Article II of this Convention, in particular:
>
> (a) killing members of the group;
>
> (b) causing serious bodily or mental harm to members of the group;
>
> (c) deliberately inflicting on the group conditions of life calculated to bring about its physical destruction in whole or in part; and

---

35. Erakat, *Justice for Some*, 196; emphasis added.
36. Erakat, *Justice for Some*, 196.

(d) imposing measures intended to prevent births within the group.[37]

The court did not determine that Israel was committing genocide, as the US State Department, coming to Israel's defense, was quick to point out.[38] Rather, the ICJ ruled that "at least some of the rights claimed by South Africa and for which it is seeking protection are plausible."[39] This finding of *plausibility* drew loud complaints from Israel. Benjamin Netanyahu called the court ruling a "vile" case of "blatant discrimination" that was both "false" and "outrageous."[40] When a March 2025 UN report accused Israel of "genocidal acts," Israeli Foreign Ministry spokesperson Oren Marmorstein described it as "one of the worst cases of blood libel the world has ever seen."[41]

Israel's evangelical defenders have likewise been scandalized, with the Philos Project referring to the "genocide slur," which they labeled "a contemporary variant of the blood libel."[42] Mike Cosper confessed, in Part Six of his podcast, that he didn't "have a lot of patience" for the charge. For Messianic Jewish apologist Michael Brown, genocide accusations were "downright scandalous."[43] Brown's recoil was understandable—given his long-standing concerns about antisemitism,[44] given the popular perception of genocide as the crime of crimes, and given that a legal determination on this matter could trigger grave global consequences for Israel.[45] His rebuttal consisted of three points:

---

37. International Court of Justice, "Summary of the Order of 26 January 2024." Updates on the South Africa-versus-Israel case before the ICJ appear on the ICJ website. https://www.icj-cij.org/case/192.

38. Magid, "US Maintains Genocide Allegations."

39. On the "plausibility" standard, see OpinioJuris, "ICJ's Findings on Plausible Genocide in Gaza."

40. Israeli PM, "Prime Minister Netanyahu Comments on the Decision of the International Court of Justice."

41. Rozovsky and Reuters, "UN Report Accuses Israel of 'Genocidal Acts' in Gaza, Israel Rejects Allegations." For the forty-nine-page UN report, see UN Office of the High Commissioner for Human Rights, "'More Than a Human Can Bear.'"

42. Philos Project, "Pope's Misled Call to Investigate Israel's 'Genocide.'"

43. Brown, "It Is Downright Scandalous to Accuse Israel of Genocide."

44. Brown regards "Jew-hatred" as "a default attitude of fallen human beings," their reaction to the Jews' status as God's chosen people. Gryboski, "'Dangerous' and 'Growing.'" See also Brown, *Christian Antisemitism*.

45. See article IV of the UN Office of the High Commissioner for Human Rights, "Convention on the Prevention": "Persons committing genocide or any of the other acts enumerated in article III shall be punished, whether they are constitutionally responsible rulers, public officials or private individuals."

1. Arab populations—in Israel, the West Bank, Gaza—are actually growing.
2. The IDF goes to great lengths to avoid civilian casualties.[46]
3. Even by Gaza Health Ministry figures, Israel (in December 2023) has killed less than 1 percent of the population, a toll "typical of civilian casualties in war—tragic, agonizing, heartbreaking—but nothing comparable to genocide in the slightest."[47]

Brown's audience may not have been aware that "genocide" is nowhere defined in terms of a percentage of the targeted population. Article Two of the Genocide Convention refers only to "acts committed with intent to destroy, *in whole or in part*, a national, ethnical, racial or religious group, as such."[48] Curiously absent from Brown's remarks is any engagement with the arguments advanced by scholars of genocide, among them Raz Segal. By October 13, 2023, the Israeli scholar of the Holocaust and genocide at Stockton University was already describing Israel's behavior in Gaza as a "textbook case of genocide," marveling that "Israel's genocidal assault on Gaza is quite explicit, open, and unashamed."[49]

It would take ten months before Omer Bartov of Brown University, a renowned Israeli-American Holocaust and genocide scholar, would invoke the G-word. By the spring of 2024, Bartov was convinced that Israel intended "to make the Gaza Strip entirely uninhabitable for its own population."[50] By June, he was noting the "utter inability of Israeli society today to feel any empathy for the population of Gaza." By August 13, 2024, Bartov was convinced that Israel had crossed the genocide line:

> At least since the attack by the IDF on Rafah on 6 May 2024, it was no longer possible to deny that Israel was engaged in systematic war crimes, crimes against humanity and genocidal actions. It was not just that this attack against the last concentration of Gazans—most of them displaced already several times by the IDF, which now once again pushed them to a so-called

---

46. On this point, see the Introduction, n16, and ch. 3 in this volume, "Bombing in the Name of the Gospel."

47. Brown, "It Is Downright Scandalous to Accuse Israel of Genocide."

48. UN Office of the High Commissioner for Human Rights, "Convention on the Prevention"; emphasis added.

49. Segal, "Textbook Case of Genocide." Segal describes the troubled state of the discipline in "Genocide Denial in Holocaust Studies."

50. Thapar, "What Israel Doing in Gaza." On the importance of preserving cultural property during armed conflict, see Donald Binder, "The Political Perils of Biblical Archaeology in the Holy Land," ch. 7 in this volume.

safe zone—demonstrated a total disregard of any humanitarian standards. It also clearly indicated that *the ultimate goal of this entire undertaking from the very beginning had been to make the entire Gaza Strip uninhabitable, and to debilitate its population to such a degree that it would either die out or seek all possible options to flee the territory.* In other words, the rhetoric spouted by Israeli leaders since 7 October was now being translated into reality—namely, as the 1948 UN Genocide Convention puts it, that Israel was acting "with intent to destroy, in whole or in part," the Palestinian population in Gaza, "as such, by killing, causing serious harm, or inflicting conditions of life meant to bring about the group's destruction."[51]

Given the findings of these researchers, to which we must add the work of Amnesty International, Human Rights Watch, Doctors Without Borders, the UN, and others,[52] defenders of Israel like Michael Brown and Melanie Phillips[53] clearly have reason to reconsider their acquittals. What is less clear, however, is whether such reconsiderations, even paired with a definitive ruling of genocide by the ICJ, would do anything to sway American foreign policy. Pulitzer Prize–winner Samantha Power lamented as much several decades ago:

> No U.S. president has ever made genocide prevention a priority, and no U.S. president has ever suffered politically for his indifference to its occurrence. It is thus no coincidence that genocide rages on.[54]

---

51. Bartov, "As a Former IDF Soldier"; emphasis added. With respect to Hamas's attack on October 7, Bartov called it a "war crime," likely a "crime against humanity" and, in light of Hamas's charter, plausibly including "genocidal aspects." See Amanpour, "Israeli-American Historian Explains."

52. Amnesty International released a 296-page report, "'You Feel Like You Are Subhuman,'" on December 5, 2024. Soon to follow, on December 19, 2024, was the 179-page report from Human Rights Watch, "Extermination and Acts of Genocide." The UN Office of the High Commissioner for Human Rights reported their assessment on November 16, 2023: "Gaza: UN Experts Call on International Community." Widely known is the ongoing case brought before the International Court of Justice by South Africa on December 29, 2023. See also "Genocide in Gaza: Analysis of International Law and Its Application to Israel's Military Actions since October 7, 2023," a report published on May 15, 2024, by the University Network for Human Rights, joined by human rights centers at the Boston University School of Law, Cornell Law School, the University of Pretoria, and Yale Law School; *UN News*, "Rights Expert."

53. Phillips, "Truth of the Palestinian Cause."

54. Power, *"Problem from Hell,"* xxi.

Debates over the applicability of "genocide" to Israel's (and Hamas's) attacks, and the challenge of establishing genocidal *intent* in the courts—all this may in any case be something of a distraction. Australian scholar A. Dirk Moses argues that our fixation on genocide as the "crime of crimes" at the top of the criminal hierarchy "blinds us to other types of humanly caused civilian death, like bombing cities and the 'collateral damage' of missile and drone strikes, blockades, and sanctions."[55]

There are plenty of reasons besides ethnic hatred, in other words, for state and para-state actors to perpetrate, or choose not to avert, civilian massacres. As Moses observes, "the deliberate destruction of a people [i.e., genocide] is a terrible crime. But why is it worse than the foreseeable destruction of many people?"[56] Countless innocents are sacrificed, he says, on the altar of "permanent security," his term for "the unobtainable goal of absolute safety that necessarily results in civilian casualties by its paranoid tendency to indiscriminate violence." It turns out that our "fetish of genocide as the 'crime of crimes'" can work to permit, rather than to prevent, other forms of systematic, industrial violence, some of which may actually be worse.[57]

Weaponizing the Bible and the Afterlife of Amalek

On October 28, 2023, Benjamin Netanyahu announced his plan for a ground offensive in Gaza by invoking the biblical clash with the Amalekites. "'Remember what Amalek did to you,'" the prime minister said. "We remember and we fight."[58]

Religiously observant soldiers and their rabbis knew well the story to which Netanyahu alluded—in which God commanded Israel to erase Amalek's memory, to "utterly destroy all that they have," and to "kill both man and woman, child and infant, ox and sheep, camel and donkey" (1 Sam 15:3). The biblically literate in his audience would also know that King Saul, by leaving the job unfinished, disqualified himself for office, and

---

55. Moses, *Problems of Genocide*, 1.

56. Moses, *Problems of Genocide*, 25.

57. Moses, *Problems of Genocide*, 1, 11–12. Also Shapiro, "Something Worse Than Genocide."

58. The official transcript (Israeli Ministry of Foreign Affairs, "Statement by PM Netanyahu") confirms that Netanyahu was alluding to Deut 25:17. The biblical Amalek saga spans multiple books of the Old Testament: Exod 17:8–16; Num 14:42–45; Deut 25:17–19; Judg 6:3; 1 Sam 15:2–33; 30:1–31; 2 Sam 1:1–16. Haman in the book of Esther is called an *Agagite* (Agag was an Amalekite king, 1 Sam 15:8) and "the enemy of the Jews" (Esth 3:1, 10; 8:1; 9:10, 24). See also Esth 3:10; 7:6, 10; 8:1–3, 7.

that Haman, who centuries later schemed to destroy Jews "young and old, women and children" in Esther (3:13), was an Amalekite survivor.

By bathing his military campaign in a biblical aura, the prime minister rendered the Palestinian nation a *perpetual* enemy. The unspoken corollary is that negotiation and compromise are ruled out. Genocide, however, is not.[59]

Christians, too, have been weaponizing Amalek.[60] Peter Leithart in a *Gospel Coalition* piece speaks of "the Amalekites of Hamas."[61] *Christianity Today*'s Mike Cosper said, "Netanyahu isn't wrong to see something of the Amalekites in the brutality of Hamas and their willingness to target women and children."[62] Jürgen Bühler of the International Christian Embassy Jerusalem sees Amalek as a demonic force, a *spirit* that *possesses* Hamas. While Israeli soldiers wage war here below, the church must hover above, like Moses on the mountain, in "persistent prayer" for Israel's victory. Hamas militants are not merely war criminals. They are hell's minions, and their destruction by Israel's band of righteous warriors is a divine mandate.[63]

David Lyle Jeffrey and Jeff Levin, in the *Christian Scholar's Review* article noted earlier, depict Amalek as the "embodiment of Jew-hatred," which embodiment they claimed to have detected not only in Hamas but

---

59. South Africa cited such statements before the ICJ as evidence of Israel's genocidal intent. See Bassist, "ICJ Genocide Hearing.'" Brian Kaylor ("Call for 'Biblical' Genocide") said it was "a call to kill everyone. Not just enemy combatants but even infants. It's a call not for a 'just war' but for a total war in the name of God." See also Kaylor, "Gaza, War, and the Christian Witness." Deploying Amalek against Palestinians on earlier occasions were ultranationalist Rabbi Meir Kahane, Gush Emunim settlers and rabbis, and Baruch Goldstein, who in 1994 gunned down Muslim men, women, and children in Hebron's Tomb of the Patriarchs, killing 29 and wounding 125 others. It was no accident that Goldstein carried out the massacre on Purim, the festival that celebrates Israel's survival and revenge on Haman-the-Amalekite (Esth 9:16).

60. Not for the first time. Puritans constructed Native Americans as Amalekites. See Warrior, "Native American Perspective," 283–84; Salaita, *Holy Land in Transit*, ch. 3.

61. Leithart, "Hamas." In a tweet on October 13, 2023, above a picture presumably showing a bomb detonating in Gaza, Leithart wrote: "Yahweh vows to fight until the memory of Amalek is blotted out from under heaven" (https://twitter.com/TGC/status/1712838183916900865?).

62. The Bulletin, "Part One: It's Complicated." One wonders if Cosper was equally troubled by Israeli bombs having killed some 10,000 of Gaza's women and children, as reported in the *New York Times* and elsewhere *before* Cosper's first episode aired.

63. Bühler, "Spirit of Amalek." Further, "This vicious spirit of Amalek arose once more on October 7th. Rabbinic literature presents Amalek as the arch enemy of the Jewish people. Today, we call it violent antisemitism." Cf. Exod 17:10–12. Tracking Messianic Jewish correlations of Amalek and Hamas is Jayson Casper, "For Messianic Jews."

also "among the ranks of faculty and students at some of our so-called elite universities." It turns out that American students are "the newest and most vociferous group of would-be Amalekites."[64]

In my judgment these Baylor scholars—an evangelical Christian and a conservative Jew—have fundamentally mischaracterized the core motivation of most campus protesters (viz., as "marching in support of Hamas and the extermination of Jews") and ignored evidence that the vast majority of students jeopardizing academic and professional futures were animated *not* by hostility toward Jews *but* by what they saw as university complicity in a real-time genocide.[65] Anti-Jewish bigotry is indeed growing in America, which should concern us all. But we only put Jews at greater risk when public discourse treats any criticism of the State of Israel as antisemitic by definition.

When Christian scholars and influencers like Peter Leithart, Mike Cosper, David Lyle Jeffrey, and Jürgen Bühler invoke Amalek, they are not riffing harmlessly on a biblical theme. Such rhetoric is incendiary, as Israel's prime minister knew well when he willfully stoked flames across Israeli society. Many responded with rage and calls for revenge.[66] Five weeks after October 7, Israeli hip-hop duo Ness & Stilla released "Harbu Darbu," a war anthem that quickly topped Israeli charts. Celebrating the military as if engaged in gang warfare, the song calls Hamas the "sons of Amalek."[67] On December 8, 2023, a video posted on X showed dancing Israeli soldiers singing, "I stick by one mitzvah [i.e., command], to wipe off the seed of Amalek."[68]

To weaponize Amalek is to locate evil entirely on one side of a conflict. It turns resistance into antisemitism and constructs Palestinians as "the reincarnation of monsters of the Jewish past, the latest manifestation of the

---

64. Jeffrey and Levin, "Anti-Semitism."

65. The Harvard Crimson article (Kim and Orakwue, "Hundreds of Harvard Protesters") Jeffrey and Levin cite as evidence that "students in the hundreds came out in public protests against Israel defending itself, even explicitly backing Hamas, some even in praise of the genocide of Jews" makes no such claims. Their best evidence of antisemitism (see their n8) comes from comments made by professors, *not* students, on social media, collected by ADL ("Some U.S. Professors Praise"). If a number of these professors' comments amount to Jew-hatred, they illustrate how antisemitism sometimes hides behind criticism of Israel. This camouflage would be more difficult if we all insisted on a rigorous distinction between Jews/Judaism/the Jewish people and Israel/Zionism/the nation-state.

66. Leal, "Don't Let Calls for Revenge."

67. Levitt, "Why the No. 1 Song in Israel Represents a Radical Shift"; Kessler, "Life During Wartime."

68. Demas, "Fact Checking Claims."

eternal, pathological, genocidal hatred that, according to the Passover Haggadah, 'in every generation rises up to destroy us.'"[69] Not only does it erase Palestinian grievances. It sanctifies Israeli behavior and implicitly claims divine sanction for mass slaughter. Israeli motivations become pure—devoid of vengeance, rage, tribalism, ethnonationalism, and territorialism. An earthly conflict—over territory, demography, and ideology—becomes a cosmic battle.

October 7 caused Israel profound and lasting trauma. Hamas showed itself capable of heinous crimes against Israeli citizens.[70] But Israel's disproportionate and indiscriminate retaliation has turned Gaza into a "'graveyard for thousands of children' and a 'living hell for everyone else.'"[71] Those for whom Gaza's war-imposed squalor is merely the setting for the latest battle between Israelites and Amalekites are unlikely to lament, much less grieve, Palestinian starvation, disease, displacement, injury, and death.[72] Those who declare Gaza's millions to be the warriors and weapons of Satan give themselves license to excuse Israel's decimation of the population and to defend US-abetted war crimes. Beware the weaponized Bible.

Praised with Faint Damnation

Israel's evangelical partisans routinely grant that Israel is not perfect. Russell Moore of *Christianity Today*, for example, assured us on the very day of the attack that he was prepared to criticize Israel.

> Many of us are quite willing to call out Israel when we believe it is acting wrongly. We don't believe the Israeli Knesset is somehow inerrant or infallible.

Yet Moore names no wrongdoings, nor does he hint that a catalog of Israel's misdeeds might provide helpful context for understanding—not

---

69. Beinart, *Being Jewish*, ch. 2.

70. On sex crimes committed and alleged on October 7, see Rozovsky, "15 Witnesses"; UN Office of the High Commissioner for Human Rights, "Commission of Inquiry"; United Nations, "Gaza"; Abunimah, "ICC Has No Evidence for 7 October Rapes."

71. Lanard, "Dangerous History"; Hasson, "Numbers Show."

72. Juergensmeyer, *Terror in the Mind of God*, 9, 191–92. Also 184: "What makes religious violence particularly savage and relentless is that its perpetrators have placed such religious images of divine struggle—cosmic war—in the service of worldly political battles."

defending—what happened on October 7 when militants broke out of Gaza and slaughtered soldiers and civilians alike.[73]

Moore is not alone in this. Almost never do Israel's apologists offer specific, substantive, public critique, much less condemnation. Writing three days after Hamas's attack, Ivan Mesa and Bernard Howard of *The Gospel Coalition* take pains to define what being "pro-Israel" does *not* mean:

> We accept that the state of Israel hasn't always acted blamelessly in its conduct toward the Palestinian people. To be pro-Israel in this situation, as we the authors are, isn't to whitewash every action Israel's government or military have taken, from its founding to today.

What Mesa and Howard "accept" is a truism—that "the state of Israel hasn't always acted blamelessly." But even while claiming not to be whitewashing Israel's "conduct toward the Palestinian people," they offer no examples and name no action that merits criticism.[74]

Equally hollow are the assurances of Anglican theologian Gerald McDermott:

> We do not mean that the state of Israel is a perfect country. Or that it should not be criticized for its failures.
>
> We . . . disagree with dispensationalism at the popular level . . . that the present state of Israel is never to be criticized.
>
> It certainly does not mean that Israel is always right or that it has never been unjust in its dealings with other nations.[75]

New Testament scholar Darrell Bock likewise claims not to be giving Israel a pass:

> To endorse Israel and a national place for the nation is *not* to give her carte blanche for everything she does. Christian Zionism is not a blind endorsement of Israel. It does not give the nation a pass on issues of justice or moral obligations.[76]

It seems fair, then, to ask: "*How* exactly has Israel been unjust?" Silence.

---

73. Moore, "American Christians Should Stand with Israel."
74. Howard and Mesa, "Israel's 9/11."
75. McDermott, *New Christian Zionism*, 12, 14, 328.
76. McDermott, *New Christian Zionism*, 309.

Rather than speak inconvenient truths to power, rather than complicate Israel's tidy morality tale, rather than thundering forth like Jeremiah, John the Baptist, and Jesus before them, their voices trail off.

Into silence.

Silence about Israel's restrictions on Palestinian movement and expropriation of Palestinian land. Silence about Israel's de facto annexation of the Jordan Valley and suffocating blockade of Gaza. Silence about the plight of imprisoned minors and Itamar Ben Gvir's efforts to punish Palestinian prisoners by reducing food rations.[77] Silence about the indiscriminate use of tear gas, about snipers shooting Palestinian aid workers and journalists with impunity,[78] and about the surging, unrestrained violence of West Bank settlers.[79] Silence about Israel's long-standing practice of collective punishment and its latest campaign to make Gaza uninhabitable.

When the Israeli government denies reports of widespread prisoner abuse, the discussion is over. When evidence exposes a governing coalition hell-bent on displacing Palestinians, demolishing homes, raiding refugee camps, annexing large portions of the West Bank, and stoking violence on the Temple Mount,[80] we hear platitudes about Israel's self-defense and security. It's as if pro-Israel zeal has made it anathema even to *imagine* a Jewish state guilty of war crimes. It's as if silence counts as penance for centuries of Christian antisemitism.

This silence is not the spiritual discipline. This is not the legal "right to remain silent." Not the echoing silence of a fragile ceasefire. It's more like the quiet that smothers a destroyed Bedouin village after the Caterpillar bulldozer departs. It's the guilty silence of complicity. Perfunctory acknowledgments of Israel's nondescript "imperfections" are vacuous. Faint damnations function as praise.

Christian Support for Israel: An Explainer

That American Christian support for Israel has not wavered throughout Gaza's decimation calls for explanation. I conclude this chapter with six observations about the American Christian context, particularly its

---

77. Breiner, "Israel Reduces Food."
78. Speri, "Israeli Forces Deliberately Killed Palestinian American Journalist."
79. In the first half of 2023, *before* the Hamas attacks of October 7, the International Crisis Group counted 591 settler attacks against Palestinians, nearly three per day. See International Crisis Group, "Rise of Settler Violence." See also Mezzofiore et al., "Israel's Military"; Bergman and Mazzetti, "Unpunished."
80. Parker, "Why Israeli Raids on Al-Aqsa Mosque Are Stoking Tensions."

various evangelical species, to help us make sense of this uncommonly fierce loyalty.[81]

1. Evangelicals feel kinship with Jews.

Christians feel solidarity with their Jewish cousins and gratitude for their gifts of monotheism, the Scriptures (both Old Testament and New), and, of course, the Messiah. Did not Isa 60:3 say that the nations shall come to the light of Israel? Did not Jesus say (John 4:22) that salvation is from the Jews?[82] Curiously, many feel stronger kinship with secular Jews than with Eastern Orthodox Christians.

2. Evangelicals feel contrition for antisemitism.

Christians with even a superficial knowledge of church history know that we have been complicit in centuries of violent antisemitism—pogroms, expulsions, false accusations, forced conversions, torture, scapegoating—culminating in the Holocaust. One way to make amends, many have decided, is by defending the modern Jewish state against its critics, or at least remaining silent about Israel's misdeeds.[83]

One problem here is the careless conflation of the ancient people (Jews) with the modern nation-state (Israel), the latter portrayed as the ever-persecuted, collective "Jew among the nations." The conflation lends weight, secondly, to the increasingly common, but dangerously flawed, contention that those who protest Israel's treatment of Palestinians are almost certainly guilty of antisemitism. Those who demand equal rights for Palestinians, who point out human rights abuses, who express solidarity with besieged Gazans, who call for an immediate ceasefire—so goes the logic—all qualify as fugitive antisemites.

With respect to the present crisis, thirdly, Peter Beinart observes that "accusing Israel's critics of antisemitism is the single best way to avert one's eyes" from Israel's crimes in Gaza.

> It's more effective than questioning death tolls, invoking human shields, or comparing Israel's bombing to other wars, because those arguments require discussing Gaza. Accusations of

---

81. See also the four factors David Crump considers in ch. 4 below, pp. 108–11.

82. See also Rom 15:25–27; Luke 7:4–5; and Smith, *More Desired*.

83. Along these lines, see the personal testimony of Suzanne Henderson in ch. 15 below.

antisemitism change the subject entirely. They turn a conversation about the war into a conversation about the motives of the people who oppose it.

By insisting that opponents of Zionism are antisemites, one is free to "depict Palestinians and their supporters as bigots, thus turning a conversation about the oppression of Palestinians into a conversation about the oppression of Jews."[84]

Evangelicals rightly lament Christianity's deep complicity in antisemitism over the centuries, and they should support the fight against it. For this very reason they should want to distinguish carefully between animus toward Jews and evidence-based criticism of the State of Israel; between an ethnic/religious identity (Jewish) and a political ideology (Zionism).[85] Ignoring this distinction actually endangers Jews around the world.

3. Evangelicals see God's hand in Middle East events.

Popular among Western Christians is the belief that the birth of modern Israel is an act of God. The hosts of heaven joined the battle; Israel's military victories in 1948 and 1967 were miraculous.[86] From which it follows that to support Israel today is to align ourselves with God's work and will.

In my experience, advocates of this view rarely consider the historical details. It is enough to profess that David once again defeated Goliath, that an improbable Jewish militia manned by refugees and Holocaust survivors somehow fought off hordes of Arab invaders. We cited Mike Cosper of *Christianity Today* earlier, along these lines. But if we do examine the historical record, a different picture emerges.

In 1948, Palestinians initially outnumbered Jews two-to-one, and they initially held the high ground. But by almost every other metric, Jews had the advantage: organization, motivation, infrastructure, war preparation,

---

84. Beinart, *Being Jewish*, 91. On the dangers of equating anti-Zionism with antisemitism, see also Crump, *Like Birds in a Cage*, 223–40; Finkelstein, *Beyond Chutzpah*, 21–85; Shabi, *Off-White*, chapter 4. It is possible, of course, for antisemites to cloak their anti-Jewish bigotry in pronouncements against the Jewish state. Crump (*Like Birds in a Cage*, 233–35) calls this "antisemitism by proxy" but contends that convincing examples are hard to find. From a Christian Zionist perspective, see Merkley, *Christian Attitudes*, 216. On antisemitic language in Hamas's 1987 charter, see Daniel Bannoura, "Hamas and Violence," ch. 5 in this volume.

85. Butler, *Parting Ways*, 114–50.

86. A 2017 LifeWay poll found that 80 percent of evangelicals believed that the birth of Israel in 1948 fulfilled biblical prophecy. Bump, "Half of Evangelicals Support Israel."

weapons production, weapons, trained fighters, command and control, and international fundraising. Prior to May 1948, combat-trained Jews outnumbered ill-equipped Arabs roughly five-to-one.[87] When the guns finally fell silent, the numerical advantage of combatants was two-to-one in Israel's favor.

Also shaping the war's outcome were clan and tribal loyalties, factionalism, secret agreements, corruption, misinformation, terrorism on both sides, collaborators, British troop withdrawals, the aspirations of Transjordan's King Abdullah, shifting American policies, and other international forces. Once again, most of these factors favored Israel. There are, in other words, solid reasons to doubt that the Zionists were the underdogs and to adopt instead the conclusion of Jewish historian Avi Shlaim: "The final outcome of the war was . . . a faithful reflection of the underlying military balance in the Palestine theater." In other words, "the stronger side prevailed."[88]

Evangelicals might *want* to tag Israel's victory in 1948 as a Sign of the Times. They might *want* to declare the birth of Israel as the fulfillment of prophecy. On closer inspection, however, hard evidence that God intervened to tip the scales and determine the outcome of the 1948 war is lacking.

4. Evangelicals view Islam as the Enemy.

Especially since Al-Qaeda's attack on 9/11, more than a few American Christian leaders have described Islam as a religion of violence. According to Texas pastor John Hagee, the problem is the Qur'an: "Islamic terrorists are not fanatics but devout followers of Muhammad who are following his example and doing what their Islamic Bible teaches them to do." Bestselling author Hal Lindsey contends similarly that "when any one of them [Muslims] gets serious about his faith and becomes zealous about what his holy books teach, he is a candidate for becoming what we know as a terrorist." Franklin Graham of Samaritan's Purse, who prayed at President Donald Trump's second inauguration, keeps it simple: Islam is a "very evil and wicked religion."[89]

---

87. There were 1.3 million Palestinians versus 630,000 Jews. On pre-war troop headcounts, see Pappé, *Ethnic Cleansing of Palestine*, 44; and Morris, *1948: A History of the First Arab-Israeli War*, 81–93.

88. Shlaim, "Israel and the Arab Coalition in 1948," 81. See also Rogan, "Jordan and 1948," 110–16; Cook, *Disappearing Palestine*, 26–27; Pappé, *Ten Myths About Israel*, ch. 5; and Smith, *Palestine and the Arab-Israeli Conflict*, 200–201.

89. Hagee, *Jerusalem Countdown*, 2006, 33; Lindsey, *Everlasting Hatred*, 2011; Merritt, "Franklin Graham's Turn Toward Intolerance."

The corollary of this characterization—that violence is intrinsic to Islam, that Muslims intend to destroy the West—is the need to support the Jewish state, America's frontline ally in the "War on Terror."

It is true that Islamic teachings do not echo Jesus's call to turn the other cheek. The Qur'an allows for justifiable retaliation and war-making in the cause of justice and peace. But this Muslim stance shares some ground with Christian notions of *Just War*, which go back, by the way, not to Jesus but to Augustine in the early fifth century, and which justify wars waged by civil authorities if waged for a just cause rather than to inflict pain upon their enemies.[90]

The vast majority of the world's 1.8 billion Muslims, in any case—be they traditional, conservative, moderate, mystic—do *not* wage holy war in Allah's name. Indeed, they fear Islamist radicals and their martyr theology like we do, and they express outrage at attacks like 9/11 in the US and the 7/7 bombings in London, England.[91] As with every other religious tradition, it is never enough simply to hold up a handful of sacred texts and claim to have found "official" Islamic thought. Other factors and influences—including non-Islamic ones—were equally weighty: "what really matters in human terms is how the Muslims of a particular time and place dealt with the vital questions of war and peace."[92]

The idea that we can detach "religion" from politics, economics and historical circumstance is, in any case, Western and modern. Modern too is the tidy distinction between the religious and the secular. We are right to critique doctrines and practices within Islam that can justify violence, as Daniel Bannoura does here in this volume. While we are at it, however, we must also scrutinize justifications of violence advanced by Christians (be they medieval Crusaders, Spanish Inquisitors, Christian nationalists, Christian Zionists, antisemites, or others), Jews (including religious nationalists), and "secular" ideologues (who champion nationalism, liberalism, capitalism, Marxism, etc.).[93]

---

90. Arguing for considerable overlap between Islamic and Western/Christian just war traditions is Kelsay, *Arguing the Just War in Islam*. Sharply critical of Kelsay's argument is Landau-Tasseron, "Is Jihad Comparable to Just War?" For a mediating position, see Johnson, "Jihad and Just War."

91. In *Missing Martyrs*, 11, Charles Kurzman, sociology professor at University of North Carolina, estimates that "global Islamist terrorists have managed to recruit . . . fewer than 1 in 100,000 Muslims since 9/11," a stunningly low 0.001 percent success rate. Islamist militants routinely insult fellow Muslims for refusing their call to arms. See Kurzman, "Islamic Statements Against Terrorism."

92. Donner, "Sources of Islamic Conceptions of War," 32.

93. See Camp, *Who Is My Enemy?*; Cavanaugh, *Myth of Religious Violence*.

5. Christian nationalists see themselves in Jewish Zionists.

Although the movement is complex and hardly monolithic, Christian nationalism is surging in America.[94] Proponents contend that America has always been, and should remain, fundamentally Christian. It's a conflation of God and country, as Paul Miller explains:

> American nationhood is and should remain defined by Christianity or Christian cultural norms; . . . the American people and their government should actively work to defend, sustain, and cultivate America's Christian culture, heritage, and values.[95]

It makes sense that many of America's Christian nationalists would feel solidarity with Jewish nationalists—also known as Zionists. That kinship has much to do with their shared theologies of chosenness. Amy Kaplan astutely observes:

> Parallel histories of settler colonialism expressed in biblical narratives of exceptionalism have formed the basis of American identification with Israel. Both nations have generated powerful myths of providential origins, drawing on the Old Testament notion of a chosen people destined by God to take possession of the Promised Land and blessed with a special mission to the world.[96]

Mark Charles and Soong Chan Rah describe "the very dysfunctional and codependent relationship that exists between the two countries." In *Unsettling Truths*, their book about the Doctrine of Discovery, they suggest that:

> The US needs Israel's Old Testament legacy of promised lands to justify the history of enslavement of African people and ethnic cleansing and genocide of Native people. The modern nation-state of Israel needs the continued flourishing of the United States as a shining city upon a hill to justify their current unjust actions against the Palestinian and Bedouin people.[97]

---

94. Pew Research Center, "45% of Americans Say U.S. Should Be a 'Christian Nation.'"

95. Miller, *Religion of American Greatness*, 4. See further Seidel, *Founding Myth*; Goldberg, *Kingdom Coming*; Miller, "What Is Christian Nationalism?"

96. Kaplan, *Our American Israel*, 4.

97. Charles and Rah, *Unsettling Truths*, 73. The "Doctrine of Discovery" is a set of fifteenth-century legal and religious principles that enabled European powers to "discover" and seize territory in the Americas from the indigenous peoples.

Both nationalisms—Christian and Jewish—tell a similar story. Both peoples suffered persecution, migrated from Europe, claimed their promised land, and displaced a hostile indigenous population. A sub-theme in both stories is perpetual crisis: Christians are ever under siege in America. So too are Jews perpetual victims in the Middle East. If Americans can protect their identity as a *Christian* nation, why shouldn't we celebrate Israel as a *Jewish* nation? "The more invested you are in America's own founding myth," Peter Beinart observed in a recent *New Yorker* interview, "the more you're going to find Israel's founding myth appealing."[98]

It seems to me both ideologies are deeply flawed, however. In order to maintain cultural supremacy, Christian nationalists in America organize to marginalize religious and non-white ethnic minorities. Zionists in Israel today likewise promote social and cultural hierarchies, and enforce legal separation from Palestinians. In both movements everyone is either insider or intruder, either family or foreigner. *The Other* is simply "too alien, too wild, too retrograde and unyielding" to be granted equal standing.[99] After all, tribal purity must be maintained.

6. Many Evangelicals embrace a form of Christian Zionism.

During the final third of the twentieth century—from Vietnam and the Six-Day War to the Gulf Wars and 9/11—a number of evangelical preachers descended from the hermeneutical bleachers onto the political playing field where they became increasingly engaged, media-savvy, and influential in support of the State of Israel. These Christian Zionists were not only spiritually vigilant and evangelistically zealous; they were increasingly active in the political arena and increasingly vocal in support of Israel. Christian Zionism today is marked not only by hermeneutical confidence, eschatological urgency, and pro-Israel zeal, but also by vigorous political engagement.[100]

---

98. Chotiner, "What Did the War in Gaza Reveal?"

99. Gitlin and Leibovitz, *Chosen Peoples*, 190. See also Cannon and Fisk, "Christian Nationalism and Christian Zionism."

100. Tracking the global rise and impact of that political action, humanitarianism, support for Jewish immigration, fund-raising for Israel, and more is Hummel, *Covenant Brothers*. In chs. 8 and 9 he discusses Christians United For Israel (John Hagee), the International Christian Embassy Jerusalem (Jan Willem van der Hoeven), Bridges for Peace (G. Douglas Young), and the International Fellowship of Christians and Jews (Yechiel Eckstein), among others. Noteworthy is the documentary about IFCJ, *'Til Kingdom Come*, produced by Maya Zinshtein, and the related Voices from the Holy Land webinar (on which I was a panelist). Several contributors to this volume have authored assessments of Christian Zionism: Gary Burge, *Whose Land? Whose Promise?*; David Crump, *Like Birds in a Cage*; Rob Dalrymple, *Land of Contention*; Lisa Loden, *Land Cries Out*; and Yousef AlKhouri, "Kingdom of God and Empires."

In *The New Christian Zionism*, Gerald McDermott identifies three tenets:

> 1. The people and land of Israel are central to the story of the Bible . . . . [T]he Bible is incoherent and salvation impossible without Israel.
>
> 2. The return of Jews from all over the world to their land, and their efforts to establish a nation-state after two millennia of being separated from controlling the land, is *part* of the fulfillment of biblical prophecy.
>
> 3. Jews need and deserve a homeland in Israel.[101]

Note that both *Jews* and *land* retain importance in "the history of redemption" and in "God's providential purposes."[102] Scripture accords to Jews, and Jews alone, standing and privileges in the Land.

Christian Zionism, like Christian nationalism, is not one thing. I distinguish three types, the most familiar of which is *apocalyptic* Christian Zionism, according to which the return of Jews to the Land after centuries of exile signals the beginning of the End. Now that Israel controls all of Jerusalem, a third Temple will surely rise where the first and second Temples once stood. Apocalyptic Zionists are pessimistic; the arc of history bends toward bedlam. To pressure Israel to trade land for peace or to restrict the growth of Jewish settlements is simply to appease Israel's enemies at a time when turmoil and violence are certain to escalate.

I call the second type *transactional* Christian Zionism. Essential here is God's promise to Abraham in Gen 12:3: "I will bless those who bless you, and the one who curses you I will curse, and in you all the families of the earth shall be blessed." One thus blesses Israel in order to be blessed by God. In this context, "*blessing*" means tangible support in the form of fundraising, lobbying, solidarity tourism, and enthusiasm for Jewish settlement expansion. The idea that divine favor can be predictable and assured in this way is popular among neo-Pentecostals. Today it is surging in the Global South where entire countries, deploying pro-Israel diplomacy, trade, and tourism, are expecting to see their fortunes rise.[103]

My third type is *covenantal* (they might prefer *post-supersessionist*) Christian Zionism. This type avoids some of the quirks and liabilities of the other two (e.g., speculative date-setting, war-mongering, prosperity theology) and has greater academic respectability. *Covenantal* Christian Zionism

---

101. McDermott, *New Christian Zionism*, 11–12.
102. McDermott, *New Christian Zionism*, 11–13.
103. B. N. Fisk, "Genesis 12:3"; and B. N. Fisk, "Response."

stresses the continuing validity of biblical covenants and promises, including the promise of land, and it maintains an abiding distinction between Jews and gentiles in God's plan. When God redeems various peoples, God preserves their particularity, or at least the distinction between Jews and non-Jews. The fact that the church today is predominantly gentile does not mean that the Jews as a people have been absorbed into an undifferentiated humanity, with no distinctive role to play in God's plan of redemption. On the contrary, the Bible promises Israel an "ethnic, national, territorial" future,[104] such that recent waves of Jewish migration and the resulting Jewish nation-state reveal God to be at work in this period prior to the consummation of all things.[105]

Common to all streams of Christian Zionism, important to note, is a preoccupation with real estate, an eagerness "to promote or preserve Jewish control over the geographic area now comprising Israel and Palestine."[106] Palestinian claims on any tract between the river and the sea, however ancient or well-documented, merit little consideration. Certainly no accommodation. When Jews compete with Palestinians for plots of land across this sacred, promised terrain, Christian Zionists pick Israel's side, every time. To test this out, count the number of self-described Christian Zionists who publicly and explicitly condemn Israel's expulsions in Gaza and creeping annexation of the West Bank. I know of one.

Moving Against the Current

This chapter has considered an array of Christian responses to Hamas's October 7 atrocities and Israel's subsequent obliteration of Gaza. The focus has been on Israel's "Christian armada," those who have weighed anchor and sailed forth to Israel's defense. Largely unacknowledged have been Christians who—preserving the marine metaphor—have been tacking into

---

104. Craig Blasing uses this phrase seventeen times in "Biblical Hermeneutics," his chapter in McDermott, *New Christian Zionism*, 79–105. On "post-supersessionism," see the definition on the post-supersessionism website (https://www.post-supersessionism.com/).

105. Note the overlap with *apocalyptic* Christian Zionism. Both forms require Jewish migration to the Land before the End of the Age. *Covenantal* Christian Zionists are agnostic about the proximity of the End, however, focusing instead on the legitimacy of Jewish claims to the Land. The modern State of Israel functions for them as an essential but *penultimate* marker in God's redemptive plan. In theory, nothing prevents them from criticizing the State of Israel for its treatment of Palestinians. In practice, they support Israel almost as predictably as do apocalyptic and transactional Christian Zionists.

106. Smith, *More Desired*, 2.

the prevailing "pro-Israel" headwinds by calling for lament, by decrying destruction, deprivation, and displacement in Gaza, by condemning it as collective punishment and ethnic cleansing, by fact-checking state and media fabrications, and by organizing to interrupt the deadly campaign waged by Israel and its enthusiastic, wealthy collaborator, the US.

I'm thinking of several North America-based Christian organizations, some of whose members have contributed to this volume. Christians for Middle East Peace, an ecumenical collective directed by Mae Elise Cannon, has been heroic and instructive throughout this crisis. Available from the Network of Evangelicals for Middle East Peace, directed by Ben Norquist, are archived webinars, a Holy Land video curriculum, and a hefty page of invaluable resources. Rob Dalrymple, founder of Determinetruth Ministries, has tirelessly tracked developments, blogged frequently, and hosted conversations we need to hear. Some of us have launched the Christian Forum on Israel-Palestine and are posting important conversations on YouTube. Inspiring too have been the efforts of the "pro-human" peacemaking team at Global Immersion, led by director Jer Swigart. Israel/Palestine has also been high on the agenda for some folks at Peace Catalyst International, and at Evangelicals 4 Justice, co-founded by Andrea Smith. Growing in impact is the *Across the Divide* podcast, co-hosted by Daniel Bannoura and Jennifer Maidrand.[107] Most of these organizations are evangelical or evangelical-adjacent; all of them are convinced that Israel will never be a safe haven for Jews if it continues to dehumanize, target, and displace Palestinians.

The obliteration of Gaza is a hinge of history. A milestone of inhumanity. A grievous moral injury, inflicted by the violence itself and by what Pankaj Mishra has called the "applause or indifference of the powerful," among whom many of us must surely be counted.

> The war will eventually recede into the past, and time may flatten its towering pile of horrors. But signs of the calamity will remain in Gaza for decades: in the injured bodies, the orphaned children, the rubble of its cities, the homeless peoples, and in

---

107. Christians for Middle East Peace (https://cmep.org/); Network of Evangelicals for Middle East Peace (https://www.neme.network/); Determinetruth Ministries (https://www.determinetruth.com/); Christian Forum on Israel-Palestine (https://www.youtube.com/@ChristianForumonIsrael-P-op9hf); Global Immersion (https://globalimmerse.org/); Peace Catalyst International (https://www.peacecatalyst.org/); Evangelicals 4 Justice (https://x.com/Evang4Justice); *Across the Divide* (https://www.youtube.com/@AcrosstheDividePodcast). Not to be overlooked are resources available from Christians for Social Action (https://christiansforsocialaction.org/), Sojourners (https://sojo.net/), Red Letter Christians (https://www.redletterchristians.org/), Theology in the Raw (https://theologyintheraw.com/), and *Clarion Journal* (https://www.clarion-journal.com/).

the pervasive presence and consciousness of mass bereavement. And those who watched helplessly from afar the killing and maiming of tens of thousands on a narrow coastal strip, and witnessed, too, the applause or indifference of the powerful, will live with an inner wound, and a trauma that will not pass away for years.[108]

Whether and how Christians' souls will begin to heal remains to be seen.

Bibliography

Abunimah, Ali. "ICC Has No Evidence for 7 October Rapes, Documents Indicate." *The Electronic Intifada*, May 21, 2024. https://electronicintifada.net/blogs/ali-abunimah/icc-has-no-evidence-7-october-rapes-documents-indicate.

ADL. "Some U.S. Professors Praise Hamas's October 7 Terror Attacks." November 8, 2023. https://www.adl.org/resources/article/some-us-professors-praise-hamass-october-7-terror-attacks.

AlKhouri, Yousef. "The Kingdom of God and Empires: A Contemporary Palestinian Christian Contextual Biblical Interpretation." PhD diss., Free University of Amsterdam, 2024.

Amanpour, Christiane. "Israeli-American Historian Explains Why He Now Believes Israel Is Committing Genocide in Gaza." *CNN*, December 19, 2024. https://edition.cnn.com/2024/12/19/Tv/video/amanpour-bartov-omer.

Amnesty International. "'You Feel Like You Are Subhuman': Israel's Genocide Against Palestinians in Gaza." December 5, 2024. https://www.amnesty.org/en/documents/mde15/8668/2024/en/.

Bartov, Omer. "As a Former IDF Soldier and Historian of Genocide, I Was Deeply Disturbed by My Recent Visit to Israel." *The Guardian*, August 13, 2024. https://www.theguardian.com/world/article/2024/aug/13/israel-gaza-historian-omer-bartov.

Bassist, Rina. "ICJ Genocide Hearing: 'You Wanted Hell, You'll Get Hell' South Africa Quotes Israel." *The Jerusalem Post*, January 11, 2024. https://www.jpost.com/israel-hamas-war/article-781705.

Beinart, Peter. *Being Jewish After the Destruction of Gaza: A Reckoning*. New York: Knopf, 2025.

Bennett, William J. *Why We Fight: Moral Clarity and the War on Terrorism*. Washington, DC: Regnery, 2003.

Bergman, Ronen, and Mark Mazzetti. "The Unpunished: How Extremists Took Over Israel." *The New York Times*, May 16, 2024. https://www.nytimes.com/2024/05/16/magazine/israel-west-bank-settler-violence-impunity.html.

Breiner, Josh. "Israel Reduces Food for Palestinian Security Prisoners, Conceals Data, Sources Say." *Haaretz*, June 26, 2024. https://www.haaretz.com/israel-news/2024-6-26/ty-article/.premium/israel-reduces-food-for-palestinian-security-prisoners-conceals-data-sources-say/00000190-542e-de5e-abd0-ff7ee9580000.

---

108. Mishra, *World After Gaza*, 5.

Brook, Larry. "My Israel Story: Ambassador Mike Huckabee." *Israel InSight Magazine: For Israel's Christian Friends*, January 8, 2025. https://israelinsight.substack.com/p/my-israel-story-ambassador-mike-huckabee.

Brown, Michael. *Christian Antisemitism: Confronting the Lies in Today's Church*. Lake Mary, FL: Charisma House, 2021.

———. "It Is Downright Scandalous to Accuse Israel of Genocide." *Townhall*, December 10, 2023. https://townhall.com/columnists/michaelbrown/2023/12/10/it-is-downright-scandalous-to-accuse-israel-of-genocide-n2632219.

Brueggemann, Walter. "The God of Joshua: An Ambivalent Field of Negotiation." In *Joshua and Judges*, edited by Athalya Brenner and Gale A. Yee, 13–25. Minneapolis: Fortress, 2013.

Bühler, Jürgen. "The Spirit of Amalek and the War on Israel." International Christian Embassy Jerusalem. https://www.icej.org/understand-israel/biblical-teachings/the-spirit-of-amalek-and-the-war-on-israel/.

The Bulletin. "Part One: It's Complicated." *Promised Land. Christianity Today*, December 20, 2023. https://www.christianitytoday.com/podcasts/promised-land/60-promised-land-israel-hamas-kibbutz-kfar-aza/.

———. "Part Two: The Zionist Story." *Promised Land. Christianity Today*, February 9, 2024. https://www.christianitytoday.com/podcasts/promised-land/68-tb-promised-land/.

———. "Part Three: Rocks in Hard Places: From the Foundation Stone to Living Stones." *Promised Land. Christianity Today*, February 27, 2024. https://www.christianitytoday.com/podcasts/promised-land/rocks-in-hard-places/.

———. "Part Four: Empire of Refugees: Victims, Villains, and Settler Colonialism." *Promised Land. Christianity Today*, March 21, 2024. https://www.christianitytoday.com/podcasts/promised-land/empire-of-refugees-victims-villains-and-settler-colonialism/.

———. "Part Five: Settlers, Sacred Cows, and the Temple." *Promised Land. Christianity Today*, June 3, 2024. https://www.christianitytoday.com/podcasts/promised-land/5-settlers-sacred-cows-and-temple/.

———. "Part Six: Vote for Peace in a Time of War." *Promised Land. Christianity Today*, June 19, 2024. https://www.christianitytoday.com/podcasts/promised-land/vote-for-peace-in-time-of-war/.

Bump, Philip. "Half of Evangelicals Support Israel Because They Believe It Is Important for Fulfilling End-times Prophecy." *The Washington Post*, May 14, 2018. https://www.washingtonpost.com/news/politics/wp/2018/05/14/half-of-evangelicals-support-israel-because-they-believe-it-is-important-for-fulfilling-end-times-prophecy/.

Burge, Gary M. *Whose Land? Whose Promise? What Christians Are Not Being Told About Israel and the Palestinians*. Cleveland: Pilgrim, 2013.

Bush, George W. "Address to a Joint Session of Congress and the American People." September 20, 2001. https://georgewbush-whitehouse.archives.gov/news/releases/2001/09/20010920-8.html.

Butler, Judith. *Parting Ways: Jewishness and the Critique of Zionism*. New York: Columbia University Press, 2012.

Camp, Lee C. *Who Is My Enemy? Questions American Christians Must Face About Islam—and Themselves*. Grand Rapids: Brazos, 2011.

Cannon, Mae Elise, ed. *A Land Full of God: Christian Perspectives on the Holy Land*. Eugene, OR: Cascade, 2017.

Cannon, Mae Elise, and Bruce N. Fisk. "Christian Nationalism and Christian Zionism: Two Sides of the Same Coin?" *Christians for Social Action*, July 28, 2021. https://christiansforsocialaction.org/resource/christian-nationalism-and-christian-zionism-two-sides-of-the-same-coin/.

Carter, Warren. "The New Testament and Moral Injury: Peter, Judas, and the Portrayals of Moral Harm and Repair." In *Moral Injury: A Guidebook for Understanding and Engagement*, edited by Brad E. Kelle, 161–71. Lanham, MD: Lexington, 2020.

Casper, Jayson. "For Messianic Jews, Debate over Hamas Gets Biblical." *Christianity Today*, December 15, 2023. https://www.christianitytoday.com/2023/12/amalekites-today-israel-hamas-war-messianic-jews-bible/.

Cavanaugh, William T. *The Myth of Religious Violence: Secular Ideology and the Roots of Modern Conflict*. New York: Oxford University Press, 2009.

Charles, Mark, and Soong-Chan Rah. *Unsettling Truths: The Ongoing, Dehumanizing Legacy of the Doctrine of Discovery*. Downers Grove, IL: InterVarsity, 2019.

Chosen People Ministries. "Chosen People Ministries' Affirmation of Israel: A Response to the War Between Israel and Hamas." https://archive.chosenpeople.com/affirmationofisrael/.

Chotiner, Isaac. "What Did the War in Gaza Reveal About American Judaism?" *The New Yorker*, February 13, 2025. https://www.newyorker.com/news/q-and-a/what-did-the-war-in-gaza-reveal-about-american-judaism.

Cook, Jonathan. *Disappearing Palestine: Israel's Experiments in Human Despair*. New York: Zed, 2008.

Cosper, Mike. "The Evil Ideas Behind October 7." *Christianity Today*, March 2024. https://www.christianitytoday.com/2024/02/evil-ideas-behind-october-7/.

Crump, David. *Like Birds in a Cage: Christian Zionism's Collusion in Israel's Oppression of the Palestinian People*. Eugene, OR: Cascade, 2021.

Daghrir, Wassim. "Binary Discourse in U.S. Presidential Speeches from FDR to Bush." *Journal of Applied Physics* 5 (2013) 25–36.

Dalrymple, Rob. *Land of Contention: Biblical Narratives and the Struggle for the Holy Land*. Eugene, OR: Cascade, 2024.

Demas, Alex. "Fact Checking Claims About Israeli Soldiers and the 'Seed of Amalek.'" *The Dispatch*, December 14, 2023. https://thedispatch.com/article/fact-checking-claims-about-israeli-soldiers-and-the-seed-of-amalek/.

Donner, Fred M. "The Sources of Islamic Conceptions of War." In *Just War and Jihad: Historical and Theoretical Perspectives on War and Peace in Western and Islamic Traditions*, edited by John Kelsay and James Turner Johnson, 31–69. New York: Greenwood, 1991.

Dylan, Bob. "With God on Our Side." Track 3 on *The Times They Are A-Changin'*. New York: Columbia, 1964.

El-Kurd, Mohammed. *Perfect Victims and the Politics of Appeal*. Chicago: Haymarket, 2025.

Erakat, Noura. *Justice for Some: Law and the Question of Palestine*. Stanford, CA: Stanford University Press, 2019.

Ethics and Religious Liberty Commission of the Southern Baptist Convention. "Evangelical Statement in Support of Israel." October 11, 2023. https://erlc.com/policy-content/israel/.

Filiu, Jean-Pierre. *Gaza: A History*. New York: Oxford University Press, 2014.

Finkelstein, Norman G. *Beyond Chutzpah: On the Misuse of Anti-Semitism and the Abuse of History*. Updated ed. Berkeley: University of California Press, 2008.

———. *Gaza: An Inquest into Its Martyrdom*. Oakland: University of California Press, 2018.

———. *"This Time We Went Too Far": Truth and Consequences of the Gaza Invasion*. New York: OR Books, 2010.

Fisk, Bruce N. "The Allure of Moral Clarity in a Time of War: A Response to Russell Moore." *Clarion Journal*, October 13, 2023. https://www.clarion-journal.com/clarion_journal_of_spirit/2023/10/the-allure-of-moral-clarity-in-a-time-of-war-a-response-to-russell-moore-by-bruce-fisk.html.

———. "Ever the Victim, Never the Aggressor: A Response to the 'Evangelical Statement in Support of Israel.'" *Clarion Journal*, November 30, 2023. https://www.clarion-journal.com/clarion_journal_of_spirit/2023/11/ever-the-victim-never-the-aggressor-a-response-to-the-evangelical-statement-in-support-of-israel-bru.html.

———. "Genesis 12:3, Christian Zionism, and Blessing Israel." *Bibliotheca Sacra* 180 (2023) 144–63.

———. "Praised by Faint Damnation: Why American Evangelical Responses to October 7 Are Dangerous." *Red Letter Christians*, November 30, 2023. https://redletterchristians.org/2023/11/30/praised-by-faint-damnation/.

———. "A Response to Darrell Bock." *Bibliotheca Sacra* 180 (2023) 176–78.

Fisk, Robert. *The Great War for Civilisation: The Conquest of the Middle East*. New York: Knopf, 2005.

Gitlin, Todd, and Liel Leibovitz. *The Chosen Peoples: America, Israel, and the Ordeals of Divine Election*. New York: Simon and Schuster, 2010.

Goldberg, Michelle. *Kingdom Coming: The Rise of Christian Nationalism*. New York: Norton, 2006.

Gordon, Neve, and Nicola Perugini. *Human Shields: A History of People in the Line of Fire*. Berkeley: University of California Press, 2020.

Gryboski, Michael. "'Dangerous' and 'Growing': Michael Brown Warns About the Rise of Christian Anti-Semitism." *The Christian Post*, February 1, 2021. https://www.christianpost.com/news/michael-brown-warns-about-the-rise-of-christian-anti-semitism.html.

Hagee, John. *Jerusalem Countdown: A Warning to the World*. Lake Mary, FL: FrontLine, 2006.

Hasson, Nir. "The Numbers Show: Gaza War Is One of the Bloodiest in the 21st Century." *Haaretz*, August 14, 2024. https://www.haaretz.com/middle-east-news/palestinians/2024-8-14/ty-article-magazine/.premium/the-death-toll-in-gaza-is-bad-even-compared-to-the-wars-in-ukraine-iraq-and-myanmar/00000191-50c6-d6a2-a7dd-d1decf340000?gift=8b4f9c707bab486a80e18c1c12898115.

Hedges, Chris. *War Is a Force That Gives Us Meaning*. New York: PublicAffairs, 2002.

Howard, Bernard N., and Ivan Mesa. "Israel's 9/11: The Need for Moral Clarity." *The Gospel Coalition*, October 10, 2023. https://www.thegospelcoalition.org/article/israel-hamas-moral-clarity/.

Human Rights Watch. "Extermination and Acts of Genocide: Israel Deliberately Depriving Palestinians in Gaza of Water." December 19, 2024. https://www.hrw.org/news/2024/12/19/israels-crime-extermination-acts-genocide-gaza.

Hummel, Daniel G. *Covenant Brothers: Evangelicals, Jews, and U.S.-Israeli Relations*. Philadelphia: University of Pennsylvania Press, 2019.

International Court of Justice. "Summary of the Order of 26 January 2024." January 26, 2024. https://www.icj-cij.org/node/203454.

International Crisis Group. "Video: The Rise of Settler Violence in the West Bank." November 14, 2024. https://www.crisisgroup.org/middle-east-north-africa/east-mediterranean-mena/israelpalestine/video-rise-israeli-settler.

Israeli Ministry of Foreign Affairs. "Opening Statement of MFA Legal Advisor Dr. Tal Becker at the International Court of Justice Proceedings." December 1, 2024. https://www.gov.il/en/pages/opening-statement-of-mfa-legal-advisor-tal-becker-at-icj-proceedings-12-jan-2024.

———. "Statement by PM Netanyahu." October 28, 2023. https://www.gov.il/en/departments/news/statement-by-pm-netanyahu-28-oct-2023.

Israeli PM. "Prime Minister Netanyahu Comments on the Decision of the International Court of Justice in The Hague." January 26, 2025. https://www.youtube.com/watch?v=keJc6ZtkXQs.

Jeffrey, David Lyle, and Jeff Levin. "Anti-Semitism, Amalek, and the American University." *Christian Scholar's Review*, August 25, 2024. https://christianscholars.com/anti-semitism-amalekand-the-american-university/#easy-footnote-55-14019.

The Jerusalem Post. "IDF: 709 of 1166 Killed in Cast Lead Identified as Hamas Terror Operatives." March 26, 2009. https://www.jpost.com/Israel/IDF-709-of-1166-killed-in-Cast-Lead-identifed-as-Hamas-terror-operatives.

Johnson, James Turner. "Jihad and Just War." *First Things*, June 1, 2002. https://firstthings.com/jihad-and-just-war/.

Juergensmeyer, Mark. *Terror in the Mind of God: The Global Rise of Religious Violence*. 4th ed. Oakland: University of California Press, 2017.

Kaplan, Amy. *Our American Israel: The Story of an Entangled Alliance*. Cambridge, MA: Harvard University Press, 2018.

Kaylor, Brian. "A Call for 'Biblical' Genocide." *A Public Witness*, October 31, 2023. https://publicwitness.wordandway.org/p/a-call-for-biblical-genocide.

———. "Gaza, War, and the Christian Witness." *A Public Witness*, October 17, 2023. https://publicwitness.wordandway.org/p/gaza-war-and-the-christian-witness.

Kelsay, John. *Arguing the Just War in Islam*. Cambridge, MA: Harvard University Press, 2007.

Kessler, Dana. "Life During Wartime." *Tablet*, January 4, 2024. https://www.tabletmag.com/sections/community/articles/life-during-wartime-tel-aviv.

Khalidi, Rashid. *The Hundred Years' War on Palestine: A History of Settler Colonialism and Resistance, 1917–2017*. New York: Metropolitan, 2020.

Kim, Joyce E., and Nia L. Orakwue. "Hundreds of Harvard Protesters Stage 'Die-In' to Demand End to Violence Following Gaza Hospital Blast." *The Harvard Crimson*, October 19, 2023. https://www.thecrimson.com/article/2023/10/19/harvard-die-in-palestine/.

Klett, Leah MarieAnn. "SBC Leaders Spearhead Evangelical Statement in Support of Israel, Condemn Hamas Attacks." *The Christian Post*, October 12, 2023. https://www.christianpost.com/news/sbc-leaders-spearhead-evangelical-statement-in-support-of-israel.html.

Kurzman, Charles. "Islamic Statements Against Terrorism." https://kurzman.unc.edu/islamic-statements-against-terrorism.

———. *The Missing Martyrs: Why There Are So Few Muslim Terrorists*. New York: Oxford University Press, 2011.

Lanard, Noah. "The Dangerous History Behind Netanyahu's Amalek Rhetoric." *Mother Jones*, November 3, 2023. https://www.motherjones.com/politics/2023/11/benjamin-netanyahu-amalek-israel-palestine-gaza-saul-samuel-old-testament/.

Landau-Tasseron, Ella. "Is Jihad Comparable to Just War? A Review Article." *Jerusalem Studies in Arabic and Islam* 34 (2008) 535–50.

Leal, Iris. "Don't Let Calls for Revenge Against Hamas Silence Our Conscience." *Haaretz*, October 24, 2023. https://www.haaretz.com/opinion/2023-10-24/ty-article-opinion/.premium/dont-let-calls-for-revenge-against-hamas-silence-our-conscience/0000018b-5d90-d8e2-a1eb-ff966bca0000.

Leatherby, Lauren. "Gaza Civilians, Under Israeli Barrage, Are Being Killed at Historic Pace." *The New York Times*, November 25, 2023. https://www.nytimes.com/2023/11/25/world/middleeast/israel-gaza-death-toll.html?.

Lefkovits, Etgar. "Huckabee Cites US Educational Fail During Gaza Border Tour." *Jewish News Syndicate*, December 21, 2023. https://www.jns.org/huckabee-cites-us-educational-fail-during-gaza-border-tour/.

Leithart, Peter. "Hamas Is Borrowing Tactics from the Amalekites." *The Gospel Coalition*, October 13, 2023. https://www.thegospelcoalition.org/article/hamas-tactics-amalekites/.

Levitt, Tani. "Why the No. 1 Song in Israel Represents a Radical Shift in Israeli Pop Music." *Forward*, December 4, 2023. https://forward.com/culture/572004/israel-pop-music-number-one-song-harbu-darbu-ness-stilla/.

Levy, Gideon. "Goldstone's Gaza Probe Did Israel a Favor." *Haaretz*, October 1, 2009. https://www.haaretz.com/2009-10-01/ty-article/goldstones-gaza-probe-did-israel-a-favor/0000017f-f879-ddde-abff-fc7d5fd80000.

Lindsey, Hal. *The Everlasting Hatred: The Roots of Jihad*. Washington, DC: WND Books, 2011.

Magid, Jacob. "US Maintains Genocide Allegations Against Israel Are Unfounded, After ICJ Ruling." *The Times of Israel*, January 26, 2024. https://www.timesofisrael.com/liveblog_entry/us-maintains-genocide-allegations-against-israel-are-unfounded-after-icj-ruling/.

McDermott, Gerald. *The New Christian Zionism: Fresh Perspectives on Israel and the Land*. Downers Grove, IL: IVP Academic, 2016.

Merkley, Paul Charles. *Christian Attitudes Towards the State of Israel*. Montreal: McGill-Queens University Press, 2001.

Merritt, Jonathan. "Franklin Graham's Turn Toward Intolerance." *The Atlantic*, July 19, 2015. https://www.theatlantic.com/politics/archive/2015/07/franklin-grahams-turn-toward-intolerance/398924/.

Mezzofiore, Gianluca, et al. "Israel's Military Called the Settler Attack on This Palestinian Town a 'Pogrom.' Videos Show Soldiers Did Little to Stop It." *CNN*, June 15, 2023. https://edition.cnn.com/2023/06/15/middleeast/huwara-west-bank-settler-attack-cmd-intl/index.html.

Miller, Paul D. *The Religion of American Greatness: What's Wrong with Christian Nationalism*. Downers Grove, IL: InterVarsity, 2022.

———. "What Is Christian Nationalism?" *Christianity Today*, February 3, 2021. https://www.christianitytoday.com/ct/2021/february-web-only/what-is-christian-nationalism.html.

Mishra, Pankaj. *The World After Gaza: A History*. New York: Penguin, 2025.

Moore, Russell. "American Christians Should Stand with Israel Under Attack." *Christianity Today*, October 7, 2023. https://www.christianitytoday.com/ct/2023/october-web-only/israel-hamas-middle-east-war-christians.html.

Morris, Benny. *1948: A History of the First Arab-Israeli War*. New Haven, CT: Yale University Press, 2008.

Moses, A. Dirk. *The Problems of Genocide: Permanent Security and the Language of Transgression*. Cambridge: Cambridge University Press, 2021.

Munayer, Salim J., and Lisa Loden. *The Land Cries Out: Theology of the Land in the Israeli-Palestinian Context*. Eugene, OR: Cascade, 2011.

National Association of Evangelicals. "NAE Condemns Violence in Middle East." October 9, 2023. https://www.nae.org/nae-condemns-violence-in-middle-east/.

NPR. "Netanyahu's References to Violent Biblical Passages Raise Alarm Among Critics." *Morning Edition*, November 7, 2023. https://www.npr.org/2023/11/07/1211133201/netanyahus-references-to-violent-biblical-passages-raise-alarm-among-critics.

Nussbaum, Martha C. *The Clash Within: Democracy, Religious Violence, and India's Future*. Cambridge, MA: Belknap, 2007.

OpinioJuris. "The ICJ's Findings on Plausible Genocide in Gaza and Its Implications for the International Criminal Court." May 4, 2024. https://opiniojuris.org/2024/04/05/the-icjs-findings-on-plausible-genocide-in-gaza-and-its-implications-for-the-international-criminal-court/.

Pappé, Ilan. *The Ethnic Cleansing of Palestine*. Oxford: Oneworld, 2006.

———. *Ten Myths About Israel*. New York: Verso, 2017.

Parker, Claire. "Why Israeli Raids on al-Aqsa Mosque Are Stoking Tensions." *The Washington Post*, October 7, 2023. https://www.washingtonpost.com/world/2023/01/05/temple-mount-al-aqsa-ben-gvir-israel/.

Pelham, Nicolas. "Gaza's Tunnel Phenomenon: The Unintended Dynamics of Israel's Siege." *Journal of Palestine Studies* 41 (2012) 6–31.

Pew Research Center. "45% of Americans Say U.S. Should Be a 'Christian Nation.'" October 27, 2022. https://www.pewresearch.org/religion/2022/10/27/45-of-americans-say-u-s-should-be-a-christian-nation/.

Phillips, Melanie. "The Truth of the Palestinian Cause." *The Jewish Chronicle*, February 20, 2025. https://www.thejc.com/opinion/if-you-support-the-palestinian-cause-in-any-form-youre-facilitating-jew-hate-shyhqyo5.

Philos Project. "The Pope's Misled Call to Investigate Israel's 'Genocide.'" November 21, 2024. https://philosproject.org/the-popes-misled-call-to-investigate-israels-genocide/.

Power, Samantha. *"A Problem from Hell": America and the Age of Genocide*. New York: Basic, 2002.

Rad, Assal. "How Western Media Has Manufactured Consent for Atrocities, from Iraq to Gaza." *Dawn*, March 4, 2025. https://dawnmena.org/how-western-media-has-manufactured-consent-for-atrocities-from-iraq-to-gaza/.

———. "I Fixed the *New York Times*' Pro-Israel Headlines on Gaza." *Zeteo*, July 18, 2024. https://zeteo.com/p/new-york-times-whitewashing-israel-genocide-gaza.

Reagan, Ronald. "Address Before a Joint Session of Congress on the State of the Union." January 27, 1987. https://www.presidency.ucsb.edu/documents/address-before-joint-session-congress-the-state-the-union-1.

Rogan, Eugene L. "Jordan and 1948: The Persistence of an Official History." In *The War for Palestine: Rewriting the History of 1948*, edited by Eugene L. Rogan and Avi Shlaim, 110–16. Cambridge Middle East Studies 15. New York: Cambridge University Press, 2001.

Rozovsky, Liza. "15 Witnesses, Three Confessions, a Pattern of Naked Dead Bodies. All the Evidence of Hamas Rape on October 7." *Haaretz*, April 18, 2024. https://www.haaretz.com/israel-news/2024-4-18/ty-article-magazine/witnesses-confessions-naked-dead-bodies-all-the-evidence-of-hamas-rape-on-oct-7/0000018e-f114-d92e-abfe-f77f7e3f0000.

Rozovsky, Liza, and Reuters. "UN Report Accuses Israel of 'Genocidal Acts' in Gaza, Israel Rejects Allegations." *Haaretz*, March 13, 2025. https://www.haaretz.com/israel-news/2025-3-13/ty-article/.premium/un-experts-accuse-israel-of-genocidal-acts-and-sexual-violence-in-gaza/00000195-8e97-d4b6-a7dd-beff33b80000.

Salaita, Steven. *The Holy Land in Transit: Colonialism and the Quest for Canaan*. Syracuse, NY: Syracuse University Press, 2006.

Samaritan's Purse. "Important Message from Franklin Graham on Israel." October 12, 2023. https://samaritanspurse.org.au/disaster-response-team-deployed-to-israel/.

———. "Samaritan's Purse Responds in Israel: Providing Ambulances and Other Life-Saving Support." November 9, 2023. https://www.samaritanspurse.org/media/israel-response-11-13-23/.

Scahill, Jeremy. "Al-Shifa Hospital, Hamas's Tunnels, and Israeli Propaganda." *The Intercept*, November 21, 2023. https://theintercept.com/2023/11/21/al-shifa-hospital-hamas-israel/.

Segal, Raz. "Genocide Denial in Holocaust Studies." *Jacobin*, January 27, 2025. https://jacobin.com/2025/01/gaza-genocide-holocaust-studies-germany.

———. "A Textbook Case of Genocide." *Jewish Currents*, October 13, 2023. https://jewishcurrents.org/a-textbook-case-of-genocide.

Seidel, Andrew. *The Founding Myth: Why Christian Nationalism Is Un-American*. New York: Union Square & Co., 2019.

Shabi, Rachel. *Off-White: The Truth About Antisemitism*. London: Oneworld, 2024.

Shapiro, Jay. "Something Worse Than Genocide and the Deadly Logic of Permanent Security." *The Dilemma Podcast*, January 2, 2025. https://www.youtube.com/watch?v=g8hNr4kUXzc&t=7133s.

Shlaim, Avi. "From the Historical Archive: Israel and the Arrogance of Power." *Irish Pages* 9 (2015) 133–80.

———. "Israel and the Arab Coalition in 1948." In *The War for Palestine: Rewriting the History of 1948*, edited by Eugene L. Rogan and Avi Shlaim, 79–103. Cambridge Middle East Studies 15. New York: Cambridge University Press, 2001.

Smith, Charles D. *Palestine and the Arab-Israeli Conflict: A History with Documents*. 7th ed. Boston: Bedford/St. Martin's, 2007.

Smith, Robert O. *More Desired Than Our Owne Salvation: The Roots of Christian Zionism*. New York: Oxford University Press, 2013.

Speri, Alice. "Israeli Forces Deliberately Killed Palestinian American Journalist, Report Shows." *The Intercept*, September 20, 2022. https://theintercept.com/2022/09/20/shireen-abu-akleh-killing-israel/.

Stefanik, Elise. "Stefanik Delivers Historic Address on Antisemitism and U.S. Support for Israel at Israeli Knesset." May 19, 2024. https://stefanik.house.gov/2024/5/stefanik-delivers-historic-address-on-antisemitism-and-u-s-support-for-israel-at-israeli-knesset.

Stevenson, Tom. "Illusions of Containment." *London Review of Books* 47 (February 6, 2025). https://www.lrb.co.uk/the-paper/v47/n02/tom-stevenson/illusions-of-containment.

Thapar, Karan. "What Israel Doing in Gaza Mix of Genocidal Action, Ethnic Cleansing, Annexation." *The Wire*, October 7, 2024. https://thewire.in/world/full-text-omer-bartov-israel-gaza-genocidal-action-ethnic-cleansing-annexation.

Thrall, Nathan. *The Only Language They Understand: Forcing Compromise in Israel and Palestine.* New York: Metropolitan, 2017.

The Times of Israel. "Pastor Hagee: 'There Is No Middle Ground in This Conflict. You're Either for the Jews or Not.'" November 14, 2023. https://www.timesofisrael.com/liveblog_entry/pastor-hagee-there-is-no-middle-ground-in-this-conflict-youre-either-for-the-jews-or-not/.

United Nations. "Gaza: Hamas, Israel Committed War Crimes, Claims Independent Rights Probe." *UN News*, June 12, 2024. https://news.un.org/en/story/2024/06/1150946.

United Nations Human Rights Council. "Report of the United Nations Fact-Finding Mission on the Gaza Conflict." September 25, 2009. https://www.ohchr.org/en/hr-bodies/hrc/special-sessions/session9/fact-finding-mission.

United Nations Office of the High Commissioner for Human Rights. "Commission of Inquiry on the Occupied Palestinian Territory Concludes That Israeli Authorities and Hamas Are Both Responsible for War Crimes." June 19, 2024. https://www.ohchr.org/en/news/2024/06/commission-inquiry-occupied-palestinian-territory-concludes-israeli-authorities-and.

———. "Convention on the Prevention and Punishment of the Crime of Genocide." December 9, 1948. https://www.ohchr.org/en/instruments-mechanisms/instruments/convention-prevention-and-punishment-crime-genocide.

———. "Gaza: UN Experts Call on International Community to Prevent Genocide Against the Palestinian People." November 16, 2023. https://www.ohchr.org/en/press-releases/2023/11/gaza-un-experts-call-international-community-prevent-genocide-against.

———. "'More Than a Human Can Bear': Israel's Systematic Use of Sexual, Reproductive and Other Forms of Gender-Based Violence Since October 2023." March 12, 2025. https://www.ohchr.org/en/press-releases/2025/03/more-human-can-bear-israels-systematic-use-sexual-reproductive-and-other.

University Network for Human Rights. "Genocide in Gaza: Analysis of International Law and Its Application to Israel's Military Actions Since October 7, 2023." May 15, 2024. https://www.humanrightsnetwork.org/projects/genocide-in-gaza.

UN News. "Rights Expert Finds 'Reasonable Grounds' Genocide Is Being Committed in Gaza." March 26, 2024. https://news.un.org/en/story/2024/03/1147976.

Verhey, Allen. "Neither Devils nor Angels: Peace, Justice, and Defending the Innocent: A Response to Richard Hays." In *The Word Leaps the Gap: Essays on Scripture and Theology in Honor of Richard B. Hays*, edited by J. Ross Wagner et al., 599–625. Grand Rapids: Eerdmans, 2008.

Voices from the Holy Land. *'Til Kingdom Come*. Webinar. February 19, 2023. https://www.youtube.com/watch?v=xr1EN1LnMuE.

Warrior, Robert Allen. "A Native American Perspective: Canaanites, Cowboys, and Indians." In *Voices from the Margin: Interpreting the Bible in the Third World*, edited by R. S. Sugirtharajah, 287–95. Maryknoll, NY: Orbis, 1991.

World Evangelical Alliance. "WEA's Statement on the Holy Land Conflict." October 9, 2023. https://worldea.org/news/23784/weas-statement-on-the-holy-land-conflict/.

Zinshtein, Maya, dir. *'Til Kingdom Come*. Ventureland, 2020.

CHAPTER THREE

Bombing in the Name of the Gospel

GARY M. BURGE

IT IS IMPOSSIBLE TO comprehend the explosive impact of a 2,000-pound bomb. Unless you have lived through it.

When the bomb is dropped, a trigger detonates 945 pounds of explosives which creates an 8,500-degree fireball and an unimaginable shockwave. The expanding hot gas in the bomb doubles in size and then explodes its shell (60 percent of the bomb) into thousands of white-hot, razor sharp pieces of metal moving at 6,000 feet per second for almost three-quarters of a mile. Ten thousand pounds of soil and debris from the twenty-foot crater are thrown into the air at supersonic speed. Few in the blast radius survive.

Physicians who meet the rare survivor in hospitals describe how they have never seen anything like this. YouTube records many testimonies of American doctors and nurses telling horrific stories of what they've seen.[1] It is not just that entire limbs are torn off or skin is shredded by massive amounts of shrapnel. The blast explodes the internal organs of anyone in the blast zone: lungs, colon, bowels, and the sinuses near the brain—anywhere there is an air cavity. Bodies are thrown enormous distances.

Oddly, physicians report something never seen before. When this bomb detonates in an urban area, it pulverizes cement and turns its grains into a million tiny weapons. Hospitals report bodies filled or pulverized by

---

1. Hamawy, "American Doctor Stuck in Gaza." The *New York Times* has reported shocking burn damage to children throughout Gaza. El-Naggar and Kerr, "They Are Burned Alive."

cement.² Once the skin is thoroughly penetrated, massive infections begin immediately.

Physicians volunteering in Gaza are telling stories almost impossible to take in. Here is Dr. Tanya Haj-Hassan from Doctors Without Borders, a pediatric intensive care surgeon, who has been working in Gaza's few remaining hospitals. She spoke in the US on August 22, 2024:

> For the past 10 months, we have witnessed civilian massacre after civilian massacre—school massacres where internally displaced people were sheltering, the flour massacre, massacres of people trying to collect water, massacres of people collecting aid at aid sites—massacre after civilian massacre, entire families exterminated in one single bomb; humanitarians, healthcare workers killed and journalists killed in record numbers; pediatric amputations, amputations in children that are breaking records; over 17,000 children who have lost one or both parents since October in Gaza.³

Dr. Haj-Hassan continued with a mind-numbing description of one of her young patients.

> I received a young boy into the emergency department during one of the mass casualties who had half of his face and neck blown off. Luckily, the organs that are vital for breathing and blood supply to the brain were preserved. They were visible, but preserved. And he was talking to us. He couldn't see himself, so he didn't know what he looked like at that point in time, and he kept asking for his sister. His sister was in the bed next to him. The majority of her body was burned beyond recognition. He didn't recognize that the girl in the bed next to him was his sister. His entire family, parents and the rest of his siblings, were killed in the same attack.
>
> That boy survived. And the next day, I went to see him. A very young plastic surgeon, one of the few remaining plastic surgeons in Gaza, because the others have either been killed or have fled, understandably, had removed part of his chest and created a graft to cover those vital organs of the neck. He was lying in his bed and mumbling, because it was so difficult to talk. And he kept saying—I got really close to him, and he said, "I wish I had died, too." And I said, "What?" And he said, "I think

---

2. To watch a 2,000-pound bomb explode, see EngineerReact, "How Powerful Is a 2000 Pound Bomb?"

3. Haj-Hassan, "So Horrific." Report begins at 26:20. Lamenting this tragedy is the poem "Rachel Still Weeps," above, xi.

my entire family has gone to heaven"—or, it's not "my entire family." His exact words were something to the effect of, "Everybody I love is now in heaven. I don't want to be here anymore." That is one of so many stories. I'm giving you—I'm so sorry, but I think people need to hear this. I'm giving you the story of one child.

Why does this matter?

Because Israel has been using these bombs routinely in Gaza's urban settings, something the bomb was not designed for. The vast majority come from American arsenals. As of July 1, Reuters reports that 14,000 of them had been shipped to Israel from the US and paid for with American's tax dollars.[4] To understand how Israel is using these bombs in Gaza, we need go no further than the *New York Times*, which provides visual evidence of Israel bombing what Israel itself had declared a "safe zone."[5] Or we might watch the musical lament of Saleh Aljafarawi as he shows us the destruction they have wrought.[6]

These bombs belong to a family of weapons called the Mark 80 Series that were created by the US following World War II. Four types fill out the roster: the Mark 81 is a 250-pound explosive; the Mark 82 carries 500 pounds; the Mark 83 is 1,000 pounds; and the Mark 84 is 2,000 pounds. Each has a signature kill zone. The Mark 83's kill zone is 600 feet from the point of impact. The Mark 84 kills within a radius of 1200 feet, the equivalent of 21 soccer fields or 25 acres. In the early 1950s these "dumb" bombs, meaning they had no guidance system, were dropped by planes on targets with a low accuracy rate. Used widely in Vietnam, they were notorious for missing the target due to wind or errant aiming. At best, about half of them came within 400 feet of their targets and often killed civilians and American troops. On January 3, 1973, in a notorious accident, the US dropped 34 Mark 82 bombs on a giant American military base in Da Nang.[7] Suddenly Americans saw up close what their bombs were doing to villages throughout the country.

In the 1960s Texas Instruments designed a guidance system called *The Paveway* for the Mark 80 series. Suddenly they were landing within ten feet of the target. These "smart bombs" were used widely in the Persian Gulf War (1990–1991) with a dramatic improvement in accuracy. A cheaper guidance

---

4. Pamuk and Stone, "US Has Sent Israel."
5. Stein et al., "Visual Evidence Shows Israel Dropped 2,000-Pound Bombs."
6. Aljafarawi, "Where Is Your Humanity?"
7. Whitney, "Da Nang Bombing Error Embarrasses U.S. Aides."

system built by Boeing[8] soon became universal, and the weapons were renamed the *Joint Direct Attack Munition* (or JDAM). In this system the bomb employs GPS guidance, and once launched it finds its target autonomously.

The American military has always used the JDAM selectively. The Mark 82 (500 lb) is the general use weapon; the Mark 84 (2,000 lb) is employed rarely and only for major fortified buildings, deep-set bunkers, or bridges. Its collateral kill rate is so large that the US avoids using it in urban settings.

The Mark 84 is Israel's weapon of choice in Gaza.

Alarm over Israel's use of Mark 84 bombs emerged shortly after October 7. According to a *CNN* report in December 2023, satellite photographs showed 900 major craters in Gaza in the month after October 7, 1,500 of them over 40 feet in diameter. This dimension is a signature of the Mark 84. In one refugee camp, nine craters can be seen with overlapping kill zones, meaning that entire sections of the densely populated region were turned into a moonscape.[9] Marc Garlasco, a former US defense intelligence analyst and UN war crimes investigator, said he had not seen anything like this since Vietnam, particularly as these targets were densely populated and urban.[10] Others reported that in two months Israel unleashed more bombs than the US dropped on the ISIS strongholds of Mosul and Raqqa in Iraq during that entire war.

The Mark 84 was clearly the wrong weapon to use widely. Nevertheless, in the first two weeks of the war, 90 percent of the bombs Israel dropped in Gaza were Mark 83s and Mark 84s. Overuse of these massive munitions has continued. In a refugee camp near Khan Younis, a Mark 84 was dropped in July 2024. It killed 90 people immediately and severely injured 300 more. Israel claimed that it was targeting one of the October 7 planners but provided no proof for this assertion.

Predictably, the Israeli military denies the indiscriminate use of these weapons. The IDF (the Israel Defense Forces) responded to *CNN*'s report saying, "In stark contrast to Hamas' intentional attacks on Israeli men, women and children, the IDF follows international law and takes feasible precautions to mitigate civilian harm."[11] This has become very difficult to believe.

Imagine taking this problem of the Mark 84 one step further. Imagine Israel dropping *three* JDAM/Mark 84 bombs on the *same* site at the *same*

---

8. America's Navy, "Joint Direct Attack Munition (JDAM)."
9. Qiblawi et al., "'Not Seen Since Vietnam.'"
10. Qiblawi et al., "'Not Seen Since Vietnam.'"
11. Qiblawi et al., "'Not Seen Since Vietnam.'"

time? This is precisely what the IDF did on August 10, 2024. The al-Tabin elementary school in the Daraj district of Gaza City had been packed with refugees seeking a safe zone. Three 2,000-pound Mark 84s simultaneously struck the campus while the community was gathered for morning prayers. The combined fireballs ripped through the building. Witnesses described the scene as "horrific."[12] Israel defended the attack because, they said, twenty Hamas "operatives" were working from the school. They backed up the claim with no evidence.

The Problem of Proportionality and Collateral Damage

The death toll in Gaza is staggering. In August 2024, it reached 40,000 (with many more buried and uncounted in the rubble of buildings). Equally dumbfounding, 90,000 have been injured. With the full destruction of Gaza's infrastructure, many more are destined to die from malnutrition or disease. In July, an article in the prestigious British medical journal *The Lancet* projected that "it is not implausible to estimate that up to 186 000 or even more deaths could be attributable to the current conflict in Gaza."[13] This is what happens when bombing happens on this scale. When Israel bombs the region's sewage and water systems, when they bomb every university and the buildings holding children's school records, it looks less like a war on Hamas and more like a war on the people of Gaza.

The moral problem here is not simply the sheer number of dead (compared with 1,200 Israeli casualties on October 7), but how they died. And whether they needed to die. The world has rarely seen such industrial-scale killing.

Militaries speak of the *kill-ratio* or, deploying a bizarre euphemism, of *civilian harm mitigation*.[14] How many non-combatants may a soldier kill to neutralize an enemy target? When Israeli government minister Amichay Eliyahu said in November 2023 that Israel should drop a nuclear bomb on Gaza, even Prime Minister Benjamin Netanyahu knew such statements were unacceptable. Eliyahu was fired. In March 2024 Rep. Tim Walberg (R-Michigan) said the same: bombs should be dropped on Gaza "like Nagasaki and Hiroshima" to "get it over quick." Walberg claimed he was misunderstood, but the damage was done.

---

12. *Al Jazeera*, "Israeli Strike on Gaza School"; Nedim, "Israel Attacked School."
13. Khatib et al., "Counting the Dead."
14. On changing American policy, see Wolfe, "Pentagon."

The concern is proportionality, a term carefully defined in international law with major implications for urban warfare.[15] We find it repugnant to kill huge numbers of people to stop an insurgency movement like Hamas *because* the proportion of civilian casualties is unacceptably high.

Try this analogy. Imagine you are at home and your family of five has been taken captive by a violent, armed terrorist. If the police proposed to bomb your house to kill the terrorist, we would instinctively recoil.

This is the kill-ratio problem or the problem of proportionality.

In December 2023, Israeli intelligence believed that they had located Wissam Farhat, the commander of Hamas's Shuja'iyeh Battalion in the neighborhood of Shuja'iyeh in Gaza City. The massive bombing there killed dozens, destroyed many residential buildings, and buried hundreds in the rubble. Inside Israel this kill-ratio was acceptable because of the perceived value of the target.[16]

On July 27, 2024, in a "safe zone" called Deir al-Balah in central Gaza, Israel bombed an elementary school where thousands were sheltering. At least thirty were killed instantly and one hundred more, mostly children, suffered profound wounds. Israel said it was destroying a Hamas "command and control center"—but again provided no evidence.[17]

In the first month of the war in Gaza, ethicists immediately saw a problem with proportionality. Israel was fighting Hamas combatants and tolerating troubling numbers of civilian casualties. By day 45 of the war, the UN reported 11,075 fatalities, 27,490 injuries, and 1.6 million displaced people. Half of the fatalities, about 6,000 people, belonged to 1,340 families wiped out *in their homes*.[18] Israel was tracking and targeting Hamas members and dropping enormous bombs on their residential buildings, generally at night. One Israeli officer who spoke on condition of anonymity said,

> Every person who wore a Hamas uniform in the past year or two could be bombed with 20 [civilians killed as] collateral damage, even without special permission. In practice, the principle of proportionality did not exist.[19]

---

15. The principle of "proportionality" prohibits attacks "which may be expected to cause incidental loss of civilian life, injury to civilians, damage to civilian objects, or a combination thereof, which would be excessive in relation to the concrete and direct military advantage anticipated." See Robinson and Nohle, "Proportionality."

16. B'Tselem, "Israel Is Not Fighting Against Hamas but Against Civilians."

17. Lilieholm et al., "At Least 30 Killed."

18. UN Office for the Coordination of Humanitarian Affairs, "Hostilities in the Gaza Strip and Israel."

19. Abraham, "'Lavender.'"

Sadly, this pattern is not new. The number of civilians killed during Israel's frequent incursions into the West Bank and Gaza is consistently indefensible. This applies to Gaza's death toll in 2008 ("Operation Cast Lead") and 2014 ("Operation Protective Edge"), and to the vastly greater number of casualties today. Oxfam, the renowned British charity, has called the current Gaza war "the deadliest conflict of the 21st century" because in the first five months Israel was killing 250 people per day.[20] In February 2024, Amnesty International reported the bombing of four residential buildings in Rafah in southern Gaza that had been declared a "safe zone." Ninety-five civilians were killed, half of them children. In June 2024, Israel bombed Nuseirat and Deir el-Balah in central Gaza killing 226 and wounding 400. The European Union called the bombing "a massacre." Dr. Tanya Haj-Hassan called it a "slaughterhouse" and "a complete bloodbath."[21]

With so many non-combatant casualties, it should come as no surprise that experts are accusing Israel of war crimes or genocide, among them the law school of Boston University.[22]

Bombing with the Gospel

In 2021, an anonymous Israeli author calling himself "Brigadier General Y.S." published *The Human-Machine Team: How to Create Synergy Between Human and Artificial Intelligence That Will Revolutionize Our World*. The general proposed building an artificial intelligence system that would label every person in Gaza on a threat scale—and thereby establish rapid targeting without bothering with the "bottleneck" of human decision making. To many the proposal was Orwellian, or reminiscent of a *Terminator* film. Machines would do both the targeting and the killing.

The author turned out to be the commander of Israel's elite unit 8200 (the military intelligence branch).[23] His day has arrived. Artificial intelligence is doing battle in Gaza, as we learned in early 2024 when Yuval

---

20. Alsaafin et al., "Israel's War on Gaza Live."
21. *Al Jazeera*, "'Bodies Scattered on Streets.'"
22. Bouranova, "Is Israel Committing Genocide in Gaza?"
23. Harel, "Top Israeli Intel Officer."

Abraham, an Israeli living in Jerusalem, published a decisive exposé,[24] backed up by both *The Guardian*[25] and *Foreign Policy Journal*.[26]

Six Israeli intelligence officers spoke to Abraham off the record to avoid incrimination. The primary AI program, labeled "Lavender," first built a database of all 2.2 million of Gaza's residents. It then tagged 37,000 people with suspected connections to Hamas and listed them as potential targets. This "kill list" has directed Israel's extensive bombing of Gazans. Before the bombs dropped, target-decisions enjoyed as little as twenty seconds of human assessment. Sometimes there was none.

Israel developed a second AI system to track the residences of these targets and supply data at night when they were likely to be at home with their families. Cynically called "Where's Daddy?" it guided the IDF to bomb countless Gazan families with their children. Whole buildings filled with people were wiped out to kill a target AI predicted was on hand. One officer shared,

> We were not interested in killing [Hamas] operatives only when they were in a military building or engaged in a military activity. On the contrary, the IDF bombed them in homes without hesitation, as a first option. It's much easier to bomb a family's home. The system is built to look for them in these situations.

A third AI program located and targeted buildings that it suspected had seen Hamas activity—though no solid evidence was ever brought forward. Called "The Gospel," this targeting program laid endless waste to homes and structures throughout Gaza. One wonders why the IDF would adopt a sacred Christian name for its final killing machine.

Together these AI programs could assess the value of a target (a junior soldier; a senior officer), give it a target ranking, and put in motion its destruction. *Lavender* tagged persons. *Where's Daddy?* located residences. *The Gospel* listed suspect buildings. If *Lavender* tagged a junior officer, the IDF used "dumb bombs" so as not to waste expensive ordinance. In this instance, the kill ratio (target to collateral deaths) could be as large as 1:20. For a senior officer, it could be 1:100. Yes. One hundred sleeping civilians could be killed in order to strike one Hamas officer. When *The Gospel* and *Where's Daddy?* were asked to locate Ayman Nofal, the central region commander

---

24. Abraham, "'Lavender.'" The e-journal *+972 Magazine* was founded in 2010 by four Israeli journalists in Tel Aviv. By 2012, fifteen journalists were on staff. Its Hebrew partner e-magazine in Israel is *Local Call* (*Sikha Mekomit*) organized by *Just Vision*, an Israeli independent news organization.

25. McKernan and Davies, "'Machine Did It Coldly.'"

26. Pratt, "When AI Decides Who Lives and Dies."

of Hamas, the accepted ratio was 1:300. Sixteen houses were bombed and destroyed. Within weeks of the war's outbreak, these AI systems were generating tens of thousands of targets. With so much data pouring in, human oversight all but disappeared. One officer said, "The rules were very lenient. They took down four buildings when they knew the target was in one of them. It was crazy."

The moral problems here are many, among them the accuracy of AI threat profiles. Criteria included potential targets' movements, their phone calls, whether they changed phones regularly, and online photos that might include another suspected target. Imagine them using the links and sublinks you have on Facebook to assess your target value. Almost immediately *Lavender* swept up ordinary civil defense workers, police, relatives of fighters, even their children, but it was speed that mattered. The pressure increased to generate targets for assassination. One anonymous officer commented, "Since it's an automatic system that isn't operated manually by humans, the meaning of [a] decision is dramatic: it means you're including many people with a civilian communication profile as potential targets." Another spoke of the efficiency of the system. "The machine did it coldly. And that made it easier."

There is something different here, unlike the horrific bombings of Hiroshima or Tokyo or Dresden in WWII. A threshold has been crossed. AI-directed killing and massive bombing have become clinical, mechanized, industrial, unsupervised, and wildly disproportionate.

Bombs, the Gospel, and the Church

The United States has deep complicity in the bombing of Gaza. The US supplies the bombs and the aircraft to deliver them. With the Mark 84 2,000-pound weapon America's token warnings about collateral damage are never enforced. The US even supplies the anti-rocket (Patriot) defense system that shields Israel while it runs its bombing campaigns.

As Christians we need to investigate the complicity of the American church. The American church has found itself at a moral crossroads in this conflict. Many are defending, even promoting, the Gaza bombing campaign. Others, particularly younger Christians, see pro-war, violence-endorsing churches losing credibility.

It is easy to become paralyzed in debates about pacifism and Just War theory. As someone who served in the military, I recognize the tragic need for armies and warfare. But war is not something to be celebrated. In a dark world we must sometimes deploy the tools of darkness to restrain evil. In a broken and disfigured world, war is a last resort.

On Tuesday, November 14, 2023, thousands of people packed the Washington Mall to "March for Israel."[27] News services reported that about 10,000 attended; organizers claimed 290,000.

A major march in Washington is not news. What *was* astounding was the number of evangelical Christians present and the number of American pastors on the stage. Speakers rightly condemned Hamas's October 7 attack on Israel. Families of Jewish hostages told their stories while Israeli leaders drew comparisons with the Holocaust. But in addition—and this is where things become disturbing—pastors and leaders of Congress, many publicly identified as Christians, celebrated the fury of Israel's response. Chants of "No Ceasefire" could be heard echoing from the crowd.

What has become of the church when it not only condones violence like what we've seen in Gaza, but calls for more of it using the apocalyptic war language of the book of Revelation? "Neutrality is not an option," said Rev. Jared Wellman during a morning sermon as he compared Gaza with Nazi Germany.[28] "When they're done with the Jews, they're coming for Christians," warned Rev. Lee Cummings of southwest Michigan. "Prepare your hearts for the rising storm because this isn't calming down."[29] Apocalyptic rhetoric instills fear, inflames audiences to endorse violence, and casts the enemy as a global threat.

What does it mean to be a peacemaker in a time like this? What prophetic voice is needed today to calm excited crowds in our churches who cheer violence in the name of God and Israel? The most grievous examples of this violence are the 2,000-pound bombs Israel is dropping on dense urban settings and the AI algorithms few war planners understand that Israel is using to target the people of Gaza and produce horrific kill-ratios.

Israel is bombing Gaza with the help of *The Gospel* while some American Christians who possess the *true Gospel* cheer them on. I see Jesus rebuking these cheerleaders and condemning their celebrations. Perhaps they would reply, from their Israeli flag–decorated churches, "Lord, did we not prophesy in your name, and cast out demons in your name, and do many mighty works in your name?" (Matt 7:21–23 ESV). Might Jesus not answer them, "I never knew you; depart from me, you workers of lawlessness"?

---

27. Lavin, "These Evangelicals Are Cheering the Gaza War."
28. Graham and Betts, "For American Evangelicals."
29. Graham and Betts, "For American Evangelicals."

PART I: War on the Land

Bibliography

Abraham, Yuval. "'Lavender': The AI Machine Directing Israel's Bombing Spree in Gaza." *+972 Magazine*, April 3, 2024. https://www.972mag.com/lavender-ai-israeli-army-gaza/.

Aljafarawi, Saleh. "Where Is Your Humanity?" December 4, 2023. https://www.youtube.com/watch?v=i91JdhuK-JM.

Al Jazeera. "'Bodies Scattered on Streets': Israel Kills 226 in Central Gaza Attacks." June 8, 2024. https://www.aljazeera.com/news/2024/6/8/many-casualties-as-israel-escalates-attacks-across-gaza.

———. "Israeli Strike on Gaza School Kills More Than 100 People." August 10, 2024. https://www.aljazeera.com/news/2024/8/10/israel-strike-on-gaza-school-kills-more-than-100.

Alsaafin, Linah, et al. "Israel's War on Gaza Live: 'Deadliest Conflict in 21st Century,' Says Oxfam." *Al Jazeera*, January 11, 2024. https://www.aljazeera.com/news/liveblog/2024/1/11/israels-war-on-gaza-live-israel-pounds-gaza-ahead-of-icj-genocide-hearing.

America's Navy. "Joint Direct Attack Munition (JDAM)." Updated October 4, 2021. https://www.navy.mil/Resources/Fact-Files/Display-FactFiles/Article/2166820/joint-direct-attack-munition-jdam/.

Bouranova, Alene. "Is Israel Committing Genocide in Gaza? New Report from BU School of Law's International Human Rights Clinic Lays Out Case." *BU Today*, June 5, 2024. https://www.bu.edu/articles/2024/is-israel-committing-genocide-in-gaza/.

B'Tselem. "Israel Is Not Fighting Against Hamas but Against Civilians, Implementing a Criminal Policy of Bombings." December 5, 2023. https://www.btselem.org/gaza_strip/20231205_israel_is_not_fighting_against_hamas_but_against_civilians_implementing_a_criminal_policy_of_bombings.

El-Naggar, Mona, and Sarah Kerr. "'They Are Burned Alive': A Doctor Captures the Toll of War on Gaza's Children." *The New York Times*, August 10, 2024. https://www.nytimes.com/2024/08/10/world/middleeast/gaza-al-aqsa-hospital-children.html.

EngineerReact. "How Powerful Is a 2000 Pound Bomb?" August 10, 2021. https://www.youtube.com/watch?v=Yvm2z6XMXMw.

Goodman, Amy. "First-Ever DNC Panel on Palestinian Rights: We Need to 'Restore the Soul of the Democratic Party.'" *Democracy Now*, August 20, 2024. https://www.democracynow.org/2024/8/20/dnc_palestinian_rights_panel.

Graham, Ruth, and Anna Betts. "For American Evangelicals Who Back Israel, 'Neutrality Isn't an Option.'" *The New York Times*, October 18, 2023. https://www.nytimes.com/2023/10/15/us/american-evangelicals-israel-hamas.html.

Haj-Hassan, Tanya. "'So Horrific': Doctor Recounts Treating Patients in Gaza Injured in Massacres Enabled by U.S. Bombs." *Democracy Now*, August 22, 2024. https://www.democracynow.org/2024/8/22/dr_tanya_haj_hassan_dnc.

Hamawy, Adam. "American Doctor Stuck in Gaza, Describes Dire State of Medical Care." *PBS Newshour*, May 16, 2024. https://www.youtube.com/watch?v=yhhv1DY-Rho.

Harel, Amos. "Top Israeli Intel Officer Goes Where No One's Gone Before. And You Can Find It on Amazon." *Haaretz*, October 1, 2021. https://www.haaretz.com/israel-news/2021-10-01/ty-article/.highlight/top-israeli-intel-officer-goes-where-no-ones-gone-before-and-its-all-on-amazon/0000017f-e1fb-df7c-a5ff-e3fb21210000.

Khatib, Rasha, et al. "Counting the Dead in Gaza: Difficult but Essential." *The Lancet* 404 (2024) 237–38. https://www.thelancet.com/journals/lancet/article/PIIS0140-6736(24)01169-3/fulltext.

Lavin, Talia. "These Evangelicals Are Cheering the Gaza War as the End of the World." *RollingStone*, November 17, 2023. https://www.rollingstone.com/politics/political-commentary/gaza-war-evangelical-leaders-cheer-end-world-1234884151/.

Lilieholm, Lucas, et al. "At Least 30 Killed in an Israeli Airstrike on a School in Gaza, Palestinian Officials Say." *CNN World*, July 27, 2024. https://www.cnn.com/2024/07/27/middleeast/israel-gaza-deir-al-balah-school-intl/index.html.

McKernan, Bethan, and Harry Davies. "'The Machine Did It Coldly': Israel Used AI to Identify 37,000 Hamas Targets." *The Guardian*, April 3, 2024. https://www.theguardian.com/world/2024/apr/03/israel-gaza-ai-database-hamas-airstrike.

Nedim, Hosni. "Israel Attacked School with 3 Massive Bombs: Gaza Media Office." *Anadolu Agency*, August 10, 2024. https://www.aa.com.tr/en/middle-east/israel-attacked-school-with-3-massive-bombs-gaza-media-office/3300419.

Pamuk, Humeyra, and Mike Stone. "US Has Sent Israel Thousands of 2,000-pound Bombs Since Oct. 7." Reuters, June 29, 2024. https://www.reuters.com/world/us-has-sent-israel-thousands-2000-pound-bombs-since-oct-7-2024-6-28/.

Pratt, Simon. "When AI Decides Who Lives and Dies: The Israeli Military's Algorithmic Targeting Has Created Dangerous New Precedents." *Foreign Policy*, May 2, 2024. https://foreignpolicy.com/2024/05/02/israel-military-artificial-intelligence-targeting-hamas-gaza-deaths-lavender/.

Qiblawi, Tamara, et al. "'Not Seen Since Vietnam': Israel Dropped Hundreds of 2,000-pound Bombs on Gaza, Analysis Shows." *CNN World*, December 22, 2023. https://www.cnn.com/gaza-israel-big-bombs/index.html.

Robinson, Isabel, and Ellen Nohle. "Proportionality and Precautions in Attack: The Reverberating Effects of Using Explosive Weapons in Populated Areas." *International Review of the Red Cross* 98 (2016) 107–45. https://international-review.icrc.org/sites/default/files/irc_97_901-9.pdf.

Stein, Robin, et al. "Visual Evidence Shows Israel Dropped 2,000-Pound Bombs Where It Ordered Gaza's Civilians to Move for Safety." *The New York Times*, December 21, 2023. https://www.nytimes.com/video/world/100000009208814/israel-gaza-bomb-civilians.html.

United Nations Office for the Coordination of Humanitarian Affairs. "Hostilities in the Gaza Strip and Israel—Reported Impact: Day 45." November 20, 2023. https://www.ochaopt.org/content/hostilities-gaza-strip-and-israel-reported-impact-day-45.

Whitney, Craig. "Da Nang Bombing Error Embarrasses U.S. Aides." *The New York Times*, January 9, 1973. https://www.nytimes.com/1973/01/09/archives/da-nang-bombing-error-embarrasses-us-aides-still-used-by-jets.html.

Wolfe, Frank. "Pentagon Removed Non-Combatant Casualty Cut-Off Value from Doctrine in 2018." *Defense Daily*, June 11, 2021. https://www.defensedaily.com/pentagon-removed-non-combatant-casualty-cut-off-value-doctrine-2018/pentagon/.

CHAPTER FOUR

Prisoner Abuse and Evangelical Indifference

David M. Crump

My friend Munther Amira shared a table with me in the small courtyard of his home in the Aida refugee camp on the outskirts of Bethlehem. We sat in shade offered by expansive grape vines covering a wooden trellis above our heads. It was a good place for a conversation about Munther's recent imprisonment.

Munther is a Palestinian Muslim social worker and long-time peace activist living and working in the West Bank. He is committed to nonviolence. He also is an important civic leader in the Aida community, sitting on numerous boards and leadership organizations overseeing the efforts of community centers and local planning committees. Munther is a true servant leader if ever I've met one.

Since the Hamas attack against Southern Israel on October 7, 2023, the West Bank has become an increasingly dangerous place to live—not that it's ever been particularly safe or peaceful since Israeli's imposition of military rule in 1967. More than 895 Palestinians were killed in the West Bank by Israeli soldiers between October 7, 2023, and March 31, 2025.[1]

Between October 7, 2023, and September 29, 2024, over 11,000 West Bank Palestinians were arrested and imprisoned.[2] Nearly 9,000 of these pris-

---

1. UN Office for the Coordination of Humanitarian Affairs, "West Bank Monthly Snapshot."

2. Palestinian Authority Commission of Detainees and Ex-Detainees Affairs, "Brief

oners were held under an extrajudicial arrangement called "administrative detention" dating back to the time of the British Mandate.[3]

On the evening of September 8, 2023, a month before the Hamas attack, Israeli soldiers burst into Munther's home, interrupting the nightly family gathering. Munther was not home. Rather than explain themselves and wait quietly for his return, the soldiers attacked the family. They handcuffed Munther's son and shoved him to the floor. They beat his brother Kareem unconscious. When Munther arrived, they handcuffed him, threw him into the back of a truck, and drove away without a word of explanation.

At an interrogation center Munther was stripped and made to stand in the center of a well-lit room with male and female guards watching. One soldier chuckled and said, "Let's get this party started." Stroking his body with their batons, giving rough, extra attention to his genitals, the soldiers peppered Munther with rapid-fire, demeaning commands that required instant obedience. It was a perverse game of Simon Says: spread your legs, wave your arms, march in place, stand on your right foot, your left foot, squat, sit down, do jumping jacks. Any time his response was too slow or otherwise unacceptable a soldier struck him with a baton.

Munther was not asked any questions during his "interrogation" because the goal of this party was not to glean information but to humiliate through random acts of violence. It was about domination: the guards were puppet masters, the prisoner their puppet. This petty and dehumanizing exercise was a forceful projection of the all-pervasive Zionist ideology that overshadows Jewish–Palestinian relations throughout Israel–Palestine. Zionist Jews are in control. Palestinians are not. They are subservient to Jewish Zionists and subject to their arbitrary power-plays.[4]

After October 7, Munther's circumstances worsened dramatically.

For the next five months, Munther was confined with twelve to fifteen other prisoners in a filthy, mildew-infested cell designed for half that number. With few blankets, the men huddled together at night to share

---

on Detention Campaigns." See also *The Cradle*, "Nearly 9,000 Palestinians Detained." By April 14, 2025, the ADDAMEER Prisoner Support and Human Rights Association tallied 16,500 arrests since October 7, 2023 (www.addameer.org/statistics/2025/04).

3. Palestine was governed by Great Britain from 1922 until 1948. Administrative detention was a common policy applied to "native" prisoners throughout the British Empire. Zionist governments in Israel have maintained this policy to the present day. Prisoners are held without charge in six month increments that can be renewed indefinitely.

4. Israeli security forces have a special term for this collective process of dehumanization. It's called the searing of consciousness. The result is a condition known as learned helplessness. For a discussion of Israel's adoption of this process of wholesale social domination, see Crump, *Like Birds in a Cage*, 163–64.

body heat. Inmates were fed once a day, given food enough for a single person that was to be shared among them all. Sometimes the military guards made their prisoners "eat like cats" on their hands and knees, licking the meager rations off the floor. Although Munther had diabetes and needed daily medication, his pleas for medical care were ignored. Unsurprisingly, my friend had lost over sixty pounds by the time he was released.

Roll call came three times each day, which often meant being stripped and forced to walk naked down a hallway lined with armed guards. Made to run the gauntlet, the prisoners were beaten as they passed between the lines of soldiers. Often they were pushed and tripped at the end of the line so that their nude bodies piled awkwardly in a bruised, contorted mass, only to be struck and further degraded with probing batons and ridicule.[5] Some prisoners chose suicide rather than endure such daily suffering and constant dehumanization.[6]

No Celebrations, No Stories, Just Fear[7]

Like Munther, Anas had been arrested and released before the recent ceasefire prisoner exchanges had begun. I had not had an opportunity to speak with him since his release, so I scheduled our conversation during my most recent visit to the camp. He remained slender and gaunt with bags under his eyes. His wife was still working at "fattening him up," he said, after losing more than fifty pounds during ten months in an Israeli prison.

Anas is the director of the Aida Youth Center located in the Aida refugee camp near Bethlehem. It may have been this work at the Center that got him arrested as he returned home one afternoon from Ramallah after taking a university language exam in the city. His car was stopped and made to pull over to the side of the road. He doesn't know if his arrest was a random detention or whether his photo appears in an Israeli wanted list. In any case, he was handcuffed, questioned, man-handled, and taken to Ofer prison with no explanation.

I know that Anas experienced the same sort of abusive mistreatment inflicted on Munther, but his different social position affected how he spoke

---

5. Several reports detail Israel's use of torture throughout its prison system and the detention camps built since October 7: Gallagher, "Strapped Down"; Kingsley and Shbair, "Inside Sde Teiman"; Zoubi, "More Horrific Than Abu Ghraib"; *Al Jazeera*, "How Does Israel Treat Thousands?".

6. Available video interviews with Munther Amira include *Mondoweiss*, "Exposing the Reality"; and Christian Forum on Israel–Palestine, "Life in an Israeli Prison."

7. The interviews in this section took place during a separate visit in February 2025.

about it. Anas is reticent to describe his abuse with the kind of detail offered by Munther. He is a young husband, father, and community leader living in a society attentive to the public values of honor and shame. Lacking the social capital of a community elder like Munther, Anas is much more circumspect in describing his mistreatment. Whereas Munther easily described the way prisoners were made to eat their food off the floor "like cats," Anas hesitated, finally explaining that "we were made to eat our food in a most uncivilized way."

Furthermore, even though Anas was released prior to the February 2025 rounds of ceasefire prisoner/hostage exchanges, he is well aware that Israel's draconian warnings to recently released prisoners—not to celebrate their newfound freedom, nor to tell their imprisonment stories to anyone, not to family or friends and least of all to the press—will be applied to him as easily as to anyone else. I was startled by the fear in his eyes when I asked if I could take his picture for my blog. He agreed. We are friends, after all. But I cannot forget the look on his face. So I've decided not to publish Anas's photo. I owe him at least that much solidarity.

It was clear that Anas preferred to work on forgetting rather than remembering. He hoped to close the door on this episode in his life and focus on enjoying his wife and eight-month-old son. Who can blame him?

Fear was the common denominator in all my encounters with recently released Palestinian prisoners. Israeli authorities repeatedly warned that there were to be no family parties, no community celebrations welcoming prisoners home. Interviews and public statements describing their time in prison were strictly forbidden. These warnings included threats of rearrest and the harassment of family members. Palestinians know that Israeli threats are not idle, and their punishments are to be avoided, if possible. I witnessed two occasions where Israeli soldiers visited prisoners' family homes to disperse the neighborhood crowds that had spontaneously gathered to welcome the prisoners home. Though I was too late to see the soldiers assault those who had gathered, I could smell the tear gas lingering in nearby alley ways. I also saw the purple welts on the face of a prisoner's uncle who was assaulted for celebrating his nephew's return.

The nephew was fourteen-year-old Mohammed, who was having the time of his life riding a dilapidated bicycle through the narrow, litter-strewn streets, his smile lighting up the sky, celebrating as only a young teenager could. Mohammed was released after serving two years of a ten-year sentence for throwing stones at soldiers. His time had been served in an adult prison, not a juvenile facility.

But Mohammed was lucky. He was able to come home to his family and remain in his community. I visited another illegal celebration that went undisturbed by soldiers only because the former prisoner had already been deported to Egypt. The family elders talked, drank coffee, and nibbled on baklava as they sat in green, plastic folding chairs arranged in neat rows along the nearest alleyway. Smiling friends of the exile shared baklava with everyone passing by, inviting all to join their celebration. Meanwhile, the immediate family hurriedly packed their belongings and finalized arrangements to reunite with their husband, father, and son somewhere in Egypt. I wondered if they had family to help them once they arrived.

Finally, my contacts arranged for me to meet with a released prisoner, another Mohammed, who might be willing to speak with me at length about his life in prison. So, late one night four of us piled into Ayed's black Camry and made our way past the smaller cinder block homes beyond the outskirts of Bethlehem. Driving through the pitch black, following a single track, gravel road through a narrow valley nestled between stony, terraced hills, we eventually saw light emanating from a small garage off to the left. A makeshift plywood door partially covered the opening to a square room with a dirt floor. Off to one side was a homemade wood burning stove with half a dozen men seated around it, holding their hands toward the flames. Ayed introduced me to the group. Mohammed shook my hand and welcomed me. Homecoming parties typically last three days; Mohammed was still greeting well-wishers on day four.

Mohammed had served seven years of a life sentence for his involvement in a bombing plot. I wanted to learn about the circumstances surrounding his crime, arrest, and imprisonment, but as soon as we began discussing the prospects of another meeting, his father firmly interrupted. Apparently, not long after Mohammed stepped off the bus at the Gaza prisoner release site, he spoke in passing to a journalist covering the event. Mohammed's brief interview had not gone unnoticed by Israeli authorities. The very next day, Mohammed's father received a threatening phone call from Israeli security. The ominous caller warned the elderly Palestinian that should Mohammed speak to anyone again about his imprisonment or release, the entire family would face dire consequences, and Mohammed would return to prison.

Though it was clear that Mohammed wanted to talk further, the additional meeting was now off the table. Israeli threats were working as intended. Instead, he showed me the old scars embedded in his left calf as permanent reminders of Israeli beatings.

We spent several hours in conversation, especially about American politics. Local men came and went, offering their greetings, hugging and kissing each other on both cheeks, sharing the Arabic coffee brewing in a large pot on the wrought iron stove. When we rose to say our goodbyes,

Mohammed thanked me for coming and said that he wished we could talk again sometime. As we drove into the night, I reflected on Israel's success at "controlling the narrative." Mohammed's home was isolated. He lived in the middle of nowhere. Yet his family knew that even there Israeli security forces would be listening. They would find you. They would hurt you—and your family.

These men and boys had been released from prison, but their punishment and incarceration continued as they navigated life in the Occupied Territories.

Who Will Condemn Israel's Abuses?

I have given only thumbnail sketches of the degrading abuse these men suffered in an Israeli prison, abuse inflicted in Israel's two-tiered legal regime only on Palestinian prisoners, not on Jewish ones. But these stories are more than examples of Israel's unjust prison system. They are windows on the grotesque inhumanity of Israel's ongoing retaliation against the Palestinian population of Gaza since October 7, 2023.

Space prevents a detailed rehearsal of the apocalyptic level of destruction meted out against the people of Gaza by the Israeli military. It is enough to remember that (as of April 3, 2025) the death toll, not counting unrecovered corpses lying beneath the rubble, exceeds 50,000 people, with over half of the victims being women, children, and the elderly.[8] In July 2024, an article in *The Lancet* medical journal concluded "it is not implausible to estimate that up to 186 000 or even more deaths could be attributable to the current conflict in Gaza."[9] The International Court of Justice ruled in January 2024 that the South African indictment brought against Israel made a compelling case that Israel is plausibly committing genocide in Gaza.[10]

In the face of this daily slaughter, the Western church remains largely silent. Worse, rather than condemn Israel's destruction of Palestinian life in Gaza and the West Bank, leaders in the evangelical branch of the Western church largely approve of Israel's behavior.

Russell Moore, senior editor at *Christianity Today* magazine, penned an editorial on the day of Hamas's assault titled "American Christians Should Stand with Israel Under Attack." He insisted that every Christian

---

8. See UN Office for the Coordination of Humanitarian Affairs, "Reported Impact Snapshot."

9. Khatib et al., "Counting the Dead in Gaza."

10. See the eighty-four-page indictment: International Court of Justice, "Application Instituting Proceedings."

should have "the moral clarity to recognize Israel's right and duty to defend itself."[11] Tragically, Moore lacks the moral clarity needed to rethink his position in light of the abundant evidence of Israel's unfolding genocide and ethnic cleansing throughout Gaza. Without doubt, the Hamas attack against civilians (not including the military personnel involved) and kidnapping of civilian hostages were acts of terrorism deserving universal condemnation. It is right to demand that Hamas release all hostages immediately. Yet Moore's ahistorical approach to the story of Gaza leads him to remain characteristically mute on a number of pressing questions. When are Palestinians allowed to exercise their right to self-defense? Why should the people of Gaza remain complacent and cooperate while living in what many international observers have described as "the largest open-air prison in the world?"[12] When can Palestinian families demand the release of *their* hostages, i.e., the thousands like Munther Amira held hostage and tortured under "administrative detention" in Israeli prisons and detention camps? Moore's article neglects all of these vital questions.

Let's look at a second example. In November 2024 the Southern Baptist Convention issued a resolution titled "On Justice and Peace in the Aftermath of the October 7th Attack on Israel" which called for "the international community to redouble its efforts to support the nation of Israel toward a just and lasting peace."[13] Again, the focus on supporting Israel is telling. To the best of my knowledge, the Southern Baptists have never condemned Israel's oppressive military blockade of Gaza, a blockade which rations caloric intake in order to keep the population on the verge of starvation. Nor have they criticized Israel's overwhelmingly disproportionate military assaults against the people of Gaza in 2008, 2012, 2014, and 2022 that killed and wounded thousands of men, women, and children.[14] Since this November resolution defending Israel the Southern Baptists, like most

---

11. Moore, "American Christians Should Stand with Israel."

12. First to describe Gaza as a prison camp was British Prime Minister David Cameron. See *BBC News*, "David Cameron." Many since have repeated the description of Gaza as an open-air prison. Historian Ilan Pappé, in *The Biggest Prison on Earth*, expanded the designation to include the West Bank. Trying to account for Gaza's dire conditions by focusing solely on the supposed economic tyranny of Hamas and their practice of diverting much-needed resources to fund "terror tunnels" does not address this fundamental issue. Israel's oppressive military blockade is the root cause of Gaza's problems; Hamas is a subsidiary concern.

13. *Baptist Press*, "On Justice and Peace."

14. See *Al Jazeera*, "Timeline: Israel's Attacks on Gaza Since 2005." On the long history of Israel's destructive military attacks on Gaza, see Chomsky and Pappé, *Gaza in Crisis*; Levy, *Punishment of Gaza*; Finkelstein, "This Time We Went Too Far"; Finkelstein, *Method and Madness*; Blumenthal, *51 Day War*; Finkelstein, *Gaza*.

evangelical denominations, have remained silent in the face of overwhelming evidence of Israel's crimes against humanity.

A third example. On November 17, 2023, thousands of evangelicals gathered on the Washington, DC, Mall to hear evangelical politicians pledge their commitment to defend the Zionist nation-state of Israel. They stood side-by-side with John Hagee, perhaps the most influential Christian Zionist leader in the United States. At one point, the massive crowd chanted "no ceasefire, no ceasefire." It's hard for me to imagine Jesus of Nazareth joining in. No evangelical gatherings on a similar scale have been held since November to condemn Israel's mass killing of over 38,000 people or its total demolition of the Gaza Strip. In fact, evangelical silence remained deafening even after Benny Gantz, Israel's Minister of Defense (at the time), boasted that Israel had "bombed Gaza back to the stone age."[15]

Evangelical voices offering a biblical critique, or any critique, of Israel's actions in Gaza and the West Bank are rare. American evangelicalism is following a long-standing pattern of trading faithfulness to Jesus's teaching for obeisance to government policies—something that is not unusual for the Christian church whose witness to the world is frequently compromised when it supports those in positions of power. To mention only one egregious example with which many are familiar, the German Christian church of the 1930s and 1940s is infamous for securely linking arms with Naziism.[16] When Hitler implemented his policy of euthanizing Germany's handicapped and mentally impaired citizens, not a single Protestant church leader stood to resist the policy or offer public protest.[17] Large sectors of the Western church are now swathed in a similar blanket of silence and moral paralysis as Israel commits blatant acts of criminality. Evangelicals remain silent in the face of genocide, discounting the accuracy of casualty figures coming from the Hamas Health Ministry (which in the past have generally been considered reliable).[18] They insist that civilian casualties in Gaza are entirely the result of Hamas's fighting methods while exonerating the Israeli targeting systems that fail to distinguish between combatants and innocent civilians (a failure readily acknowledged by Israeli officials).[19] All of these malicious acts of special pleading are akin to Holocaust denialism.

---

15. Abunimah, "Israeli Election Ad."

16. Barnett, *For the Soul of the People*; Gushee, *Righteous Gentiles of the Holocaust*; Bergen, *Twisted Cross*; Haffner, *Defying Hitler*; Steigmann-Gall, *Holy Reich*.

17. Steigmann-Gall, *Holy Reich*, 202.

18. McGreal, "Can We Trust Casualty Figures?"; and Debre, "What Is Gaza's Ministry of Health?"

19. Israel's AI (artificial intelligence) missile targeting programs are called The Gospel, Lavender, and Where's Daddy? See Yuval Abraham's reports: "'Mass Assassination

Why are Western evangelicals generally indifferent, even hostile, to the plight of the Palestinian people? Why is it so difficult to find evangelical leaders willing publicly to denounce Israel's brutal treatment of prisoners under "administrative detention," not to mention its campaign to destroy Gaza, conquer additional territory, and displace more and more Palestinians in Gaza and the West Bank?

Why Do Evangelicals Support Israel?

The answer has at least four parts. First is American evangelical devotion to the ideology of *Christian Zionism*, a devotion that has spread worldwide wherever evangelical missionaries have left their mark on local churches. What is Christian Zionism? Christian Zionism maintains that all land between the Jordan River and the Mediterranean Sea belongs to the Jewish people by divine promise. As a result of God's territorial commitment to the descendants of Abraham, Jews are free to take whatever measures they deem necessary to acquire territory in the Holy Land and displace non-Jews living there.[20] Consequently, both the assault against Gaza and the displacement of Palestinian residents in the West Bank are not merely permissible. They are desirable steps toward the fulfillment of God's promise to Israel.

Space does not allow for a full refutation of Christian Zionist ideology. I have tried to do that in *Like Birds in a Cage: Christian Zionism's Collusion in Israel's Oppression of the Palestinian People*. Here I pose a single question. What is it about Christian Zionism that prevents criticism of Israel's behavior, no matter how horrendous? Why do Christian Zionists only act as Israel's cheerleaders? I see no logical or theological rationale for this wall of Christian Zionist silence.

No group has been more committed to Israel's (and Judah's) welfare than were the Old Testament prophets. Yet these pious men devoted to the God of Israel were also the nation's harshest critics. According to the Bible, their prophetic critique of Israel and Judah was God's own critique of a covenant people gone astray. Why doesn't Christian Zionism allow room for such prophetic critique today?

Factory'" and "'Lavender.'" Israel's decision to strike suspected Hamas targets (while admitting that the AI system has a 10 percent error rate which is not monitored or verified by human oversight) in their homes after dark when the entire family is gathered together guarantees massive civilian casualties. See further ch. 3 above, pp. 94–96.

20. The conflation of the biblical descendants of Abraham, Isaac, and Jacob with the modern nation-state of Israel is one of Zionism's most problematic claims. For a good analysis of this problem, see Sand, *Invention of the Jewish People*. See also chapters 1 and 2 in Crump, *Ten (Christian) Myths*.

The second reason for evangelical silence is *disinterest*. American society is notoriously parochial and intellectually crippled by something I call the "American Entertainment Disorder." We are narrow-minded, socially and politically apathetic, and happy to devour the newest video games, entertainment programs, reality shows, and sporting events. American Christians often express little concern for world affairs and fail to see that faithful discipleship must be radically counter-cultural. Pro-Israel activism is one of the few causes motivating American evangelicals to concern themselves with the affairs of a foreign country. Sadly, the average American is woefully uninformed, if not thoroughly misinformed, about Israel and its place in the Middle East. Armed with Christian Zionist talking points, the average evangelical may find herself attending rallies at the Washington Mall with extremists like John Hagee, dutifully chanting "no ceasefire" in the face of untold human suffering.

Israel is the largest cumulative recipient of foreign aid in US history. The United States provides Israel with nearly four billion dollars every year.[21] The vast majority of the weapons destroying Gaza and murdering its populace are supplied by American companies.[22] Since October 7, 2023, the US Congress has allocated over twenty-three billion dollars in additional military aid to Israel.[23] America's complicity in facilitating Israel's genocide should concern every US citizen, and it should be profoundly disturbing for the people of God. No follower of Jesus should support ethnic cleansing.

If American citizenship alone is insufficient motivation, God's people have a calling to serve as prophets to the nations. In the Old Testament prophets we see a pattern of godly men and women confronting the evil policies of national leaders. Nathan confronted King David (2 Sam 12:1–15), Elijah rebuked King Ahab (1 Kgs 18:16–46), Daniel openly disobeyed King Darius (Dan 6:6–16), John the Baptist condemned King Herod (Mark 6:14–20). These prophets confronted both the personal immorality and the unjust policies of rulers. They remind us that as citizens of God's kingdom, we are called to speak prophetically to every empire (especially our own), not to offer supine servitude as polite, chastened chaplains. The Christian church abdicates its role as a prophetic community whenever we are silent in the face of flagrant injustice.

Fear is a third factor that keeps evangelical leaders from standing against Israel's genocidal behavior. The divisive politicization of American Christianity throughout the years of Donald Trump's presidency and

---

21. Masters and Merrow, "US Aid to Israel."
22. See Gritten, "Gaza War."
23. Masters and Merrow, "US Aid to Israel."

COVID-19 have shown how quickly congregations can fracture when a leader's political views are out-of-step with the strongly held convictions of members.[24] Pastors have learned how quickly they can be fired when they ruffle too many congregational feathers.

Not long after October 7, I gave a presentation offering a Palestinian perspective on life under Israeli domination. A senior member of my church was outraged. The man interrupted my talk, pounded his fist, and raised his voice to prevent me from speaking. Later, by phone, he chided the pastor for allowing me to speak in the first place. Church discipline, internal revolt, and outright dismissal are real threats faced by many pastors and evangelical leaders who dare to condemn Israel's actions in Gaza or defend the Palestinian right to self-defense.

The final factor motivating evangelical silence is *anti-Arab racism*, which is arguably embedded in much Christian Zionism in America.[25] Whether or not we recognize this problem, the cultural-racial construct Edward Said called "Orientalism" permeates Western societies.[26] Orientalists stereotype the "Arab mind" as primitive, unsophisticated, quick tempered, naturally combative, inherently antisemitic, deceitful, and untrustworthy. They have no explanation for someone like my friend Munther Amira.

In his 2011 book *Everlasting Hatred: The Roots of Jihad*, best-selling Christian Zionist author Hal Lindsey explained that the antagonistic character of the "Arab Bedouin nature" is best represented by the "wild donkey"—out of control and difficult to tame.[27] Furthermore, Lindsey claims that the biblical "enmity of Ishmael and Esau toward Isaac and Jacob" continues today with a "supernatural" hatred of all Arabs against all Jews.[28] So perpetual warfare between Israel and the Arabs is inevitable because of God's plan and the deficiencies of Arab DNA. Lindsey represents the worst sort of Orientalist racism.

Orientalist prejudice was on full display in early news reports contrasting the war in Ukraine with Israel's assault on Gaza. Western broadcasters explicitly reminded viewers that Ukraine is "European," "white," "Christian," and "civilized." Ukrainian refugees are "like us." They didn't look like your "typical refugees" because they were "relatively prosperous, well-dressed and middle-class." Dark-skinned Arab refugees, on the other

---

24. Eighty percent of white evangelical Christians voted for Donald Trump in November 2016 and 82 percent in 2024.

25. See my "Echoes of Slavery."

26. Said, *Orientalism*.

27. Lindsey, *Everlasting Hatred*, 62.

28. Lindsey, *Everlasting Hatred*, 70–71. A subheading in chapter 6 (p. 86) is titled "The Arabs' Warring Nature."

hand, were "the Other"; they were nothing at all like us, but were representatives of undeveloped "third-world nations" dominated by chaos, strife and unthinking sectarianism.[29]

Orientalism is a deep-seated prejudice against Arab people, and a partner to the incipient anti-black racism running throughout American history. If Western, white, Christian Zionist evangelicals remain unmoved after hearing about the violent deaths of over 50,000 Palestinians, the erasure of 15,000 Palestinian children, and the apocalyptic devastation of Gaza, racism is partly to blame.

Carrying Our Cross Against the Current

Jesus warns every potential disciple about the high cost of following him. Every disciple is to "take up their cross" and follow a path of self-denial, possible rejection, and suffering (Mark 8:34). Just as obedience to the Father led Jesus to Calvary, so our obedience to Christ will lead us to painful self-denial, and for some, it will lead to an early death. Jesus never asks his followers to do anything that he does not first do himself. Thus, Jesus demonstrates something of what it means to take up our cross when he endures hostility for his provocative teachings.

Carrying one's cross means marching out of step with the cultural, social, moral, and political status quo that prevails in the fallen world around us—and too often in the Christian church as well. Jesus warns, "Woe to you when everyone has only good things to say about you" (Luke 6:26, my translation). We are in trouble when our proclamation never offends anyone.

The overarching theme of Jesus's teaching was the arrival of the kingdom of God.[30] He began his ministry with a command: "Repent and believe for the kingdom of God is at hand" (Mark 1:14–15). Jesus's understanding of God's kingdom diverged significantly from the conventional expectations of his contemporaries. In fact, one reason Jesus gave so much attention to the kingdom of God was because he offered a version that no one had anticipated.[31] Skeptics questioned him. Crowds and disciples misunderstood him (Mark 4:13; 8:17–21; 9:32), took offense, and sometimes opposed him (Mark 8:33). As for Judas Iscariot, the off-putting nature of Jesus's kingdom

---

29. Words and phrases in quotation marks taken from *NowThis*, "Hypocritical Media Coverage."

30. Malina, *Social Gospel of Jesus*, 1: "Even the most skeptical historian would agree that if Jesus spoke about anything, he spoke about the kingdom of heaven."

31. See my book *I Pledge Allegiance*, 13–15, 22–23.

teaching led to outright betrayal (Mark 14:10–11). Yet Jesus stayed the course knowing how much personal antagonism his kingdom teaching would stir up, as well as how much this hostility served to validate his own faithfulness.

Sometimes being faithful to God's kingdom means confronting those who reject Jesus's teaching. In John 8:44 Jesus identifies hostile religious authorities as "children of the devil," a most undiplomatic accusation to be sure. But the truth must be spoken even when it provokes a hostile reaction. Jesus reminds us that sometimes our opposition will come from within the family of faith, even from those who appear especially devout. Jesus remained undeterred by the fact that his opponents were keeping score, knowing he would pay a price for his words of judgment when the chief priests and Pharisees determined that he must be eliminated.

Perhaps Jesus's most egregious offense appears in John 6:35–66, when he urged his followers to "eat his flesh and drink his blood," words he knew would sound repulsive to religious Jews known for their abhorrence of consuming blood (see Lev 17:10–14). Jesus immediately found himself alienated from many who had previously pledged allegiance: "from this time many of his disciples turned back and no longer followed him" (6:66 NRSV). Nor was Jesus surprised by their response. Yet his determination to tell the truth took precedence over any fears Jesus may have had about losing followers or antagonizing enemies.

Steadfastness in the face of opposition is what it means to take up our cross. Truthfulness during storms of misinformation is the Christian's prophetic calling. Moral conviction that denounces evil is a sign of maturity. Silence in the face of genocide—or worse, using theology to defend genocide—is complicity in monstrous evil.

Christian discipleship requires us to overcome whatever obstacles are keeping us silent. If that silence is due to the moral anesthesia of Christian Zionism, we must wake up and speak out in defense of those under attack. If our silence stems from a general indifference to world affairs due to the "American Entertainment Disorder," we must seek a cure. If we are silent for fear of standing alone when declaring "No more," we must pray for courage. If our silence is driven by prejudice against people not like us, we must repent. In the midst of Israel's war on the people of Gaza, Christians cannot remain silent.

Bibliography

Abraham, Yuval. "'Lavender': The AI Machine Directing Israel's Bombing Spree in Gaza." *+972 Magazine*, April 3, 2024. https://www.972mag.com/lavender-ai-israeli-army-gaza/.

———. "'A Mass Assassination Factory': Inside Israel's Calculated Bombing of Gaza." *+972 Magazine*, November 30, 2023. https://www.972mag.com/mass-assassination-factory-israel-calculated-bombing-gaza/.

Abunimah, Ali. "Israeli Election Ad Boasts Gaza Bombed Back to 'Stone Ages.'" *The Electronic Intifada*, January 21, 2019. https://electronicintifada.net/blogs/ali-abunimah/israeli-election-ad-boasts-gaza-bombed-back-stone-ages.

Al Jazeera. "How Does Israel Treat Thousands of Palestinians in Its Prisons?" July 1, 2024. https://www.aljazeera.com/program/inside-story/2024/7/1/how-does-israel-treat-thousands-of-palestinians-in-its-prisons.

———. "Timeline: Israel's Attacks on Gaza Since 2005." August 7, 2022. https://www.aljazeera.com/news/2022/8/7/timeline-israels-attacks-on-gaza-since-2005.

The Associated Press. "Middle East Latest: Death Toll in Gaza Passes 46,000 and Lebanon Ends Presidential Deadlock." January 9, 2025. https://apnews.com/article/israel-hamas-war-syria-lebanon-news-01-09-2025-a6ffc6e062d81f57e13682d35d562b02.

Baptist Press. "On Justice and Peace in the Aftermath of the October 7 Attack on Israel." www.baptistpress.com/wp-content/uploads/2024/05/4-On-Justice-and-Peace-in-the-Aftermath-of-the-October-7-Attack-on-Israel.pdf.

Barnett, Victoria. *For the Soul of the People: Protestant Protest Against Hitler.* Oxford: Oxford University Press, 1992.

BBC News. "David Cameron Describes Blockaded Gaza as 'a Prison.'" July 27, 2010. https://www.bbc.com/news/world-middle-east-10778110.

Bergen, Doris L. *Twisted Cross: The German Christian Movement in the Third Reich.* Chapel Hill: University of North Carolina Press, 1996.

Blumenthal, Max. *The 51 Day War: Ruin and Resistance in Gaza.* New York: Nation, 2015.

Chomsky, Noam, and Ilan Pappé. *Gaza in Crisis: Reflections on Israel's War Against the Palestinians.* Chicago: Haymarket, 2010.

Christian Forum on Israel–Palestine. "Life in an Israeli Prison: Munther Amira Tells His Story." July 12, 2024. https://www.youtube.com/watch?v=EYXuwuUNJ-k.

The Cradle. "Nearly 9,000 Palestinians Detained in West Bank Since 7 October." May 27, 2024. https://thecradle.co/articles-id/25108.

Crump, David M. "Echoes of Slavery, Racial Segregation and Jim Crow: American Dispensationalism and Christian Zionist Bible-Reading." *Journal of Holy Land and Palestine Studies* 23 (2024) 1–17.

———. *I Pledge Allegiance: A Believer's Guide to Kingdom Citizenship in 21st-Century America.* Grand Rapids: Eerdmans, 2018.

———. *Like Birds in a Cage: Christian Zionism's Collusion in Israel's Oppression of the Palestinian People.* Eugene, OR: Cascade, 2022.

———. *Ten (Christian) Myths About Israel-Palestine.* Eugene, OR: Cascade, forthcoming.

Debre, Isabel. "What Is Gaza's Ministry of Health and How Does It Calculate the War's Death Toll?" Associated Press News, November 6, 2023. https://

apnews.com/article/israel-hamas-war-gaza-health-ministry-health-death-toll-59470820308b31f1faf73c703400b033.

Finkelstein, Norman G. *Gaza: An Inquest into Its Martyrdom*. Oakland: University of California Press, 2018.

———. *Method and Madness: The Hidden History of Israel's Assaults on Gaza*. New York: OR Books, 2014.

———. *"This Time We Went Too Far": Truth and Consequences of the Gaza Invasion*. New York: OR Books, 2010.

Gallagher, Patrick. "Strapped Down, Blindfolded, Held in Diapers." *CNN*, May 11, 2024. https://www.cnn.com/2024/05/10/middleeast/israel-sde-teiman-detention-whistleblowers-intl-cmd/index.html.

Gritten, David. "Gaza War: Where Does Israel Get Its Weapons?" *BBC News*, April 15, 2024. https://www.bbc.com/news/world-middle-east-68737412.

Gushee, David. *The Righteous Gentiles of the Holocaust: A Christian Interpretation*. Minneapolis: Fortress, 1994.

Haffner, Sebastian. *Defying Hitler: A Memoir*. London: Phoenix, 2003.

International Court of Justice. "Application Instituting Proceedings in the Name of the Republic of South Africa Against the State of Israel." https://icj-cij.org/sites/default/files/case-related/192/192-20231228-app-01-00-en.pdf.

Khatib, Rasha, et al. "Counting the Dead in Gaza: Difficult but Essential." *The Lancet* 404 (2024) 237–38. https://www.thelancet.com/journals/lancet/article/PIIS0140-6736(24)01169-3/fulltext.

Kingsley, Patrick, and Bilal Shbair. "Inside Sde Teiman, the Base Where Israel Detains Gazans." *The New York Times*, June 6, 2024. https://www.nytimes.com/2024/06/06/world/middleeast/israel-gaza-detention-base.html.

Levy, Gideon. *The Punishment of Gaza*. London: Verso, 2010.

Lindsey, Hal. *The Everlasting Hatred: The Roots of Jihad*. Washington, DC: WND, 2011.

Malina, Bruce. *The Social Gospel of Jesus: The Kingdom of God in Mediterranean Perspective*. Minneapolis: Fortress, 2001.

Masters, Jonathan, and Will Merrow. "US Aid to Israel in Four Charts." Council on Foreign Relations, May 31, 2024. https://www.cfr.org/article/us-aid-israel-four-charts.

McGreal, Chris. "Can We Trust Casualty Figures from the Hamas-Run Gaza Health Ministry?" *The Guardian*, October 27, 2023. https://www.theguardian.com/world/2023/oct/26/can-we-trust-casualty-figures-from-the-hamas-run-gaza-health-ministry.

Mondoweiss. "Exposing the Reality: Life Inside an Israeli Prison." May 29, 2024. https://www.youtube.com/watch?v=Rrl-ZxnH6ys&t=11s.

Moore, Russell. "American Christians Should Stand with Israel Under Attack." *Christianity Today*, October 7, 2023. https://www.christianitytoday.com/ct/2023/october-web-only/israel-hamas-middle-east-war-christians.html.

NowThis. "Hypocritical Media Coverage of Ukraine vs. the Middle East." March 1, 2022. https://www.youtube.com/watch?v=2z9UyPurVok.

Palestinian Authority Commission of Detainees and Ex-Detainees Affairs. "Brief on Detention Campaigns Carried Out in the West Bank Since the Beginning of the Genocide." https://cda.gov.ps/index.php/en/commission-activities/report-and-achivements/18484-brief-on-detention-campaigns-carried-out-in-the-west-bank-since-the-beginning-of-the-genocide-3.

Pappé, Ilan. *The Biggest Prison on Earth: A History of the Occupied Territories.* London: Oneworld, 2017.
Said, Edward W. *Orientalism.* New York: Vintage, 1979.
Sand, Shlomo. *The Invention of the Jewish People.* London: Verso, 2009.
Steigmann-Gall, Richard. *The Holy Reich: Nazi Conceptions of Christianity, 1919–1945.* Cambridge: Cambridge University Press, 2003.
United Nations Office for the Coordination of Humanitarian Affairs. "Reported Impact Snapshot: Gaza Strip (3 April 2025)." https://www.ochaopt.org/content/reported-impact-snapshot-gaza-strip-3-april-2025.
———. "West Bank Monthly Snapshot—Casualties, Property Damage and Displacement: March 2025." https://www.ochaopt.org/content/west-bank-monthly-snapshot-casualties-property-damage-and-displacement-march-2025.
Zoubi, Baker. "More Horrific Than Abu Ghraib." *+972 Magazine,* June 27, 2024. https://www.972mag.com/sde-teiman-prisoners-lawyer-mahajneh/.

CHAPTER FIVE

Hamas and Violence

Ideology, Militarism, and the Quest for Liberation

Daniel Bannoura

Since the Hamas attack on Israel on October 7, 2023, and the ensuing genocidal war Israel has waged on the Palestinians in Gaza, it has been extremely difficult to speak objectively about Hamas. Western discourse about Hamas, both public and academic, in the political sphere and in the media, is fraught with simplistic and distorted descriptions of Hamas as a violent and antisemitic terrorist group sworn to the eradication of Israel and the annihilation of the Jews. Such reductionist—and false—discourse has impeded any thoughtful and nuanced analysis that might make sense of Hamas's ideology and motivations. Even worse, this discourse has been used by politicians and media pundits to shut down critical conversations about the oppressive policies, war crimes, violations of international law, and genocide Israel is committing in the Gaza Strip.

How should we think about Hamas? And what is the appropriate Christian response to its ideology and militarism? This essay is a modest attempt to explain Hamas to the general Christian audience. It summarizes the beliefs and political aspirations of Hamas, and assesses critically aspects of its contentious ideology, particularly its adoption of violence as a tactic for liberation. The goal is to help the reader understand Hamas's *raison d'être*, religious ideology, and political vision, and move beyond reductionist and simplistic attitudes often found in Western political discourse. The essay concludes with a Christian Palestinian reflection on the place of violence within the Palestinian struggle for justice and liberation.

What Is Hamas?

Hamas is the acronym of *ḥarakat al-muqāwama al-islāmiyya*, or "Islamic Resistance Movement."[1] It was founded in Gaza in 1988, during the first Intifada, by Sheikh Ahmad Yassin and others, the majority of whom were refugees whose families had been forced to settle in Gaza during the Nakba of 1948.[2] From its inception, Hamas rejected the peace process adopted by the Palestinian Liberation Organization (PLO) and regarded it as capitulation to the Israeli occupation. Hamas has maintained that resistance, in the form of military struggle, is the most effective way to counter the occupation. Its ideology is built on Islamic Nationalism, as understood by the Muslim Brotherhood of Egypt, in contradistinction to the secularist model adopted by the PLO and other Palestinian resistance groups and political parties.[3]

Hamas participated in the 2006 Palestinian legislative election and secured a majority in the Palestinian Legislative Council. After a brief civil war in 2007 between Hamas and its rival party Fatah, Hamas seized control of the Gaza Strip from Fatah and has since governed the territory separately from the Palestinian National Authority. After Hamas's takeover, Israel imposed a complete blockade on the Gaza Strip, which has had a crippling socioeconomic impact on the territory. Such a blockade is legally an act of war.[4] Moreover, it constitutes collective punishment and is a "flagrant contravention of international human rights and humanitarian law."[5]

---

1. The term ought to be capitalized since it is an acronym. Here it is rendered Hamas, instead of HAMAS, following long-standing convention.

2. Among those founders are Abdel Aziz al-Rantisi (d. 2004), Mahmoud al-Zahar, Mohammad Taha (d. 2014), Abdul Fatah Dukhan (d. 2023), and Hassan Yousef. Most of these founders were refugees from outside the Gaza Strip whose families had endured the trauma of the Nakba.

3. For more on the rise of Hamas and Islamic Nationalism, see Baconi, *Hamas Contained*, 1–28.

4. Bisharat et al., "Israel's Invasion of Gaza," 59.

5. UN Office of the High Commissioner for Human Rights, "How Can Israel's Blockade of Gaza Be Legal?"

The Political Vision of Hamas

In August of 1988, a few months after its creation, Hamas detailed its ideology and political vision through its charter, "The Charter of God: The Platform of the Islamic Resistance Movement (Hamas)." Comprising thirty-six articles, the document introduces the movement; outlines its mission, values, and political vision; and provides a motto: "God is its goal, the messenger [Muḥammad] is its leader, the Qur'an is its constitution, *jihād* is its way, and death for the sake of God is its most coveted desire."[6]

This original charter, widely criticized for some of its content, particularly its use of antisemitic tropes, was replaced in 2017 with a forty-two-article manifesto entitled "The Document of General Principles and Policies of Hamas." This updated or "new" charter advances a rather mature political position that eliminates much of the fervent religious rhetoric of the original charter and corrects earlier antisemitic tropes by framing the struggle as an anti-colonial one against Zionism and not against Judaism or Jews.[7]

Islamic Nationalism

According to the original charter, Hamas is a "distinct Palestinian movement" whose nationalism is "part and parcel of its religious ideology." It defines itself as allied with other Islamist parties and movements that draw on Islam to define a particular political agenda and national identity, a stance referred to as Islamo-nationalism.[8]

The charter further describes all of historic Palestine as an Islamic *waqf*, an inalienable religious endowment, no part of which could be relinquished. Accordingly, Islamic law (*sharī ʿa*) should be the law of the land (Article 11).

The new charter defines Palestine as "Arab Islamic land. It is a blessed sacred land that has a special place in the heart of every Arab and every Muslim" (Article 3), and "an integral territorial unit" stretching between the Jordan and Mediterranean, and "from Ras al-Naqurah in the north to Umm al-Rashrash in the south" (Article 2). When it comes to the Palestinian people, the new charter adopts an Arabist definition of the people that

---

6. English excerpts of the 1988 charter provided by the author. For the full text in English, see Maqdsi, "Charter."

7. For an English translation of the 2017 charter, see *Middle East Eye*, "Hamas in 2017."

8. On Islamicist political ideology and Islam, see Tibi, *Islamism and Islam*; Osman, *Islamism*.

includes all of the inhabitants of Palestine up to 1947 (before the establishment of Israel), including, presumably, native Arab Jewish populations:

> The Palestinians are the Arabs who lived in Palestine until 1947, irrespective of whether they were expelled from it, or stayed in it; and every person that was born to an Arab Palestinian father after that date, whether inside or outside Palestine, is a Palestinian. (Article 5)[9]

The old charter offers no explicit vision for an Islamic Palestinian state in terms of its theological and political structures, nor any indication of how Hamas views nation-states more generally.[10] At the same time, in discussing its relationship to the PLO, the charter spells out Hamas's attitude toward secularism. While considering the PLO an ally—"our homeland is one, our struggle is one, our fate is one, and the enemy is a joint enemy to all of us"—the charter is nevertheless critical of the PLO's secularist identity, a product of "the ideological confusion prevailing in the Arab world as a result of the ideological invasion" infiltrating the Arab world since the Crusades (Article 27).

This apparent tension between Islamic nationalism and secularism is part of the larger debate that has continued in Muslim-majority societies since the late nineteenth century about the applicability of secular ideals and the appropriateness of separating Islamic rulings from civic and legal affairs of the state.[11] Similar to theonomic political formulations of Christian states such as the Kingdom of Armenia or the Holy Roman Empire—or to modern conceptions of Christian nationalism found among members of the Christian Right in the West—Islamic political discourse is generally perceived by its critics to be illiberal and an obstacle to the guarantee of equal treatment under the law of all citizens, particularly ethnic and religious minorities, within the pluralistic societies of the Middle East.[12]

There is wide diversity of opinion among Muslims over how to implement and apply Islamic precepts as the basis of civil and religious laws and rights. Today there are several self-defined Islamic states, such as Pakistan,

---

9. The following article, Article 5, further reflects on the Palestinian identity as an "authentic and timeless" identity that cannot be erased due to the Nakba of 1948 and continual efforts by "the Zionist occupation" to displace Palestinians and erase or negate their identity. Article 6 continues: "The Palestinian people are one people, made up of all Palestinians, inside and outside of Palestine, irrespective of their religion, culture or political affiliation."

10. On Islam and nation-states, see Piscatori, *Islam in a World of Nation-States*; Esposito and Voll, *Islam and Democracy*.

11. See Salem, "Rise and Fall"; and al-Azmeh, *Secularism in the Arab World*.

12. See Roy, *Failure of Political Islam*.

Saudi Arabia, Iran, Oman, and Mauritania. Many other Muslim-majority countries, like Jordan, Egypt, Syria, and Morocco, affirm in their constitutions that Islamic *sharī'a* forms the foundation of their laws, or that Islamic jurisprudence (*fiqh*) is a principal source of legislation. Other states, like Lebanon, Turkey, Sudan, Indonesia, and Uzbekistan, are explicitly secular or do not make constitutional declarations about any specific religion, while affirming plurality and freedom of religion and worship.[13]

Returning to Hamas, far from their political vision necessitating the oppression or annihilation of Jewish people, as is frequently claimed in the West, the charter asserts that "Islam confers upon everyone his legitimate rights. Islam prevents the incursion on other people's rights" (Article 31). As such, it describes its vision of coexistence between Islam, Christianity, and Judaism as "humanistic":

> [Hamas] is a humanistic movement that upholds human rights and adheres to tolerance as prescribed by Islam in its view of the followers of other religions. It is only hostile towards those who are hostile to it.... Under the wing of Islam, it is possible for the followers of the three religions—Islam, Christianity and Judaism—to coexist in peace and quiet with each other. Security and safety would not be possible except under the wing of Islam. (Article 31)

The new charter further develops this moderate understanding of Islam in terms of *wasaṭiyya*, or "the middle way":[14]

> By virtue of its justly balanced middle way and moderate spirit, Islam for Hamas provides a comprehensive way of life and an order that is fit for purpose at all times and in all places. Islam is a religion of peace and tolerance. It provides an umbrella for the followers of other creeds and religions who can practice their

---

13. Secular Muslim-majority states are not necessarily models of religious freedom or liberal democracy. Clearly, a constitutional declaration is not sufficient to ensure equality under the law or to guarantee religious freedom or freedom of expression in practice. For more on Islamic constitutions, see Ahmed and Abbasi, "What Is an Islamic Constitution?" Incidentally, the official Palestinian constitution, amended in 2003, states that "the principles of Islamic law (*sharī'a*) are a primary source of legislation," and goes on to state that the "followers of 'heavenly messages'" (understood broadly as monotheistic religions) can organize their personal conditions and religious matters according to their religious and denominational regulations "within the framework of [Palestinian] law, and in keeping of the unity of the Palestinian people and their independence" (Article 7).

14. For more about Hamas's model of *wasaṭiyya* pragmatism that upholds core Islamic principles while maintaining flexibility in achieving its long-term goals, see Polka, "Hamas as a *Wasati* (Literally: Centrist) Movement."

beliefs in security and safety. Hamas also believes that Palestine has always been and will always be a model of coexistence, tolerance and civilizational innovation. (Article 8)

Hamas's political vision, as expressed in the original charter, to establish a Palestinian state guided by Islamic law clearly necessitates the dismantling or "abolishing" of Israel as a Jewish state (Article 2). In a sense, Hamas aspires for what is commonly referred to as a "one-state solution," whereby a Palestinian state would exist over the whole area between the Jordan River and Mediterranean Sea.

Hamas shifted pragmatically toward a version of the two-state solution in their new charter. While affirming that "no part of the land of [historic] Palestine shall be compromised or conceded," Hamas expresses its openness to coexisting alongside Israel.

> However, without compromising its rejection of the Zionist entity and without relinquishing any Palestinian rights, Hamas considers the establishment of a fully sovereign and independent Palestinian state, with Jerusalem as its capital along the lines of the 4th of June 1967, with the return of the refugees and the displaced to their homes from which they were expelled, to be a formula of national consensus. (Article 20)

Hamas's surprising acceptance of the pre-1967 borders and a two-state solution was likely a pragmatic attempt to appease Palestinians.[15] Either way, it is important to highlight that Hamas's language about abolishing Israel did not threaten Jewish existence in the land or necessitate their exodus or expulsion. The charter does not include any language of displacing Jewish people, much less exterminating them, and it denies that violence would befall Jewish people living in the land. Instead, the charter emphatically asserts that Jews, as a religious group, would be protected within the Palestinian state envisioned by Hamas. This is spelled out in Article 6 of the original charter that imagines coexistence among the different religious groups in Palestine:

> [Hamas] strives to raise the banner of God over every inch of Palestine, for under the wing of Islam followers of all religions can coexist in security and safety where their lives, possessions and rights are concerned. In the absence of Islam conflict arises, oppression spreads, evil prevails and schisms and wars break out.

---

15. Hass, "Why Hamas' New Charter."

Hamas reaffirms this pluralistic and tolerant understanding in the new charter, in Article 9:

> Hamas believes that the message of Islam upholds the values of truth, justice, freedom and dignity and prohibits all forms of injustice and incriminates oppressors irrespective of their religion, race, gender or nationality. Islam is against all forms of religious, ethnic or sectarian extremism and bigotry. It is the religion that inculcates in its followers the value of standing up to aggression and of supporting the oppressed; it motivates them to give generously and make sacrifices in defense of their dignity, their land, their peoples and their holy places.

Whether this religious language and utopian political vision should be deemed credible or practical is not clear.[16] Such language of coexistence between religions is standard in Muslim-majority countries in the Middle East. In some respects, it is analogous to what exists in countries like Jordan, Tunisia, and Indonesia, where protection and equality are offered, at least officially, to all citizens irrespective of religious affiliation. Ironically, Hamas's proposal approximates the flipside of Israel's self-understanding as a Jewish state, for both Hamas and Israel adhere to a religious definition of statehood while claiming to provide equality and protection for other religious minorities.[17]

---

16. Reports about torture and unlawful killings against Palestinians in 2014 challenge the charter's idealistic language. See for example, Amnesty International, "Gaza: Palestinians Tortured." For human rights violations in the West Bank, Gaza, and Israel proper, see US Department of State, "2023 Country Reports."

17. This is not to equate the two political visions. On the one hand, while Israel could claim to be both Jewish and democratic, nowhere in this charter does Hamas mention pluralism or democracy. A clear shift, however, is evident in its 2017 document, which states that Hamas adheres to principles of pluralism and democracy (Article 28) and is committed to the building of Palestinian institutions on "sound democratic principles, foremost among [which] are free and fair elections" (Article 30). On the other hand, understanding Israel as an "ethnic democracy" complicates, and at many times contradicts, its reputation as a Western liberal democracy, particularly with regard to the limited rights offered to its Palestinian citizens. For more see Smooha, "Model of Ethnic Democracy"; White and Zoabi, *Palestinians in Israel*. More recently, discrimination against Palestinian citizens of Israel has become *de jure*. The passing of the nation-state basic law in 2018 limits the right of self-determination to Jewish citizens of the state and denies it to its Palestinian citizenry that comprise around 20 percent of the population. The designation of Israel as a liberal democracy is further repudiated when considering the legal and civil rights of the Palestinian populations living under Israeli military control in the West Bank and Gaza—a political system of Jewish supremacy that is now understood to satisfy the legal definition of apartheid. See Amnesty International, "Israel's Apartheid."

Hamas and Anticolonialism

Hamas's political vision is informed by what it sees as a continuation of historic and ongoing invasions of Palestine by foreign entities: "Expansionists have more than once put their eye on Palestine which they attacked with their armies to fulfill their designs on it" (Article 34).[18] Accordingly, Hamas views "the present Zionist onslaught" to be a continuation of these previous invasions and expresses confidence in Muslim determination and ability "to confront the Zionist invasion and defeat it" (Article 35). Followers of other religions ought "to stop disputing the sovereignty of Islam in this region, for when they take over there will be nothing but carnage, displacement and terror" (Article 31). Hamas's struggle is fundamentally with "global Zionism and imperial powers" who have been isolating and oppressing Palestinians (Article 32).

This *longue durée* reading of colonialist history in the Middle East is further developed in the new charter of Hamas that identifies Zionism with historic colonialism, with its preamble declaring that "Palestine is a land that was seized by a racist, anti-human and colonial Zionist project based on a false promise (the Balfour Declaration), on recognition of a usurping entity, and on imposing a *fait accompli* by force." Article 14 describes "the Zionist project" as

> a racist, aggressive, colonial and expansionist project based on seizing the properties of others; it is hostile to the Palestinian people and to their aspiration for freedom, liberation, return and self-determination. The Israeli entity is the plaything of the Zionist project and its base of aggression.[19]

---

18. The old charter recounts the importance of learning from the lessons of various historic invasions: "The Islamic Resistance Movement views seriously the defeat of the Crusaders at the hands of [Saladin] and the rescuing of Palestine from their hands, as well as the defeat of the Tatars at [the Battle of] Ain Jalut, and breaking their power at the hands of [the Mamluk sultans Sayf al-Dīn] Qutuz and Baybers and thus saving the Arab world from the Tatar onslaught which aimed at the destruction of human civilization. The Movement draws lessons and examples from all this" (Article 35).

19. In the following article, the charter explains that Israel ("the Zionist project") is a threat not only to Palestinians, but also to all Arabs and Muslims: "The Zionist project does not target the Palestinian people alone; it is the enemy of the Arab and Islamic Ummah posing a grave threat to its security and interests. It is also hostile to the Ummah's aspirations for unity, renaissance and liberation and has been the major source of its troubles. The Zionist project also poses a danger to international security and peace and to mankind and its interests and stability" (Article 15).

Hamas and Jews

Hamas's detractors readily point to its charter of 1988 as a clear indication of Hamas's attitudes toward the Jewish people. While most of its critics resort to sensationalist and distorted caricatures—and perhaps intentional misrepresentation—of Hamas's ideology and political ambitions, it is true that a number of statements in that charter display odious antisemitic tropes and stereotypes about Jews.

Most obviously, there is a tendency in the 1988 charter to blur the line between Jews, as a diverse group of individuals and communities residing within and outside of Israel, and the State of Israel whose policies and actions Hamas repudiates. For instance, the charter begins with a passage from the Qur'an (Āl 'Imrān 3:110–12) followed directly by a quote from Hasan al-Banna, the founder of the Egyptian Muslim Brotherhood,[20] claiming that "Israel will be established and will remain established until Islam abolishes it, just as it abolished others before it."[21] The introduction continues: "Our struggle against the Jews is very great and very serious," and in Article 7, the charter quotes a well-known—and problematic—*ḥadīth* attributed to the prophet Muḥammad about an apocalyptic war between Muslims and Jews where Jews would hide behind stones and trees, and the stones and trees would tell Muslims where Jews were hiding.[22]

This apocalyptic *ḥadīth* narrates one of the signs preceding the day of judgment (*'alamāt al-sā'ah*), along with the splitting of the moon, the coming of the Imam Mahdi, and the appearance of the Antichrist (*al-masīḥ al-dajjāl*).[23] The *ḥadīth* remains controversial, and its appearance in the charter

---

20. Hamas was founded by members of the Egyptian Muslim Brotherhood in Gaza; the old charter defines Hamas as a constituent member of the Brotherhood (Article 2). Hamas has since distanced itself from the Brotherhood and asserted its own Palestinian national identity. There is no mention in the new charter of the Muslim Brotherhood or Egypt.

21. The Arabic verb translated here "abolish" is *yubṭil*, which could also be translated as "invalidate" or "put an end to." English translations use the term "obliterate," which is normally the translation of different words in Arabic, namely *yaṭmus* or *yuzīl*. Hasan al-Banna asserted that the struggle of the Muslim Brotherhood with the Jewish people is not religious since the *Qur'an* enjoins Muslims to befriend Jews and since Islam is a humanitarian doctrine, not an ethnic one. See 'Abd al-Ḥalīm, *al-Ikhwān al-muslimūn* 1:409.

22. "The Day of Judgement will not come about until Muslims fight the Jews, and Jews will hide behind stones and trees, and the stones and trees will say, 'O Muslims, O Abdulla, there is a Jew behind me, come and kill him.' Only the *gharqad* [Nitraria] tree would not do that because it is one of the trees of the Jews." This *ḥadīth* is attested in the main collections of *ḥadīth*, namely those of Bukhārī (#2926) and Muslim (#2922).

23. For more on the Islamic signs of the day of judgment, see Ostransky, "Lesser Signs of the Hour."

is doubly problematic as it furthers the myth of perpetual enmity between Muslims and Jews. Hamas has conflated an apocalyptic *ḥadīth* with their own stated political struggle with Zionism, as attested in the paragraph where the *ḥadīth* is cited (Article 7).[24]

This sloppy conflation of Jews with Zionism and the State of Israel peppers the charter: it speaks of the "Jews' usurpation of Palestine" (Article 15), of "the warmongering Jews" (lit., "the merchants of war," Article 32), and of the Jewish conquerors of Jerusalem in 1967 who prove that "Israel, with its Judaism and its Jews, challenge Islam and Muslims" (Article 28).

Some of these statements are intolerable to Western audiences, especially in light of historic Western Christian hostility toward Jewish people. At the same time, this sloppy conflation of Jews with Israel should be understood in the context of the limited Palestinian experience of Jewish people, not as a historically marginalized and persecuted minority in Europe, but as a conquering and powerful majority that has taken over Palestine by force and oppressed its native populations for decades. In common Palestinian parlance, people generally do not distinguish between Israelis and Jews, or between Zionism and Judaism, because their experience of systematic oppression and violence has been perpetrated by the self-described Jewish state and by a people group that defines itself as Jewish.

Furthermore, while discussing the spirit of generosity and mutual responsibility that marks Muslim societies, Article 20 of the original Hamas charter states that this society ought to be animated by that Muslim spirit as it "confronts a vicious enemy which acts in a way similar to Nazism, making no differentiation between man and woman, between children and old people." It then goes on to describe the methods of this enemy, including collective punishment, deprivation, breaking bones, demolition of houses, and cruel sentencing of young people. Soon after, the charter specifies the identity of this enemy:

> The Nazism of the Jews has included women and children. Their policy of striking fear in the heart is meant for all. They attack people in their livelihood, extorting their money and trampling over their honor. They deal with people as if they were the worst war criminals.

---

24. Many of Hamas's critics conveniently avoid mentioning that this is an apocalyptic *ḥadīth* and simply attribute it to Hamas without noting the diversity of Islamic interpretations. See, for instance, Hoffman, "Understanding." On Muslim apocalyptic literature, see Cook, *Studies in Muslim Apocalyptic*.

The conflation of Jews with Nazis is inappropriate considering the Holocaust and Nazi treatment of European Jews in the twentieth century. It is noteworthy, however, that some Jewish and Israeli intellectuals have also used the term "Judeo-Nazi" to describe Israel's violent conduct in occupied Palestine, and more recently in response to atrocities committed against the Palestinians in Israel's genocidal war in Gaza.[25]

More significantly, the charter traffics in odious antisemitic tropes. Chief among these is that of "the perfidy of the Jews" and their allegedly oversized global influence and power. This is elaborated in Article 22, which channels fanciful allegations found in the infamous—and apocryphal—*Protocols of the Elders of Zion*, Hitler's *Mein Kampf*, and various neo-Nazi writings about Jewish wealth and domination, involvement in secret societies, and instigation of global wars.

Article 28 continues this theme, citing various civic organizations and fraternal orders as the malign vessels through which the Jewish people relentlessly pursue global domination, including the Freemasons, Rotary and Lions clubs, and other "espionage groups." They aim at "undermining societies, destroying values, corrupting consciences, deteriorating character and destroying Islam. [They are] behind the drug trade and alcoholism in all its kinds so as to facilitate its control and expansion" (Article 28). The charter also argues that "world Zionism," along with imperial powers, attempts to isolate Palestinians and expand from the Nile to the Euphrates. That plan "is embodied in the *Protocols of the Elders of Zion*,[26] and their present conduct is the best proof of what we are saying" (Article 32).

---

25. Prominent among these was the Israeli public intellectual and biochemist Yeshayahu Leibowitz (d. 1994), who coined the phrase. See Feldhay, "Fragile Boundary," 5; Greenberg, "Yeshayahu Leibowitz." In response to Israel's killing of sixty villagers of Qibya in 1953, most of whom were women and children, Leibowitz was quoted as saying: "We must ask ourselves: where does this teenager come from, the one who has no qualms about committing such an atrocity, when was he pushed from within or without to commit revenge? The teen, after all, is not part of the rabble, but rather someone who grew up and was educated on Zionist principles, alongside human and societal values" (Brown, "How the Israeli Media Covers Massacres"). Holocaust survivor Yehuda Elkana warned in 1988 that the Israeli tendency to see potential threats as existential and opponents as Nazis would lead to Nazi-like behavior by Jews (Bartov, "National Narratives," 192). Jewish American linguist Noam Chomsky has made similar comments (*Middle East Monitor*, "Chomsky Echoes Prominent Israeli"), and Israeli writer Jonathan Ofir ("I Used to Think") has reflected on the term "Judeo-Nazi" in response to Israeli conduct in Gaza.

26. *Protocols of the Elders of Zion* is a well-documented fraudulent, conspiratorial, and antisemitic document created by the Tsarist Russian secret police in the early twentieth century. Despite this, it continues to circulate, particularly online, and remains a potent source of antisemitism.

Claims about Zionist ambitions for a "greater Israel" that would include the conquest of the areas between the Nile and the Euphrates have become the stuff of legend and can be traced back to the Hebrew Bible as well as to claims made by early Zionists and to reported statements by Israeli politicians.[27]

Clearly these antisemitic tropes are damaging and problematic, and ought to be repudiated and rejected. It is also noteworthy that such attitudes of "Jewish domination" and over-sized power come as a natural Palestinian response to their lived reality whereby their homeland was taken from them in 1948. Moreover, Israel continues to enjoy, seventy-seven years later, impunity and diplomatic protection in the West, particularly through unwavering political and military support from the US government and the various lobby and political groups, such as AIPAC, that continue to influence American foreign policy in the Middle East and American-Israeli relations.[28]

In the new charter of 2017, Hamas distanced itself from the antisemitic tropes expressed in the original charter, and clarified an important distinction between Zionism as a political project and between Jews as a religious

---

27. The claim is grounded in the famous verses in the Hebrew Bible describing God's promise to Abraham and his descendants of the land from the Nile to the Euphrates (Gen 15:18; see Deut 11:24). As Jewish American professor Daniel Pipes argues, early Zionist leaders had grand territorial hopes: "Theodor Herzl and Isidore Bodenheimer routinely referred to Jewish settlement in 'Palestine and Syria,' as did organizations like the Jewish National Fund and the Zionist Congress. In 1898, Herzl [allegedly] planned to ask the Ottoman sultan for a territory stretching from the Egyptian frontier to the Euphrates. Four years later he spoke of settling Jews in Mesopotamia. Vladimir Jabotinsky, the founder of Revisionist Zionism, was quoted in 1935 stating, 'We want a Jewish Empire.'... Moshe Dayan's visit to the Golan Heights soon after its capture by Israeli troops in 1967 has become the stuff of legends" due to reports in the Arab press that he had declared Israel's intention to take over Yathrib (Medina in Saudi Arabia) and Babylon. "Prime Minister Menachem Begin was later quoted to the effect that the Bible predicts the Israeli state will eventually include portions of Syria, Iraq, Turkey, Saudi Arabia, Sudan, Lebanon, Jordan and Kuwait" (*Hidden Hand*, 54). Pipes minimizes the importance of statements by early Zionists and discredits statements attributed to Jabotinsky, Begin, and Dayan as "second-hand and at best dubious" (55). Famously, at the UN Security Council session convened in Geneva on May 25, 1990, and throughout the nineties, Yasser Arafat claimed that the obverse design on the Israeli ten agorot coin displays a map of greater Israel representing Zionist expansionist goals (238). Another common perception among Palestinians and others is that the two horizontal blue lines on the Israeli flag represent the Nile and the Euphrates, while in fact David Wolffsohn (d. 1914), second president of the Zionist Organization, wrote in 1897 in preparation for the First Zionist Congress in Basel that the flag would have two blue lines to represent the *talith*, the traditional Jewish prayer shawl (53).

28. For more on the influence of the "Israel lobby" on the US government, see Mearsheimer and Walt, *Israel Lobby*. For a history, see Pappé, *Lobbying for Zionism*.

group: "Hamas affirms that its conflict is with the Zionist project not with the Jews because of their religion. Hamas does not wage a struggle against the Jews because they are Jewish but wages a struggle against the Zionists who occupy Palestine." Hamas claimed it was in fact Zionists who conflated Judaism with "their own colonial project and illegal entity" (Article 16).[29] The charter further clarified Hamas's position against the persecution of people groups and against antisemitism as an essentially Western problem, whereby Zionism is continuation of Western colonialism and domination:

> Hamas rejects the persecution of any human being or the undermining of his or her rights on nationalist, religious or sectarian grounds. Hamas is of the view that the "Jewish problem," anti-Semitism and the persecution of the Jews are phenomena fundamentally linked to European history and not to the history of the Arabs and the Muslims or to their heritage. The Zionist movement, which was able with the help of Western powers to occupy Palestine, is the most dangerous form of settlement occupation which has already disappeared from much of the world and must disappear from Palestine. (Article 17)

Hamas and Violence

As a movement established to resist the Israeli occupation where *"jihād* is our way," as its original charter states, Hamas follows a long line of militia organizations from around the world, such as the Irish Republican Army and African National Congress (ANC) of South Africa that adopted armed struggle as a tactic for liberation. The military wing of Hamas is called the "brigades of Izz ad-Din al-Qassam, which is named after a Syriac preacher who organized armed resistance groups against early Zionist settlement in Palestine."[30] Formed in 1991, the brigades claimed responsibility for carry-

---

29. In an interview with *Al Jazeera* soon after the new charter was published, Khaled Meshaal, current chairman of the Hamas political bureau, insists that Hamas's struggle is with Israel and not with Jews ("Khaled Meshaal").

30. Izz ad-Din al-Qassam was initially involved in the Syrian resistance against French colonialism and later moved to Palestine in the 1920s. He presented military *jihād* as a religious responsibility for all Muslims to resist the British Mandate government and Zionism. See Baconi, *Hamas Contained*, 5–7. Al-Qassam was killed in a manhunt by the British authorities in 1935, an event that helped to foment the 1936–1939 Arab revolt in Palestine. Israeli historian Tom Segev (*One Palestine*, 362–63) has called him "the Arab Joseph Trumpeldor," referring to the famed Russian Zionist (d. 1920) who helped organize "The Jewish Legion" made up of Russian Jewish émigrés from Palestine that participated in the effort to seize Palestine from the Ottoman Empire and worked to bring Jewish immigrants into Palestine.

ing out bombings and "homicide attacks"[31] against Israelis in the 1990s, and particularly during the second Intifada (2000–2005). Hamas's adherence to armed struggle against Israel is based on its religious understanding of *jihād*. In discussing nationalism as an intrinsic part of its religious beliefs, the original charter states that

> Nothing in nationalism is more significant or deeper than in the case when an enemy should tread upon Muslim land. Resisting (*jihād*) and quelling the enemy become the individual duty of every Muslim, male or female. (Article 12)

This is further detailed in Article 15, in which *jihād* is a response to imperialism and Israeli usurpation of Muslim lands: "In response to the Jews' usurpation of Palestine, it is imperative to raise the banner of *Jihād*."

Hamas's adoption of *jihād* as a legitimate method for liberation is confirmed again in the new charter as an inalienable right and duty of Palestinians:

> Hamas stresses that transgression against the Palestinian people, usurping their land and banishing them from their homeland cannot be called peace. Any settlements reached on this basis will not lead to peace. Resistance and jihad for the liberation of Palestine will remain a legitimate right, a duty and an honor for all the sons and daughters of our people and our Ummah. (Article 23)

Later in the new charter, Hamas articulates its understanding of *jihād* in terms of struggle and resistance whereby armed resistance is one method of resisting the occupation:

> The liberation of Palestine is the duty of the Palestinian people in particular and the duty of the Arab and Islamic Ummah in general. It is also a humanitarian obligation as necessitated by the dictates of truth and justice. (Article 24) . . .

---

31. Like the term "terrorism," the term "suicide attack" is problematic since it obfuscates the motivations (and desperation!) of the people engaging in these attacks, reducing them to radical zealots, with no regard to the long-standing oppression and violence that has traumatized and radicalized individuals to resort to a horrible action that all but guarantees their own death. A better term might be "homicide" bombing or attack. Alternatively, Islamist supporters of such attacks use the Arabic term *istishhād* or "martyrdom operation." Similar to the etymology of "martyrdom," *istishhād* signifies "witnessing" in the sense that the attacker dies to testify to their faith in God. Suicide is wholly rejected in Islam and is considered a major sin as attested in the Qurʾan (e.g., Q 3:129; 4:29) and in the Ḥadīth (e.g., *Bukhārī*, #3276, #5442, #5700).

Resisting the occupation with all means and methods is a legitimate right guaranteed by divine laws and by international norms and laws. At the heart of these lies armed resistance, which is regarded as the strategic choice for protecting the principles and the rights of the Palestinian people. (Article 25) . . .

Hamas rejects any attempt to undermine the resistance and its arms. It also affirms the right of our people to develop the means and mechanisms of resistance. Managing resistance, in terms of escalation or de-escalation, or in terms of diversifying the means and methods, is an integral part of the process of managing the conflict and should not be at the expense of the principle of resistance. (Article 26)

It is important to underscore here that Hamas employs *jihād* in its classical sense, as the act of "striving" or "doing one's utmost" against any sort of oppression or evil, whether it be selfishness, greed, or political oppression.[32] For example, the old charter mentioned that it is *jihād* for mothers to take care of their homes and educate their children (Article 18). At the same time, Hamas is explicit about the militaristic application of *jihād* against Israeli oppression as a duty for Muslims who need to "confront their enemies and join the ranks of fighters" (Article 15). In this sense, Hamas's usage of *jihād* is the militaristic equivalent of the Christian "Just War" model—both of which have much in common in terms of justifying war in ethical and religious terms, offering ethical rules and constraints in warfare, and defending war deontologically rather than analyzing its direct consequences.[33]

A Terrorist Organization?

Perhaps the most common description of Hamas in the West is that it is a terrorist organization. There is no doubt that Hamas has carried out terror-inducing activities within Israel and the Palestinian territories. Its military activities fit into the definition of terrorism used by the US Department of State, which defines terrorism as "premeditated politically motivated violence perpetrated against noncombatant targets by subnational groups or clandestine agents."[34] While Hamas itself admits that it has used such

---

32. On the term *jihād* and the distinction between "greater *jihād*" and "lesser *jihād*," see Cook, *Understanding Jihad*, 32–48. On the history of *jihād*, see Bonner, *Jihad in Islamic History*.

33. See Johnson, *Holy War*, 4–10; Johnson, "Jihad and Just War."

34. In 2001, in US Department of State Executive Order 13224, President George W. Bush defined terrorism as "an activity that (1) involves a violent act or an act dangerous to human life, property, or infrastructure; and (2) appears to be intended to

tactics, it rejects being designated a terrorist organization,[35] and frames its militancy within a project of liberation and ending the Israeli occupation, as noted above in both charters.

The term "terrorism" itself is malleable and subjective since there is no single definition about what constitutes terrorism. In fact, the term has become a powerful device to undermine any legitimacy that organizations may have and to dismiss their tactics wholly with little nuance or critical analysis. For example, why is terrorism limited to subnational groups if states are the biggest perpetrators of organized violence against civilians? What criteria are used to distinguish between acts of indiscriminate violence solely intended to terrorize civilians and acts of armed resistance aimed at securing internationally recognized rights, when such resistance results in civilian casualties?[36] More importantly, the term has been used numerous times as a tool of war, and has been consistently and cynically manipulated to justify illegal and morally reprehensible military measures, in this case by Israel.[37] While the label of "terrorism" is easily applied to Hamas, it fails to account for the terror and harm caused by Israel's relentless military regime over the Palestinians. Or as Lawrence Freedman puts it, "labelling is part of the strategy."[38]

Classifying Hamas as a terrorist organization has justified sweeping and brutal military action against the Palestinians, particularly during this latest genocidal war against Gaza. The label "terrorism" has been an effective weapon in dehumanizing and depoliticizing the Palestinian struggle for liberation, and has prevented us from viewing Palestinian armed struggle as self-defense within the context of war and violent oppression. This dismissal of Palestinian self-defense came to the fore during Israel's latest onslaught on Gaza where the whole war—including war crimes, human rights violations, and breaches of international law—was framed as Israel's legitimate

---

intimidate or coerce a civilian population; to influence the policy of a government by intimidation or coercion; or to affect the conduct of a government by mass destruction, assassination, kidnapping, or hostage-taking."

35. On April 8, 2025, Hamas applied to the British Home Secretary under Terrorism Act 2000 to have its name removed from the government's list of proscribed organizations, an effort intended in part to "stop criminalizing the open discussion of and support for the right to self-determination of the Palestinian people and the use of armed struggle pursuant to that right by Hamas." The full application is available at https://hamascase.com/.

36. On the distinction between "civilized violence" and "barbaric violence," see Asad, "Thinking About Terrorism."

37. See Teichman, "How to Define Terrorism"; Primoratz, "What Is Terrorism?"

38. On manipulation of the label as a war strategy, see Freedman, "Terrorism as Strategy."

self-defense, with no corresponding allowance for Palestinian self-defense during the war and during the Israeli occupation in general.

The asymmetry here follows a well-established mythology in the West about war and peace in Palestine-Israel. Tareq Baconi comments,

> For [Israel] war begins when rockets fall on its territory or when suicide bombers invade its streets. For the [Palestinians], war is constant, manifest through a brutal military occupation that has persisted for more than half a century. The transition between war and peace for Palestinians is an imaginary one. Where rocket attacks and suicide bombs trigger claims of self-defense and ostensibly justify Israeli military operations, no similar mechanisms are in place for Palestinians reacting against the act of war inherent in an occupation that is both terror inducing and intentional. While international law has made exceptions for viewing Israeli military operations in Gaza through the lens of a security paradigm, security for Palestinians against consistent Israeli aggression appears to be absent.[39]

Very often, discussions about the morality of Palestinian armed resistance disregard the historical precedent of violence within many anticolonial movements. This omission obscures the specific context that fostered Hamas's emergence as a resistance movement within the larger Palestinian struggle for liberation. Consequently, Palestinians are collectively demonized and their legitimate political struggle for self-determination is overshadowed by the indictment of being inherently violent.[40]

Once the power dynamics in Palestine-Israel are understood to involve an occupier and an occupied, or a colonizer and a colonized, armed struggle by Palestinian military resistance can be framed as legitimate action against a violent and illegal occupation that systematically terrorizes Palestinians and systematically denies them their basic rights and freedoms. The adoption of armed struggle by some Palestinian resistance movements is grounded in their own legal, political, and religious justifications for military struggle against the occupation.[41] Without justifying their adoption of violence, especially toward innocent civilians, we need to understand it

---

39. Baconi, *Hamas Contained*, xix. For Israel's justification of prolonged occupation in the name of security, see Moses, "Empire, Resistance, and Security."

40. This pervasive stereotyping of Palestinians, especially among Christians in the West, recalls the "victim blaming" of African Americans during slavery and segregation, on which see National Museum of African American History and Culture, "Popular and Pervasive Stereotypes." On the equation of Blackness with criminality in the US, see Smiley and Fakunle, "From 'Brute' to 'Thug.'"

41. Asad, "Thinking About Terrorism," 14.

within the Palestinian experience and not a Western one. We need to grapple with the thoughts, emotions, and experiences of many Palestinians that shape a reality which is often at odds with the dominant Western-centric framing of political violence. This is especially important when much Western violence (the Crusades, colonialism, American wars in the Middle East) is rationalized, normalized, and defended. It is incumbent on us, therefore, to abandon reductionist and polemical approaches associated with charged terms like "terrorism," acknowledge the devastation, suffering, and trauma, and develop healthy attitudes and perspectives motivated by a desire for understanding and the pursuit of goodness and justice.[42]

Violence as a Tactic of the Oppressed

It is important therefore to demythologize Hamas's adoption of armed struggle as a legitimate tactic for liberation particularly if we understand the history of seventy-seven years of Israeli ethnic cleansing, settler colonialism, apartheid, and a violent military occupation.[43] As Rashid Khalidi explains, "the modern history of Palestine can best be understood in these terms: as a colonial war waged against the indigenous population, by a variety of parties, to force them to relinquish their homeland to another people against their will."[44]

If this context is understood properly, we should not be surprised when oppressed populations resort to violence, even acts of extreme violence. In his seminal work *Jesus and the Disinherited*, African American educator and theologian Howard Thurman reflected on the appeal for the oppressed to pick up arms:

> Armed resistance is apt to be a tragic last resort in the life of the disinherited. Armed resistance has an appeal because it provides a form of expression, of activity, that releases tension and frees the oppressed from a disintegrating sense of complete impotency and helplessness. "Why can't we do something? Something must be done!" is the recurring cry. By "something" is meant action, direct action, as over against words, subtleties,

---

42. Devji, *Terrorist in Search of Humanity*, moves beyond traditional explanations of Islamic militancy, such as poverty or specific regional conflicts, and argues that militant movements are driven by a desire for global agency and a sense of humanitarianism, albeit a distorted one, on behalf of a victimized global Muslim community.

43. On what Palestinian life is like under Israeli settler colonialism and occupation, see Isaac, *Christ in the Rubble*, 37–71.

44. Khalidi, *Hundred Years' War on Palestine*, 9.

threat, and innuendoes. It is better to die fighting for freedom than to rot away in one's chains, the argument runs.

> Before I'd be a slave
> I'd be buried in my grave,
> And go home to my God
> And be free![45]

Similarly, Martin Luther King Jr. understood the conditions that motivated African American violence during the civil rights struggle. In the wake of urban race riots in Detroit, King reflected:

> A million words will be written and spoken to dissect the ghetto outbreaks, but for a perceptive and vivid expression of culpability I would submit two sentences written a century ago by Victor Hugo: "If the soul is left in darkness, sins will be committed. The guilty one is not he who commits the sin, but he who causes the darkness." The policy makers of the white society have caused the darkness; they created discrimination; they created slums; they perpetuate unemployment, ignorance and poverty. It is incontestable and deplorable that Negroes have committed crimes; but they are derivative crimes. They are born of the greater crimes of the white society.[46]

It is no surprise then that history is replete with examples of violence by the oppressed. Consider, for instance, the three Servile revolts against the Roman Empire, the last of which was led by Spartacus (73–71 BCE), or the various Jewish uprisings like the Bar Kokhba revolt (132–136 CE), the Gallus revolt (351–352), and the Jewish revolt against Heraclius (614–617) that sought to establish Jewish autonomy in Palestine. There are also ample examples of notable revolts by enslaved people, including the Zanj Rebellion of east African slaves who rose up in 869 CE against the Abbasid caliphate, the 1570 rebellion of Gaspar Yagna against Spanish colonial rule,[47] the 1733 St. John insurrection in the Danish West Indies, and the Haitian slave revolt of 1791 that ended with the founding of the independent republic of Haiti, inspiring countless other revolts throughout the Caribbean and the United States. Significant among these were the "Baptist War" of 1831–1832 in

---

45. Thurman, *Jesus and the Disinherited*, 15–16.

46. From King's speech on August 15, 1967, at the gathering of the Southern Christian Leadership Conference in Atlanta. For the full text, see King, "Crisis in America's Cities."

47. It is named after African slave Gaspar Yagna, or Nyanga (d. 1618), who is dubbed "the first liberator of the Americas" (*el primer libertador de América*) and considered a national hero in Mexico.

Jamaica, led by an enslaved Black Baptist deacon, Samuel Sharpe, and Nat Turner's rebellion of 1831 in Virginia, in which an intelligent and devout Christian slave, along with a small band of seventy fellow slaves, killed over fifty white slavers, women, and children before they were captured and executed by the state.[48]

It is significant that a number of these slave revolts, particularly those of Samuel Sharpe and Nat Turner, were organized by Christians, while many white abolitionists who resorted to violence were devout Christians as well.[49] With the benefit of more than two centuries of hindsight, and one hundred and fifty years after the abolishment of slavery in the US, it is not surprising that we would feel sympathy toward these rebels. We object to the killing of innocents or "civilians" in these rebellions, but we recognize that the rebels were slaves seeking emancipation. Does the justice of their cause make the death toll understandable? Even justified? If the term "terrorist" had been available, the ancient Romans would surely have applied it to Jewish rebels—as would slavers in North America in reference to rebelling slaves.

Moving forward, we understand why Hindu nationalists resorted to violence against British colonial rule, why European Jews staged prisoner revolts and ghetto uprisings against Nazi forces during World War II, and why the African National Congress (ANC) of South Africa, in response to the Sharpeville massacre of 1960, formed "uMkhonto weSizwe," Nelson Mandela's paramilitary force, which carried out "terrorist attacks" against the apartheid regime. How is Hamas different?

None of the examples from this historical survey justifies Hamas's adoption of militarism and armed struggle, or the attack on October 7. But if the historical context of past revolts helps us understand the despair that led oppressed and dehumanized people (including Christians) to lash out, the Palestinian context—marked by decades of violent oppression,

---

48. For more on this, and how abolitionists understood the effectiveness of violence and insurrections for ending slavery and producing social change, see Jackson, *Force and Freedom*.

49. The most famous of these white abolitionists was John Brown (d. 1859), an evangelical Christian who was heavily influenced by Puritan piety. He is known for the failed 1859 raid on the Harpers Ferry armory in Virginia that resulted in his execution. On John Brown's influence, see Reynolds, *John Brown*. The abolitionist movement was not thoroughly violent; the white abolitionist William Lloyd Garrison (d. 1879) was known as a leading proponent of nonviolent ideology within the antislavery movement, and many of the early abolitionists believed that moral suasion would work to end slavery. However, the use of violence became more pervasive as moral suasion failed to protect Black people and lead to liberation, particularly after the passing of the Fugitive Slave Law in 1850.

brutal blockades, and legal and military structures of racism, Jewish ethnic supremacy, and apartheid—helps to explain why some Palestinians also choose to resort to violence. The lessons of the past and our understanding of the present should temper our response to violence and inform our advocacy for justice and peace.

A Palestinian Christian Response

While a thorough analysis of the October 7 attack cannot be provided here, one notes that Palestinians and their allies are expected not to justify the attack, while so many people, particularly Western Christians, use October 7 to justify everything that Israel has done to the Palestinians since then—including war crimes, violations of international law, state-engineered famine, and mass killing—in what is now considered by legal experts and human rights organizations to be a clear case of genocide. There is a persistent double-standard in Western, particularly Christian, circles regarding what is considered to be justifiable violence by states, on the one hand, and by non-state actors and liberationist movements (e.g., Hamas, ANC), on the other. This was the point pressed home in an open letter written by Palestinian Christians a few weeks after the beginning of the Israeli assault on Gaza in October 2023:

> Time and again, we are reminded that western attitudes towards Palestine-Israel suffer from a glaring double standard that humanizes Israeli Jews while insisting on dehumanizing Palestinians and whitewashing their suffering. It seems to us that this double standard reflects an entrenched colonial discourse that has weaponized the Bible to justify the ethnic cleansing of indigenous peoples in the Americas, Oceania, and elsewhere, the slavery of Africans and the transatlantic slave trade, and decades of apartheid in South Africa. Colonial theologies are not passé; they continue in wide-ranging Zionist theologies and interpretations that have legitimized the ethnic cleansing of Palestine and the vilification and dehumanization of Palestinians—Christians included—living under systemic settler-colonial apartheid.[50]

Whatever critique one has of violence, it must be calibrated by a nuanced analysis of power dynamics and an ethical standard grounded in the pursuit of truth and justice. In response to the political realities in Palestine, Palestinian Christians have consistently advocated nonviolence, a position

---

50. Kairos Palestine et al., "Call for Repentance."

articulated years ago by Rev. Naim Ateek in his seminal work, *Justice and Only Justice: A Palestinian Theology of Liberation*:

> The fundamental Christian attitude toward conflict and war familiar to the Christians in the Middle East is that of Jesus—the way of nonviolence. It is very difficult to study the life of Jesus in the Gospels and not conclude that nonviolence was his philosophy. This is substantiated in the Sermon on the Mount. For Eastern Christians, this is their tradition, their Gospel milieu, their heritage.[51]

Christian Palestinians hold firmly to a principled position of pacifism—a Christian pacifism that regards violence against civilians and combatants as a violation of the sanctity of life and an inexcusable assault on the image of God (Gen 1:26–27). We attempt to follow the ethic of the kingdom of God as revealed through Christ and grounded in the love of God and neighbor. It is abundantly clear to us that if one loves an enemy, one does not attempt to kill that enemy or inflict pain on them or their loved ones.

Today's widespread practice of vilifying Hamas has led many to demonize millions of Palestinians in the Gaza Strip and throughout historic Palestine and to dismiss their plight. I have sought to explore Hamas's worldview and present an objective yet critical portrayal of a marginalized group that, for good or ill, will remain central to the Palestinian national movement. My goal has been to advance our understanding of Hamas by explaining its core beliefs and its development over the course of more than three decades, from its inception in 1987 onward. Understanding Hamas is key to understanding the larger Palestinian struggle to restore our rights during more than a century of struggle for freedom and self-determination.

For their part, the Palestinian Christians have consistently rejected the religious ideology of Hamas and its framing of the Palestinian struggle as a religious one. The state, according to the Kairos Palestine document, must be for all its citizens, a pluralistic state with equal rights for all:

> Trying to make the state a religious state, Jewish or Islamic . . . confines it within narrow limits, and transforms it into a state that practices discrimination and exclusion, preferring one citizen over another. We appeal to both religious Jews and Muslims: let the state be a state for all its citizens, with a vision constructed on respect for religion but also equality, justice, liberty and respect for pluralism and not on domination by a religion or a numerical majority.[52]

---

51. Ateek, *Justice and Only Justice*, 134.
52. Kairos Palestine, "Moment of Truth," 9.3.

At the same time, Palestinian Christians are committed to the hard work of creative nonviolent resistance that is grounded in love of neighbor and enemy, resistance that grounds itself in the humanity and dignity of everyone involved, as stated by Kairos:

> We say that our option as Christians in the face of the Israeli occupation is to resist. Resistance is a right and a duty for the Christian. But it is resistance with love as its logic. It is thus a creative resistance for it must find human ways that engage the humanity of the enemy. Seeing the image of God in the face of the enemy means taking up positions in the light of this vision of active resistance to stop the injustice and oblige the perpetrator to end his aggression and thus achieve the desired goal, which is getting back the land, freedom, dignity and independence.[53]

If the church is truly committed to the work of justice and peace, we need to be telling truthful stories about each other. Instead of adopting ideologies of supremacy, violence, and dehumanization, we must follow Christ on the path of love and mercy. For so long, Christians have failed to be Christlike when it matters—whether historically toward Native people, Blacks, and Jews, or toward Palestinians today.

Bibliography

ʿAbd al-Ḥalīm, Maḥmūd. *al-Ikhwān al-Muslimūn: Aḥdāth Ṣanaʿat al-Tārīkh* [*The Muslim Brotherhood: Events That Made History*]. Vol. 1. Alexandria: Dār al-Daʿwah, 1979.

Ahmed, Dawood, and Muhammad Zubair Abbasi. "What Is an Islamic Constitution?" In *Democracy Under God: Constitutions, Islam and Human Rights in the Muslim World*, 26–72. Cambridge: Cambridge University Press, 2023.

al-Azmeh, Aziz. *Secularism in the Arab World: Contexts, Ideas and Consequences*. Edinburgh: Edinburgh University Press, 2020.

Al Jazeera. "Khaled Meshaal: Struggle Is Against Israel, Not Jews." May 6, 2017. https://www.aljazeera.com/program/talk-to-al-jazeera/2017/5/6/khaled-meshaal-struggle-is-against-israel-not-jews.

Amnesty International. "Gaza: Palestinians Tortured, Summarily Killed by Hamas Forces During 2014 Conflict." May 27, 2015. https://www.amnesty.org/en/latest/news/2015/05/gaza-palestinians-tortured-summarily-killed-by-hamas-forces-during-2014-conflict/.

———. "Israel's Apartheid Against Palestinians." February 1, 2022. https://www.amnesty.org/en/latest/campaigns/2022/02/israels-system-of-apartheid/.

Asad, Talal. "Thinking About Terrorism and Just War." *Cambridge Review of International Affairs* 23 (2010) 3–24.

---

53. Kairos Palestine, "Moment of Truth," 4.2.3.

Ateek, Naim. *Justice and Only Justice: A Palestinian Theology of Liberation.* Maryknoll, NY: Orbis, 1989.

Baconi, Tareq. *Hamas Contained: The Rise and Pacification of Palestinian Resistance.* Redwood City, CA: Stanford University Press, 2018.

Bartov, Omer. "National Narratives of Suffering and Victimhood: Methods and Ethics of Telling the Past as Personal Political History." In *The Holocaust and the Nakba: A New Grammar of Trauma and History,* edited by Bashir Bashir and Amos Goldberg, 187–205. New York: Columbia University Press, 2018.

Bisharat, George, et al. "Israel's Invasion of Gaza in International Law." *Denver Journal of International Law and Policy* 38 (2009) 41–114.

Bonner, Michael. *Jihad in Islamic History: Doctrines and Practice.* Princeton, NJ: Princeton University Press, 2006.

Brown, John. "How the Israeli Media Covers Massacres: Lessons from 1953." *+972 Magazine,* October 18, 2014. https://www.972mag.com/how-the-media-covers-massacres-lessons-from-1950/.

Bukhārī, Muḥammad ibn Ismāʿīl. *Ṣaḥīḥ al-Bukhārī.* Translated by M. Muhsin Khan. https://sunnah.com/bukhari.

Cook, David. *Studies in Muslim Apocalyptic.* Berlin: Gerlach Press, 2021.

———. *Understanding Jihad.* Berkeley: University of California Press, 2015.

Devji, Faisal. *The Terrorist in Search of Humanity: Militant Islam and Global Politics.* New York: Columbia University Press, 2008.

Esposito, John L., and John Obert Voll. *Islam and Democracy.* New York: Oxford University Press, 1996.

Feldhay, Rivka. "The Fragile Boundary Between the Political and the Academic." *Israel Studies Review* 28 (2013) 1–7.

Freedman, Lawrence. "Terrorism as Strategy." *Government and Opposition* 42 (2007) 314–39.

Greenberg, Joel. "Yeshayahu Leibowitz, 91, Iconoclastic Israeli Thinker." *The New York Times,* August 19, 1994. https://timesmachine.nytimes.com/timesmachine/1994/08/19/999121.html?pageNumber=25.

Hass, Amira. "Why Hamas' New Charter Is Aimed at Palestinians, Not Israelis." *Haaretz,* May 3, 2017. https://www.haaretz.com/middle-east-news/palestinians/2017-5-03/ty-article/.premium/why-hamas-new-charter-is-aimed-at-palestinians-not-israelis/0000017f-eabf-d0f7-a9ff-eeffc7ec0000.

Hoffman, Bruce. "Understanding Hamas's Genocidal Ideology." *The Atlantic,* October 10, 2023. https://www.theatlantic.com/international/archive/2023/10/hamas-charter-israel-attack-war-genocide/675602/.

Ibn al-Ḥajjāj, Muslim. *Ṣaḥīḥ Muslim.* https://sunnah.com/muslim.

Isaac, Munther. *Christ in the Rubble: Faith, the Bible, and the Genocide in Gaza.* Grand Rapids: Eerdmans, 2025.

Jackson, Kellie Carter. *Force and Freedom: Black Abolitionists and the Politics of Violence.* Philadelphia: University of Pennsylvania Press, 2019.

Johnson, James Turner. *The Holy War Idea in Western and Islamic Traditions.* University Park, PA: Pennsylvania State University Press, 1997.

———. "Jihad and Just War." *First Things,* June 2002. https://www.firstthings.com/article/2002/06/jihad-and-just-war.

Kairos Palestine. "A Moment of Truth: A Word of Faith, Hope and Love from the Heart of Palestinian Suffering." Bethlehem: Kairos Palestine, 2009. https://kairospalestine.ps/index.php/about-kairos/kairos-palestine-document.

Kairos Palestine, et al. "A Call for Repentance: An Open Letter from Palestinian Christians to Western Church Leaders and Theologians." October 20, 2023. https://www.change.org/p/an-open-letter-from-palestinian-christians-to-western-church-leaders-and-theologians.

Khalidi, Rashid. *The Hundred Years' War on Palestine: A History of Settler Colonialism and Resistance, 1917–2017*. New York: Metropolitan, 2017.

King, Martin Luther, Jr. "The Crisis in America's Cities." August 15, 1967. *The Atlantic*, February 2018. https://www.theatlantic.com/magazine/archive/2018/02/martin-luther-king-jr-the-crisis-in-americas-cities/552536/.

Maqdsi, Muhammad. "Charter of the Islamic Resistance Movement (Hamas) of Palestine." *Journal of Palestine Studies* 22 (1993) 122–34.

Mearsheimer, John J., and Stephen M. Walt. *The Israel Lobby and U.S. Foreign Policy*. New York: Farrar, Straus and Giroux, 2008.

Middle East Eye. "Hamas in 2017: The Document in Full." May 2, 2017. https://www.middleeasteye.net/news/hamas-2017-document-full.

Middle East Monitor. "Chomsky Echoes Prominent Israeli, Warns of the Rise of 'Judeo-Nazi Tendencies' in Israel." November 12, 2018. https://www.middleeastmonitor.com/20181112-chomsky-echoes-prominent-israeli-warns-of-the-rise-of-judeo-nazi-tendencies-in-israel/.

Moses, A. Dirk. "Empire, Resistance, and Security: International Law and the Transformative Occupation of Palestine." *Humanity: An International Journal of Human Rights, Humanitarianism, and Development* 8 (2017) 379–409.

National Museum of African American History and Culture. "Popular and Pervasive Stereotypes of African Americans." https://nmaahc.si.edu/explore/stories/popular-and-pervasive-stereotypes-african-americans.

Ofir, Jonathan. "I Used to Think the Term 'Judeo-Nazis' Was Excessive. I Don't Any Longer." *Mondoweiss*, December 8, 2023. https://mondoweiss.net/2023/12/i-used-to-think-the-term-judeo-nazis-was-excessive-i-dont-any-longer/.

Osman, Tarek. *Islamism: What It Means for the Middle East and the World*. New Haven, CT: Yale University Press, 2016.

Ostransky, Bronislav. "The Lesser Signs of the Hour: A Reconstruction of the Islamic Apocalyptic Overture." *Archiv Orientální* 81 (2013) 235–84.

Pappé, Ilan. *Lobbying for Zionism on Both Sides of the Atlantic*. London: Oneworld, 2024.

Pipes, Daniel. *The Hidden Hand: Middle East Fears of Conspiracy*. New York: St. Martin's, 1996.

Piscatori, James. *Islam in a World of Nation-States*. New York: Cambridge University Press, 1986.

Polka, Sagi. "Hamas as a *Wasati* (Literally: Centrist) Movement: Pragmatism Within the Boundaries of the Sharia." *Studies in Conflict and Terrorism* 42 (2019) 683–713.

Primoratz, Igor. "What Is Terrorism?" *Journal of Applied Philosophy* 7 (1990) 129–38.

Reynolds, David S. *John Brown, Abolitionist: The Man Who Killed Slavery, Sparked the Civil War, and Seeded Civil Rights*. New York: Random House, 2005.

Roy, Olivier. *The Failure of Political Islam*. Cambridge, MA: Harvard University Press, 1994.

Salem, Paul. "The Rise and Fall of Secularism in the Arab World." *Middle East Policy* 4 (1996) 147–60.

Segev, Tom. *One Palestine, Complete: Jews and Arabs Under the British Mandate*. New York: Metropolitan, 2000.

Smiley, Calvin John, and David Fakunle. "From 'Brute' to 'Thug': The Demonization and Criminalization of Unarmed Black Male Victims in America." *Journal of Human Behavior in the Social Environment* 26 (2016) 350–66.

Teichman, Jenny. "How to Define Terrorism." *Philosophy* 64 (1989) 505–17.

Thurman, Howard. *Jesus and the Disinherited*. 1949. Repr., Boston: Beacon, 1996.

Tibi, Bassam. *Islamism and Islam*. New Haven, CT: Yale University Press, 2012.

Smooha, Sammy. "The Model of Ethnic Democracy: Israel as a Jewish and Democratic State." *Nations and Nationalism* 8 (2003) 475–503.

United Nations Office of the High Commissioner for Human Rights. "How Can Israel's Blockade of Gaza Be Legal? UN Independent Experts on the 'Palmer Report.'" September 13, 2011. https://www.ohchr.org/en/press-releases/2011/09/how-can-israels-blockade-gaza-be-legal-un-independent-experts-palmer-report.

US Department of State. "2023 Country Reports on Human Rights Practices: Israel, West Bank and Gaza." https://www.state.gov/reports/2023-country-reports-on-human-rights-practices/israel-west-bank-and-gaza/.

———. "Executive Order 13224." September 23, 2001. https://www.state.gov/executive-order-13224/.

White, Ben, and Haneen Zoabi. *Palestinians in Israel: Segregation, Discrimination and Democracy*. London: Pluto, 2012.

CHAPTER SIX

Palestinian Citizens of Israel in the Shadow of the War on Gaza

Lamma Mansour

Introduction

THE BRUTALITY THAT ISRAEL has unleashed on the Gaza Strip since Hamas's attack on Southern Israel on October 7, 2023, has dominated the global coverage of the crisis. And rightly so. The Israeli army, supported and funded by Western powers, has sought to obliterate Gaza, killing thousands of its inhabitants, wounding hundreds of thousands, and displacing millions. Israel has destroyed the vast majority of Gaza's infrastructure, decimating water and electricity lines and bombing homes, shops, hospitals, clinics, schools, universities, mosques, and churches—while simultaneously restricting food, water, medical supplies, and other vital humanitarian aid from entering the Strip.[1]

As the world witnesses the devastation in Gaza, Israel has used this period of war and upheaval to further solidify its apartheid regime across the land.[2] In the West Bank, settlers have intensified their violence and harassment of Palestinians, acting with impunity and with the support of the

---

1. Oxfam, *Gaza: 1 Year On*; UN Office for the Coordination of Humanitarian Affairs, "Reported Impact Snapshot."

2. Al-Haq, *Israeli Apartheid*; Amnesty International, "Israel's Apartheid."

Israeli army.[3] The state has also accelerated its land grabs, approving the confiscation of thousands of acres of Palestinian land in the West Bank.[4]

This chapter, however, focuses on the reality inside Israel. Palestinian citizens of Israel, who make up around a fifth of the Israeli population, have found themselves in a precarious situation, facing levels of state repression reminiscent of earlier periods of Israeli control and domination. Israel has criminalized public empathy toward fellow Palestinians, and severely curtailed political activities like protests, vigils, and online expressions of political dissent. This chapter will trace the historical context within which Palestinian citizens of Israel emerged as a category and examine the challenges we face in the shadow of the ongoing war on Gaza. As a Palestinian citizen of Israel myself, I speak to this reality not only from research expertise but from lived experience.

Historical Context of Palestinian Citizens of Israel

Nakba and Military Rule (1948–1966)

The category of "Palestinian citizen of Israel" emerged in the aftermath of the 1948 *Nakba*, a catastrophe for Palestinians that involved the mass expulsion of over 750,000 people from their homes, the depopulation and destruction of villages and towns, and the creation of the Israeli state. The Nakba of 1948 was more than mere loss of land; it deeply fractured and fragmented Palestinian society, culture, and identity. It created different groups of Palestinians, separated by geographical location and civil status. One group, those who remained within the newly established borders of Israel—some internally displaced and others whose towns survived, in total around 150,000—received Israeli citizenship. They turned from a majority into a minority almost overnight, forcing them to navigate a new reality of subjugation.[5]

After the Nakba, my own hometown of Nazareth became the unofficial capital of Palestinian citizens of Israel, having survived almost intact. Nazareth became a refuge for thousands of internally displaced Palestinians from surrounding villages, yet its geographical boundaries remained

---

3. UN Office for the Coordination of Humanitarian Affairs, "West Bank"; and "Humanitarian Situation Update."

4. *Middle East Monitor*, "In Largest Land Grab." Months before this latest seizure of land, Peace Now observed that "the year 2024 marks a peak in the extent of declarations of state land" ("Government Declares").

5. Pappé, *Forgotten Palestinians*.

unchanged. For example, the residents of *Saffuriya*, who were forcibly expelled from their lands, settled in the *Safafra* neighborhood on the outskirts of Nazareth, where they continue to live today. Saffuriya's lands were confiscated and transformed into the Jewish settlement of Tzipori.[6]

Another example is the village of Ma'alul, which was also ethnically cleansed during the Nakba, and its residents resettled in Nazareth as internally displaced refugees unable to return to their homes.[7] The Jewish National Fund planted pine trees over most of the village site. The church building still stands; second- and third-generation Ma'alulites still hold their annual Easter celebrations there. The stories of these villages—and others too many to name here—are not faraway histories. My friends, relatives, classmates, and colleagues all hail from these sites of dispossession, and carry its impact even today.

For the first two decades of Israeli statehood, these Palestinian citizens were subject to military rule, which severely restricted movement, political expression, and economic opportunities. They were isolated from the rest of the Palestinian—and Arab—world, with their movement constrained and their resources and land confiscated to make room for Jewish settlement.[8] Again, my hometown of Nazareth is a prime example. In the 1950s, the state established the Jewish settlement of Nazareth Illit (later renamed Nof HaGalil) on land confiscated from Nazareth and surrounding villages in order to "Judaize the Galilee" and "swallow up" Nazareth, as one military governor phrased it.[9]

The end of military rule in 1966 did not end the marginalization of Palestinian citizens of Israel; it subjected them to a more covert apartheid regime within a state that described itself as a democracy. The legacy of the Nakba and military rule still looms large for Palestinian citizens of Israel, whose political, economic, and social marginalization persists today.

Structural Discrimination and Marginalization

While equality for all inhabitants of Israel was promised in the Declaration of Independence, numerous Israeli laws and practices are biased against Palestinian citizens of Israel.[10] Despite having Israeli citizenship, Palestin-

---

6. See "Institutional Discrimination in Israel. Case Study: Nazareth," in Human Rights Watch, *Threshold Crossed*, 159–68. See further pp. 162–63 below.
7. See https://www.zochrot.org/villages/village_details/49281/en.
8. Rouhana and Sabbagh-Khoury, "Settler-Colonial Citizenship."
9. Human Rights Watch, *Threshold Crossed*, 159, 162.
10. Jamal, "Palestinian Citizens of Israel."

ians in Israel face systematic discrimination in all areas of life, including housing, employment, education, and political representation. Palestinian localities in Israel, from Nazareth to Lydd to Al-Naqab, are systematically underfunded and underdeveloped. They suffer from poor infrastructure, high unemployment, and inadequate access to essential services.[11]

One prominent example of this discrimination is Israel's policy of "boxing in" Palestinian localities within Israel by refusing Palestinian citizens building permits and by confiscating the land surrounding the localities for the exclusive use of nearby Jewish towns. This practice severely limits housing expansion required by natural population growth and turns these localities into overcrowded enclaves with little horizon for development. Such policies explain why Palestinian citizens of Israel, who make up about 20 percent of Israel's population, reside in communities that cover about 3.5 percent of Israel's territory.[12]

Once again, my hometown of Nazareth vividly illustrates these discriminatory policies. Since the Nakba, Nazareth's population has grown more than fivefold, yet the city remains confined to nearly the same land area. For us residents, this has resulted in a severe housing crisis, unbearable overcrowding, and inadequate public services—all contributing to a sense of suffocation and a desire to leave. This feeling is magnified when compared to the nearby settlement of Nazareth Illit, which continues to expand at Nazareth's expense, benefiting from industrial zones, green spaces, and government offices that were once located in Nazareth.[13]

In 2018, the Israeli parliament passed a "basic law"—a law with constitutional authority—that declared Israel the national homeland of the Jewish people, reserved the right of national self-determination to Jewish citizens alone, and asserted Jewish settlement as a national value that the state must advance and promote. In passing this law, the inferior status of Palestinian citizens of Israel was enshrined in law.[14]

Turning Points: The Events of October 2000 and May 2021

In October 2000, following the outbreak of the second Intifada, protests erupted across Palestinian communities in Israel to express solidarity with Palestinians in East Jerusalem, the West Bank, and Gaza, as well as to protest

---

11. Sultany, "Making of an Underclass."

12. Human Rights Watch, "Israel: Discriminatory Land Policies"; Iraqi, "Israel's Housing Policy for Arabs."

13. Human Rights Watch, *Threshold Crossed*; Cook, "Welcome to Nazareth."

14. Jabareen, "Nation-State Law."

the long-standing state neglect, inequality, and discrimination permeating every aspect of Palestinian life in Israel. Israeli police responded with live ammunition and sniper fire, wounding thousands of unarmed Palestinian protesters. Thirteen Palestinian citizens were killed—almost all from gunshots to the chest, head, or eyes.

The events of October 2000 constituted "one of the most pronounced manifestations of institutionalized racism and discrimination"[15] by the Israeli state against its Palestinian citizens, defining the relationship between them for the following decades. These events laid bare the state's perception of the Palestinians inside Israel as an enemy population, and revealed its readiness to suppress dissent among its own citizens with the same lethal force it uses in the West Bank and Gaza.

Following pressure from families of the victims and from Palestinian political leadership and civil society, the Israeli government established the Or Commission to investigate the events of October 2000. Released in 2003, the commission's report criticized police conduct, stressing that there had been no justification for the use of lethal force against the protesters. Importantly, the commission also acknowledged the deep-rooted discrimination faced by Palestinian citizens—the first official recognition of this—recommending that the government act to end discrimination. However, despite these findings, the commission's recommendations went largely unheeded. In 2005, Israel's internal investigations division closed the cases without any indictments. In 2007, the attorney general officially ended all investigations into the events of October 2000, ensuring full impunity for the police and commanders responsible. This lack of accountability has fueled mistrust between Palestinian citizens and the Israeli state, with the community perceiving the government's inaction as a green light for future police brutality.[16]

In May 2021, Palestinian citizens of Israel again took to the streets, this time in solidarity with Palestinians in East Jerusalem facing eviction from the neighborhood of Sheikh Jarrah and in response to Israeli police raids into Al-Aqsa Mosque during Ramadan. Known as the Uprising of Dignity or the Unity Intifada, the solidarity protests spread through mixed (Palestinian–Jewish) cities, including Lydd, Haifa, and Acre. Protests were accompanied by intense grassroots social media activity that connected Palestinians across the land and the diaspora.

The Israeli state's response was once again severe, echoing the brutality of October 2000. The police sought to disperse protests using "unnecessary

---

15. Association for Civil Rights in Israel, "Reflections on October 2000."
16. Iraqi, "Thirteen Killed, No One Punished."

and excessive force" including tear gas, rubber bullets, and mass arrests.[17] Jewish far-right groups also mobilized, attacking Palestinian neighborhoods and businesses, and doxing Palestinian activists online.[18] The events on the streets turned deadly, with two protesters killed: one in Umm Al-Fahem and one in Lydd—both cases closed without indictments. After the protests died down, the police launched a campaign of mass arrests to crack down on Palestinian citizens, with disproportionate sentencing for their participation in the protests.[19] Subsequently, intelligence units monitoring social media activity, primarily that of Palestinian citizens, were technologically upgraded and their personnel were increased.[20]

The historical context of the Palestinian citizens of Israel reveals the infrastructure of repression that the State of Israel built to intimidate and control Palestinians. This history of unchecked violence, surveillance, crackdowns on free speech, and lack of police accountability laid the groundwork for the state's aggressive attitude toward Palestinian citizens after October 7, 2023.

In the Shadow of the War on Gaza: Intimidation, Silencing, Political Persecution, and Abandonment

Since the events of October 7, 2023, the systemic discrimination, marginalization and repression that Palestinian citizens of Israel face has only intensified. State institutions have effectively criminalized expressions of empathy with Palestinians in Gaza.

Intimidation and Silencing: Criminalizing Solidarity

On October 7, 2023, during the attack of Hamas and other Palestinian armed groups on Southern Israel, twenty-seven Palestinian citizens of Israel were killed: twenty by gunfire and seven by rockets. Additionally, six Palestinian citizens were taken hostage to Gaza.[21] Of the hostages, two were returned in a hostage deal in November 2023, one was returned in a rescue

---

17. Amnesty International, "Israeli Police Targeted Palestinians."
18. Mansour, "Echoes of Violence."
19. Amnesty International, "Israeli Police Targeted Palestinians."
20. Barron, "How Four Posts on Instagram Destroyed Her Life."
21. Statistics from the Israeli site NewMedia (in Hebrew): https://newmedia.calcalist.co.il/magazine-16-11-23/m03.html.

operation, one was killed accidentally by Israeli military fire, and two were found killed in Gaza.

These events, as well as the killing of fellow Jewish-Israeli citizens, left Palestinian citizens reeling and bracing themselves for the unprecedented Israeli aggression that was to follow. State institutions made it known to the Palestinian citizens of Israel that empathy with Palestinian Gazans will not be tolerated. On October 17, ten days after the attack on Southern Israel, Police Commissioner Kobi Shabtai said, "Anyone who wants to be a citizen of Israel, *ahlan wa sahlan* [welcome]. Anyone who wishes to identify with Gaza, is welcome to—I will put him on the buses that are heading there now."[22] Through his statement, similar to those made by other Israeli officials, Shabtai defined what it meant to be an Israeli citizen—i.e., showing no sympathy for Gaza—and threatened to expel any who transgressed these boundaries. The police also banned anti-war protests, significantly diminishing the "democratic margins" that Palestinian citizens have.

Over the following months, hundreds of Palestinian citizens of Israel were detained, arrested, and interrogated for a variety of social media posts construed as incitement—including verses from the Qur'an, the Palestinian flag, and pictures of Gazan children. These arrests are particularly humiliating and degrading. Detainees are handcuffed, blindfolded, and photographed under the Israeli flag. Photographs are leaked and circulated widely. One such case is Intisar Hijazi from the town of Tamra in Galilee. Intisar is a teacher and a school counselor who was accused by the police of incitement to terrorism for posting a dancing video—construed as celebrating the events of October 7. She was arrested and kept in detention for seventy-two hours, with National Security Minister Itamar Ben-Gvir posting a picture of her blindfolded and handcuffed, and personally taking credit for her arrest.

Non-state institutions joined in the campaign of political persecution, contributing to the atmosphere of intimidation and fear. Retaliating against social media posts, employers dismissed Palestinian workers and universities launched disciplinary procedures against Palestinian students and academics—dismissing some without due process and transferring some cases to the police, resulting in numerous arrests.[23] Far-right groups further fueled this campaign, crawling through Palestinians' old social media posts, doxing and harassing those who voiced support for Palestinians in Gaza or protested Israeli policies.

---

22. Shimoni et al., "Israel Police Commissioner."

23. Academia for Equality, "Academy for Equality Report"; Adalah, "Repression of Palestinian Students."

Some of my friends and acquaintances were the target of such retaliations. This instilled a sense of fear in me: I often felt forced to self-censor; I curtailed my social media activity and turned down speaking and advocacy engagements. I was even wary of speaking in Arabic, my mother tongue, in public spaces.

This crackdown on Palestinian freedom of expression contrasts starkly with the impunity granted to Jewish Israeli citizens who incite violence against Palestinians. Palestinian non-profit 7amleh documented ten million instances of violent incitement against Palestinians in Hebrew.[24] Yet, as Adalah, another Palestinian non-profit, reports, there are virtually no cases of Jewish Israeli citizens facing repercussions (legal or otherwise) over hate speech.[25] Furthermore, public figures and politicians have openly called for the destruction of Gaza, with high level decision-makers and known personalities adopting genocidal rhetoric. Starting at the very top, Israel's president Isaac Herzog declared the whole Palestinian nation as guilty: "It's an entire nation out there that is responsible. This rhetoric about civilians not aware, not involved, it's absolutely not true." Defense Minister Yoav Gallant characterized Palestinians as "human animals," ordering a total siege on the Gaza Strip: "no electricity, no food, no fuel, everything is closed." Calls for wiping Gaza off the face of the earth appear regularly on TV shows, and a sticker declaring "finish them!" can be seen on many cars in Israel.[26] None of this incitement is punished. For Palestinian citizens of Israel, this is not only a matter of injustice, it is also a matter of safety. The prevalence of these violent expressions is terrifying.

Abandonment: Lack of Protection and Emergency Infrastructure

Israel's systemic neglect and underdevelopment of Palestinian communities, particularly in terms of emergency preparedness, attests to the profound abandonment faced by Palestinian citizens in Israel. This abandonment is costing Palestinian lives: of the thirty-four civilian deaths due to rocket fire in Northern Israel between October 7, 2023, and November 2024, nineteen were Palestinian. This can be traced back to the lack of available safe spaces in Palestinian localities: while 26 percent of Israeli civilians overall lack proper shelters, this figure nearly doubles to 46.5 percent in

---

24. 7amleh, "Racism and Incitement Index."

25. Adalah, "Repression of Palestinian Students."

26. Law for Palestine keeps a database of such instances, available on their website: https://law4palestine.org/law-for-palestine-releases-database-with-500-instances-of-israeli-incitement-to-genocide-continuously-updated/.

non-Jewish areas, reflecting stark disparities in infrastructure. Tamra and Safad are a case in point: Tamra, a Palestinian town with 37,000 residents, has no public shelters, while Safad, a Jewish-majority city with a comparable population of 42,000 residents, has 138.[27] Moreover, only 11 percent of Arabic-speaking schools and educational institutions are equipped for emergencies, and a quarter of Palestinian students lack the technological means to access remote education.[28]

The state's neglect is especially stark in the Naqab region in the south. The 100,000 Bedouin Palestinian citizens living in unrecognized villages are 2,200 times more likely than other citizens to be harmed by rocket fire.[29] Due to the lack of recognition of these villages by the state, these areas are often considered open areas, meaning that they do not receive rocket alerts and are not covered by aerial defense mechanisms such as the Iron Dome. Their residents are thus left without any warning in the event of a rocket attack.[30] Furthermore, these communities severely lack adequate safe rooms, and often rely on charity donations from civil society organizations for makeshift shelters.[31] Makeshift shelters are either large bags of sand organized in a circle shape (there is no roof) or large concrete cylinders that hold up to twelve people at a time. The state does not provide proper mobile shelters for unrecognized villages, for fear that these structures would be used for residential purposes and further solidify the residents' connection with the land. Home demolitions continue even amid the war.

Social and Emotional Consequences

The ongoing war on Gaza has taken a profound social and emotional toll on Palestinian citizens of Israel, touching nearly every aspect of daily life. Watching the devastation unfold in Gaza is intensely distressing, not only due to the direct family ties many Palestinian citizens have in Gaza but also because Gaza represents a central pillar of Palestinian identity, culture, and memory. The sense of connection with Gaza amplifies the trauma of witnessing the violence and destruction, which many feel powerless to stop and unable to mourn publicly due to the state's repression of solidarity.

This trauma resonates deeply across generations, evoking intergenerational memories of the Nakba and creating the sense that it is ongoing. For

---

27. Yahia and Hashmonai, "Israeli Government."
28. Follow-Up Committee on Arab Education in Israel, "Status Report."
29. Knesset News, "2200 Times More Likely."
30. Association for Civil Rights in Israel, "Absence of Warning."
31. Negev Coexistence Forum for Civil Equality, "Lack of Protection."

older generations, the situation reawakens the pain of dispossession, while younger generations feel intensifying disenfranchisement and despair. The inability to express grief or solidarity without risking arrest forces Palestinian citizens to internalize their emotions, exacerbating feelings of isolation and helplessness.

The unique position of Palestinian citizens inside Israel itself means that we face a host of challenges while sharing public spaces with Jewish Israelis. Whereas Palestinians in the West Bank and Gaza see Israelis primarily in a military context, Palestinian citizens inside Israel meet Jewish Israelis in workplaces, government offices, shops, universities, and other public spaces. Thus, Palestinian professionals, especially those working in mixed Jewish-Palestinian environments, grapple with complex emotions. For example, a report by the Palestinian NGO Ad'ar describes the experiences of Palestinian social workers during the war who often found themselves walking a psychological tightrope between their Palestinian identity and their daily relationships with Jewish colleagues.[32] Many reported feeling compelled to suppress their emotions and even prove their loyalty to the state, fearing that "every word could be counted against" them. In moments of intense grief, some professionals resorted to self-imposed isolation, retreating from shared spaces to process their sorrow privately. This need to compartmentalize emotions and avoid scrutiny creates an exhausting inner conflict, complicating their work and social interactions.

Another psychological toll arises from public encounters with uniformed soldiers who may have perpetrated violence in Gaza and Lebanon. For Palestinian citizens, the knowledge that coworkers, neighbors, or acquaintances may have directly committed violence against Palestinians introduces another distressing layer of trauma.

Furthermore, since the events of October 7, National Security Minister and far-right politician Itamar Ben-Gvir has significantly eased the restrictions on citizens' eligibility to possess firearms. In six months, the number of licensed gun owners soared from 150,000 to 230,000.[33] Expected soon to surpass 300,000, this surge in armed civilians, combined with minimal regulation or training, creates a volatile and dangerous environment. For Palestinian citizens, the presence of an increasingly armed civilian population is especially terrifying, given the backdrop of a society energized by nationalist (and racist) sentiments since October 7. This arms buildup, largely unchecked, represents a human rights risk that leaves Palestinian citizens feeling even more vulnerable to potential violence.

---

32. Mansour et al., "War, Welfare, and Resilience."
33. Association for Civil Rights in Israel, "Civilian Armament in Israel."

Conclusion: Where to Go from Here?

The war on Gaza and the Israeli escalation of violence in the region by Israelis have forced Palestinian citizens of Israel to question their place within the land. Excluded from core Palestinian political discussions in the West Bank and Gaza, and disillusioned by Israeli politics, even left-leaning parties that once nominally opposed the occupation have shifted rightward and registered minimal opposition to the devastation in Gaza. This leaves Palestinian citizens of Israel politically isolated, caught between a marginalized identity and the hostile atmosphere of Israeli society.

Within this environment, a near-totalitarian expectation of silence prevails. Palestinian citizens are pressured to conform publicly to the state's narratives, with severe consequences for perceived deviations extending beyond social ostracism to job loss, surveillance, and legal persecution. Palestinian students, doctors, teachers, and other professionals are systematically targeted, with a disproportionate focus on women[34]—an approach that resonates deeply in a community still shaped by patriarchal structures. These tactics communicate that Palestinian identity itself is under attack, heightening feelings of vulnerability and alienation.

In response, many Palestinian citizens, including many of my own friends and acquaintances, feel an urge to seek a new life abroad, though this option comes with its own emotional weight. Leaving would mean distancing from family, culture, and the land we continue to love despite the adversity. This internal conflict captures the essence of their current position: isolated and at risk in Israel, yet deeply bonded to the Palestinian identity we are expected to relinquish. The future remains uncertain, yet the resilience and continued connection to Palestinian identity persist, even amid profound societal repression.

Bibliography

7amleh. "Racism and Incitement Index: 7amleh Documents 10 Million Instances of Violent Content in Hebrew Throughout the Year 2023." February 26, 2024. https://7amleh.org/2024/02/26/racism-and-incitement-index-7amleh-documents-10-million-instances-of-violent-content-in-hebrew-throughout-the-year-2023.

Academia for Equality. "Academy for Equality Report for the UN Special Rapporteur on Freedom of Expression." July 15, 2024. https://en.academia4equality.com/post/academy-for-equality-report-for-the-un-special-rapporteur-on-freedom-of-expression.

---

34. Adalah, "Repression of Palestinian Students."

Adalah. "Repression of Palestinian Students in Israeli Universities and Colleges." May 9, 2024. https://www.adalah.org/en/content/view/11116.

Al-Haq. *Israeli Apartheid: Tools of Zionist Settler Colonialism*. November 29, 2022. https://www.alhaq.org/advocacy/20931.html.

Amnesty International. "Israeli Police Targeted Palestinians with Discriminatory Arrests, Torture and Unlawful Force." June 2021. https://www.amnesty.org/en/latest/press-release/2021/06/israeli-police-targeted-palestinians-with-discriminatory-arrests-torture-and-unlawful-force/.

———. "Israel's Apartheid Against Palestinians: Cruel System of Domination and Crime Against Humanity." London: Amnesty International, 2022. https://www.amnesty.org/en/documents/mde15/5141/2022/en/.

Association for Civil Rights in Israel. "The Absence of Warning and Shelter Systems in the Unrecognized Villages in the Negev." October 12, 2023. https://www.english.acri.org.il/post/the-absence-of-warning-and-shelter-systems-in-the-unrecognized-villages-in-the-negev.

———. "Civilian Armament in Israel." April 2, 2024. https://www.english.acri.org.il/post/civilian-armament-in-israel.

———. "Reflections on October 2000." October 7, 2008. https://law.acri.org.il/en/2008/10/07/reflections-on-october-2000/.

Barron, Jesse. "How Four Posts on Instagram Destroyed Her Life." *The New York Times*, November 3, 2024. https://www.nytimes.com/2024/11/03/magazine/israel-free-speech.html.

Cook, Jonathan. "Welcome to Nazareth." https://www.jonathan-cook.net/2012-8-03/welcome-to-nazareth/.

Follow-Up Committee on Arab Education in Israel. "Status Report: The Education System in Arab Localities in the Shadow of the Emergency Situation." October 30, 2023. https://arab-education.org/uploads//releases_pdf/15427794622023110 71146181803753150.pdf.

Human Rights Watch. "Israel: Discriminatory Land Policies Hem in Palestinians." May 2020. https://www.hrw.org/news/2020/05/12/israel-discriminatory-land-policies-hem-palestinians.

———. *A Threshold Crossed: Israeli Authorities and the Crimes of Apartheid and Persecution*. April 27, 2021. https://www.hrw.org/report/2021/04/27/threshold-crossed/israeli-authorities-and-crimes-apartheid-and-persecution.

Iraqi, Amjad. "Israel's Housing Policy for Arabs Is Designed to Fail." *+972 Magazine*, February 2016. https://www.972mag.com/israels-housing-policy-for-arabs-is-designed-to-fail/.

———. "Thirteen Killed, No One Punished: Remembering October 2000." *+972 Magazine*, October 4, 2015. https://www.972mag.com/thirteen-killed-no-one-punished-remembering-october-2000/.

Jabareen, Yousef. "The Nation-State Law and Jewish Supremacy." *Palestine-Israel Journal of Politics, Economics, and Culture* 23 (2018) 16–22.

Jamal, Amal. "Palestinian Citizens of Israel." In *Routledge Handbook on the Israeli-Palestinian Conflict*, edited by Joel Peters and David Newman, 278–91. London: Routledge, 2012.

Knesset News. "2200 Times More Likely Than Any Other Citizen to Be Killed by a Rocket." December 6, 2023. https://main.knesset.gov.il/news/pressreleases/pages/press06.12.23s.aspx.

Mansour, Lamma. "Echoes of Violence: Experiences of Palestinian Arab Students in Israeli Academia During the Violent Events of May 2021." *Higher Education*, October 1, 2024. https://doi.org/10.1007/s10734-024-01315-w.

Mansour, Lamma, et al. "War, Welfare, and Resilience: Insights from Professionals in the Shadow of War." *Ad'ar*, January 2024. https://adar3.org/wp-content/uploads/2024/01/WarWelafreandResilience.pdf.

Middle East Monitor. "In Largest Land Grab Since Oslo, Israel Confiscates 6,000 Acres in West Bank." December 6, 2024. https://www.middleeastmonitor.com/20241206-in-largest-land-grab-since-oslo-israel-confiscates-6000-acres-in-west-bank/.

Negev Coexistence Forum for Civil Equality. "Lack of Protection Against Missiles and Rockets in the Unrecognized Villages in the Negev." November 15, 2023. https://www.dukium.org/wp-content/uploads/2023/11/NCF-Lack-of-protection-against-missiles-and-rockets_position-paper_15.11.23_ENG_FINAL2-Photos.pdf.

Oxfam. *Gaza: 1 Year On: Accountability Report*. October 3, 2024. https://www.oxfam.org/en/research/gaza-one-year-accountability-report.

Pappé, Ilan. *The Forgotten Palestinians: A History of the Palestinians in Israel*. New Haven, CT: Yale University Press, 2011.

Peace Now. "The Government Declares 12,000 Dunams in the Jordan Valley as State Lands." July 3, 2024. https://peacenow.org.il/en/state-land-declaration-12000-dunams.

Rouhana, Nadim, and Areej Sabbagh-Khoury. "Settler-Colonial Citizenship: Conceptualizing the Relationship Between Israel and Its Palestinian Citizens." *Settler Colonial Studies* 5 (2015) 205–25.

Shimoni, Ran, et al. "Israel Police Commissioner: 'Those Who Identify with Gaza Can Be Escorted There on Buses.'" *Haaretz*, October 19, 2023. https://www.haaretz.com/israel-news/2023-10-19/ty-article/.premium/israel-police-commissioner-those-who-identify-with-gaza-can-be-escorted-there-on-buses/0000018b-4735-df22-a5eb-4f7dca0c0000.

Sultany, Nimer. "The Making of an Underclass: The Palestinian Citizens of Israel." *Israel Studies Review* 27 (2012) 190–200.

United Nations Office for the Coordination of Humanitarian Affairs. "Humanitarian Situation Update #279: West Bank." April 10, 2025. https://www.ochaopt.org/content/reported-impact-snapshot-gaza-strip-3-april-2025.

———. "Reported Impact Snapshot: Gaza Strip (3 April 2025)." https://www.ochaopt.org/content/reported-impact-snapshot-gaza-strip-3-april-2025.

———. "West Bank: Violence, Destruction and Displacement: September 2024." October 5, 2024. https://www.ochaopt.org/content/west-bank-violence-destruction-and-displacement-september-2024.

Yahia, Deiaa Haj, and Adi Hashmonai. "The Israeli Government Neglected to Build Shelters in Arab Towns. Now Deaths Are Piling Up." *Haaretz*, November 4, 2024. https://www.haaretz.com/israel-news/2024-11-04/ty-article-magazine/.premium/israeli-govt-neglected-to-build-shelters-in-arab-towns-now-deaths-are-growing/00000192-f8af-d51d-a5d3-febf0b530000.

CHAPTER SEVEN

The Political Perils of Biblical Archaeology in the Holy Land

Donald D. Binder

IN A VOLUME THAT seeks to plumb the depths of the Gaza War's many horrors, the inclusion of an essay on biblical archaeology might seem to be woefully out of place.[1]

But it's not. That's because wars are fought for reasons. Some of these are obvious, and they include such considerations as personal and economic survival as well as disputes over land, freedom of movement, and self-determination.

Yet there is also a galaxy of other overarching justifications that are often not fully recognized or appreciated by the general public. This cluster forms a broad category that we might label as the *Preservation of Cultural Heritage*. Some of the constellations within this galaxy are mostly

---

1. In using the term "biblical archaeology," I adopt the modern definition embraced in the academic discipline as set forth in the digital edition of the *Oxford Classical Dictionary* (*OCD*), which summarizes the much larger entry on the term as follows: "Biblical archaeology is defined as the study of the archaeological remains of the peoples, cultures, and periods in which the biblical texts were formed. While in the past biblical archaeology was often seen as an ideologically motivated field of inquiry, currently, a balanced and scientifically advanced approach is common among most practitioners. The large body of research in this field, continuing to the present, provides a broad range of finds, insights, and understanding of the relevant cultures, peoples and periods in which the biblical texts were formed" (Maeir, "Biblical Archaeology"). As we will see in the subsequent discussion, not all recent practitioners have in fact held to this more modern ideal. Hence the title of this essay.

intangible. They include oral histories, customs, beliefs, language, music, and folklore. Others, however, are more fully manifested in the physical world. Among these are historical sites, buildings, monuments, artifacts, and texts. Together they constitute the unique history and character of a particular human group or society.

While the field of anthropology focuses on the first of the constellations, archaeology concerns itself primarily with the second. Through unearthing ancient sites and artifacts, archaeologists first seek to reconstruct the history of a local group and then to connect it with the histories of similar contemporaneous groups in order to form a broader understanding of a larger civilization and its interactions with others across time.[2]

In both of these exploratory and synthetic tasks, the archaeologist or historian is sometimes assisted (or at least influenced) by ancient texts that have been preserved from the distant past. One such text, of course, is the Bible. And here, even in the twenty-first century, it is impossible to speak of archaeology in the "Holy Land" apart from the Bible. Indeed, its contents are the very reason this relatively tiny geographic region has been given its sacred designation. And so, from the first quasi-scientific digs in Ottoman Palestine during the nineteenth century to the more rigorous excavations of the present day, the Bible has loomed large. Not only has it fueled the international interest (and financing) that has led to the Holy Land becoming the most excavated region in the world, but it has also guided excavators in their methodologies, identifications, interpretations, and final presentations of archaeological sites.

And therein lies a problem. The Bible, either as a whole or in part, is sacred to each of the world's three great monotheistic religions: Judaism, Christianity, and Islam.[3] Nearly two millennia after its final production, present-day members of these faith-traditions, including those now living in Israel/Palestine, trace their religious and/or ethnic heritages to peoples described in the Bible—peoples frequently depicted there as being in conflict over possession of the Land.

This alone would be enough to tempt the inheritors of these traditions to appeal to ancient control or ownership of the land in order to justify their

---

2. For an example of this reconstructive process being applied to nascent Judaism, see my various writings on the development of the earliest synagogues, e.g., Binder, *Into the Temple Courts*; Runesson et al., *Ancient Synagogue*.

3. While the Bible is the most consequential of the ancient texts held as sacred by the three Abrahamic faiths, others also exert their influence in archaeological work. In Judaism, these include the Mishnah and the two Talmuds; in Christianity, the early church fathers (esp. Eusebius of Caesarea); and in Islam, the Qur'an and Hadith. For an exploration of the variety of theologies within these three traditions vis-à-vis the Holy Land, see Munayer, *Reconciling Justice*.

present-day claims. Yet to many, this temptation becomes irresistible when coupled with an unqualified reading of certain biblical passages seen as conferring a divine bequest of the Land in perpetuity to a particular religious or ethnic group (e.g., Gen 15:18–21, 48:3–4).[4] Added to this influence is the great interest that each tradition's adherents have in preserving ancient sites associated with certain sacred figures or events mentioned in the Bible.

This is where archaeology enters in. For not only must archaeologists decide where to dig, they also have to choose which layers of civilization to focus upon. And because this region of the Levant forms a hotly contested land-bridge between three continents, the stratigraphy of its habitation sites often dates back many millennia, with dozens of occupation levels piled on top of each other. Thus, while some layers are chosen to be preserved intact, others are either destroyed outright or dismantled, with those pieces deemed preservation-worthy carted away to a secure warehouse and only a tiny fraction of them ending up inside a display case in some museum. In both instances, detailed evidence of these occupational layers continues to exist (at best) only in unpublished field notes or specialized academic tomes. Additionally, once a level of civilization has been chosen to be presented to the public, the remains of earlier civilizations are often left to languish beneath the featured layer, mostly unexplored and unheralded.

As we will see, one's interpretation of the Bible has demonstrably played a key role in making such determinations throughout the Holy Land, especially since 1948. As archaeologist Jodi Magness writes in the introduction of her recently published book (2024) on the archaeology of Jerusalem, "Archaeology is neither neutral nor objective . . . . Nowhere is this more evident than in Jerusalem, where archaeology has been employed from the beginning of modern exploration for religious and nationalistic purposes."[5] After noting the biases of early Christian explorers in this regard, she continues:

> For many Israelis archaeology is a means of (re)establishing a physical connection to the land by bringing to light remains

---

4. For example, when the Archbishop of Canterbury, Justin Welby, issued a statement supporting the ICJ's Advisory Opinion on Israel's Occupation of the Occupied Palestinian Territories—"The Advisory Opinion by the International Court of Justice (19 July 2024) makes definitively clear that Israel's presence in the Occupied Palestinian Territories is unlawful and needs to end as rapidly as possible"—the Chief Rabbi of South Africa, Rabbi Warren Goldstein, was quoted as saying, "By ignoring God's promise of the land of Israel to the Jewish people, Welby [is] rejecting the Bible" (Welby, "Archbishop of Canterbury Statement "; *The Jerusalem Post*, "S. Africa Chief Rabbi"). A group of Christian leaders similarly called Welby's statement "unbiblical" (Treharne et al., "Christian Leaders").

5. Magness, *Jerusalem Through the Ages*, 11–12.

associated with the ancient Israelite and Jewish populations. Religious and political interests influence many of the controversies surrounding archaeological finds discussed in this book, such as the claimed discovery of King David's palace or the road along which Jesus may have walked from the Pool of Siloam to the Temple Mount. In addition, religious and political motivations often dictate which excavated remains are preserved and how they are presented to the public. For example, the City of David Visitors' Center, which is in the midst of a Palestinian neighborhood, prioritizes remains of the Iron Age—the period of David and Solomon and their successors—in an attempt to establish Israeli claims to this part of the city.[6]

In this study, we will survey a small sample of excavated sites in Israel/Palestine from 1948 onward where such biblically driven political considerations have clearly played a role. Here, however, we must pause to note that a power imbalance has existed in the Holy Land during most of this period, especially since 1967, with the Israeli government exercising control over many more archaeological sites than those of its Palestinian (or Jordanian) counterparts. As a result, the majority of our examples emerge from the Israeli side. Nevertheless, when given the opportunity, Palestinian leadership has also not been immune from indulging in similarly driven behavior. And so we will also look at one instance where this has played itself out in a major dig, while citing other examples of culturally destructive behavior. The essay will then highlight the recent case of a more culturally sensitive excavation, one that might serve as a model for others. It will conclude by offering a list of practical suggestions to help promote the greatest possible preservation of the tangible cultural heritages of both Israelis and Palestinians living in the Land—as well as those of Jews, Christians, and Muslims (and other faith traditions) worldwide.

Before we embark on this exploration, however, it is first necessary to examine legal considerations touching on this overall topic.

---

6. Magness, *Jerusalem Through the Ages*, 12. Cf. Maeir, "Biblical Archaeology," who notes: "Another controversial issue is the use or misuse of biblical archaeology in the context of modern political and religious ideologies. In the past, and in some cases even presently, discoveries or lack of discoveries have been used to promote or support ideological views. Claims that certain finds prove the Land of Israel *belongs* to the Jews, or that it does not, are part of this controversy. Likewise, claims that certain finds corroborate or disprove specific biblical stories, thus strengthening or weakening various religious beliefs, are also controversial" (emphasis original).

Considerations of International Law

Recent media commentary on South Africa's case against Israel in the International Court of Justice (ICJ, South Africa v. Israel, 2023–) has reminded the general public that the term *genocide* was first coined during WWII by Raphael Lemkin, a Polish Jew who was greatly alarmed by the Nazis' annihilation of his people—and by the failure of the world to do anything about it. But he was not merely distressed at the physical attacks being orchestrated against his fellow Jews. Among the acts Lemkin viewed as being potentially genocidal were those suppressing "artistic and cultural values." Lemkin recounted in his writings the Nazis' destruction in Poland of "national monuments" and their looting of "libraries, archives, museums, and galleries of art."[7] One such casualty was the historic Jewish Theological Seminary at Lublin, Poland, whose destruction Lemkin conveys through the report of a supervising German officer:

> For us it was a matter of special pride to destroy the Talmudic Academy which was known as the greatest in Poland . . . . We threw out of the building the great Talmudic library, and carted it to market. There we set fire to the books. The fire lasted for twenty hours. The Jews of Lublin were assembled around and cried bitterly. Their cries almost silenced us. Then we summoned the military band and the joyful shouts of the soldiers silenced the sound of the Jewish cries.[8]

Although political opposition thwarted Lemkin's efforts to include cultural genocide in the UN Genocide Convention of 1948,[9] his championing of the concept eventually led to the matter being addressed in the 1954 Hague Convention for the Protection of Cultural Property in the Event of Armed Conflict, together with its First and Second Protocols (1954 and 1999, respectively).[10] The Convention and First Protocol broadly stipulate the protection of cultural properties during times of conflict, including those in lands held under military occupation. In regard to this last consideration, Article 5 of the Convention allows for salvage excavations by the occupying power only if "the competent national authorities [are] unable to take such measures"—the national authorities, that is, of the occupied

---

7. Lemkin, *Axis Rule in Occupied Europe*, 85.
8. Quoted in Lemkin, *Axis Rule in Occupied Europe*, 85.
9. See Bachman, "Historic Perspective."
10. UNESCO, "Convention for the Protection"; UNESCO, "[First] Protocol"; UNESCO, "Second Protocol."

people.[11] Even then, the occupying power is only permitted to "take the most necessary measures of preservation . . . as far as possible, and in close co-operation with such authorities."[12]

Despite the fact that both Israel and Palestine are signatories to the Convention and its First Protocol, the document's ambiguous wording ("as far as possible") has enabled Israel to undertake more than a thousand archaeological excavations throughout the Occupied Palestinian Territories (OPT) since 1967.[13] Such abuses there and worldwide eventually led to the issuing of the Second Protocol, which greatly tightens the above wording:

> [A] Party in occupation of the whole or part of the territory of another Party shall prohibit and prevent in relation to the occupied territory: (a) any illicit export, other removal or transfer of ownership of cultural property; (b) any archaeological excavation, save where this is strictly required to safeguard, record or preserve cultural property; (c) any alteration to, or change of use of, cultural property which is intended to conceal or destroy cultural, historical or scientific evidence.[14]

Notably, Israel has refused to become a signatory to the Second Protocol, which Palestine signed in 2012. Indeed, doing so would immediately put Israel in violation of its terms, not only with respect to most of its excavations inside the OPT, but also with respect to the Israeli settlements surrounding a number of such sites.[15]

In addition to explicitly protecting cultural sites under occupation, Articles 5–8 of the Second Protocol establish similar safeguards for such locations during periods of active conflict. Given the extensive bombing and rocket fire that have taken place from the very start of the Gaza War, it should come as no surprise that Blue Shield International, the UN organization tasked with overseeing adherence to the Hague Convention, issued a

---

11. UNESCO, "Convention for the Protection," Article 5, para. 2.

12. UNESCO, "Convention for the Protection," Article 5, para. 2 (clauses transposed).

13. Shiff, *Six Feet Under*, 13. In a related move, Israel took steps to formally annex East Jerusalem beginning on June 28, 1967, and concluding on July 30, 1980. A number of UN Security Council resolutions have rejected this annexation (e.g., UNSC Resolutions 476 and 478 [1980]), as has the "Advisory Opinion" (July 19, 2024) of the International Court of Justice, par. 179, 252–54. Israel justifies its excavations in East Jerusalem by maintaining that such international rulings are biased.

14. UNESCO, "Second Protocol," Article 9, para. 1.

15. See Abdullah, "Century of Cultural Genocide," as well as the various examples cited by the Israeli NGO Emek Shaveh (see p. 171 below) in publications on their website, e.g., Emek Shaveh, "Susya."

warning statement to the warring parties on October 30, 2023—less than a month after the war's start. Noting "the destruction of the mosque of Jabalia and significant damage to the historic center of Gaza," the statement called on all parties in the conflict to take

> all feasible actions to safeguard and respect cultural property located in areas where armed conflict is taking place; avoid using cultural property and its immediate surroundings as part of their military operations in a way that may cause or lead to damage and destruction; avoid targeting cultural property unless there is military necessity; prevent looting; avoid reprisals directed at cultural property; and protect and support those involved in the protection of cultural heritage.[16]

The statement also called for Israel to become a signatory to the Second Protocol as soon as possible. Although at this writing it is too early to determine the total extent of the damage or destruction of archaeological sites in Gaza, news reports published since the issuing of the above warning strongly suggest that it has been considerable.[17]

A matter related to the preceding discussion concerns Israel's troubled relationship with UNESCO, the United Nations agency that promotes science and culture throughout the world. Its World Heritage Center is responsible for selecting World Heritage Sites, properties that meet a number of criteria for outstanding historical or cultural contributions and are worthy of special attention and protection. In 1999, Israel became a signatory of the associated Convention Concerning the Protection of World Cultural and Natural Heritage.[18] Since that time, it has managed to have sixteen sites from within its internationally recognized territories successfully listed as World Heritage Sites. However, partly because of disputes with UNESCO over the safeguarding of archaeological sites in the Old City of Jerusalem (a World Heritage Site sponsored by Jordan) and the organization's admission of Palestine as a member in 2011, Israel withdrew its membership from

---

16. Blue Shield International, "Current Events."

17. See *Middle East Eye*, "War on Gaza"; *Al Jazeera*, "'Cultural Genocide'"; *The Times of Israel*, "Gaza's Archaeology Experts."

18. UNESCO, "Convention Concerning the Protection."

UNESCO in January of 2019.[19] Nevertheless, Israel's listed World Heritage Sites continue to trumpet their elite status.[20]

Although the preceding maneuvers have seemingly allowed Israel to skirt its legal responsibilities with respect to the control of Palestinian cultural properties, it nevertheless remains a signatory to the International Covenant on Economic, Social and Cultural Rights (ICESCR), as does Palestine. This document enshrines the right to self-determination of a people, including their "cultural development" (Article 1, para. 1). Importantly, the International Court of Justice's recent Advisory Opinion on Israel's occupation of the OPT, including East Jerusalem (July 2024), quotes this agreement at several points, culminating in a paragraph mandating Israel's return of "all cultural property and assets taken from Palestinians and Palestinian institutions."[21]

It remains to be seen how the United Nations and the various members of the international community will seek to enforce this and other components of the ICJ's ruling. Nevertheless, the foregoing discussion should be enough to establish for the reader both the letter and the spirit of international law's expectations of Israel and Palestine with regard to the treatment and protection of cultural properties, including archaeological sites.[22]

Biblical Archaeology and the Lure of Religious and Political Sirens

We begin our review of potentially problematic archaeological digs with a confession: I myself helped excavate one such site in the 1990s. As a young PhD candidate, I participated in the University of South Florida (USF) excavations at Sepphoris in Galilee, perhaps best known to ancient history as Herod Antipas's first capital city. In the years leading up to 1948, however, this

---

19. *The Times of Israel*, "69 Years After Joining." Although Israel has not formally voided its signature on the associated convention, it nevertheless no longer cooperates with UNESCO. Under the Trump administration, the United States also withdrew from UNESCO in concert with Israel, though during the subsequent presidency of Joe Biden, it filed for readmission (which was granted) in July of 2023. See also Shiff, *Six Feet Under*, 16–17.

20. Israel Nature and Parks Authority, "World Heritage Sites." As of August 30, 2024, the website has still not been updated to reflect Israel's withdrawal from UNESCO.

21. International Court of Justice, "Advisory Opinion" (July 19, 2024), para. 270. Cf. paras. 97, 233, 256.

22. Those religionists who do not recognize the validity of international law might consider the so-called *Golden Rule* of Christ: "Do to others as you would have them do to you" (Luke 6:31), which has parallels in Judaism (Lev 19:18; B. Shabbat 31a) and Islam (Kitab al-Kafi, vol. 2, bk. 1, ch. 66:10) as well.

site existed as the Palestinian town of Saffuriya, home to a population of some 4,300. In fact, it had served as such a village for nearly seven centuries, since the time the Mamluks captured it from the Crusaders sometime between 1263 and 1266 CE. By the middle of the twentieth century, it was the largest town in Galilee by both population and area (see figure 1 below). Yet after being attacked by Israeli forces in July of 1948, Saffuriya's residents all fled or were expelled during and after the 1948 War, never allowed to return.²³

Figure 1. The village of Saffuriya, 1931. Of the buildings pictured, only the Crusader citadel on the acropolis survives.

By the time our excavations took place, the Israeli government had long since demolished their homes and public buildings, removing even the very name of their town from newly published maps. Today the site has been re-established as an Israeli National Park. In a visit there, tourists and pilgrims will encounter the ruins of Herod's market basilica (the field USF excavated) as well as a Roman theater and drinking hall, a Byzantine-era synagogue, a Crusader citadel, and other ancient structures. And while much attention is paid to the city's history during the periods of Jesus (who lived in nearby Nazareth) and Judah ha-Nasi, the principal compiler of the Mishnah (who lived in Sepphoris for a time), there is scant if any reference to the Palestinian villagers who resided there in most recent centuries. Their cultural presence has been almost entirely erased from the archaeological record.²⁴

Sadly, Saffuriya is not an isolated case in this regard. The same if not worse happened to other Palestinian towns and villages during and after the War of 1948, including those once located at the current Israeli National Parks of Beit She'an (Beisan), Tel Dor (Tantura), Ashkelon (al-Majdal), Maresha/Beit Guvrin (Bayt Jibrin), and Belvoir Fortress (Kawkab al-Hawa), to name

---

23. Schechla, "Forced Eviction," 95.

24. See Khalidi, *All That Remains*, 350–53. Of the above-ground structures standing before the outbreak of war in 1948, only the Church of St. Anne and the Crusader citadel on the acropolis survive.

PART I: War on the Land

only a few.[25] Of particular note for the focus of this volume is that most of the fleeing residents of al-Majdal (Ashkelon) ended up becoming refugees inside Gaza, where they and their descendants have remained until the present day.[26]

During this same war, the Jordanian Arab Legion, fighting against Israeli forces on the opposing side, also destroyed many buildings in the Jewish Quarter of Jerusalem's Old City, including dozens of synagogues. The most iconic of these was the Hurva synagogue, itself constructed over the ruins of a previous incarnation erected in the fifteenth century (see figure 2 below). It would only be rebuilt decades after Israel's capture of the Old City during the 1967 Six Day War.[27]

Figure 2. The Hurva Synagogue, ca. 1933. Arab League forces demolished this Jewish place of worship following its capture of Jerusalem's Old City in 1948.

While the destruction of cultural sites and erasure of archaeological vestiges began during and immediately after the 1948 War, more recent

---

25. Khalidi, *All That Remains*, s.v.; Kadman, *Erased*. In most cases, Jewish settlements were also built on adjacent or nearby village lands.

26. See Cheal, "Refugees." Approximately 80 percent of Gaza's present population consists of refugees or descendants of refugees from towns and villages inside the current State of Israel that were forcibly depopulated in 1948.

27. Morris, *1948: A History*, 218. For additional documentation of Jordanian vandalism of the Jewish Quarter, see Azaryahu and Golan, "Photography." The newly rebuilt Hurva Synagogue was officially opened on March 15, 2010.

operations in this vein have focused on East Jerusalem, including the Old City, captured by Israel in June of 1967. Two days after that war, the Israeli government ordered the near complete destruction of the Mughrabi (Moroccan) Quarter of the Old City in order to make way for the current Western Wall Plaza (see figure 3 below). The demolition of this 700-year-old neighborhood with its 135 homes and several historic mosques began in the middle of the night, leaving 650 fleeing residents homeless and at least one person dead amid the collapsing rubble. Today, while the thousands of visitors to that plaza and its adjoining museums encounter innumerable plaques and interpretive signs harkening back to the days of Herod, Solomon, and David, they will not find a single mention of the destroyed Quarter that existed for seven centuries in Jerusalem's more recent history. It has been erased from the map.[28]

Figure 3. Upper Photo: The Mughrabi Quarter, mid-twentieth century. Lower Photo: The Mughrabi Quarter being bulldozed to make way for the Western Wall Plaza in June 1967.

---

28. See Lawler, *Under Jerusalem*, 133–46; Teller, *Nine Quarters*, 218–25.

PART I: War on the Land

Part of the destroyed Mughrabi Quarter presently lies within the archaeological park connected to the Davidson Center in an area just south of the Western Wall Plaza. As for the excavation of this site, Andrew Lawler documents how, in March 1968, Israeli archaeologist Meir Ben-Dov "secured a bulldozer and scraped away the dense layers left by a full millennium of Ottoman, Arab, and Crusader residents, remains that were sent largely unexamined to a municipal dump."[29] According to Lawler, when Ben-Dov finally reached a massive Umayyad palace complex dating to the seventh century CE, fellow archaeologist Yigael Yadin advised him to bulldoze it also.[30] Although Ben-Dov refused to do so, most of the ancient remains of this structure are presently inaccessible or lie buried under a paved plaza. By way of contrast, they are surrounded by fully open and exposed ruins from the period of the second Jewish temple, replete with detailed signage. The Muslim Umayyad palace, on the other hand, is referenced in a solitary descriptive sign whose site plan has been allowed to deteriorate to near invisibility.[31]

On the Palestinian side of things, the principal example of archaeological abuse can be seen with respect to one of the few multi-period historical sites over which they have a modicum of control: the Haram esh-Sharif ["Noble Sanctuary"]. Presently, this is the location of the iconic Dome of the Rock and Al-Aqsa Mosque, both initially built in the seventh century CE (with the latter being subsequently reconstructed numerous times). For Muslims, this thirty-five-acre complex is a holy site where the Night Journey of Muhammed took place. For Jews, on the other hand, this is the ancient location of the sacred temples of Solomon and Zerubbabel/Herod, both later destroyed by the Babylonians (586 BCE) and Romans (70 CE), respectively. To them, the site is known as the Temple Mount.[32]

Yet despite solid historical and archaeological evidence supporting the truth of this latter claim, numerous Palestinian public and religious officials have denied the past existence of the Jewish temples on the Haram. Indeed, the denial has been repeated so often that it has become almost dogma in

---

29. Lawler, *Under Jerusalem*, 142.

30. Lawler, *Under Jerusalem*, 144.

31. To the Davidson's credit, the inside of the Center now displays fragments of "A Lintel from the Umayyad Period" (as it is labeled), though the accompanying sign makes no specific mention of the massive Umayyad palace excavated below the southwest corner of the Haram/Temple Mount.

32. See Gonen, *Contested Holiness*; Mizrachi, *Temple Mount/Haram al-Sharif*. Notably, Hamas code-named their attacks of October 7, 2023, "Al-Aqsa Flood," implying their active defense of this holy site in Jerusalem. For background on Hamas's underlying theological justifications, see Munayer, *Reconciling Justice*, 152–63; and Daniel Bannoura, "Hamas and Violence," ch. 5 in the present volume.

some Muslim circles—though it has gained little traction elsewhere.[33] Such denial of the earlier history of the site eventually led to tangible archaeological damage there.

In 1999, in order to reclaim for worshipers the subterranean level of the existing Marwani mosque, the governing Islamic Waqf [Trust] used heavy equipment to remove tons of earth. However, this was no mere modern renovation project: This area on the southeast corner of the Haram/Temple Mount is also known as "Solomon's Stables." As such, it potentially held archaeological evidence from the periods of the first and second Jewish temples (as well as from the time of the Crusaders, who actually used the location as a stable). Yet since there was no archaeological oversight of the project, significant amounts of stratigraphic data were forever lost.[34]

A quarter of a century later, one might think that the use of such "bulldozer archaeology" would have long since passed into the dustbin of primitive archaeological methodologies. After all, as even the novice dig volunteer knows from the introductory lecture, "Archaeology is destruction." That is why modern archaeological excavations proceed painstakingly across each four-by-four meter square, slowly peeling away each layer. While doing this, excavators carefully document shifts in soil color and pottery deposits in order to preserve the record of each level of civilization. It goes without saying that the use of bulldozers precludes such a careful and precise methodology.

Despite this, the author himself recently witnessed the resuscitation of these crude instruments in a governmentally sanctioned "excavation" of one of the world's most sensitive historical sites: the ancient Pool of Siloam, mentioned in both the Old and New Testaments of the Bible (Isa 22:9, John 9:7).

---

33. See Gold, *Fight for Jerusalem*, 199–230.

34. See Lawler, *Under Jerusalem*, 244–47; Mizrachi, *Temple Mount/Haram al-Sharif*, 9–11. Some of the artifacts are being recovered through the volunteer-driven "Temple Mount Sifting Project," but without specific stratigraphic context. For Palestinian-inflicted damage to an Iron Age site on Mt. Ebal (north of Nablus), see Emek Shaveh, "Response."

Figure 4. A bulldozer being used to "excavate" the upper 3+ meters of the 1.25-acre site of the Pool of Siloam. Photo taken by the author on March 10, 2023, just over two months after the settler group Elad had seized the site.

On December 27, 2022, the Israeli settler group Elad, aided by police, raided land in East Jerusalem situated over top of the area believed to be part of the Pool of Siloam. Although the estate had been a Greek Orthodox Church–owned property for more than a century, the settler group alleged that they were the actual owners. And so the police forcibly evicted the Palestinian family that had been renting and cultivating the property as a fruit orchard since 1933.[35]

When I visited the site just over two months later, I was shocked by what I discovered. The settler group, under the purview of the Israel Antiquities Authority (IAA), had almost completely dug out the 1.25-acre property using bulldozers and dump trucks (see figure 4 above). From a visual inspection, the heavy equipment appeared to have dug down at least three meters below the surface of the site, displacing tons of historical evidence spanning two millennia. By modern archaeological standards, work at such an historically significant site should have required years of meticulous excavations. And yet it was dug out in just over two months.

---

35. For details concerning the eviction, see Emek Shaveh, "Alert"; Terrestrial Jerusalem, "Update"; Hasson, "Israel Razed the Last Orchard in Silwan."

A month and a half after my site visit, the Israeli newspaper *Haaretz* published a summary article about the dig bearing the title "Israel Razed the Last Orchard in Silwan in Search of Siloam Pool. It Still Can't Be Found." The article described the shock of excavators at not unearthing the Second Temple period pool they had been so earnestly seeking. That's because an adjoining plot had earlier revealed evidence of stairs leading down to the hypothesized structure. Thus Israeli archaeologist Ronny Reich, who was not involved in the dig and who also expressed his surprise at the use of bulldozers, was quoted as saying:

> I can't explain it. For years, I had wanted to dig a trench between the trees to get to answers—how far beneath the surface the pool lies and whether there are steps on the other side. Now they made a godly mess there, and we didn't get any answers, I hope that in the heat of battle, no data was lost there.[36]

That excavators failed to find the presumed presence of the ancient structure apparently matters little to the overseeing settler group. On my last visit to the site in August of 2024, workers were busy reconstructing the pool that they had expected to find from modern stone blocks, each cut to appear ancient. When completed and filled with water, this reconstructed "Pool of Siloam" will almost certainly be marketed as a crown jewel of Elad's "City of David" archaeological park nestled in the heart of the modern Palestinian village of Silwan.

The Case of Tel Hadid/Al-Haditha: A Way Forward?

Although the preceding section could be greatly expanded to include other examples of abuse in biblical archaeology,[37] it should nevertheless be sufficient to make the following point clear: each party in the Israeli-Palestinian dispute has sought through archaeological and rhetorical means to highlight its own ancestral and religious history at the expense of the other's. In far too many cases, biblical archaeology has become warfare by other means.

To consider a potentially more constructive model than those previously reviewed, we turn now to the work of Ido Koch of Tel Aviv University (TAU), director of excavations at Tel Hadid.[38] Located not far from today's

---

36. Hasson, "Israel Razed the Last Orchard."

37. See the discussion of resources from the website of the Israeli NGO Emek Shaveh on p. 171 below.

38. The contents of this section are indebted to a lecture by Dr. Koch, attended by

Ben Gurion Airport, the ancient town of Hadid is mentioned in 2 Kings 17 and elsewhere in the Bible as one of the places from which the invading Assyrians had deported the resident population in the late eighth century BCE. However, as we have seen in other instances in this essay, up until 1948 the site had also served as a Palestinian village—in this case, one named Al-Haditha. During the 1948 War, Israeli forces intentionally drove out its 900 residents, later destroying the village's existing buildings and planting pine trees over top of the ruins.[39]

Early in the TAU dig, a live hand-grenade from 1948 suddenly emerged from the top layer of an excavation square, its pin fortunately not dislodged by the chopping of the worker's pickaxe. This grenade's discovery led Koch and his fellow excavators to conclude that they could not ignore this stratum of history in their excavations, especially given the convergence of ancient and modern deportations at the site. And so Koch and his associates sought and received permission from TAU and the IAA to expand the scope of their excavations to include the remains of the destroyed village of Al-Haditha. They were eventually even awarded a four-year grant to do so.

With this all in hand, the team then did something else extraordinary: they reached out to the refugee families in Jordan, seeking to record their experiences, as well as to receive permission to excavate their former family homes at Al-Haditha. The families were at first angry and suspicious, as one might expect. But after it became clear that the excavators were looking to document the history of their village as well as their own refugee experiences, the family members began to assist in the team's work.

Obviously, the Al-Haditha/Tel Hadid project will not undo any of the injustices of the past. Nor does it constitute anything resembling a political solution that will lead to a just and lasting peace between Israelis and Palestinians. No single research project could or should bear the weight of such expectations. Nevertheless, it is a start. Moreover, it is the embodiment of what biblical archaeology and the discipline as a whole ideally seeks to do: to uncover and reconstruct histories of past societies, along with their wider contexts across time. As such, the Al-Haditha/Tel Hadid project is a welcome sea-change in archaeological methodology and a potential model for future excavations in Israel/Palestine.

---

the author, given at the W. F. Albright Institute of Archaeological Research in Jerusalem on June 15, 2023. The lecture was entitled "Home and Away: Studying the Deportations to and from the Southern Levant during the Age of the Neo-Assyrian and the Neo-Babylonian Empire." For the project description, see Tel Hadid Expedition, "Al-Haditha."

39. See Khalidi, *All That Remains*, 381.

Conclusion

This study is by no means the first to highlight the many abuses of archaeology in the Holy Land over the past eight decades.[40] Nevertheless, it has sought to place these abuses more prominently among the many grievances contributing to the outbreak of armed conflicts between Israel and Palestine, including the 2023–2025 Gaza War. As stated earlier, wars begin for reasons. One of these reasons is the suppression or even destruction of one group's cultural heritage by another. From tragic personal experience in Nazi-controlled Poland, Raphael Lemkin rightly discerned this to be true. And he devoted most of his adult life to promoting a universal respect for these and other human rights not just on behalf of the Jewish people, but for the sake of all peoples.

In a similar vein, the Israeli NGO Emek Shaveh was established in 2008 to monitor the violation of cultural heritage rights and to advocate for ethical practices in archaeology within Israel/Palestine. The organization's statement of purpose makes this clear:

> Emek Shaveh is an Israeli NGO working to defend cultural heritage rights and to protect ancient sites as public assets that belong to members of all communities, faiths and peoples. We object to the fact that the ruins of the past have become a political tool in the Israeli-Palestinian conflict and work to challenge those who use archaeological sites to dispossess disenfranchised communities. We view heritage sites as resources for building bridges and strengthening bonds between peoples and cultures and believe that archaeological sites cannot constitute proof of precedence or ownership by any one nation, ethnic group or religion over a given place.[41]

In concert with these laudable aspirations, readers of this essay can help advance these goals by embracing the following action points:

- Become informed by reading through resources on the abuses of archaeology in the Holy Land published by groups such as Emek Shaveh.

- Advocate for preserving the rich historical and cultural heritage of all ethnic and religious groups in Israel/Palestine.

---

40. E.g., Abdullah, "Century of Cultural Genocide"; Stahl, *Appropriating the Past*; Shiff, *Six Feet Under*.

41. Emek Shaveh, "About Us."

- Look beyond the highlighted archaeological remains of popular tourist and pilgrimage sites when visiting the Holy Land, inquiring about the history of other periods, especially more recent ones.
- Seek to encounter the "living stones" of the Land, the people who continue to preserve the culture and traditions associated with archaeological sites visited, so that the richness of the past can be experienced in the abundant variety of its manifestations in the present.

By committing to the above program, the conscientious reader will not only gain a greater appreciation for the wider history and culture of the Holy Land, but also help promote a greater respect and understanding between peoples of different traditions—ultimately enhancing the possibility for realizing a just and lasting peace here in this otherwise troubled and war-torn region.

Bibliography

Abdullah, Daud. "A Century of Cultural Genocide in Palestine." In *Cultural Genocide: Law, Politics, and Global Manifestations*, edited by Jeffery S. Bachman, 227–45. London: Routledge, 2019.

Al Jazeera. "A 'Cultural Genocide': Which of Gaza's Heritage Sites Have Been Destroyed?" January 14, 2024. https://www.aljazeera.com/news/2024/1/14/a-cultural-genocide-which-of-gazas-heritage-sites-have-been-destroyed.

Azaryahu, Maoz, and Arnon Golan. "Photography, Memory, and Ethnic Cleansing: The Fate of the Jewish Quarter of Jerusalem, 1948—John Phillips' Pictorial Record." *Israel Studies* 17 (2012) 62–76.

Bachman, Jeffery S. "An Historic Perspective: The Exclusion of Cultural Genocide from the Genocide Convention." In *Cultural Genocide: Law, Politics, and Global Manifestations*, edited by Jeffery S. Bachman, 45–61. London: Routledge, 2019.

Binder, Donald D. *Into the Temple Courts: The Place of the Synagogues in the Second Temple Period.* Atlanta: SBL, 1999.

Blue Shield International. "Current Events in Israel and Palestine." October 30, 2023. https://theblueshield.org/current-events-in-israel-and-palestine/.

Cheal, Beryl. "Refugees in the Gaza Strip, December 1948–May 1950." *Journal of Palestinian Studies* 18 (1988) 138–57.

Emek Shaveh. "About Us." https://emekshaveh.org/en/about-us/.

———. "Alert: Border Police with Settlers Raided Plots of Land This Morning in Silwan near Pool of Siloam." December 27, 2023. https://emekshaveh.org/en/pool-of-siloam/.

———. "Response to the Destruction of Antiquities at the Iron Age Site of Mount Ebal/el-Burnat." February 17, 2021. https://emekshaveh.org/en/mount-ebal-el-burnat/.

———. "Susya: The Displacement of Residents Following the Discovery of an Ancient Synagogue." September 12, 2016. https://emekshaveh.org/en/susiya-2016/.

Gold, Dove. *The Fight for Jerusalem: Radical Islam, the West, and the Future of the Holy City*. Washington, DC: Regnery, 2007.

Gonen, Rivka. *Contested Holiness: Jewish, Muslim, and Christian Perspective on the Temple Mount in Jerusalem*. Jersey City, NJ: Ktav, 2003.

Hasson, Nir. "Israel Razed the Last Orchard in Silwan in Search of Siloam Pool. It Still Can't Be Found." *Haaretz*, April 28, 2023. https://www.haaretz.com/israel-news/2023-4-28/ty-article-magazine/.highlight/israel-razed-the-last-orchard-in-silwan-in-search-of-siloam-pool-it-still-cant-be-found/00000187-c6d0-d9b4-abaf-eefe23910000.

International Court of Justice. "Advisory Opinion on Legal Consequences Arising from the Policies and Practices of Israel in the Occupied Palestinian Territory, Including East Jerusalem." July 19, 2024. https://www.un.org/unispal/document/advisory-opinion-icj-19jul24/.

Israel Nature and Parks Authority. "World Heritage Sites." https://en.parks.org.il/article/world-heritage-sites/.

The Jerusalem Post. "S. Africa Chief Rabbi Slams Pope, Archbishop of Canterbury over Israel." August 27, 2024. https://www.jpost.com/diaspora/article-816638.

Kadman, Noga. *Erased from Space and Consciousness: Israel and the Depopulated Palestinian Villages of 1948*. Bloomington: Indiana University Press, 2015.

Khalidi, Walid. *All That Remains: The Palestinian Villages Occupied and Depopulated by Israel in 1948*. Washington, DC: Institute for Palestine Studies, 1992.

Lawler, Andrew. *Under Jerusalem: The Buried History of the World's Most Contested City*. New York: Doubleday, 2021.

Lemkin, Raphael. *Axis Rule in Occupied Europe: Analysis, Proposals for Redress*. Washington, DC: Carnegie Endowment for International Peace, 1944.

Maeir, Aren. "Biblical Archaeology." *Oxford Classical Dictionary*. https://oxfordre.com/classics/view/10.1093/acrefore/9780199381135.001.0001/acrefore-9780199381135-e-8308.

Magness, Jodi. *Jerusalem Through the Ages: From Its Beginnings to the Crusades*. New York: Oxford University Press, 2024.

Middle East Eye. "War on Gaza: Important Archaeological Site 'Mostly Destroyed' by Israeli Invasion." December 19, 2023. https://www.middleeasteye.net/news/war-gaza-important-archaeological-site-destroyed-israeli-invasion.

Mizrachi, Yonathan. *The Temple Mount/Haram al-Sharif—Archaeology in a Political Context*. Jerusalem: Emek Shaveh, 2017.

Morris, Benny. *1948: A History of the First Arab-Israeli War*. New Haven, CT: Yale University Press, 2008.

Munayer, Salim J. *Reconciling Justice: Concepts of Justice in the Multireligious Context of Palestine/Israel*. Eugene, OR: Cascade, 2024.

Runesson, Anders, et al. *The Ancient Synagogue from Its Origins to 200 CE: A Source Book*. Leiden: Brill, 2008.

Schechla, Joseph. "Forced Eviction as an Increment of Demographic Manipulation." *Environment and Urbanization* 6 (1994) 89–105.

Shai, Aron. "The Fate of Abandoned Arab Villages in Israel, 1965–1969." *History and Memory* 18 (2006) 86–106.

Shiff, Chimi. *Six Feet Under: The Cultural Heritage of Minorities in Jerusalem*. Jerusalem: Emek Shaveh, 2019.

Stahl, Ziv. *Appropriating the Past: Israel's Archaeological Practices in the West Bank.* Jerusalem: Emek Shaveh, 2017.

Tel Hadid Expedition. "Al-Haditha: A Historical–Archaeological Study of a Depopulated Arab Village." https://hadidexpedition.org/al-haditha-a-historical-archaeological-study-of-a-depopulated-arab-village/.

Teller, Matthew. *Nine Quarters of Jerusalem: A New Biography of the Old City.* London: Profile, 2022.

Terrestrial Jerusalem. "Update: An Important Breaking Development in Silwan." December 27, 2022. https://t-j.org.il/2022/12/27/update-an-important-breaking-development-in-silwan/.

The Times of Israel. "69 Years After Joining, Israel Formally Leaves UNESCO; So, Too, Does the US." January 1, 2019. https://www.timesofisrael.com/69-years-after-joining-israel-formally-leaves-un-cultural-body/.

———. "Gaza's Archaeology Experts Say Enclave's Historic Treasures Saved by 'Irony of History.'" April 15, 2024. https://www.timesofisrael.com/gazas-archaeology-experts-say-enclaves-historic-treasures-saved-by-irony-of-history/.

Treharne, Michael, et al. "Christian Leaders Criticise Justin Welby's 'Unbiblical' Statement on Israel." *Premier Christianity*, August 12, 2024. https://www.premierchristianity.com/opinion/exclusive-christian-leaders-criticise-justin-welbys-unbiblical-statement-on-israel/18056.article.

UNESCO. "Convention Concerning the Protection of the World Cultural and Natural Heritage." Adopted November 16, 1972, Paris. https://whc.unesco.org/en/conventiontext/.

———. "Convention for the Protection of Cultural Property in the Event of Armed Conflict with Regulations for the Execution of the Convention." Adopted May 14, 1954, The Hague. https://www.unesco.org/en/legal-affairs/convention-protection-cultural-property-event-armed-conflict-regulations-execution-convention?hub=415#item-1.

———. "[First] Protocol to the Convention for the Protection of Cultural Property in the Event of Armed Conflict." Adopted May 14, 1954, The Hague. https://www.unesco.org/en/legal-affairs/protocol-convention-protection-cultural-property-event-armed-conflict?hub=66535.

———. "Second Protocol to the Hague Convention of 1954 for the Protection of Cultural Property in the Event of Armed Conflict." Adopted March 26, 1999, The Hague. https://www.unesco.org/en/legal-affairs/second-protocol-hague-convention-1954-protection-cultural-property-event-armed-conflict?hub=66535.

Welby, Justin. "Archbishop of Canterbury Statement on the ICJ's Advisory Opinion on Israel and the Occupied Palestinian Territories." August 2, 2024. https://www.archbishopofcanterbury.org/news/news-and-statements/archbishop-canterbury-statement-icjs-advisory-opinion-israel-and-occupied.

PART II

The Bible and the Land

Listening for God's Voice in the Tempest

CHAPTER EIGHT

How Can We Sing the Lord's Song?

LISA LODEN

FOR FIFTY YEARS MY home has been the land of Israel/Palestine, a land that has been in conflict longer than I have lived. Over centuries, this conflict has become deeply embedded in the memories, hopes, dreams, and lives of those who call this land their home. Together with my husband, both of us Jews who believe in Jesus, I immigrated to Israel in 1974. Many who regard this land as their "ancestral" homeland are not currently residing here. This is for a variety of reasons, including the millions of Jews who choose to live outside of Israel, the expulsion of hundreds of thousands of Palestinians between 1947 and April 1949, and for both peoples, emigration, economic issues, and the seventy-year plus intractable conflict between the two peoples who claim indigeneity in the land of their forefathers.

For me, a Jewish believer in Jesus who chose to immigrate to Israel, both peoples are my people. From childhood, I have had a sense of being a part of the entire human race. The image of God is present in all of humanity. For that reason, I see all people as my people. We are united at the core of our being. Although our lives differ in many ways, the suffering of Israelis and Palestinians is that of my people. Hence, my life in this land and my identity are a multicolored mosaic. For the past fifty years I have prayed, wept, worked, and advocated for reconciliation within the Body of Christ in this divided land. What follows stems from and is embedded in this perspective.

The focus of this chapter is the Israel-Hamas war that began on October 7, 2023, and the struggle to know how to respond to the devastation that this war has caused in the lives of the two peoples in this land.

Remembering October 7, 2023

October 7 will forever be etched in the minds and hearts of the Jewish and Palestinian people. Like the destruction of the Twin Towers in New York City or the assassinations of John F. Kennedy and Yitzhak Rabin, it is one of those exceptional days when millions will remember where they were when they first heard the report of the massacre that inaugurated the Israel-Hamas war.

The Israel-Hamas war has cast its shadow over the entire globe and has personally affected the lives of all who live in Israel and Palestine. The title of this chapter is taken from Ps 137:4. "How shall we sing the Lord's song?" continues with the words "in a strange land." The land of Israel/Palestine has become a land lacerated by war, covered in loss, grief, and trauma. This land has become unrecognizable, a strange land from which arise cries for justice, mercy, and revenge.

On October 7, my husband and I sat down for an early breakfast at 6:30. I turned to him and asked a question. "Do you think we are close to having a war? Is it imminent or still distant?" We spoke for a few minutes, and he said, "I think it isn't imminent, but it is close." After finishing breakfast, we left for a gathering of Messianic Jewish and Arab Christian families for a day of joint activities and teaching. We were looking forward to seeing old friends and making new ones. We arrived at eight and began preparing for the day.

Families began to slowly trickle in. By around ten o'clock, the numbers were still small. Some of us were preparing activities and food for the day. The children were outside playing together. Then sirens began shrieking. We watched missiles streaking overhead. The village administration came and told us that we would have to leave and that something was happening in the south. Everyone, children and adults, gathered inside. Someone picked up a guitar, and we began to sing these words in Hebrew and Arabic: "God is our refuge and strength, a very present help in trouble" (Ps 46:2).[1] We wept together, shared hugs as brothers and sisters, and left without knowing the scope of what was happening in the south.

---

1. Unless otherwise stated, all biblical quotations are taken from the New American Standard Bible 1995.

While we had been singing, thousands of Hamas fighters were invading Southern Israel beginning in the early morning hours. They murdered 1,139 men, women, and children and abducted approximately 250 others.[2] Israel retaliated the same day, declaring a war of self-defense and placing a total siege on the 2.3 million inhabitants of the Gaza Strip. On October 28, the Israel Defense Forces (IDF) launched the "Operation Iron Swords" war and invaded the Gaza Strip.

On October 13, less than a week after Hamas's attack, I was compelled to compose the following reflection. I knew I had to make it public. I am a poet, and this piece flowed like a stream of living fire.

Under the Shadow of Death

> In the shade of the mango tree,
> beside the rosebush,
> stands an ancient plowshare,
> a symbol of peace
> created from forged iron.
> Perhaps it was once iron swords.
>
> Under the lengthening shadow of death
> live seventeen million Israelis, Gazans, Palestinians,
> divided by impenetrable walls.
> Walls of suspicion, hatred, fear.
> Grief and suffering stalk their streets.
>
> At the Gazan border, by the sea,
> untold thousands, soldiers,
> stand ready to invade.
> A million ordered to evacuate.
> Each one a mother, father,
> brother, sister, daughter, son.
>
> The dream of peaceful plowshares,
> scent of roses, redolence of ripe mango
> obliterated by smoke, shrapnel
> and ash, fallen on once holy ground,
> stained now by death's red shadow,
> and the double-sided stab of iron swords.

---

2. *France 24*, "Israel Social Security Data Reveals True Picture."

What do we see when we see the faces, when we look into the eyes of the "other?" Do we see the Gazan mother fleeing with her children, the dead children downed by bombs or massacred in their beds, the lost youth of both peoples growing up with the legacy of war upon war upon war, or the pilots who rained death from the skies on defenseless people, or the soldier faced with the impossible choice to protect or kill? What do we see?

I cannot discern the difference. Israeli, Arab, Palestinian, Jew, Christian, Muslim, secular, religious, men, women. We are all one, all human, members of the vast and beautiful human family. We stand this day, divided, sundered by the forces of hatred, fear, pride, and our common need to survive.

What will be the cost of this war? Will it be the hearts and minds of our youth, the calcification of our views about the "other"—us the Jews and them the other, us the Arabs and them the other? Will it be the end of peace, the further distancing of citizens—Jewish and Arab, left and right, secular and religious, Jewish/Christian/Muslim, after we've "won" another war?

As I write these words, we are on the threshold of an irrevocable decision. Yes, Israel has the right to defend itself. In this current operation, entitled "Iron Swords," Israel has already rained death and destruction on thousands of innocent citizens, and wounded thousands more. Will it ever be enough to erase the multiplying trauma? There is no balance in this equation, nor has there ever been. Today, to "eradicate" the enemy at any cost, Israel has justified all further civilian deaths for those who may yet choose to remain in Gaza. We've denied them the basic necessities of food, water, and electricity for days. There are no machines to dig through the rubble, to rescue any who may yet be alive. And time is passing.... How long can they live under the rubble of war? How long can we live in the rubble of war?

There is no exit, there are no shelters, all borders are closed, one million people are "advised" to evacuate to nowhere. And we pride ourselves on our humanitarian stance to warn them of the imminent devastation of their world.

Our war is not with flesh and blood but with the powers of darkness that seek to destroy. The wrath of man never works the will of God.

In the words of journalist Nicholas Kristof: "If we owe a moral responsibility to Israeli children, then we owe the same moral responsibility to Palestinian children. Their lives have equal weight." And "If you care about human life only in Israel or only in Gaza, then you don't actually care about human life."[3]

> We, the most privileged of all,
> we who know the grace,
> the mercy of the living God,
> called to walk in love,
> to do justice, to love mercy,
> to walk humbly with our God.
> What will we do this day?
> Will we weep? Will we lament?
> Will we rejoice in victory?
> Will we cry out for life?
> Will we choose to see
> the open wounds of our Saviour,
> bleeding still for all his children?

The Aftermath of October 7

Israel chose to invade Gaza, and the trajectory of war was set. One year later, the words I wrote on October 13 are as true today as they were then. Nothing, except the increase of carnage, has changed. The Gaza Strip continues to be occupied by the IDF, and it is attacked daily by ground, air, and sea forces. The air attacks use guided missiles that can carry bombs weighing up to two thousand pounds and drones with smaller loads; this is in addition to the street battles between Hamas fighters and Israeli soldiers. Of the 251 hostages who were taken to Gaza, 146 have been released or rescued, and those remaining alive are estimated to be fewer than twenty-five.[4] They and their captors are my people.

At various times throughout this war, over one thousand Israeli believers in Jesus were called up into military service. Throughout the Israel-Hamas war, the IDF has also been engaged in an exchange of fire with Hezbollah on the Lebanese border. Israeli believers serve on both fronts. I cannot imagine what they see. I am friends with some of their mothers who have had one child serving in Gaza and another on the northern border with Lebanon. They are my brothers and sisters.

At the onset of the war, North Gaza was the focal point. This area was home to one of the oldest Christian communities in the world. Before

---

3. Kristof, "Moral Compass."
4. Bisset et al., "Hamas Took 251 Hostages."

October 7, this small group was a vibrant worshiping community, with approximately one thousand Orthodox, Catholic, and Protestant Christians living in harmony with their Muslim neighbors. In previous wars, Israel had not targeted the Christian area in North Gaza. This time, the area was a major target for the IDF, and much of the area was destroyed by the Israeli forces. The majority of Gazan Christians took refuge in the churches. Fewer than six hundred Christians remain. Those who were able to do so have left Gaza, and at least thirty have died. They are my brothers and sisters.

As of April 3, 2025, approximately two million Gazans have repeatedly been displaced internally, and 92 percent of the housing units have been destroyed or damaged.[5] A reported 53,523 have been killed (including at least 15,613 children)[6] and 114,776 have been wounded, the majority by IDF air and ground forces. A year and a half later, the devastation and loss continue unabated, with no end in sight. Israeli sources report a total of more than 6,600 casualties in Israel from October 7. This number includes 1,162 identified fatalities, of which at least 33 were children, and approximately 5,400 wounded. In addition, 407 soldiers have been killed in Gaza and 2,584 wounded. An estimated 58 hostages remain in Gaza, either dead or still in confinement. The number of casualties climbs daily. Israel and Hamas are both determined to win this war. Hamas militants were well prepared, and although weakened they continue to prevent the "total victory" that the Israeli war machine determinedly seeks.

In the context of the Israel-Hamas war, suffering is a constant theme. The entire populations of both Israel and Palestine have been upended. In the early months of the war, one million Israeli soldiers were uprooted from their lives, homes, and families and conscripted into active duty. Many did not return home for up to six months. Approximately 250,000 Israelis have been internally displaced in hotels in the center of Israel while their homes in the borderlands are undergoing daily attacks by missiles coming from Hamas in the south, Hezbollah in the north, and even from the Houthis in Yemen. All of the Gazan population remains under massive attack. The situation is volatile, and food shortages are a major problem. Access to what humanitarian aid Israel allows into the enclave is often delayed by Israeli military protocol. The residents of northern Gaza were ordered to vacate

---

5. Statistics in the paragraph are taken from UN Office for the Coordination of Humanitarian Affairs "Reported Impact Snapshot," and World Health Organization: Occupied Palestinian Territory, "Casualties." In the main, Gaza numbers come from the Gaza Ministry of Health and Israeli numbers from Israeli media citing government sources.

6. In February 2024, UNICEF estimated that at least 17,000 children were unaccompanied or separated from their families ("Stories of Loss and Grief").

and go south through a "humanitarian corridor" that was often randomly attacked by the Israeli air force.[7]

Since October 7, 2023, Palestinians resident in the West Bank have frequently and for long periods been prohibited from crossing the separation barrier. The result has been extreme economic suffering for the thousands of families who before the war were employed in Israel. In addition, Israeli settlers have mobilized militias that have attacked Palestinian villages, leaving devastation in their wake. The IDF has mobilized battalions of soldiers to clamp down on any suspected "terrorists." By October 7, 2024, Israeli authorities had "destroyed, confiscated, sealed or forced the demolition of 1,777 Palestinian structures across the West Bank, including East Jerusalem, displacing more than 4,574 Palestinians, including about 1,919 children," and the number of West Bank Palestinians killed by the IDF or by Israeli settlers since October 7, 2023, had risen to 719 persons.[8]

Brief Historical Context

Today, Israel is governed by the most extreme right-wing coalition in its history. Israel has a mixed citizen population of 73 percent Jews, 6 percent undifferentiated others, and 21 percent Arabs, many of whom choose to be identified as Israeli Palestinians. During the year prior to the outbreak of the Israel-Hamas war, the country had been experiencing social division and upheaval that resulted in massive demonstrations protesting the government's attempt to pass undemocratic legislation. The war temporarily stopped the demonstrations. As the war continues, protests and anti-government demonstrations have resumed, joined by massive crowds demonstrating against the government's failure to secure the hostages' return.

The Israel-Hamas war is but one of the many wars between Israel and Palestine since the foundation of Israel as a secular state in 1948. Nothing happens in a vacuum, and there is a history behind every conflict. It lies

---

7. Relief Web, "Pauses."

8. UN Office for the Coordination of Humanitarian Affairs, "Humanitarian Situation." On April 3, 2025, the UN High Commissioner for Human Rights reported, "Israeli operations in the northern West Bank [Jan.–Feb. 2025] have killed hundreds of people, destroyed entire refugee camps and makeshift medical sites, and displaced over 40,000 Palestinians. . . . Since 7 October 2023, my Office has verified that State and settler violence has killed 909 Palestinians across the West Bank, including 191 children and 5 people with disabilities, some of which may amount to extrajudicial and other unlawful killings. In the same period, 51 Israelis, including 15 women and 4 children, were killed in Palestinian attacks or armed clashes, 33 in the West Bank and 18 in Israel" ("Türk Warns UN Security Council").

beyond the scope of this chapter to give an extensive overview of the history of the relationship between Israel and Palestine. However, a few words can capture the character of this history: exile and return, Nakba, military occupation, status, settlement, colonialism, promise, loss, and suffering. The two peoples living side by side have much in common, the experience of loss being one of the most pervasive common denominators. Both peoples have suffered much in the years since the modern Jewish immigration and settlement of what was then officially known as Palestine. Before 1948, Palestinian identity cards and passports were issued to both Jews who had settled in the land and Arabs who were already residents in the land of Israel/Palestine.

Since the signing of the Oslo II agreement in 1995, the 5.5 million Palestinians who live in the Palestinian Territories (the West Bank and Gaza Strip)[9] do not have a recognized state and are governed by several authorities. Oslo II divided the Palestinian Territories into three distinct units. Area A, comprising the Gaza Strip and 17 percent of the West Bank, is under full Palestinian control (the Palestinian Authority has oversight of the West Bank, and since 2007 Gaza has been governed by Hamas). Area B is under shared Israeli and Palestinian control and covers approximately 25 percent of the West Bank. Area C is under full Israeli control. It comprises East Jerusalem and the largest portion of the West Bank, including 700,000 Israelis living in over 300 settlements,[10] 200 of which are illegal.[11] The pursuit of citizenship and the recognition of Palestinian status as a nation remains an unrealized dream.

What Is the Lord's Song?

Given the reality described here, how can we sing the Lord's song? Indeed, what *is* the Lord's song? In these dark times, numerous questions occupy the hearts and minds of many. "Where is God?" is the underlying cry heard echoing across seventy years of intractable conflict and ten months of inconceivable war.

For those who have faith in the God of the Bible, the Bible is life and truth for all creation. The Bible, particularly the book of Psalms, contains

---

9. Worldometer, "State of Palestine Population."

10. According to International Law, all the settlements are illegal. However, Israel officially recognizes 146 of them as "legal." In addition, there are 224 "illegal" settlements: 119 "outposts" and 105 "farm outposts." Israel regularly recognizes numbers of these illegal settlements, thereby giving them legal status.

11. Robinson, "Who Governs the Palestinians?"

many different types of song: love, praise, thanksgiving, worship, lament, and protest. Depending on the situation, God's people sing different songs. However, close to 50 percent of the biblical Psalms are songs of individual and corporate lament or protest.[12] The prophets and poets lived in difficult times, and their writings contain many songs of lament. For example, the entire second book of Jeremiah, Lamentations, is (as the name suggests) a book of laments.

Just as our forefathers in biblical times questioned God, so do we in these dark times. Since the first day of this war, Israelis and Palestinians alike have been living in a land that has suddenly become strange, where it seems impossible to sing the Lord's song. Daily we lament the ongoing loss. We grieve with all those who mourn the loss of life, health, and property, and we grieve for the devastation and hopelessness of this war. My peoples stand divided, with both claiming the rightness of their positions. The same holds true for many within the worldwide Christian community. This is seen in their rhetoric and participation in pro- or anti-Israel and pro- or anti-Palestinian demonstrations around the world.

Lament in times of uncertainty, suffering, and war is a profound reaction to the evil, injustice, and suffering that surrounds and threatens to overwhelm. It is a very human response. Lament tells it like it is. Lament is most often a cry wrenched from the hearts of those who suffer injustice. The laments of Job, Elijah, and Jeremiah expressed their deep anguish in terms that resonate throughout human history. Where is God? Why is this happening?

However, lament, whether personal or corporate, is incomplete if it only decries evil, injustice, and suffering. Biblical laments end with a declaration of hope and trust in the face of anguish, uncertainty, and darkness where, to all appearances, God is absent or, worse, uncaring. Lament, without hope, offers no answers.

For those, especially Christians, who believe in a God of mercy and compassion, the ongoing Israel-Hamas war is intolerable. Christian responses to this war have divided the Body of Christ. This is true in both Israel and Palestine as believers passionately embrace one side—their side—and strongly advocate for it. Both sides rightly lament the horrendous situation and grieve the results of this war—for their "own people." Relationships forged over decades have become dormant at best and, at worst, are being shattered beyond recovery.

Within the Body of Christ in Israel and Palestine, the polarization and division are an open wound. In May 2024, my husband and I were the only

---

12. Sweeney, *TANAK*, 377.

Jewish believers in Jesus present at the *Christ at the Checkpoint* conference hosted by Palestinian Christians in Bethlehem. Standing against much censure from some of our Israeli Messianic brothers and sisters and others who hold to a Christian Zionist political stance, we chose to join our Palestinian brothers and sisters. We love them. Their pain is ours.

Although lament alone is not enough in the midst of suffering, we cannot but lament. Neither can we stand silent in the face of evil and injustice. We must let our voices be heard. At the same time, we can choose to trust and believe that God is present. Jesus is our Suffering Savior. There is a reason that Jesus' wounds remained open after his resurrection when he appeared to his grieving disciples. He bears his wounds into eternity. He suffers with us, not just for us. He is present in Gaza with the refugees as they are evacuated time and again from "safe places." He is with each child who no longer has a home. He is with those in Palestine whose hearts grieve for the loss of livelihood and who mourn for their families in Gaza. He is with the displaced and homeless in Israel. He is with the hostages and their grieving families. He is with all who mourn and all who suffer.

Toward a Theology of Suffering and Hope

From the first day of the Israel-Hamas war, I knew two things. First, there was nothing good about this war. And second, every individual would need to find their own way to endure what was to come. What was once familiar has become incomprehensible. The shock and horror of the suffering of both peoples was and remains overwhelming. How was I to relate to this? Could I sing any song, much less the Lord's song, in the midst of such suffering?

Suffering is not something one would choose to endure. Yet it is an inseparable part of what it means to be human and to be a follower of Jesus. The scriptures repeatedly inform us that suffering is an ever-present reality in a fallen world. The New Testament makes it clear that God has not only destined us to suffer (1 Pet 4:1, 12–18, 1 Thess 3:2–4) but has also borne our suffering in himself (Isa 53:4). Jesus, Peter, Paul, and James all speak of the reality of suffering, its purpose and its meaning (John 16:22, 33; 1 Pet 2:19–21, 4:12–14; Rom 5:3, 8:18, 35, Jas 1:2–4). Rather than deny or escape the inevitable, we need to embrace a theology of suffering.

Suffering is a generic word that holds many meanings. It is not a concept that can be abstracted from the reality of life as a human being. Suffering is up close and personal, whether it is individual or collective. Suffering engages the whole person, and each person's experience is unique. No one is immune. Suffering makes us vulnerable; it challenges and changes us.

Jesus was no stranger to suffering. His life was that of an itinerant, homeless teacher without "a place to lay his head" (Matt 8:20). He was vilified and rejected by those in power, and his final journey was through inner anguish so intense that he "sweat drops of blood" (Luke 22:44). His death on the cross entailed physical and emotional suffering beyond anything we will ever experience. We who know and love God are called to follow this "man of suffering who is acquainted with grief" (Isa 53:3).

Jesus invites each one who desires to follow him to "deny himself, and daily take up his cross" (Luke 9:23). This is not a suggestion nor is it a command; it is an invitation to surrender one's life and follow God's often inscrutable ways. Our Father who gave his only son to suffer death invites us into his suffering, the suffering of Jesus; to walk with him in the dark places of our world, to identify with him, and to share his suffering.

As a very young believer, I passionately wanted to know my Savior, the one who gave his life for me. I earnestly prayed "that I may know Him and the power of His resurrection and the fellowship of His sufferings, being conformed to His death" (Phil 3:10). At that time, I had no idea what I was asking. Over the years, he has answered my prayer in ways I could not have comprehended. The experience of the Israel-Hamas war has deepened my understanding of what this verse implies, "Christ also suffered for you, leaving you an example for you to follow in His steps" (1 Pet 2:21).

As I follow Jesus in this context, suffering is in the air I breathe. The land is strange and the air is toxic. The Lord's song has become a requiem for the dead. Those who are not on the front lines suffer the pain, fear, anger, grief, violence, and hatred that pollute the trauma-laden atmosphere. The injustice, the devastation of an entire population, the erosion of all moral standards, religious extremists on both sides cursing the infidels, and a mad government resolved to "win" a war at any cost—all militate against a speedy end to the suffering. Suffering doesn't lend itself to analysis. It is often mysterious. And yet it has power to transform.

Only by living in the power of the resurrection can we endure suffering. This is our hope. A theology of suffering is incomplete without an adjacent theology of hope. When one is suffering, the need is to understand and make sense of the reasons, and the dynamics of the question "Where is God?" The enigma of how he, who is all-powerful, a God of mercy and justice, can be at the heart of our struggle to discern how to respond in this war.

Of the three things that remain—faith, hope, and love (1 Cor 13:13)—hope is often neglected. These three qualities are rooted in the character of God. We know that "without faith it is impossible to please God" (Heb

11:6), and we confess that "love is the greatest of them all" (1 Cor 13:13). Why, then, do we need hope?

Biblical hope differs greatly from hope as it is commonly understood. According to the dictionary, to hope is "to want something to happen or be true and think that it could happen or be true." As a noun, hope is "the feeling of wanting something to happen and thinking that it could happen: a feeling that something good will happen or be true."[13] According to this understanding, hope is a feeling and a desire for something positive to happen.

Biblical hope, in contrast, is a certainty that is not conditional, nor is it dependent on external circumstances. The words translated as "hope" from Hebrew and Greek describe a process of waiting, expectation, and trust in God. Hope in God is founded on the reality of his character and his promises. Biblical hope, by definition, looks to the future. Hope maintains that, regardless of present suffering, our future is assured (Heb 11:1).

Hope is essential for all who have faith in God and have chosen the way of love. Jesus's life, death, and resurrection demonstrate that hope will endure despite the circumstances. One of Jesus's last words, spoken from the cross, instilled hope in a convicted thief who was awaiting death.[14] Jesus spoke to this condemned man and told him that they would be together in paradise that same day (Luke 23:43).

The New Testament, particularly the letters to the early churches and the book of Revelation, repeatedly remind the church of a promised future, encouraging them in times of suffering. Hope looks beyond the present and sees a future that is glorious and secure (Jer 29:11). In this life, hope is meant to be as active as faith and love. Using a soldier's metaphor, Paul advised the Thessalonians to put on the hope of salvation as a helmet, and faith and love as a breastplate (1 Thess 5:8). The allusion to armor resonates with Paul's instructions to the Ephesians. They were enjoined to put on the whole armor of God, being reminded that the enemies they faced were (and are) rulers, powers, world forces of darkness, and spiritual forces of wickedness in the heavenly places (Eph 6:11–12). Our enemies are not people; rather they are the powers of evil that run rampant in this world. People are to be loved, and the powers of evil are to be resisted.

In times of war, the struggle to make sense of what is happening can eclipse the basic truth that faith, hope, and love remain. Of these three,

---

13. *Britannica Dictionary*, "Hope."

14. Given our context, it is worth noting that some would have called this thief (*lēstēs*), like Barabbas "who had committed murder in the insurrection" (Mark 15:7), a "terrorist," and others a "freedom fighter."

love and faith are given to us by grace to live our daily lives. Hope leads us beyond the visible and enables us to endure suffering.

As I ask, "Where is God?" amid unspeakable horror, and as I ponder how God can let the carnage of this war continue in my land, hope has become my anchor. Without hope—without the secure knowledge that what I see with my eyes and experience in the depths of prayer, supplication, and lament is not all there is—I would be shipwrecked. I've learned to pick up the anchor of hope and thrust it into the deep sea of suffering. I have learned a new song in the raging storm of this war. Hope in the midst of suffering has taught me that there is another song, a song that remains for eternity. I can sing this song and let it be heard because it is his. This is the Lord's song in a strange land.

Bibliography

Bisset, Victoria, et al. "Hamas Took 251 Hostages from Israel into Gaza. Where Are They?" *The Washington Post*, updated May 13, 2025. https://www.washingtonpost.com/world/interactive/hamas-hostages-israel-war-gaza/.

The Britannica Dictionary. "Hope." Encyclopædia Britannica, Inc., 2024. https://www.britannica.com/dictionary/hope.

France 24. "Israel Social Security Data Reveals True Picture of October 7 Deaths." December 15, 2023. https://www.france24.com/en/live-news/20231215-israel-social-security-data-reveals-true-picture-of-oct-7-deaths.

Kristof, Nicholas. "Seeking a Moral Compass in Gaza's War." *The New York Times*, October 12, 2023. https://www.nytimes.com/2023/10/11/opinion/israel-gaza-hamas.html.

ReliefWeb. "Pauses, Corridors, and Safe Zones in Gaza: Rhetoric vs. Reality." November 22, 2023. https://reliefweb.int/report/occupied-palestinian-territory/pauses-corridors-and-safe-zones-gaza-rhetoric-vs-reality.

Robinson, Kali. "Who Governs the Palestinians?" Council on Foreign Relations, May 28, 2024. https://www.cfr.org/backgrounder/who-governs-palestinians.

Sweeney, Marvin. *TANAK: A Theological and Critical Introduction to the Jewish Bible*. Minneapolis: Fortress, 2011.

UNICEF. "Stories of Loss and Grief: At Least 17,000 Children Are Estimated to Be Unaccompanied or Separated from Their Parents in the Gaza Strip." February 2, 2024. https://www.unicef.org/press-releases/stories-loss-and-grief-least-17000-children-are-estimated-be-unaccompanied-or.

United Nations Office for the Coordination of Humanitarian Affairs. "Humanitarian Situation Update #228: West Bank. October 10, 2024." https://www.ochaopt.org/content/humanitarian-situation-update-228-west-bank.

———. "Reported Impact Snapshot: Gaza Strip (3 April 2025)." https://www.ochaopt.org/content/reported-impact-snapshot-gaza-strip-3-april-2025.

United Nations Office of the High Commissioner for Human Rights. "Türk Warns UN Security Council of Increasing Risk of Atrocity Crimes Being Committed in the Occupied Palestinian Territory." April 3, 2025. https://www.ohchr.org/en/statements-and-speeches/2025/04/turk-warns-un-security-council-increasing-risk-atrocity-crimes-opt.

Worldometer. "State of Palestine Population (Live)." https://www.worldometers.info/world-population/state-of-palestine-population.

World Health Organization: Occupied Palestinian Territory. "Casualties: Conflict-related Direct Casualties as Reported by the Palestinian Ministry of Health (since the 7th of October 2023)." Updated Wednesday, April 2, 2025. https://app.powerbi.com/view?r=eyJrIjoiODAxNTYzMDYtMjQ3YS00OTMzLTkxMWQtOTU1NWEwMzE5NTMwIiwidCI6ImY2MTBjMGI3LWJkMjQtNGIzOS04MTBiLTNkYzI4MGFmYjU5MCIsImMiOjh9.

CHAPTER NINE

Theologizing and De-theologizing Genocide

Yousef Kamal AlKhouri

Genocide is arguably the most horrific crime in the history of humanity.[1] Its trauma moves across generations.[2] Genocide becomes even worse when legitimized and justified theologically and biblically. In this essay I showcase the ways Israel, as a Zionist settler-colonial project,[3] has invoked biblical stories to justify its genocide in Gaza. Those stories have become

---

1. Some would debate which is worse, crimes against humanity or genocide; nevertheless, both crimes constitute gross violations of the sacredness of human life and of international law. See Ratner, "Can We Compare Evils?"

2. Genocide results in cross-generational trauma to victims and their children. Darya Rostam Ahmed, "From Holocaust to Anfal," describes inter- and cross-generational trauma and PTSD evident among Kurds in Iraq during—and even years after—the genocide. See also Wyatt, "Intergenerational Trauma."

3. Some object to calling Israel "settler-colonial" because Jews claim to have a religious connection to the land of Palestine. Others argue that a settler-colonial project must erase the entire native population in order to succeed. See Shah, "Is Israel a 'Settler-Colonial' State?" Nevertheless, the majority of Zionist Jews are Europeans, colonizers or refugees who migrated to Palestine in the nineteenth and twentieth centuries. The cases of North America and South Africa show that settler-colonialism need not eliminate the entire native population to succeed. Scholars of settler-colonial studies such as Lorenzo Veracini ("Other Shift") and Rashid Khalidi (*Hundred Years' War on Palestine*) make a compelling case that Israel has the character and politics of a settler-colonial project.

the metanarrative[4] by means of which Zionists and their Christian Zionist supporters theologize the ongoing mass-slaughter of the Palestinian people. First, however, it is an imperative to name the un-named and define what is being debated and denied, namely, the genocide itself. I also explore the context of Palestine with an eye on the stories of two other contexts. The first is Turtle Island, the indigenous name for North America, whose native peoples share a history of victimization by settler-colonial regimes. The second is Rwanda, which is still recovering from the genocide of 1994. Like the natives of Turtle Island and the Hutu and Tutsi of Rwanda, Palestinians have suffered under the weight of abusive biblical metanarratives constructed to undergird ideologies of domination and extermination. The primary question this essay aims to answer is: How have Zionism and the Christian Zionist lobby turned biblical stories into a blueprint for genocide and made God its mastermind?

During the early weeks of Israel's genocidal campaign in Gaza, after days of telecommunication outages, I had a phone call with my family, who are native to and still resident in the coastal strip. The magnitude of destruction, fear, starvation, and death had shaken them to the core. My elderly parents were describing the horrors they had witnessed when one of my relatives interrupted our conversation to say that the Israeli military radio station had reported about a group of Christians who were at the borders of Gaza to pray for and bring supplies to the Israeli military. Zionists groups and their Western Christian allies have been offering unconditional support to the Zionist regime, even calling for nuking Gaza, destroying its people, and turning Gaza into a parking lot, echoing statements made by Israeli officials.[5] The Bible has been an integral part of their propaganda to promote genocide as an act of holy war between "sons of light and sons of darkness," as the Israeli prime minister Benjamin Netanyahu stated in his speech on October 16, 2023.[6] Such rhetoric recycles the same narrative dehumanizing and demonizing Palestinian people that was used to legitimize the ethnic cleansing of the 1948 Nakba.[7]

---

4. See Raheb, *Decolonizing Palestine*, ch. 2, on how the metanarrative of biblical texts is constructed to justify the Israeli colonization of Palestine.

5. For a catalog of genocidal statements made by Israeli Zionists, see the report "Bearing Witness" by Israeli historian and professor at the Hebrew University of Jerusalem Lee Mordechai.

6. Israeli Ministry of Foreign Affairs, "Excerpt from PM Netanyahu's Remarks."

7. See Pappé, *Ethnic Cleansing*; Masalha, *Palestine Nakba*.

Genocide Defined and Denied

In a broadcast speech in 1941 addressing Nazi atrocities during WWII, Winston Churchill said, "We are in the presence of a crime without a name."[8] In response, Raphael Lemkin, a Polish Jewish scholar, conceptualized and coined the term *genocide*. The history of humanity over the past few centuries documents several agonizing crimes involving the mass killing of indigenous and/or ethnic groups such as Black African slaves, Armenians, European Jews during the Holocaust, the Herero and Namaqua of Namibia, the Tutsis of Rwanda, and many others.

Nevertheless, settler-colonial regimes and imperial powers have refused to name some of these crimes as genocides. The United States for years wouldn't define the mass killing in Rwanda as a genocide. Successive US governments have declined to denounce its own settler-colonial history and confess its genocidal campaigns against the indigenous peoples of Turtle Island and against Black African slaves.[9] The Western world, with its long, dark era of colonialism and settler-colonialism during the age of Christendom, has yet to recognize and acknowledge the atrocities it committed against indigenous peoples in the name of Christianization and civilization.

Today, the State of Israel, armed with its settler-colonial ideology, is actively committing a genocide, one that is incited by Israel's highest-ranking officials, live-streamed by its military, prosecuted with Western weapons, permitted by Western powers, and defended and justified by the powerful Christian Zionist lobby. That the war on Gaza amounts to genocide has been argued by many officials of the United Nations,[10] by international human rights organizations,[11] by the Lemkin Institute for Genocide Prevention,[12] and by scholars of genocide.[13] Moreover, the charge of genocide has also been made in the South African application before the International Court of Justice,[14] and the University Network for Human Rights has recently of-

---

8. Vasel, "In the Beginning."

9. In a similar fashion, successive Turkish governments have continued to deny the Armenian genocide, which the Ottoman Empire perpetrated against the Armenian people in 1915–1916. See Republic of Türkiye Ministry of Foreign Affairs, "Armenian Allegation of Genocide."

10. *UN News*, "Rights Expert."

11. Malik, "Consensus Is Emerging."

12. Lemkin Institute for Genocide Prevention, "SOS Alert."

13. *Democracy Now*, "'Total Moral, Ethical Failure.'"

14. Republic of South Africa, "Application."

fered a thorough legal analysis that makes a solid case for classifying the Israeli campaign in Gaza as a genocide.[15]

The refusal of many, despite the evidence, to name Israel's crimes in Gaza a genocide highlights the need to identify who has the right and the power to name and define. Naming a genocide requires admitting a genocide is taking place. Is it logical to expect colonial regimes to incriminate themselves? Will a regime founded on a genocidal ideology and engaged in genocidal actions willingly confess its crimes and allow itself to be held accountable? Unlike Europe in 1941, the crime in Gaza today does have a name, for we have the 1948 Genocide Convention and clear historical precedents to help us identify a genocide. The term is legally hefty, and a determination requires unique expertise, but it is reasonable for non-experts to cite the arguments of respected international organizations who have characterized Israeli war atrocities as genocide.

Yet it is sobering to observe that churches in the West, and many of their allies in the Global South, continue to deny the charge of genocide. They can do so only by ignoring and discrediting the voices of reputable human rights organizations as well as the testimony of Palestinian Christians. It seems that churches in the West have chosen the easier path of turning a blind eye to genocide rather than confessing and repenting of their complicity, despite calls for repentance made by Palestinian Christian organizations.[16] These Western Christians and churches may attempt to assume a posture of neutrality in order to excuse themselves from liability. But should it not be crystal clear, for those who hold to the Bible as their moral authority, that genocide is both a crime and a sin against God and against those created in God's image, people who carry within them a divine spark? Denying a sin does not redeem it, but it does render those who deny it irredeemable (Isa 59:2).

The Story and History of Genocide

In his insightful 2009 book, *Mirror to the Church: Resurrecting Faith After Genocide in Rwanda*, the Rwandan-Ugandan theologian Emmanuel Katongole recounts the history of the genocide in Rwanda and points to the underlying story that drove this atrocity. He observes, "One cannot understand any nation and its politics without getting to the heart of the story that shapes that people."[17] According to Katongole, European colonizers sowed

---

15. University Network for Human Rights, "Genocide in Gaza."
16. Kairos Palestine et al., "Call for Repentance."
17. Katongole, *Mirror to the Church*, 66.

the seeds of racial supremacy and stirred up divisions among the Hutu and Tutsi, and they aided the Rwandan genocide not only by means of arms, but also by means of the theology they had brought with them. Thus, the story of Rwanda cannot be understood apart from European colonialism and the role Christianity played in it.

The story that shaped Zionism and its quest to find in Palestine an answer to Europe's "Jewish Question" is informed by Western colonialism and Orientalism. Zionism is inherently an extension and manifestation of European colonialism with its long history of domination, subjugation, and extermination of indigenous peoples. As a settler-colonial project, Zionism aimed at colonizing Palestine with the intention of displacing or exterminating its indigenous population. It is thus a genocidal project par excellence.[18] The Zionist story is nearly identical to the stories of European colonization and settlement of Turtle Island. The prominent Palestinian theologian and Lutheran pastor Mitri Raheb rightly argues that the unconditional support of the United States for the Israeli Zionist regime is due, in no small part, to the fact that the US story and Israel's story are fundamentally one and the same: that of settler colonialism.[19]

Genocide against the Palestinian people did not begin in October 2023; it has been ongoing for more than a century.[20] Genocide, after all, is a story, a narrative, long before it is put into practice. This ideology began in the minds of the proto-Zionist Christians, Jewish Zionists, and Orientalists who claimed that Palestine was a land without people. In 1841, for example, the Scottish clergyman Keith Alexander, arguing for the restoration of the Jews to Palestine, reported to European Protestant monarchs on behalf of the Church of Scotland that Palestine "is in a great measure a country without a people," a wildly misleading notion that eventually morphed into the infamous slogan, "a land without people for a people without a land."[21]

A decade later, Lord Shaftesbury, the British clergyman and statesman, recorded a similar sentiment, one that eventually guided British imperial policies toward Palestine:

> The Turkish Empire is in rapid decay; every nation is restless; all hearts expect some great things. . . . No one can say that we are

---

18. Wolfe, "Settler Colonialism," 387, argues that "settler colonialism is inherently eliminatory but not invariably genocidal." Building on Wolfe's analysis, we can characterize Zionist settler colonialism as genocidal due to its stated desire to demolish and eliminate the native Palestinians as a people.

19. Raheb, *Decolonizing Palestine*, 45–49; Kaplan, *Our American Israel*.

20. So Khalidi, *Hundred Years' War on Palestine*.

21. Shafir, "Theorizing Zionist Settler Colonialism," 339.

anticipating prophecy; the requirements of it (prophecy) seem nearly fulfilled; Syria "is wasted without an inhabitant";[22] these vast and fertile regions will soon be without a ruler, without a known and acknowledged power to claim domination. The territory must be assigned to someone or other; can it be given to any European potentate? to any American colony? to any Asiatic sovereign or tribe? Are these aspirants from Africa to fasten a demand on the soil from Hamath to the river of Egypt? No, no, no! *There is a country without a nation; and God now, in His wisdom and mercy, directs us to a nation without a country. His own once loved, nay, still loved people, the sons of Abraham, of Isaac, and of Jacob.*[23]

The examples of Alexander and Shaftesbury show that the Palestinians, as a people indigenous to their ancestral land, were perceived as non-existent or inferior in comparison to the European Zionist settlers. The narratives and stories that Western imperial powers and Zionist Christians constructed to justify the colonization of Palestine are genocidal in nature. For despite their claim about "a land without a people," Western imperialists and Zionists knew very well that Palestine was inhabited. In the words of two rabbis who went on a fact-finding mission after the 1897 Zionist Congress in Basel, "The bride [Palestine] is beautiful, but she is married to another man [the Palestinian nation]."[24] It thus became imperative to murder the "man" so that "the bride" could be given to another. In essence, since its earliest days, the settler-colonial project of Zionism aimed at the elimination of the native Palestinian people, in whole or in part, in order to replace them with Zionist settlers.

The church in the West and its Zionist allies invented a story, a myth, of a land without a people. This story colonized their minds before they colonized the Palestinians' land. In his critique of Western Christian rationalizations of the genocide in Rwanda, Katongole points to their claim that Hutus and Tutsis killed each other due to a long history of tribal conflict. The same story has been told about Palestinians and Israelis. This version maintains that Arabs and Jews have been fighting since time immemorial—despite the lack of evidence for this in historical archives or in living memory. In fact, as Katongole shows, "Western Christianity is overeducated in a story that holds their minds captive."[25] In other words, the stories they

---

22. Cf. Isa 6:11.
23. Hodder, *Life and Work*, 493 (emphasis added).
24. Shlaim, "Iron Wall." See also Karmi, *Married to Another Man*.
25. Katongole, *Mirror to the Church*, 72.

tell about Palestinians and Rwandans are not representative of the peoples, cultures, and histories of the two nations. Rather, they are modeled on a pattern tailored to fit the imagination of Western Christians.

Theologizing Genocides

Stories can kill. For over a century, Zionists have used biblical stories as theological justification for their settler-colonial conquest of Palestine. This includes Christian Zionists, a powerful lobby that frequently abuses sacred texts to justify colonial violence and domination. In his recent book, *Decolonizing Palestine*, Mitri Raheb offers a new definition of Christian Zionism that expands on the classical definitions that focus on dispensationalism and evangelicals. According to Raheb, Christian Zionism "should be defined as a Christian lobby that supports the Jewish settler colonialism of Palestinian land by using biblical/theological constructs within a metanarrative while taking glocal considerations into account."[26]

As a settler-colonial ideology, Christian Zionism has weaponized the Bible and cherry-picked theological themes to promote its project as a biblical mandate. The creation of such a metanarrative is not unique to the case of Palestine. The tactic has also been employed in other settings. R. S. Sugirtharajah, a scholar of post-colonial hermeneutics, argues that colonial powers have repeatedly turned conquest and colonialism into a biblical enterprise.[27] In the process, the biblical stories of divine intervention, liberation, and redemption that have long been a source of life and comfort to the people of Palestine are transformed into a blueprint for their genocide, ethnic cleansing, and dispossession.

Christian Zionist theologians, church leaders, scholars, and politicians have rationalized the Zionist genocide by appealing to ancient biblical stories. I highlight two themes in particular as examples of the ways genocide has been—and still is—theologized in these circles. First, ancient stories of divine love and favoritism expressed in terms of chosenness, election, and promised land have become the "software," that is, the ideology, running the imperial colonial military "hardware" of Zionism and its Christian enablers in the West.[28] Shaftesbury's statement shows clearly the role stories of divine love played in shaping his own ideology (as well as that of other proto-Zionists and later Christian Zionists). Shaftesbury identified the European Jews who were supposed to be given the land of Palestine as

---

26. Raheb, *Decolonizing Palestine*, 31.
27. Sugirtharajah, *Exploring*, 32.
28. Raheb, *Faith in the Face of Empire*, 24.

"[God's] own once loved, nay, still loved people, the sons of Abraham, of Isaac, and of Jacob."[29]

Similar narratives were deployed against the indigenous peoples of Turtle Island. The European colonizers viewed themselves as the new Israel, God's beloved, a chosen people conquering a promised land by defeating God's enemies, the Canaanites and Philistines. Mike Pence's statement at the Israel Knesset in 2018 illustrates this connection well:

> In the story of the Jews, we've always seen the story of America. It is the story of an exodus, a journey from persecution to freedom, a story that shows the power of faith and the promise of hope. My country's very first settlers also saw themselves as pilgrims, sent by Providence, to build a new Promised Land. The songs and stories of the people of Israel were their anthems, and they faithfully taught them to their children, and do to this day. And our founders, as others have said, turned to the wisdom of the Hebrew Bible for direction, guidance, and inspiration.[30]

Pence's statement reflects a common sentiment among Christian Americans who adhere to Zionist ideology. Their "Manifest Destiny" is interlocked with the Zionist settler-colonial project. They have transformed the very biblical stories they celebrate as an inspiration for their liberation into instruments for the colonization and oppression of others.

Second, Zionists have refashioned biblical stories of ancient hostilities into a biblical mandate for genocide. Netanyahu has repeatedly identified the Palestinians as "Amalek," the ancient enemy of biblical Israel, invoking the divine command to "blot out the remembrance of Amalek from under heaven" (Exod 17:14; Deut 25:19; cf. 1 Sam 15:3) in order to portray the settler-colonial genocide against the Palestinian people as a holy war.[31] Significantly, this is not the first time these particular texts have been weaponized against the Palestinians. In 2004, Benzi Lieberman, the chairman of the council of settlements, stated unequivocally, "The Palestinians are Amalek!"[32] Likewise, in 2009, the Chief Rabbi of Safed claimed that the Israeli war on Gaza is a war "against Amalek."[33] Later on, however—and days before Netanyahu made his own remarks—it was Christian leaders of the International Christian Embassy Jerusalem (ICEJ) who provided the theological cover and biblical justification for a war against the Palestinians

---

29. Hodder, *Life and Work*, 493.
30. *The Jerusalem Post*, "Full Transcript."
31. *Middle East Eye*, "Netanyahu Faces Backlash."
32. Goldberg, "Among the Settlers."
33. Shragai, "Gaza Campaign."

in Gaza![34] David Parsons, the vice president and senior spokesperson of ICEJ, argued that "the Amalek spirit is driving Hamas to unspeakable atrocities against the Jews."[35]

Interestingly, the story told to legitimize European settler-colonization of Turtle Island was also inspired by the Amalek narrative and by the colonists' self-identification as the new Israel. In his book *Religious Intolerance, America, and the World: A History of Forgetting and Remembering*, John Corrigan observes that European settlers "saw themselves in the Bible, and imagined that they were reenacting the providentially guided campaigns of the Jews against their enemies."[36] Corrigan dedicates an entire chapter in his monograph to examining the references made by European settler-colonizers to the natives—and sometimes other groups—as Amalek, people worthy of annihilation. They invoked the story of Amalek "as inspiration and justification for violence between the British and Native Americans, American Protestants and Roman Catholics, and Mormons and various other American religious groups."[37] The Zionist settler-colonial project in Palestine and European settler-colonialism on Turtle Island share the shameful history of a genocidal ideology that weaponized biblical stories against indigenous peoples.

In addition to these two themes and stories, one can also observe that many Zionist Christians view Palestinian Arab resistance to Israeli colonization as the extension of an ancient rivalry between two brothers, Isaac and Ishmael. Ishmael, the "wild man" (cf. Gen 16:12) is taken to be the father of the Arabs, including the Palestinians, while Isaac, the "chosen one" (cf. Gen 21:12) is identified as the father of the Jews. For example, a Jewish group cursed then-prime minister Yitzhak Rabin (later assassinated by a pro-settlement Jewish extremist in 1995) for signing a peace agreement with the Palestinian Liberation Organization. As part of their cursing ritual, they anathematized Rabin "for handing over the Land of Israel to our enemies, the sons of Ishmael."[38] Similarly, European colonizers of Rwanda used the Hamitic myth to turn Hutu and Tutsi against one another, describing the Tutsis as Semitic and thus superior to the majority, supposedly Hamitic, Hutus.[39]

---

34. Parsons, "Israel, Hamas and the Spirit of Amalek."
35. Parsons, "Israel, Hamas and the Spirit of Amalek."
36. Corrigan, *Religious Intolerance*, 31.
37. Corrigan, *Religious Intolerance*, 34.
38. Dahlburg, "Assassination."
39. Katongole, *Mirror to the Church*, 56–58.

De-theologizing Genocide

Zionist Christians have either denied or sought theological justifications for the ongoing genocide of Palestinians. Like the (settler-)colonial regimes in Turtle Island and Rwanda, they have made sacred texts into pretexts for genocide. When people of faith encounter biblical stories abused to support a crime against humanity—a sin against humans created in the image of God—it is critical to challenge these ideologies, theologies, and interpretations of scripture.

First, genocide cannot be justified theologically. Theology, according to the various Christian traditions, is the study of the God who revealed God's self in and through Christ. There is no "Theo" in a "logy" that endorses and justifies genocide and colonialism. It neither glorifies God nor acknowledges the humanity of those created in the image of God. There is no way to reconcile some Western theologians', pastors', and politicians' justification of genocide in Palestine as the lesser of two evils with the clear teaching of the Bible:

> Repay no one evil for evil, but give thought to do what is honorable in the sight of all. If possible, so far as it depends on you, live peaceably with all. Beloved, never avenge yourselves, but leave it to the wrath of God, for it is written, "Vengeance is mine, I will repay, says the Lord." To the contrary, "if your enemy is hungry, feed him; if he is thirsty, give him something to drink; for by so doing you will heap burning coals on his head." Do not be overcome by evil, but overcome evil with good. (Rom 12:17–21 ESV)

> Do not repay evil for evil or abuse for abuse; but, on the contrary, repay with a blessing. It is for this that you were called— that you might inherit a blessing. (1 Pet 3:9 ESV)

Rather than adopt the playbook of imperial powers, Christian theology must reflect on and abide by the teaching of Christ and the precepts of the Kingdom of God. This is not idealism, but faithful realism grounded in God's sovereign purpose to bring about a new humanity and a new creation.[40]

Second, genocide cannot be rationalized by an appeal to biblical stories. Raheb offers a powerful critique of the abuse of biblical texts to legitimize Israeli settler colonialism. He states, "No one should be allowed to use 'biblical rights' to violate human rights; not Jewish settlers, Israeli politicians, or naïve Christian theologians."[41] So-called biblical rights have

---

40. See AlKhouri, "Kingdom of God and Empires."
41. Raheb, *Decolonizing Palestine*, 80.

frequently been invoked as ordinances of God that override human rights. Put another way, settler-colonial ideologies such as Zionism and its Christian counterparts have turned genocides into holy wars and God into the mastermind behind them.

But the God encountered throughout the Bible, and preeminently in the person of Christ, is one who demonstrates solidarity with God's creation, even to the point of experiencing oppression and suffering a brutal death together with them; a God who prioritizes saving human life over keeping a biblical commandment. In response to the Pharisees' criticism that he was breaking the Sabbath, Jesus answered their complaints with a rhetorical question: "I ask you, is it lawful on the Sabbath to do good or to do harm, to save life or to destroy it?" (Luke 6:9 ESV). In the same way, a claim of "biblical rights" does not override the biblical prohibitions against killing and stealing or the biblical commandments to do justice and not to shed the blood of the innocent (Isa 59:7). It is critical to listen to the prophets and to take Jesus seriously. In his critique of the church's complicity in the Rwandan genocide, Katongole rightly critiques Western individualism for its focus on knowing rather than doing. He states, "We've gone out preaching Jesus, but we haven't been able to 'teach them to obey everything' he commanded (Matt. 28:20)."[42] The Western fixation on biblical literacy over orthopraxy has led to a departure from the teaching of Christ as Christians have "abused power in the name of Jesus and gone to battle with crosses on our shields."[43]

Third, it is imperative to speak and to act prophetically in the face of injustice and genocide. This is a moment of truth. Christians cannot remain silent or claim neutrality while people are being killed in the name of God. The church cannot refuse to take a stand. Dietrich Bonhoeffer, the German Lutheran pastor and theologian, himself a victim of a genocidal ideology, boldly confronted the church's silence in the face of National Socialism:

> But to put off acting and taking a position simply because you are afraid of erring, while others—I mean our brethren in Germany—have to reach infinitely difficult decisions daily, seems to me to almost go against love. To delay or fail to make decisions may be more sinful than to make wrong decisions out of faith and love . . . . [A]nd in this case it really is now or never. "Too late" means "never." . . . Let us shake off our fear of this world— the cause of Christ is at stake; are we to be found sleeping?[44]

---

42. Katongole, *Mirror to the Church*, 93.

43. Katongole, *Mirror to the Church*, 111.

44. Letter to Henry Louis Henriod (April 7, 1934), in Goedeking et al., *Dietrich Bonhoeffer Works*, 13:127; discussed in Schlingensiepen, *Bonhoeffer*, 159.

In a similar manner, the anti-apartheid South African theologian Allan Boesak calls for prophetic courage and resistance in the face of church and state theologies that are complicit in injustice. He provocatively states:

> Because Christians participate in and benefit from the oppression of others while claiming faith in the God of Jesus Christ who came to establish justice in the earth, that faith, the integrity of that Gospel, and the credibility of the witness of the church are at stake. The moment of truth is a moment to act for the sake of justice and humanity, but also for the sake of the integrity of the Gospel.[45]

The Palestinian theologian and Lutheran clergyman Munther Isaac, in his now-famous Christmas sermon "Christ in the Rubble" preached on Sunday, December 23, 2023, likewise criticized Western silence as complicity in the genocide in Gaza. He insisted, "If we, as Christians, are not outraged by this genocide, by the weaponizing of the Bible to justify it, there is something wrong with our Christian witness, and [we are] compromising the credibility of the Gospel!"[46]

Finally, genocide and the ideologies of settler-colonialism must be actively resisted. Palestinian Christians have long offered an example of faithful commitment to Jesus and to God's kingdom. They have taken Jesus seriously, even when it has been costly. Palestinian Christians refuse to deny the humanity of their neighbors or their enemies. They reject all justifications offered for violence, along with theologies of domination and exclusion. They challenge all forms of demonization and dehumanization and boldly proclaim liberty for all. Palestinian Christians resist evil with the logic of love. The Palestinian Christian ecumenical statement of Kairos Palestine, "A Moment of Truth: A Word of Faith, Hope and Love from the Heart of Palestinian Suffering," makes this clear:

> Resistance to the evil of occupation is integrated, then, within this Christian love that refuses evil and corrects it. It resists evil in all its forms with methods that enter into the logic of love and draw on all energies to make peace. We can resist through civil disobedience. We do not resist with death but rather through respect for life. We respect and have a high esteem for all those who have given their life for our nation. And we affirm that every citizen must be ready to defend his or her life, freedom and land.[47]

---

45. Boesak, *Kairos, Crisis, and Global Apartheid*, 17.
46. Isaac, "Christ in the Rubble."
47. Kairos Palestine, "Moment of Truth," 4.2.5.

The genocide in Gaza is a crisis moment that Christ can transform into a moment of truth, a *kairos*. The church and Christians must commit themselves to prophetic courage. Boesak puts it beautifully:

> The discovery of a moment of truth in history is not the result of our intelligence and extraordinary cleverness. It is revelation, the gift of the Holy Spirit. We are not the truth: the truth has found, recovered, and reclaimed us. We are not the light: the light illumines and leads us. We are not the voice: we speak and act because we heard the Voice that calls us to do justice, love mercy, and walk humbly with our God.[48]

The church in the West, with its history of settler colonialism and weaponization of the Bible, is in urgent need of rediscovering a moment of truth—a *kairos* moment that could lead to confession, repentance, and a journey of healing and reconciliation.

Conclusion

In this essay I have argued that genocide cannot be legitimized theologically. Christian theology cannot justify mass murder. Rather, it is crucial to question the legitimacy and orthodoxy of Christian groups that deploy biblical texts and Christian symbols to rationalize the genocide underway in Gaza. Christians, in the West and around the globe, must listen to and imitate Palestinian Christians as they offer a living example of prophetic courage, nonviolent resistance, and faithful resilience in the face of settler-colonial oppression.

Bibliography

AlKhouri, Yousef Kamal. "The Kingdom of God and Empires: A Contemporary Palestinian Christian Contextual Biblical Interpretation." PhD diss., Vrije Universiteit Amsterdam, 2024.

Boesak, Allan. *Kairos, Crisis, and Global Apartheid: The Challenge to Prophetic Resistance*. London: Palgrave Macmillan, 2015.

Corrigan, John. *Religious Intolerance, America, and the World: A History of Forgetting and Remembering*. Chicago: University of Chicago Press, 2020.

Dahlburg, John-Thor. "Assassination in the Middle East: Jewish Mystic Put a Curse on Rabin, Magazine Reports." *Los Angeles Times*, November 5, 1995. https://www.latimes.com/archives/la-xpm-1995-11-05-mn-65263-story.html.

---

48. Boesak, *Kairos, Crisis, and Global Apartheid*, 11.

Democracy Now. "'Total Moral, Ethical Failure': Holocaust Scholar Omar Bartov on Israel's Genocide in Gaza." December 30, 2024. https://www.democracynow.org/2024/12/30/omer_bartov_israel_gaza_genocide.

Goedeking, Hans, et al., eds. *Dietrich Bonhoeffer Works.* Vol. 13: *London: 1933–1935.* Edited by Keith Clements and translated by Isabel Best. Minneapolis: Fortress, 2007.

Goldberg, Jeffrey. "Among the Settlers." *The New Yorker,* May 24, 2004. https://www.newyorker.com/magazine/2004/05/31/among-the-settlers.

Hodder, Edwin. *The Life and Work of the Seventh Earl of Shaftesbury, K. G.* London: Cassell & Co., 1887.

Isaac, Munther. "Christ in the Rubble: A Liturgy of Lament." *Red Letter Christians,* December 23, 2023. https://redletterchristians.org/2023/12/23/christ-in-the-rubble-a-liturgy-of-lament/.

Israeli Ministry of Foreign Affairs. "Excerpt from PM Netanyahu's Remarks at the Opening of the Winter Assembly of the 25th Knesset's Second Session." October 16, 2023. https://www.gov.il/en/pages/excerpt-from-pm-netanyahu-s-remarks-at-the-opening-of-the-knesset-s-winter-assembly-16-oct-2023.

The Jerusalem Post. "Full Transcript of Pence's Knesset Speech." January 22, 2018. https://www.jpost.com/Israel-News/Full-transcript-of-Pences-Knesset-speech-539476.

Kairos Palestine. "A Moment of Truth: A Word of Faith, Hope and Love from the Heart of Palestinian Suffering." Bethlehem: Kairos Palestine, 2009. https://kairospalestine.ps/index.php/about-kairos/kairos-palestine-document.

Kairos Palestine, et al. "A Call for Repentance: An Open Letter from Palestinian Christians to Western Church Leaders and Theologians." October 20, 2023. https://www.change.org/p/an-open-letter-from-palestinian-christians-to-western-church-leaders-and-theologians.

Kaplan, Amy. *Our American Israel: The Story of an Entangled Alliance.* Cambridge, MA: Harvard University Press, 2018.

Karmi, Ghada. *Married to Another Man: Israel's Dilemma in Palestine.* London: Pluto, 2007.

Katongole, Emmanuel, with Jonathan Wilson-Hartgrove. *Mirror to the Church: Resurrecting Faith After Genocide.* Grand Rapids: Zondervan, 2009.

Khalidi, Rashid. *The Hundred Years' War on Palestine: A History of Settler Colonialism and Resistance, 1917–2017.* New York: Picador, 2020.

Lemkin Institute for Genocide Prevention. "SOS Alert Gaza, Palestine." October 13, 2023. https://www.lemkininstitute.com/_files/ugd/9bc553_75f9de53d6a34ea7b119b86dcbcf637d.pdf.

Malik, Nesrine. "A Consensus Is Emerging. Israel Is Committing Genocide in Gaza. Where Is the Action?" *The Guardian,* December 23, 2024. https://www.theguardian.com/commentisfree/2024/dec/23/israel-gaza-war-genocide-where-is-the-action.

Masalha, Nur. *The Palestine Nakba: Decolonising History, Narrating the Subaltern, Reclaiming Memory.* London: Zed, 2012.

Middle East Eye. "Netanyahu Faces Backlash for Evoking Biblical Amalek amid Heavy Civilian Casualties in Gaza." October 29, 2023. https://www.youtube.com/watch?v=pMVs7akyMho.

Mordechai, Lee. "Bearing Witness to the Israel-Gaza War." Version 6.6.0. March 9, 2025. https://witnessing-the-gaza-war.com/wp-content/uploads/2025/03/Gaza_English-v6.6.0-9.3.25.pdf.

Pappé, Ilan. *The Ethnic Cleansing of Palestine*. Oxford: Oneworld, 2006.

Parsons, David. "Israel, Hamas and the Spirit of Amalek." International Christian Embassy in Jerusalem, October 26, 2023. https://www.icej.org/blog/israel-hamas-and-the-spirit-of-amalek.

Raheb, Mitri. *Decolonizing Palestine: The Land, the People, the Bible*. Maryknoll, NY: Orbis, 2023.

———. *Faith in the Face of Empire: The Bible Through Palestinian Eyes*. Maryknoll, NY: Orbis, 2014.

Ratner, Steven R. "Can We Compare Evils? The Enduring Debate on Genocide and Crimes Against Humanity." *Washington University Global Studies Law Review* 6 (2007) 583–89. https://repository.law.umich.edu/articles/2922/.

Republic of South Africa. "Application Instituting Proceedings and Request for the Indication of Provisional Measures." December 29, 2023. https://www.icj-cij.org/sites/default/files/case-related/192/192-20231228-app-01-00-en.pdf.

Republic of Türkiye Ministry of Foreign Affairs. "The Armenian Allegation of Genocide: The Issue and the Facts." https://www.mfa.gov.tr/the-armenian-allegation-of-genocide-the-issue-and-the-facts.en.mfa.

Rostam Ahmed, Darya. "From Holocaust to Anfal: The Impact of Genocide and Cross-Generational Trauma on the Mental Health of Kurds." *International Journal of Social Psychiatry* 70 (2023) 621–25.

Schlingensiepen, Ferdinand. *Dietrich Bonhoeffer 1906–1945: Martyr, Thinker, Man of Resistance*. Translated by Isabel Best. London: T. & T. Clark, 2010.

Shafir, Gershon. "Theorizing Zionist Settler Colonialism in Palestine." In *The Routledge Handbook of the History of Settler Colonialism*, edited by Edward Cavanagh and Lorenzo Veracini, 339–52. Oxford: Routledge, 2017.

Shah, Haleema. "Is Israel a 'Settler-Colonial' State? The Debate, Explained." *Vox*, April 17, 2024. https://www.vox.com/world-politics/24128715/israel-palestine-conflict-settler-colonialism-zionism-history-debate.

Shlaim, Avi. "Prologue." In *The Iron Wall: Israel and the Arab World Since 1948*. New York: Norton, 2000. https://archive.nytimes.com/www.nytimes.com/books/first/s/shlaim-wall.html.

Shragai, Nadav. "Gaza Campaign Is War Against Amalek, Says Chief Rabbi of Safed." *Haaretz*, January 16, 2009. https://www.haaretz.com/2009-1-16/ty-article/gaza-campaign-is-war-against-amalek-says-chief-rabbi-of-safed/0000017f-f486-d47e-a37f-fdbeb51e0000.

Sugirtharajah, R. S. *Exploring Postcolonial Biblical Criticism*. Chichester, West Sussex: Wiley-Blackwell, 2012.

University Network for Human Rights. "Genocide in Gaza: Analysis of International Law and Its Application to Israel's Military Actions Since October 7, 2023." https://www.humanrightsnetwork.org/genocide-in-gaza.

UN News. "Rights Expert Finds 'Reasonable Grounds' Genocide Is Being Committed in Gaza." March 26, 2024. https://news.un.org/en/story/2024/03/1147976.

Vasel, Johann Justus. "In the Beginning, There Was No Word . . . ." *European Journal of International Law* 29 (2018) 1053–56.

Veracini, Lorenzo. "The Other Shift: Settler Colonialism, Israel, and the Occupation." *Journal of Palestine Studies* 42 (2013) 26–42.
Wolfe, Patrick. "Settler Colonialism and the Elimination of the Native." *Journal of Genocide Research* 8 (2006) 387–409.
Wyatt, Zoë. "Intergenerational Trauma in the Aftermath of Genocide." *European Journal of Theoretical and Applied Sciences* 1 (2023) 72–78.

CHAPTER TEN

Doing Justice
The Unequivocal Calling of God's People

Ruth Padilla DeBorst

If you visit a Costa Rican town at the end of October, you will be welcomed by people wearing colorful masks. A blend of pre-Columbian, Afro, and Spanish colonial traditions, the masquerades have grown to become national symbols of Costa Rica. Music and brightly colored masks create a festive atmosphere in the popular celebrations. Colorful and fun as they might look, masks express meaning. They also conceal.

I suggest that religiosity—religious rites and practices that appear pious but lack deep heart commitment and ethical teeth—has served through the ages and still serves as a mask. It conceals what should be seen, named, lamented, resisted, and changed in the light of God's good purposes for the world. I invite you to unmask.

In the days of the prophet Micah, the farming people of Judea were suffering. They were not only anxious about the impending invasion of enemy forces. They also faced the daily oppression of corrupt governing elites. They were being forced to pay taxes and abandon their fields to build cities for the wealthy few. Their lands were being expropriated to feed the greed of the rich. Their young men were being recruited into the army, and their young women taken into the royal court. What made matters worse was that these injustices were masquerading as religiosity. Religious practices, rites, and sacrifices were covering up social corruption. False prophets were deaf to the cries of the people, while priests cozied up to the wealthy and blessed the weapons of oppression.[1]

Similar was the role of the religious establishment in the Argentina of my youth. The country was ruled by an oppressive military dictatorship that was arbitrarily "disappearing" people under the pretext of ridding the country of communism. Roman Catholic leaders blessed instruments of torture in clandestine sites. Protestant and evangelical leaders, with a few valiant exceptions, pretended nothing was wrong. Masses and liturgies, evangelistic campaigns and exuberant worship celebrations—it all proceeded with no one denouncing the social injustice raging out of sight. Religiosity was a useful mask: numbing, distracting, distorting, and shielding people from reality.

Still today, the darkest feature of our beautiful continent is inequality. In no other region of the world is the gap between wealthy and poor as gaping as it is in Latin America and the Caribbean.[2] We also suffer the malady of violent power. Together, from Mexico to Argentina, we constitute the murder capital of the world. The region's homicide rate is three times higher than the world average.[3] Latin America boasts forty-three of the fifty cities with the most murders in the world, including the top ten.[4] State and gang violence, drug cartels, crimes of passion; the murder of journalists, social and environmental activists; murder by exclusion, hunger, and institutionalized injustice; femicides and official extrajudicial killings.

No one is safe. The shadow of violence is long. Fear forces thousands to flee. Additional thousands are uprooted by the changing climate, a crisis to which they have not contributed. And still today, churches mask the brokenness. They carry out worship business as usual while religious leaders climb megachurch ladders of popularity and public influence without ever questioning the oppressive status quo.

Your world may or may not resemble life in the Judea of Micah's time or the Latin America I described, but we are all part of a global system. Capital interests and military power span oceans and cross borders. Within this system, religious jargon, symbols, and rituals serve as masks, covering unjust and violent social realities. Religiosity can insulate believers from reality, inducing indifference, passivity, and compliance. It can also generate theological justifications for active, complicit support of oppression.

---

1. See Mic 2:2; 3:1–3; 3:9–11; 6:10–12; 7:2–4.
2. Inter-American Development Bank, "Complexities of Inequality"; World Economic Forum, "Latin America."
3. Inter-American Development Bank, "Citizen Security."
4. World Population Review, "Most Violent Cities."

A case in point is the growing number of Christians across Latin America who are a-critically embracing Zionism. Israeli flags wave outside many Pentecostal and neo-pentecostal churches in Central America. The second largest church in El Salvador is called *The Biblical Baptist Tabernacle of the Friends of Israel*; their logo is a menorah; and several annual pilgrimages to the Holy Land lead hundreds of parishioners to "stand with Israel" and to unquestionably pray for its army. Often unaware of the existence and plight of Palestinian Christians, they side with the modern, secular State of Israel as if it equaled the Israel of the Old Testament. Through all these means they become accomplices in the injustices perpetrated against Palestinians in Gaza and West Bank.

Bethlehem, where I first delivered this address, is a city emblematic of the story of God's people. Near that city, Jacob buried his wife Rachel. There too Ruth, the widowed Moabite, followed her widowed mother-in-law, Naomi, in search of sustenance. It was there that David, Ruth's great-grandson, was born. And there, many generations later, Jesus was born.

Bethlehem is also emblematic of the West Bank where Israeli settlers, backed by Israel's security forces, have dramatically increased their attacks on Palestinians since Hamas's brutal assault on October 7, 2023, and Israel's relentless onslaught in Gaza. The US government, Germany, the UK, and many people who claim to be Christian are turning a blind eye or actively supporting Israel with weapons, solidarity, and prayer. Politics masquerading as theology is denying the most basic human rights, and the most basic human rights are being blatantly violated. This mask must be ripped off!

Once the mask is peeled off, we must explore, who does Scripture reveal to be God's people, if it is not the modern State of Israel? The Bible portrays a Sovereign Creator and Sustainer of life reaching into history, establishing a series of covenants with God's creatures, and summoning a people who will reflect the character of God. Let's review that history.

In the beginning, God creates diverse forms of life and calls humanity to care for the created order. When humanity disregards that calling and violence escalates, God renews the covenant with Noah and all living creatures (Gen 9). God then calls a "wandering Aramean" to begin a family that would bless all families of the earth by living according to God's good purposes (Gen 12:1–3). God provides for Abraham's descendants when famine strikes. Four centuries later we find this clan and others living under Egyptian oppression. God calls these suffering slaves "my people" (Exod 3:7) and frees this "mixed crowd" of foreigners, aliens, and descendants of Abraham (Exod 12:38, Num 11:4, Lev 24:1–23, Josh 8:35). Whoever they were, they were counted among God's people if the males were circumcised and if everyone submitted to God's law (Exod 12:43–49).

At Sinai God renews the covenant, fashioning this mixed collection of freed slaves into a people and providing them with clear instructions in the Torah for how to live. What makes this new people distinct, says Chris Wright, is "not their ethnic exclusiveness (there were all kinds of ways that foreigners could be incorporated into the worshiping community of Israel)."[5] What makes this people distinct is their allegiance to God, not to Pharaoh or other powerful figures; their worship of God as ultimate and uniquely sovereign; and their engagement in reciprocally loving relationships in obedience to God (Exod 20:6).

This is the crux. The people of God are above all marked by their submission to God's sovereignty, their response to God's love, and their outworking of that love in social, ethical terms. This is the message Micah delivers to the empowered people of his day to challenge their religious masks and unjust behavior. Famously, he asks and answers his own question:

> He has told you, O mortal, what is good; and what does the Lord require of you but to do justice, and to love kindness, and to walk humbly with your God? (Mic 6:8 NRSV)

Micah has already reminded the people of Judea about God's gracious intervention on their behalf throughout history. He exhorts them to remember, to listen, to repent, and to act in accord with God's character. What God requires of God's people then and now is no secret! God's intent was clear from the beginning and is made clear throughout Scripture, for them and for us. Long before Micah's day, referring to Abraham, God said: "For I have chosen him, that he may charge his children and his household after him to keep the way of the Lord by doing righteousness and justice" (Gen 18:19 NRSV). Centuries later Moses, using language that reminds us of Mic 6:8, addresses the mixed group of freed slaves being fashioned by the law into a new people:

> So now, O Israel, what does the Lord your God require of you? Only to fear the Lord your God, to walk in all his ways, to love him, to serve the Lord your God with all your heart and with all your soul, and to keep the commandments of the Lord your God and his decrees that I am commanding you today, for your own well-being. (Deut 10:12–13 NRSV)

The prophets consistently echo this call. Jesus makes it explicit to his early followers: "If you love me, you will keep my commandments" (John 14:15). There is no room for doubt. God is worshiped, not merely by rites, religious festivities, or sacrifices—practices that can mask injustice—but by ethical

---

5. Wright, *Mission of God*, 257.

obedience. What marks God's people are not superficial expressions of religious piety, "Christianese" jargon, worship jingles, or colonialist theologies that justify and finance oppression under the guise of certain eschatologies.

What then are the markers of God's people? When we review Micah's summary in reverse, focusing on what God expects, we see first God's people, then and now, called to "walk humbly with our God." This is to live in deep reverence, acknowledging God as the Sovereign reality that lies outside self and independent of human will.[6] It requires unmasking self-sufficient pride and acknowledging utter dependence on God. It entails questioning any power that might challenge our ultimate allegiance and submission to God. There is no room for elevating the claims of nation or ethnicity over the claims of God's reign of justice for all.

The second expectation is to "love mercy" or "kindness." This points to the core motivation that should underlie all our actions: deep solidarity and love. It means unmasking our selfish, self-protective drives and allowing God's compassion to move us. "Solidarity," says Jewish theologian Marc Ellis,

> is the movement of the heart, mind, and body toward those who are suffering. Though often seen as a movement outward toward others . . . solidarity actually is a journey to ourselves as well. It is an attempt to reclaim our own humanity, bruised and alienated when our lives are built on the exploitation of others.[7]

Kindness and solidarity rule out indifference toward the uprooted and beleaguered peoples of the earth—not least the people of Gaza—toward those mourning lost loved ones, toward hostages held by both Israel and Hamas and their families, toward Palestinians threatened in their own territories, toward all who are suffering the scourge of war and violence the world round.[8] Their pain is our pain if we are God's people.

---

6. Brueggemann, *Theology of the Old Testament*, 461.

7. Ellis, *Toward a Jewish Theology*, 178.

8. When I voiced this very call at Lausanne IV, in Incheon, South Korea, in September of 2024, the CEO of Jews for Jesus and others in the conference objected emphatically, angered especially that I would mention hostages held by Israel, and demanded an apology. For years Amnesty International has recorded "unlawful attacks and collective punishment of civilians in the besieged Gaza Strip and the use of torture, arbitrary detention and other violations of the rights of Palestinian prisoners" (Amnesty International, "Israel/OPT: Horrifying Cases"). Though Israel uses terms like "administrative detention," and "security inmates" for the thousands of people they are holding indefinitely without charge or trial, I believe it is appropriate to use the term "hostage" since they are being used as pawns in Israel's intimidation campaign.

The third marker of God's people is the pursuit of justice, the practice of socio-economic and political action for the common good. We unmask our self interest for the sake of others. In Walter Brueggemann's words, this entails the "venturesome enactment of positive good, whereby human solidarity is maintained and enhanced." It is the "enhancement of the human community by mobilizing social power, especially the power and resources of the strong for the well-being of the whole community."[9] The supreme model for this practice is God, the Sovereign Lord, as is clear from Deuteronomy:

> For the Lord your God is God of gods and Lord of lords, the great God, mighty and awesome, who is not partial and takes no bribe, who executes justice for the orphan and the widow, and who loves the strangers, providing them with food and clothing. You shall also love the stranger, for you were strangers in the land of Egypt. (Deut 10:17–19 NRSV)

There is no room for silence when fellow human beings are being robbed of home, land, livelihood, and life itself. Not in the Judea of Micah's day. Not in the Latin America of my youth. Not in the Gaza of today and across the beautiful but troubled West Bank. Those of us who dare—with fear and trembling—to identify as God's people must unmask every religious justification for oppression. We must name our masks, lament, and resist with all means at our disposal.

What is the mission of God's people in the context of oppression? To do justice, to love kindness, and to walk humbly with our God. May God have mercy as we tear off our masks. May God's Spirit breathe truth and strength into us so that we may live out God's good purposes in God's world, sowing seeds of justice until the Lord returns and justice finally prevails.

Bibliography

Amnesty International. "Israel/OPT: Horrifying Cases of Torture and Degrading Treatment of Palestinian Detainees amid Spike in Arbitrary Arrests." November 8, 2023. https://www.amnesty.org/en/latest/news/2023/11/israel-opt-horrifying-cases-of-torture-and-degrading-treatment-of-palestinian-detainees-amid-spike-in-arbitrary-arrests/.

Brueggemann, Walter. *Theology of the Old Testament: Testimony, Dispute, Advocacy.* Minneapolis: Fortress, 1997.

Ellis, Marc H. *Toward a Jewish Theology of Liberation: The Challenge of the 21st Century.* 3rd ed. Waco, TX: Baylor University Press, 2004.

---

9. Brueggemann, *Theology of the Old Testament*, 461.

Inter-American Development Bank. "Citizen Security in Latin America and the Caribbean." March 7, 2024. https://www.iadb.org/en/who-we-are/about-idb.

———. "The Complexities of Inequality in Latin America and the Caribbean." March 6, 2024. https://www.iadb.org/en/news/complexities-inequality-latin-america-and-caribbean#.

World Economic Forum. "Latin America Is the World's Most Unequal Region." January 17, 2016. https://www.weforum.org/stories/2016/01/inequality-is-getting-worse-in-latin-america-here-s-how-to-fix-it/.

World Population Review. "Most Violent Cities in the World 2024." https://worldpopulationreview.com/world-city-rankings/most-violent-cities-in-the-world.

Wright, Christopher J. H. *The Mission of God: Unlocking the Bible's Grand Narrative*. Downers Grove, IL: IVP Academic, 2006.

CHAPTER ELEVEN

Missiology After Gaza
Christian Zionism, God's Character, and the Gospel

Anton Deik

During the first few months of Israel's war on Gaza, my family and I were based in Cambridge, UK. To our dismay, the community where we lived and studied had strong Zionist leanings. One Sunday, we decided to take a break from that environment and visit our favorite church in central London—a church well known for its influence on global evangelicalism. We went there to be encouraged in a period of distress.

That Sunday was Mission Sunday, and the church had a guest speaker: the director of a key evangelical ministry. The subject of his sermon was Bible translation. Gaza, to our surprise, was mentioned several times. But it was mentioned as an example of things that could distract the church from accomplishing its mission. To our horror, Gaza was mentioned alongside Taylor Swift and Donald Trump, both in the news that week. The preacher's admonition to the church was to remain focused on its mission. Christians, according to him, should not distract themselves with "the things of the world," such as Gaza, Taylor Swift, and US elections. Rather, the church should get busy in the work of God's kingdom—for this Christian leader, mainly Bible translation.

This sermon horrified us. How could a Christian leader so easily dismiss human suffering in Gaza, which the International Court of Justice considers a plausible case of genocide? What kind of mission was he talking about? Even more troubling was this leader's failure to acknowledge the role his church, the Western evangelical church, has played in offering the Zionist settler-colonial project theological legitimacy since its inception. As demonstrated by scholars of Christian Zionism, if it weren't for the theology and activism of Western evangelicals, especially in Britain and the US, the Zionist settler-colonial project would not have succeeded.[1] Further, since October 7, 2023, many Western evangelicals have unashamedly continued to provide theological justification for Israel's genocidal war on Gaza. Yet here we were, in a church we thought was a beacon of hope, listening to an evangelical leader dismissing the suffering of the Palestinians and completely ignoring the huge responsibility evangelicals bear for justifying that suffering. All this on Mission Sunday.

As a response to this flawed missiology—sadly shared by many evangelicals worldwide—I offer here two missiological reflections in the shadow of Israel's genocide in Gaza. First, I will argue that Christian Zionism's distorted conception of God undermines the gospel. I will develop my argument by focusing on support for Zionism in three theological traditions: liberal/mainline, dispensational evangelical, and non-dispensational evangelical. Second, I will suggest a constructive way forward in three steps: proclaiming God's goodness, calling for repentance, and working for justice.

Christian Zionism's Conception of God

Thirty-five years ago, Palestinian theologian Naim Ateek identified what is perhaps the most dangerous implication of Christian Zionism. In 1989, he wrote: "theologically speaking, what is at stake today in the political conflict over the land of the West Bank and Gaza is nothing less than the way we understand the nature of God."[2] Yet the implications of Christian Zionism are not only theological—shaping our doctrine of God—but also missiological, for at the heart of what Christians are commissioned to proclaim to the world, in word and deed, is the goodness, righteousness, and love of God embodied in the person of Jesus Christ.

Genuine gospel proclamation is incompatible with Christian Zionist theologies that misuse biblical notions of "chosen people" and "promised land" to legitimize the Zionist settler-colonial project. Such theologies proclaim neither God's goodness nor God's love, let alone God's justice and righteousness. Rather, these theologies proclaim God as a racist, tribal deity.

---

1. See Sizer, *Christian Zionism*, 254–55; Smith, *More Desired*, esp. chs. 5–8.
2. Ateek, *Justice*, 111.

This may seem like a strong accusation, but I am not attacking a straw man. The burden of proof is on Zionist theologians to show otherwise: to explain how, after Jesus Christ, God can still have a special relationship with a particular nation or race—one that includes giving them land inhabited by other people—and not be racist.[3] On what basis does God favor one nation over another after Jesus Christ?

When I was a high school student at the Lutheran school in Bethlehem, I often found myself troubled by the biblical notion of election. I once asked our religious education teacher, "Why did God choose the Jews over everyone else?" His answer was simple yet to my mind persuasive: "God chose a particular tribe to prepare them for the coming of Christ."[4] How God prepared for Jesus to appear as the Savior of all peoples might appear tribal and ethnocentric to some. Nonetheless, now that Jesus has come, how can God maintain a special relation with a particular tribe, granting them divine rights to a land already inhabited by others, and still be good and just?

Zionist theologies do even more than defend divine racism. In their justification of the ethnic cleansing of Palestine, these theologies conceptualize God not as a god of justice and mercy but as a god of colonialism, oppression, and mass killing. In the words of Mitri Raheb, Christian Zionism provides "the theological software that enables Israeli oppression of the people of Palestine."[5] This applies across the spectrum of Christian Zionist theologies that justify the Zionist settler-colonial project, including (1) mainline/liberal Protestant; (2) dispensational evangelical; and (3) non-dispensational evangelical.

Mainline Protestant Christian Zionism

Among Palestinian theologians, Mitri Raheb has been one of the most vocal in addressing the influence of liberal and mainline Christian Zionism. In *Decolonizing Palestine*, he provides numerous examples of how Zionist

---

3. In saying that Christian Zionist theologies depict God as "racist," I have in mind the definition of "racism" offered by the *Oxford English Dictionary*: "Prejudice, antagonism, or discrimination by an individual, institution, or society, against a person or people on the basis of their nationality or (now usually) their membership of a particular racial or ethnic group.... Also: beliefs that members of a particular racial or ethnic group possess innate characteristics or qualities, or that some racial or ethnic groups are superior to others."

4. See below, pp. 225–27, on the biblical concept of election.

5. Raheb, *Decolonizing Palestine*, "Introduction."

theology has taken root in these circles.⁶ For instance, in 1962, theologian Karl Barth described the establishment of Israel as a sign of God's faithfulness to the seed of Abraham. In 1970, the General Synod of the Dutch Reformed Church published a statement affirming that the establishment of Israel is a fulfillment of the Abrahamic covenant. In 1980, the German Protestant *Evangelische Kirche im Rheinland* adopted a resolution asserting the enduring significance of Israel in salvation history and affirming that the establishment of the State of Israel is a sign of God's covenant faithfulness. In 2015, Walter Brueggemann acknowledged, "Like many Christians, progressive and evangelical, I was grateful (and continue to be so) for the founding and prospering of the state of Israel as an embodiment of God's chosen people."⁷

To establish the State of Israel, which these mainline theologians and churches celebrate, Zionist militias committed no fewer than 30 massacres against the people of Palestine, destroyed more than 530 Palestinian villages, and forcibly displaced 750,000 Palestinians (almost 90 percent of those living in what eventually became the State of Israel).⁸ Contrary to popular perception, these atrocities were not simply the outcome of a national conflict, but the result of a particular kind of colonialism known as *settler-colonialism*: when colonizers immigrate to a territory not to live among and integrate with the local population, but *to replace them*. The Arabic term, *al-istiʿmār al-istīṭānī al-iḥlālī* ("substitutional settler colonialism"), conveys this idea perhaps more clearly than the English.⁹

In the late nineteenth and early twentieth centuries, European Jews sought to mirror the settler-colonial paradigm that their Christian compatriots had followed in the Americas, Oceania, and parts of Africa. These European Jews began a movement known as Zionism, spearheaded by Theodor Herzl, an Austro-Hungarian journalist.¹⁰ The goal of Zionism was to address Europe's entrenched antisemitism by establishing what Herzl called *der Judenstaat* ("the Jewish state"). With the support of Western powers,

---

6. Raheb, *Decolonizing Palestine*; see ch. 2, esp. the section titled "Liberal Christian Zionism and the Holocaust"; see also ch. 3, under "Settler Colonialism: The Blind Spot of Land Theology."

7. Brueggemann, *Chosen?*, xiv.

8. Numbers from Israeli historian Ilan Pappé. See *Ethnic Cleansing*, 258; *History*, 128; *Ten Myths*, 64. See also the work of Palestinian historian Nur Masalha, esp. *Expulsion of the Palestinians*.

9. For the inherent connection between settler-colonialism and "the logic of elimination," see Wolfe, "Settler Colonialism."

10. On the relation between Zionism and settler-colonialism, see Khalidi, *Hundred Years' War on Palestine*; Pappé, *Ten Myths*, 41–49.

the Zionist movement began promoting and facilitating the mass migration of Jews from Europe to Palestine. These settlers did not arrive as immigrants intending to integrate with us but as colonizers seeking to establish an ethnostate—an ethnically exclusive *Judenstaat*—on a land inhabited by Palestinians.

This contrasted sharply with the long-standing Palestinian Jewish community, which had lived alongside Muslims and Christians for centuries as an integral part of Arab society, with no colonial agenda. The Zionist dream of an ethnostate also differed from the intentions of Armenian and Syriac Christians who fled Ottoman genocides in the early twentieth century. These came to Palestine to take refuge *among us* rather than to *replace us* and appeal to their suffering, ancient traditions, and texts to justify their plan. (Therefore, today, there is no "Armenian-Palestinian conflict.")

So, how did Zionist colonizers establish their exclusivist *Judenstaat* on Palestinian land? Not through peaceful coexistence, but through mass killing and displacement—tactics characteristic of settler-colonial projects. As Palestinians, we remember the atrocities committed by Zionist colonizers in 1947–1949 as the *Nakba* ("catastrophe"), but renowned Israeli historian Ilan Pappé aptly demonstrates—using Israeli military archives—that these atrocities were part of an intentional plan: "the ethnic cleansing of Palestine."[11]

Christian churches and theologians who claim that Israel's founding is an expression of God's covenant faithfulness thereby associate God's name and character with a vicious settler-colonial project that led to the ethnic cleansing of Palestine. Thus, theologies that justify Zionism should be labeled as what they are: *colonial theologies*.

Importantly, the mainline theologians and churches noted above are *not* merely saying that the establishment of modern Israel—inseparable from the ethnic cleansing of Palestine—falls under the umbrella of God's sovereignty. This, for me, would be a truthful statement that does not associate God's character with evil. Instead, these theologians and churches are claiming that the founding of Israel is an act of God, a sign of God's faithfulness to the Abrahamic covenant. The latter is a key moment in salvation history and an expression of God's love for humanity: "in your offspring shall all the nations of the earth be blessed" (Gen 22:18 ESV). Further, the Abrahamic covenant is central to the gospel; the good news of Jesus fulfills God's promises to Abraham (Luke 1:54–55, 72–73; Acts 3:25–26; Gal 3:14, 16, 29). Therefore, to claim that the Palestinian *Nakba* is an expression of God's covenant faithfulness is to confuse God's goodness with human evil,

---

11. Pappé, *Ethnic Cleansing*.

the good news of Jesus with the ethnic cleansing of Palestine. Such a confusion has catastrophic consequences for our gospel witness.

Dispensational Evangelical Christian Zionism

Among evangelicals, the most predominant form of Christian Zionism is dispensationalism: a theological and hermeneutical system at the heart of which is the distinction between "God's purposes for the church" and "God's purposes for Israel."[12] A missionary from a dispensationalist church once shared with me how he struggled mightily in his devotional Bible reading to distinguish between texts that are applicable to his life and those that are relevant only to the modern State of Israel.

Insofar as dispensationalists support Israel *spiritually, theologically,* and *practically,* the damaging implications of their Christian Zionism for the gospel are profound.

(1) Spiritually, many dispensationalists pray for Israel to conquer and defeat its enemies. I first encountered such prayers when I worked as a missionary with a Western mission agency, and I continue to encounter them in evangelical circles. The most recent instance occurred at Lausanne IV, a historical gathering of over 5,000 evangelical leaders from more than 200 countries, held in Incheon, South Korea, in September 2024. To my dismay, at a conference aiming to encourage Christians "to declare and display Christ," I found posted on the prayer wall of the congress this petition: "Pray for Israel: let them conquer their enemies." To me, such prayers are genocidal and stand in stark opposition to the gospel of Christ, for "conquering the Palestinians" in Israeli military doctrine often equates to the ethnic cleansing of Palestine, as my grandfather and his family witnessed in 1948,[13] and as we are witnessing today in Israel's genocidal war on Gaza.

At the same gathering of Lausanne IV, a group of us wanted to meet to pray for Palestine. Unfortunately, the organizers did not give us a room, so we ended up meeting outside of Exit 18 of the Songdo Convensia venue where the congress was taking place. Just as we were about to begin praying, a conference participant interrupted the meeting by shouting at us. Even prayer for Palestine is unacceptable to some evangelicals.

(2) Theologically, according to Pew Research (May 2022), 70 percent of white evangelicals in the US believe that "God gave the land that is now

---

12. One of the best treatments of dispensational Christian Zionism is found in Sizer, *Christian Zionism.*

13. For the Nakba story of my family, see Deik, "Palestinian Counterstory."

Israel to the Jewish people."[14] Ernest Sandeen notes that "this particular emphasis within dispensationalism accounts for the enthusiastic Zionism manifested by many Fundamentalists."[15] This belief is an outcome of the basic dispensational presupposition that God has two "chosen peoples" (the church and Israel) with two distinct sets of promises and purposes. For the dispensationalist, God's promises to biblical Yisrael[16] are not simply fulfilled in Christ. Like the liberal/mainline positions discussed above, dispensationalism sees God's promise of land to Abraham and his offspring fulfilled in Theodor Herzl and the Zionist movement (*contra* Gal 3:16). Further, the more Israel succeeds in defeating its enemies (us) and conquering land, the more some dispensationalists are "excited." This "excitement" comes not only from the perceived fulfillment of "God's promises to his chosen people," but also from the near dawn of the eschaton, for the "Jewish return to the promised land" forms part of dispensationalist end times schemes.

Sadly, one cannot agree with N. T. Wright that this strange theology is confined to the US.[17] Due to the missionary fervor of American dispensationalists, this harmful theology has spread around the world. Wherever I have resided, including in the Philippines, the UK, and Bolivia, I have encountered dispensational Christian Zionism. We currently live in Cochabamba, Bolivia, and the church next to our home displays no Christian symbols but, instead, a large Israeli flag. The former dean of the main seminary of the Bolivian evangelical denomination we belong to was an American dispensationalist missionary. What subjects did he teach? The book of Revelation and eschatology. As he told me once, he teaches his Bolivian students that "it all hangs on what we believe about Israel." The situation is no better in Africa, as demonstrated in an edited volume by Cynthia Holder Rich.[18]

Like the mainline theological positions discussed above, so too does dispensational Christian Zionism conceptualize God as a racist, tribal deity. Further, claims such as "God gave the land to the Jewish people" depict God

---

14. Pew Research Center, "Modest."

15. Sandeen, "Toward a Historical Interpretation," 21.

16. For disambiguation, I consistently use "Yisrael" when referring to the ancient people of God and "Israel" for the modern state. My spelling, "Yisrael," is based on a straight-forward transliteration of the Hebrew יִשְׂרָאֵל (*yisrā'ēl*) and is close to the Middle English "Ysrael" used in the fourteenth-century early Wycliffite Bible. The reason for this disambiguation in spelling is that conflating biblical Yisrael with the modern State of Israel is part and parcel of the colonial software used to legitimize the Zionist settler-colonial project and the bloodshed and oppression that accompany it.

17. Fuller Studio, "N. T. Wright."

18. Holder Rich, *Christian Zionism*.

as a real estate agent who, instead of legally buying and selling land, uses violence and ethnic cleansing to seize land inhabited by the Palestinians and give it to his "chosen people." During the 2014 Israeli war on Gaza, a Palestinian friend confronted a Christian Zionist who was studying with me at London School of Theology, highlighting Israel's indiscriminate killing of women and children, along with its widespread ecological destruction in Gaza. In response, the Christian Zionist referred my friend to the *ḥērem* wars of the book of Joshua. The gravity of such abuse of the Scriptures cannot be overstated.[19] Who would want to worship a god who favors one nation over another and sanctions the slaughter and displacement of an indigenous people for the benefit of his chosen ones?

(3) Practically, one of the primary emphases of evangelicalism is "activism."[20] As such, we might expect Zionist evangelicals, who pray for the defeat of Israel's enemies and who believe that Israel has a divine right to historical Palestine, to act upon their theological and spiritual convictions. Among dispensationalists, Zionist activism can range from expressing political support for Israel's oppressive and genocidal policies to mobilizing human and material resources for the benefit of Israel's settler-colonial project. Two examples illustrate this.

One year into Israel's genocidal war on Gaza—which by then had claimed the lives of well over 41,000 Palestinians, more than half of whom were identified as children, women, or the elderly[21]—prominent dispensationalist Darrell Bock unashamedly described Israel's policy of disproportionate warfare as "understandable."[22]

In terms of political action, a few years ago a young woman shared with me how "the Holy Spirit" led her to contact the Israeli embassy in her country to organize a big mobilization conference in support of Israel. She explained that her initiative was inspired by Christians United for Israel (CUFI), an influential US dispensationalist lobby that claims ten million

---

19. Even the most conservative scholarly treatment of the OT *ḥērem* wars does not allow their application to any modern-day context. For different approaches to the subject, see Cowles et al., *Show Them No Mercy*. On the topic of Old Testament violence in general, see Paynter, *God of Violence*.

20. Bebbington, *Evangelicalism*, 10–12.

21. These figures from the Gaza Ministry of Health were reported by the UN Office for the Coordination of Humanitarian Affairs in their "Reported Impact Snapshot" of October 2, 2024. On February 3, 2025, the head of the Gaza Government Information Office released an updated estimate of 61,709 dead, of whom 17,881 are children, including 214 newborn infants. *Al Jazeera*, "Deaths from Israel's Attacks." There is good reason to believe these horrific figures are far too low; see Jamaluddine et al., "Traumatic Injury Mortality."

22. Casper, "Gaza War."

members. CUFI's website gives numerous examples of the type of material support these evangelicals extend to Israel, including political lobbying, financial donations, and sponsoring political trips to Israel to "transform pastors from spiritual pilgrims into passionate Zionists."[23] CUFI works tirelessly to oppose Palestinian rights, to support Israeli settlements, and to lobby for more US weapons sales to Israel.[24]

Non-Dispensational Evangelical Christian Zionism

Evangelical Christian Zionism extends far beyond dispensationalist circles. Since October 7, we have witnessed a surge in the weaponization of theology and Scripture even by evangelicals whose covenantal theology depicts God neither as racist nor as a real estate agent. For example, Russell Moore of *Christianity Today*, in an article published on October 7, 2023, begins his defense of Israel with a profession: "We believe the promises of God are fulfilled in Christ, not in the 1948 Israeli Declaration of Independence."[25] Yet Moore goes on to provide Israel with the theological software it needs for its war machine, relying mainly on a version of Just War Theory and quoting from Rom 13:1–4. Notwithstanding Moore's understanding of Old Testament promises, his justification of Israel's war on Gaza—like the Christian Zionist views discussed above—portrays God as a warmonger, a depiction that seriously undermines the gospel of Christ.[26]

If Moore's article were the only piece published by *Christianity Today* about Israel's ongoing war on Gaza, one might excuse it as a hasty, mistaken reaction to the atrocities of October 7. However, *Christianity Today* has persisted in publishing articles and podcasts with a clearly Zionist editorial slant. To our dismay, *Christianity Today* has consistently rejected articles sharing the Palestinian narrative, whether by Palestinians or by sympathetic Western authors. Sadly, a respected evangelical leader attempted to arrange a meeting between Russell Moore and Palestinian Christian leaders

---

23. Christians United for Israel, "Programs."

24. Kuttab, "CUFI"; Christians United for Israel, "Policy Accomplishments."

25. Moore, "American Christians." *Christianity Today*'s pro-Israel bias is also discussed in chs. 1, 2, 4, and 14.

26. Although Moore does not identify as a dispensationalist, his views may be considered as "Christian Zionist" in the broad sense. Colin Chapman, for example, defines Christian Zionism as the "Christian support for Zionism that is based on theological reasons" (Chapman, *Whose Promised Land?*, 369). For Moore, these "theological reasons" are grounded in a version of Just War Theory and a misinterpretation of Rom 13; for dispensationalists, they are based on a false reading of the Abrahamic covenant (for example, Gen 12:1–7; 15:18–21), among others.

and theologians, myself included, but was unsuccessful. As of this writing, *Christianity Today* refuses to reconsider its Zionist editorial stance, to platform Palestinian voices, or even to engage in dialogue with us. I recently expressed my concern to a *Christianity Today* editor about being tokenized if interviewed by the magazine. Lamenting the lack of Arab Christian voices in the publication post-October 7, the editor responded by saying that I would be lucky if even that much happened.

Moore's misuse of Romans 13 to justify Israel's war on Gaza warrants a brief response here, as the passage is often weaponized to legitimize imperial and colonial violence by depicting God not as just and good, but as unjust and oppressive. In his interpretation of Romans 13, Moore employs a classical political hermeneutic by which the interpreter aligns the sociopolitical realities of the biblical text with those of our world.[27] To pull this off the interpreter must thoroughly understand both ancient and modern contexts as well as be able to discern differences between them. Unfortunately, Moore naïvely equates the modern State of Israel with the idealized civil authorities to whom Paul encourages Roman Christians to submit, thereby legitimizing Israel's ongoing war on Gaza under the pretext that a government can use the sword to punish wrongdoers.

Unfortunately for Moore, the idealized civil authorities that Paul refers to in Romans 13 are *not* equivalent to the Israeli authorities. Moore rightly indicates that Romans 13 applies to governments "acting justly," and he acknowledges that "every state is accountable to the justice of God and, if it acts unjustly, is subject to the judgment of God." However, Moore fails to acknowledge that Israel does, in fact, act unjustly and oppressively against the Palestinians.

A state with no declared borders, Israel applies brutal, iron-fist policies against the people of Palestine with the aim of achieving a clear, strategic goal: "maximum land, minimum Palestinians."[28] In Gaza, the Israeli government has weaponized the reprehensible events of October 7 to achieve this goal—hence the ongoing, disproportionate, genocidal war. In the West Bank, Israel's ruthless system of settler-colonial apartheid, which severely discriminates between Jewish settlers and native Palestinians, facilitates the ongoing seizure of Palestinian land and the expansion of Israeli settlements to accommodate the continuous influx of Jews into Palestine.[29] Already, no less than 60 percent of Palestinian land in the West Bank has been

---

27. Brazilian theologian Clodovis Boff calls this hermeneutic "the model of 'correspondence of terms,'" which he critiques for its naïveté. See Boff, *Theology and Praxis*, 143–46.

28. Shakir, "Israeli Apartheid."

29. For an introduction to Israeli apartheid, see White, *Israeli Apartheid*.

confiscated by Israel.[30] (Consider that the West Bank, Gaza, and East Jerusalem—the so-called Occupied Palestinian Territories, where the Palestine Liberation Organization agreed to establish a Palestinian state—comprise only 22 percent of historical Palestine.) At a personal level, my family and I were forced to leave our home in Bethlehem and have been living in forced exile for the last seven years due to Israel's policies of apartheid and displacement.[31] In contrast, Israel gives an American Jew born in New York, for example, the "right" to live with their family in the West Bank—on land stolen from Palestinians.

In a nutshell, the expulsion of Palestinians and the ethnic cleansing of Palestine have persisted since the Nakba of 1948. This is to be expected when a settler-colonial state, continuously expanding, clings to its foundational vision of maintaining an exclusivist *Judenstaat* on land inhabited by others. In 2018, Israel reaffirmed its exclusivist identity by passing the "Nation-State law," which declares Israel "the Nation-State of the Jewish People."[32] As an expanding, settler-colonial ethnostate, Israel cannot achieve its goals through peaceful, well-intended means. Instead, it must forcibly displace Palestinians, wage genocidal wars, implement brutal apartheid policies, and expand settlements aggressively.

The least that can be said, using Moore's words, is that the State of Israel has been "acting unjustly" against the Palestinians since its inception. Moore rightly asserts that a government "acting unjustly" becomes "a 'beast' state to be opposed" (Rev 13:1–18). If Moore had been careful to listen to his Palestinian Christian siblings or to reputable human rights organizations like Amnesty International and Human Rights Watch,[33] he would have likened Israel to the rogue state of Revelation 13 rather than to the idealized authorities of Romans 13. Unfortunately, by weaponizing Paul to sanction Israel's war on Gaza, Moore has depicted God as a warmongering deity who supports ethnic cleansing and oppression. It goes without saying that this stands in sharp contradiction to the good news of Jesus.

A Way Forward: Goodness, Repentance, and Justice

The discussion thus far leads us to the key question: What to do? What is a proper missiological response to theologies of apartheid and death?

---

30. For an excellent visualization of Israeli land grabs, see Haddad, "Visualising."
31. My personal story can be found in Deik, "Palestinian Counterstory."
32. For an in-depth analysis of this law, see Ghanim, "Israel's Nation-State Law."
33. See the reports on Israel's apartheid: Amnesty International, "Israel's Apartheid"; Human Rights Watch, *Threshold Crossed*.

I suggest that the way forward entails three steps: (1) proclaiming God's goodness and justice; (2) calling Christian Zionist theologians to repentance; and (3) working for justice.

Proclaiming God's Goodness and Justice

I first encountered Christian Zionism while working with a Western mission agency. My first reaction was to cry out, "Father, hallowed and sanctified be your name."

Christian Zionism defiles God's name. Anyone zealous for God's name should proclaim with Deuteronomy that "the great, the mighty, and the awesome God . . . is not partial" (Deut 10:17 ESV). As the Song of Moses declares, "The Rock [God], his work is perfect, for all his ways are justice. A God of faithfulness and without iniquity, just and upright is he" (Deut 32:4 ESV). One of my favorite translations of this verse is from the tenth-century Egyptian Rabbi Saadia ben Iosef al-Fayyoumi (known as Saadia Gaon). In his Judeo-Arabic translation of the Torah, Saadia renders the latter part of Deut 32:4 as *huwa al-ʿadl al-mustaqīm*, "he is upright justice."[34] Not only is God just, but God *is* justice.

The proof that God is just and impartial is found in the Scriptures, both Old and New Testaments, and ultimately in the person of Jesus Christ. In spite of this, some Western theologians read the Old Testament through the eyes of race and nationalism. They believe that Old Testament Yisrael continues today in an ethnostate with a divine mandate to claim a "promised land." Such theologians fail to understand the biblical notion of election (and of land).[35] They fail to see how Yisrael in the Hebrew Bible is a multiethnic community called to display God's justice to the world. They also fail to understand the centrality of Jesus in New Testament Christianity.

Why did God choose Abraham?[36] Neither for the color of his eyes nor for the complexion of his skin. God chose Abraham so that Abraham would "charge his children and his household after him to keep the way of the Lord by doing righteousness and justice" (Hebrew: *tzedakah* and *mishpat*; Greek: *dikaiosynē* and *krisis*; Gen 18:19 NRSV).

---

34. Saadia Gaon's Judeo-Arabic translation of the Torah can be found in Derenbourg, *Version Arabe*. English translation mine.

35. For excellent works on land theology by Palestinian Christians, see Isaac, *Land*; Katanacho, *Land*; Katanacho, "Christ."

36. The discussion of Scripture here draws on my PhD dissertation, provisionally titled *On Justice: A Study of the Wealth Ethics of the Acts of the Apostles in Conversation with Greek Deuteronomy and Graeco-Roman Philosophy*.

God's story with Abraham continues with the founding of Yisrael in the exodus event and the Mosaic covenant. Exodus 12:38 reminds us that people from mixed ethnicities came out of Egypt with the Hebrews. All those who said "Amen" to the Mosaic law became God's people. Significantly, the law of Moses in the Old Testament is the primary expression of God's justice (*tzedakah, dikaiosynē*), best understood as God's all-encompassing vision for righteous living. Displaying God's justice is the purpose of Yisrael's existence (Deut 4:5–8).

In the ancient world, there were competing conceptions of justice. So the crucial question is: what is *God's* conception of justice (*tzedakah, dikaiosynē*)? Deuteronomy sums it up in the injunction to love God with one's whole heart, soul, and strength (Deut 6:5; cf. 11:13, 22; 19:9). When Yisrael loves and clings to God, it *imitates God* in extending love and liberative justice (*mishpat/krisis*) to the oppressed (Deut 10:17–19). Some people, failing to grasp the full meaning of the latter kind of justice (*mishpat/krisis*), emphasize the penal rather than the liberative sense of the term. Nonetheless, the two meanings of *mishpat/krisis* are two sides of one coin: for the oppressor, justice (*mishpat/krisis*) is judgment; for the oppressed, justice is liberation and vindication.

Consider the exodus event. In *mishpat/krisis*, God punished the Egyptian oppressors and rescued the oppressed Hebrews. Crucially, the liberative *mishpat/krisis* that Yisrael receives from God in the exodus becomes central to Yisrael's social ethic: as God liberated Yisrael from oppression in Egypt, so Yisrael should imitate God by standing in solidarity with the oppressed (see, e.g., Deut 10:17–19; 24:17–22).

From a New Testament perspective, we find ultimate proof of God's goodness and justice in the person of Jesus Christ. In John 15:1, Jesus declares, "I am the true vine." The vine is a well known symbol of Yisrael (see Isa 5:1–7; Jer 2:21; Hos 9:10; Ps 80:8). Jesus was saying, "I am the true Yisrael." Likewise for Paul, Jesus is the true offspring of Abraham (Gal 3:16). Jesus is the fulfillment of what Old Testament Yisrael failed to do: he is the *dikaios*, "the just," Son of God (Luke 23:47; Acts 3:14; 7:52; 22:14; 1 Pet 3:18; 1 John 2:1), who fulfills all *dikaiosynē* (all justice, all righteousness; Matt 3:15). He is the true Yisrael, the true liberator of all the oppressed (Luke 4:16–21).

In the face of theologies that distort the holy name of God, the first step is to persist in proclaiming God's goodness and justice in our theology and biblical interpretation, keeping Jesus at the center. Heresies are measured by the distance between our theological center and Jesus. Genuine gospel proclamation does not replace Jesus with a settler-colonial project; Jesus is not in competition with Theodor Herzl. Zionism does not fulfill any of God's covenants. Rather, as Paul declared 2,000 years ago, in Jesus Christ "*every one* of God's promises is a 'Yes.'"[37]

Calling Christian Zionist Theologians to Repentance

In addition to proclaiming God's goodness and justice, we should call Christian Zionist theologians to repentance, as we emphasized in our 2023 "Call for Repentance."[38] Western theologians must discard Christian Zionism, in all its shapes and colors, and return to a theology that proclaims God's goodness and justice in Jesus Christ for all people.

The earliest Christians grappled with something comparable to Christian Zionist theology.[39] Jesus's Jewish followers faced the strong nationalist theology of Second Temple Judaism. Like other Jewish sects at the time (cf. Matt 3:7–9), they regarded themselves as special because of their ethnicity. They did not fully understand at first that the gospel included gentiles.

This is why in the first nine chapters of the book of Acts we do not see the gospel reaching gentiles. We hear the first evangelistic sermon to the gentiles in Acts 10, in the house of a Roman centurion by the name of Cornelius. This story, commonly known as the conversion of Cornelius, tells of another conversion as well: Peter's.

Before Peter could start declaring the good news about Jesus to Cornelius and his household, he had something to confess: "I truly understand that God shows no partiality, but in every nation anyone who fears him and does justice [*dikaiosynē*] is acceptable to him" (Acts 10:34–35, translation mine). This theological statement is not new; Deuteronomy clearly taught that God is not partial (Deut 10:17).[40] Peter's assertion, therefore, is a type of theological repentance—a return to the right conception of God and God's justice: God is not tribal, God does not show favoritism, and anyone who does justice is acceptable to him. This kind of repentance is a prerequisite to proclaiming God's love to the world.

Although Christian Zionism may be compared to the arguably racist theology espoused by some of the earliest Christians, Christian Zionism is actually much more dangerous. First, the earliest Christians did not use their ethnocentric theology to legitimize killing and ethnic cleansing.

---

37. 2 Cor 1:20 NRSV, emphasis mine.

38. Kairos Palestine et al., "Call for Repentance." The letter was co-authored by my colleagues Munther Isaac, Daniel Bannoura, Yousef AlKhouri, and me, and it was endorsed and signed by twelve Palestinian Christian institutions.

39. The discussion in this section is partly based on Deik, "Christian Zionism."

40. With Lundbom, *Deuteronomy*, 94.

Second, they did not place their theology in the service of an imperial agenda that contradicted the teachings of Jesus. On the contrary, the earliest Christians were a minority vulnerable to persecution from various quarters, including Rome itself. (Remember that Cornelius was a Roman centurion.) Yet even this non-colonial and non-imperial ethnocentric theology needed to be discarded for the advancement of the gospel. How much more do we—2,000 years after Peter's confession—need to discard racist theologies that legitimize ethnic cleansing and settler-colonial apartheid? If we are to proclaim God's love and goodness to the world, we must remove Christian Zionism from our midst.

The historical evangelical gathering of Lausanne IV in September 2024 was part of a process that included three major milestones: (1) the "State of the Great Commission" report, a pre-conference document of more than 500 pages, with contributions from 150 authors covering a wide range of topics;[41] (2) the gathering itself in Incheon, South Korea; and (3) the Seoul Statement that was released during the congress.[42] Unfortunately, neither the "State of the Great Commission" report nor the Seoul Statement properly addressed the challenge of Christian Zionism. During the congress, however, esteemed Latin American theologian Ruth Padilla DeBorst critiqued dispensational Christian Zionism with the following words:

> What makes God's people such are not superficial expressions of religious piety, "Christianese" jargon, worship jingles, or colonialist theologies that justify and finance oppression under the guise of some dispensational eschatology.[43]

Less than forty-eight hours after Padilla DeBorst's plenary talk, conference director David Bennett issued an apology statement that was circulated to all the congress participants on behalf of the Lausanne leadership:

> We ask speakers to submit scripts in advance, for the sake of clearer expression . . . . But sometimes we have failed to review carefully enough in advance the precise wording or tone used by a presenter . . . . As Congress Director, I would like to offer an apology for a presentation this week which singled out "dispensational eschatology" in a critical tone, implying that it contributed to violence and injustice, and which failed to note that many theologies have been misused and misapplied as

---

41. Niermann et al., "State."
42. Lausanne Movement, "Seoul."
43. Padilla DeBorst's full manuscript can be found in Atencio, "Speech." See also Padilla DeBorst's essay, "Doing Justice: The Unequivocal Calling of God's People," ch. 10 in this volume.

justifications for violence . . . . Our Lausanne team, including me, failed to review the wording of the presentation carefully enough in advance . . . . I ask for your forgiveness.[44]

Bennett's statement of apology came as a shock. However, I personally felt encouraged by the conference participants who expressed solidarity with us after the incident. I witnessed firsthand how many evangelicals, from both the Global South and North, genuinely love God and deeply care about God's justice and righteousness. Unfortunately, however, these evangelicals were not heeded. Instead, Lausanne's leadership capitulated to a vocal minority employing coercive tactics reminiscent of Zionist lobbyists in Washington, DC, leveraging threats to pressure decision-makers.

Sadly, the leaders of the congress gave in to Christian Zionist pressure, a fact that raises many questions. How can the organizers of a *global* Christian gathering issue such an apology for a perspective shared by a respected Global South theologian? Is Lausanne a place for genuine dialogue or is it simply a mobilization conference where those adhering to the same missiological paradigm gather together to energize one another toward fulfilling a specific understanding of mission? What is Lausanne about?

Further, one must wonder whether Lausanne's leaders fully grasp the goal of the congress, i.e., to "declare and display Christ together to a watching world." Do they realize that the world is *indeed* watching? Do they understand that the world is watching the evangelical justification of Israel's crimes, including the genocidal war on Gaza? How can we be serious about declaring and displaying Christ while leaving a racist theology unchallenged in our midst? Even worse: how dare we silence those who critique theologies of death and apartheid?

It is high time for evangelicals who are genuine about declaring and displaying Christ to work together to remove Christian Zionism from our midst—unless we want to declare and display to the world a god of favoritism and ethnic cleansing. If the early church had to remove non-colonial, non-imperial, ethnocentric theologies to enable the progress of the gospel, we today must dismantle Christian Zionism in all its forms.

---

44. Bennett, "Apology." In Padilla DeBorst's open letter of September 25 she responded: "This is not in any way a blanket dismissal of dispensational theology and, even less, of sisters and brothers who subscribe to that stance. For the pain my statement might have caused, I am sorry. What I am naming is the troubling theological rationale sustained by some people to perpetrate injustice against certain other people."

Working for Justice

The third step on the way forward is to work for justice for the Palestinians. I have already addressed, albeit briefly, the biblical foundation for such work. To those who are triggered by talk about justice—and there are many—we say: *love (agapē)*! Jesus summed up Old Testament justice in two simple commandments: love God and love your neighbor (Mark 12:28–34 and parallels). So, those who find injunctions to liberate the oppressed difficult (e.g., Ps 82:2–4; Isa 58:6; Luke 4:18–19) or the Sermon on the Mount impossible can heed the Old Testament call *to love God and neighbor*. "Do this," said Jesus to the teacher of the Law, "and you will live" (Luke 10:28).

In the face of a brutal Israeli occupation harming a defenseless population, Palestinians find themselves with two options: either violent resistance or nonviolent resistance. While some of our Western siblings may condone the use of violence, as Palestinian Jesus-followers we condone neither the violence of imperial powers (Israel and its Western allies) nor of zealots (the military brigades of Hamas and other factions within the Palestinian liberation movement). We believe that our duty and responsibility is to resist the oppressive Israeli occupation and apartheid system imposed on our people by adhering to Jesus's ethic of love. In the words of Kairos Palestine:

> We say that our option as Christians in the face of the Israeli occupation is to resist. Resistance is a right and a duty for the Christian. But it is resistance with love as its logic.[45]

Further, as we said in our 2023 "Call for Repentance," we urge our Western siblings to join us in "reject[ing] all theologies and interpretations that legitimize the wars of the powerful."[46] Instead, we invite our sisters and brothers to walk alongside us in nonviolent resistance against apartheid and all other forms of injustice and oppression perpetrated by Israel. For us, this is not an empty slogan but an invitation to witness to the risen Lord together by embodying his ethics in a fallen world. Could followers of Jesus once again unite in rejecting imperial and colonial violence, working together to end injustice and become the peacemakers Jesus has called us to be?

In Palestine, we say *al-dīn akhlāq*, "religion is [embodied in] ethics." As Palestinian Christians, we have been raised from childhood on the ethics of Jesus, especially the Sermon on the Mount. Growing up, I did not know much about the Bible, but thanks to my Catholic school and church I knew Matthew 5–7. At my Lutheran high school, nonviolent resistance was part of our curriculum. For Palestinian Christians, "love your neighbor" and

---

45. Kairos Palestine, "Moment of Truth," 4.2.3.
46. Kairos Palestine et al., "Call for Repentance."

"love your enemy" are community markers integral to our gospel witness. We are not a perfect community, but for us, Jesus's ethic of love is what makes a Christian, Christian. This is what sets us apart. So it is difficult for us to understand how some Western Christians can claim to follow Jesus without taking his teachings and ethics seriously—not only in their private lives but also in the public square.

In the early church, Jesus's ethic of love was inseparable from gospel witness. This is clearly seen in the book of Acts, especially in chapter 2. There, Peter preaches his first evangelistic sermon (Acts 2:14–36), as a result of which three thousand people come to faith in Jesus (2:41). Immediately afterward, we see how these earliest Christians live in a way that actualizes Jesus's ethic of love (2:42–47), subverting established sociopolitical patterns and structures in the Greco-Roman world (such as patronage, oppressive social stratification, and merit-based wealth distribution). As an outcome, "day by day the Lord added to their number those who were being saved" (2:47 NRSV). Living out the ethics of Jesus in the public square is a gospel witness that attracts people to God.

In one of the plenary talks at Lausanne IV, the speaker stressed how young people today are searching for *goodness* in Christianity; that is what attracts them to Jesus. When Christian leaders baptize reprehensible wars against people long oppressed, who will be drawn to the Christian faith? Who would want to follow a warmongering god that sanctions colonial violence and genocidal wars? If Christians are serious about the gospel, we should distance ourselves from the evil ways of the world and cling to the ethics of Jesus. Christians, including evangelicals, are already heavily engaged in politics; the question is, do they represent the politics of the world or the politics of Jesus?

Over the last year, I have noticed that Christians who consider the carnage in Gaza to be "just" (perhaps in accord with some version of Just War Theory) are fixated on destroying Hamas.[47] They have uncritically adopted the Israeli narrative. Not only have they dehumanized Hamas and encouraged their slaughter, but they have also reduced tens of thousands of innocent Palestinians to necessary and justified "collateral damage."

Someone in Cambridge once overheard me criticizing those who legitimize Israel's war on Gaza. He came to me upset, pointed his finger at me, and said: "So you don't want Hamas to be destroyed!" For such Christians, it seems, violence is the only solution imaginable. In the words of Nikki Haley, "Finish them!"[48]

---

47. On Hamas, see Bannoura, "Hamas and Violence," ch. 5 in this volume.
48. Singh, "Nikki Haley."

It goes without saying that such a posture has nothing to do with Jesus's ethic of love, which is God's solution to the problems of the world. This ethic is applicable not only to one's private life, but also to the church and to the *polis*. In other words, Jesus's ethic of love is *politikos*—"having relation to public life, political, public"[49]—and is, therefore, applicable not only to us as individuals but also to our political positions and conduct in the public square.

So, to our Christian siblings fixated on Hamas, I say: do you want to dismantle Hamas's al-Qassam brigades? Try Jesus. Try loving the Palestinians. Try giving them dignity and justice. Since you are already involved from afar, pressure your governments to end Israel's brutal occupation and apartheid. Believe me, the Palestinians themselves will then be the ones to dismantle not only the al-Qassam brigades but also the rest of the Palestinian militias, including the Abu Ali Mustafa brigades, al-Quds brigades, and al-Aqsa Martyrs' brigades.

Palestinians are not born violent. Like all human beings, Palestinians are made in the image of God. As a nation like any other nation, they want to live in dignity and freedom. They do not want to be treated like animals. Palestinians have endured oppression and injustice for seventy-seven years under the watch of the so-called "free world." Sadly, evangelical Christians have played an active role in that oppression by providing theological legitimization and lending practical support to Israel's apartheid regime. This must stop. It is high time that evangelicals discard Zionism, work for justice, and love our neighbors as Jesus did. This is the only way to lasting peace.

Bibliography

Al Jazeera. "Deaths from Israel's Attacks on Gaza Close to 62,000 as Missing Added." February 3, 2005. https://www.aljazeera.com/news/2025/2/3/gaza-death-toll-rises-close-to-62000-as-missing-added.

Amnesty International. "Israel's Apartheid Against Palestinians: Cruel System of Domination and Crime Against Humanity." London: Amnesty International, 2022. https://www.amnesty.org/en/documents/mde15/5141/2022/en/.

Ateek, Naim. *Justice and Only Justice: A Palestinian Theology of Liberation*. Maryknoll, NY: Orbis, 1989.

Atencio, Mitchell. "A Speech on Justice Criticized Israel; the Global Evangelical Conference Apologized." *Sojourners*, September 30, 2024. https://sojo.net/articles/news/speech-justice-criticized-israel-global-evangelical-conference-apologized.

Bebbington, David W. *Evangelicalism in Modern Britain: A History from the 1730s to the 1980s*. London: Unwin Hyman, 1989.

---

49. Liddell et al., *Lexicon*, s.v. πολιτικός, §IV.

Bennett, David. "An Apology from the Congress Director." Email sent to the participants of Lausanne IV, September 25, 2024.
Boff, Clodovis. *Theology and Praxis: Epistemological Foundations*. Maryknoll, NY: Orbis, 1987.
Brueggemann, Walter. *Chosen? Reading the Bible Amid the Israeli-Palestinian Conflict*. Louisville, KY: Westminster John Knox, 2015.
Casper, Jayson. "Gaza War Strains Bible Scholars' Model of Christian Conversation." *Christianity Today*, October 7, 2024. https://www.christianitytoday.com/2024/10/gaza-war-israel-palestine-conflict-christian-zionism-bible-scholars/.
Chapman, Colin. *Whose Promised Land? The Continuing Conflict over Israel and Palestine*. Rev. ed. Oxford: Lion Hudson, 2015.
Christians United for Israel. "Policy Accomplishments." https://cufi.org/about/policy/policy-accomplishments/.
———. "Programs." https://cufi.org/about/programs/.
Cowles, C. S., et al. *Show Them No Mercy: Four Views on God and Canaanite Genocide*. Counterpoints. Grand Rapids: Zondervan, 2003.
Deik, Anton. "Christian Zionism and Mission: How Does Our Understanding of Christianity Impact Our Witness in the World?" In *The Religious Other: A Biblical Understanding of Islam, the Qur'an and Muhammad*, edited by Martin Accad and Jonathan Andrews, 74–81. IMES. Carlisle: Langham, 2020.
———. "A Palestinian Counterstory." Centre for the Study of Bible and Violence, October 11, 2023. https://www.youtube.com/watch?v=B_dFCLFqPys.
Derenbourg, J., ed. *Version Arabe du Pentateuque de R. Saadia ben Iosef al-Fayyoûmî*. Vol. 1. *Oeuvres Complètes de R. Saadia ben Iosef al-Fayyoûmî*. Paris: Leroux, 1893.
Fuller Studio. "N. T. Wright on Discipleship and the Future of the Church." YouTube, October 12, 2020. https://www.youtube.com/watch?v=ptrsd3hJXNc.
Ghanim, Honaida. "Israel's Nation-State Law: Hierarchized Citizenship and Jewish Supremacy." *Critical Times* 4.3 (2021) 565–76.
Haddad, Mohammed. "Visualising How Israel Keeps Stealing Palestinian Land." *Al Jazeera*, July 11, 2024. https://www.aljazeera.com/news/2024/7/11/how-israel-keeps-stealing-palestinian-land.
Holder Rich, Cynthia, ed. *Christian Zionism in Africa*. Lanham, MD: Lexington, 2021.
Human Rights Watch. *A Threshold Crossed: Israeli Authorities and the Crimes of Apartheid and Persecution*. April 27, 2021. https://www.hrw.org/report/2021/04/27/threshold-crossed/israeli-authorities-and-crimes-apartheid-and-persecution.
Isaac, Munther. *From Land to Lands, from Eden to the Renewed Earth: A Christ-Centered Biblical Theology of the Promised Land*. Carlisle: Langham, 2015.
Jamaluddine, Zeina, et al. "Traumatic Injury Mortality in the Gaza Strip from Oct 7, 2023, to June 30, 2024: A Capture–Recapture Analysis." *The Lancet* 405 (2025) 469–77. https://www.thelancet.com/journals/lancet/article/PIIS0140-6736(24)02678-3/fulltext.
Kairos Palestine. "A Moment of Truth: A Word of Faith, Hope and Love from the Heart of Palestinian Suffering." December 15, 2009. https://www.kairospalestine.ps/index.php/about-kairos/kairos-palestine-document.
Kairos Palestine, et al. "A Call for Repentance: An Open Letter from Palestinian Christians to Western Church Leaders and Theologians." October 20, 2023. https://www.change.org/p/an-open-letter-from-palestinian-christians-to-western-church-leaders-and-theologians.

Katanacho, Yohanna. "Christ Is the Owner of *Haaretz*." *Christian Scholar's Review* 34 (2005) 425–41.

———. *The Land of Christ: A Palestinian Cry*. Eugene, OR: Pickwick, 2013.

Khalidi, Rashid. *The Hundred Years' War on Palestine: A History of Settler Colonialism and Resistance, 1917–2017*. New York: Metropolitan, 2022.

Kuttab, Jonathan. "CUFI and Two Vastly Different Theologies." FOSNA. https://www.fosna.org/the-fosna-blog/cufi-and-two-vastly-different-theologies.

Lausanne Movement. "The Seoul Statement." Lausanne Movement, 2024. https://lausanne.org/statement/the-seoul-statement.

Liddell, Henry George, et al. *A Greek-English Lexicon*. 9th ed. with revised supplement. Oxford: Clarendon, 1996.

Lundbom, Jack R. *Deuteronomy: A Commentary*. Grand Rapids: Eerdmans, 2013.

Masalha, Nur. *Expulsion of the Palestinians: The Concept of "Transfer" in Zionist Political Thought, 1882–1948*. Washington, DC: Institute for Palestine Studies, 1992.

Moore, Russell. "American Christians Should Stand with Israel Under Attack." *Christianity Today*, October 7, 2023. https://www.christianitytoday.com/2023/10/israel-hamas-middle-east-war-christians/.

Niermann, Matthew, et al., eds. "State of the Great Commission: Report Prepared for Lausanne Global Congress Seoul-Incheon 2024." Lausanne Movement, 2024. https://lausanne.org/report.

Pappé, Ilan. *The Ethnic Cleansing of Palestine*. Oxford: Oneworld, 2007.

———. *A History of Modern Palestine*. 3rd ed. Cambridge: Cambridge University Press, 2022.

———. *Ten Myths About Israel*. Updated ed. London: Verso, 2024.

Paynter, Helen. *God of Violence Yesterday, God of Love Today? Wrestling Honestly with the Old Testament*. Eugene, OR: Wipf & Stock, 2019.

Pew Research Center. "Modest Warming in U.S. Views on Israel and Palestinians." May 2022. https://www.pewresearch.org/religion/2022/05/26/modest-warming-in-u-s-views-on-israel-and-palestinians/.

Raheb, Mitri. *Decolonizing Palestine: The Land, the People, the Bible*. Maryknoll, NY: Orbis, 2023.

Sandeen, Ernest R. "Toward a Historical Interpretation of the Origins of Fundamentalism." In *Fundamentalism and Evangelicalism*, edited by Martin E. Marty, 19–36. Modern American Protestantism and Its World 10. Munich: Saur, 1993.

Shakir, Omar. "Israeli Apartheid: 'A Threshold Crossed.'" *Zenith Magazine*, July 19, 2021. https://www.hrw.org/news/2021/07/19/israeli-apartheid-threshold-crossed.

Singh, Kanishka. "Nikki Haley Writes 'Finish Them' on Israeli Artillery Shell, Drawing Criticism." Reuters, May 29, 2024. https://www.reuters.com/world/us/nikki-haley-writes-finish-them-israeli-artillery-shell-drawing-criticism-2024-5-29/.

Sizer, Stephen. *Christian Zionism: Road-Map to Armageddon?* Leicester: InterVarsity, 2004.

Smith, Robert O. *More Desired Than Our Owne Salvation: The Roots of Christian Zionism*. New York: Oxford University Press, 2013.

United Nations Office for the Coordination of Humanitarian Affairs. "Reported Impact Snapshot: Gaza Strip." October 2, 2024. https://www.ochaopt.org/content/reported-impact-snapshot-gaza-strip-2-october-2024.

White, Ben. *Israeli Apartheid: A Beginner's Guide*. 2nd ed. London: Pluto, 2014.

Wolfe, Patrick. "Settler Colonialism and the Elimination of the Native." *Journal of Genocide Research* 8 (2006) 387–409.

CHAPTER TWELVE

October 7 and Armageddon
Misreading Revelation, Justifying Genocide

Rob Dalrymple

> *The sixth angel poured out his bowl on the great river, the Euphrates; and its water was dried up, so that the way would be prepared for the kings from the east. And I saw coming out of the mouth of the dragon and out of the mouth of the beast and out of the mouth of the false prophet, three unclean spirits like frogs; for they are spirits of demons, performing signs, which go out to the kings of the whole world, to gather them together for the war of the great day of God, the Almighty. ("Behold, I am coming like a thief. Blessed is the one who stays awake and keeps his clothes, so that he will not walk about naked and men will not see his shame.") And they gathered them together to the place which in Hebrew is called Har-Magedon. (Rev 16:12–16)*[1]

On October 8, one day after Hamas terrorists broke through the security fence and brought devastation to Israel, pastor Greg Laurie told his congregation, "We should be looking up" because "your redemption is drawing near," at which point some of the congregants broke out in applause.[2]

---

1. All Scripture citations in this chapter are from the NASB.
2. Laurie, "Terror Attacks."

> *Half of evangelicals support Israel because they believe it is important for fulfilling end-times prophecy.*[3]

SEVERAL YEARS AGO, A parishioner in the church I was serving arranged to meet with me. Excited to share insights he had discovered that confirmed the imminent return of Jesus, he arrived with printouts of charts and all sorts of data. Moreover, he was adamant about his conclusions. Everything, he explained, would transpire within the next five years. That was more than twenty years ago.

I wish I had had a magic wand that would have transported us into the future to show him that he was wrong. After all, there was nothing I could have said at the time that would have made any difference. Then again, I wonder if time travel would have done much good. When events prove such prognosticators wrong, instead of issuing a *mea culpa* they simply return to their studies to discern where they made the mistake. Then they emerge with a new, refined prediction that is held even more adamantly than before.[4]

Similar claims to discern the signs of the times are on the rise today. In particular, some have maintained that Hamas's terror attack against Israel on October 7, 2023, and Israel's assault on Gaza mark the beginning of the war of Armageddon.[5]

Was October 7 a Prelude to, or Even the Beginning of, Armageddon (Rev 16:12–16)?

On October 7, 2023, when Hamas terrorists breached the security fence around Gaza and launched a terror attack on Israel, I was overwhelmed with disbelief and grief. There was disbelief that something like this could ever happen. The nation of Israel is a global leader in security, and its billion-dollar security fence was said to be impenetrable. That the people of Gaza had been living for almost two decades under an oppressive blockade in conditions increasingly deemed "unlivable"[6] made some sort of attack almost inevitable. Yet who would have believed that an attack of this scale could be launched?

---

3. Bump, "Half of Evangelicals."

4. This sort of reasoning is apparent in Harold Camping's repeated failures, over the course of decades, to predict the end of the world. See McFadden, "Harold Camping."

5. See André, "American Evangelicals."

6. The UN declared in 2018 that Gaza would be "unlivable" by 2020. See United Nations, "Gaza 'Unliveable.'"

There was grief for the more than 1,100 Israelis who were killed and the 251 who were taken to Gaza as hostages. There was also grief because, as I wrote on October 8,[7] anyone familiar with this situation knew that Israel had consistently responded to such terror attacks in the past with a policy of overwhelming deterrence. Israel would again ensure that those who attempted to harm them suffered far greater harm than what they had been able to inflict on Israel. I grieved on October 7 because I knew what this would all mean for the people of Gaza.[8]

In the days that followed, my grief only increased as I became aware of Christian pastors and leaders who were capitalizing on the suffering of others and using Hamas's attack as a pretense for espousing their eschatological convictions. On October 8, evangelical pastor Greg Laurie told his congregation that they must "look up" (cf. Luke 21:28) because the deaths of over 1,100 Israelis were a clear sign that the day of Jesus's return was drawing near,[9] to which news Laurie's congregation responded with a spattering of applause. Applause? More than a thousand Israelis had just died—and who knew then how many thousands of Palestinians were about to meet a similar fate—and this was grounds for rejoicing?[10]

For evangelicals such as Laurie, the eschatological clock is winding down rapidly toward the end.[11] They are convinced that the war on Gaza is only the beginning. For these end times speculators, Hamas's attack on October 7 and Israel's resultant siege on Gaza serve as a clear indication that the famed war of Armageddon (Rev 16:12–16) is underway. Hopeful times indeed.

In this brief essay, I aim to counter such claims by providing insights into the book of Revelation and its description of the war of Armageddon. I will argue that in the book of Revelation, the war of Armageddon represents Satan's efforts to deceive the people of God in order to thwart their mission of imitating Christ in sacrificial love for the other. As a result, to engage in end-time speculation is not only a waste of time. It is actually to stumble unawares into the devil's snare in a way that renders the church's witness impotent in the face of evil and injustice.

---

7. Dalrymple, "My Thoughts."

8. Tragically, my fear that Israel would inflict a ten-fold suffering on Gaza woefully underestimated the scale of the Israeli response.

9. Laurie, "Terror Attacks."

10. On November 5, 2023, less than one month after the attack of October 7, the popular pastor at First Baptist Church in Dallas asked his congregation, "Are we actually living in what the Bible calls the End Times?" Cited in André, "American Evangelicals."

11. See Jaffe-Hoffman, "Israel-Hamas Conflict."

Understanding the Book of Revelation

The first step in understanding the book of Revelation is to recognize that it tells a story—a story that centers on Jesus Christ. It is, after all, "the revelation of Jesus Christ" (Rev 1:1). At the heart of the Apocalypse is the affirmation that Jesus is the world's true King and that through his death and resurrection the kingdom—the rule—of God has begun.[12]

In one sense, the book of Revelation is no different from the rest of the New Testament (NT). Revelation affirms, as does the Gospel of Mark, that Jesus's rule is not like that of the kings of the nations:

> Calling them to Himself, Jesus said to them, "You know that those who are recognized as rulers of the Gentiles lord it over them; and their great men exercise authority over them. But it is not this way among you, but whoever wishes to become great among you shall be your servant; and whoever wishes to be first among you shall be slave of all. For even the Son of Man did not come to be served, but to serve, and to give His life a ransom for many." (Mark 10:42–45)[13]

Whereas the nations rule by power, force, and violence (Rev 18:24), Christ rules as the Lamb that was slain (Rev 5:5–6, 9). As the narrative unfolds, we learn that the victorious Christ calls his people and appoints them to follow the Lamb (Rev 14:4) by faithfully, lovingly, and sacrificially laying down their lives, too, for the sake of the nations. Revelation adds, however, that the efforts of the people of God meet with fierce opposition. A dragon (identified as Satan, Rev 12:9) and his minions wage war against them (i.e., "Armageddon"; Rev 16:12–16) in an effort to hinder their cruciform witness to God's kingdom.

Armageddon and "the War" in the Book of Revelation

John's account of "the war of Armageddon" (Rev 16:12–16)[14] is one aspect of his extensive description of "the war" in the book of Revelation. Thus, to understand John's account of Armageddon, we must discern his comprehensive understanding of "the war."

---

12. This is the clear message from Rev 4–5. See my *Revelation: A Love Story*.

13. See parallels in Matt 20:25–28 and Luke 22:25–27.

14. The NASB and the NRSV render it "Har-Magedon" (though the NRSV uses the unhyphenated "Harmagedon"), meaning the "mount of Megiddo." The ESV, NET, NIV, NKJV, and the NLT all read "Armageddon," meaning the "battle of Megiddo." For further discussion, see my *Understanding*, 155–65.

The noun "war" (*polemos*) occurs nine times in the book of Revelation (Rev 9:7, 9; 11:7; 12:7, 17; 13:7; 16:14; 19:19; 20:8). The first two occurrences (Rev 9:7, 9) refer to war in a generic sense,[15] which leaves us with seven (not surprisingly) uses of the noun "war," each of which appear to reference "*the* war." These seven occurrences of "war" share several features, two of which are especially important.

First, setting aside for a moment "the war" of Rev 16:12–16 (our Armageddon passage), we see that each of the other six instances of *polemos* refers to a war that Satan and his minions wage. Thus, in Rev 12:7, 17, and 20:8,[16] "the war" is explicitly said to be waged by Satan (the dragon; Rev 12:9):

> And there was war in heaven, Michael and his angels waging war with the dragon. The dragon and his angels waged war. (Rev 12:7)

> So the dragon was enraged with the woman, and went off to make war with the rest of her children, who keep the commandments of God and hold to the testimony of Jesus. (Rev 12:17)

> When the thousand years are completed, Satan will be released from his prison, and will come out to deceive the nations which are in the four corners of the earth, Gog and Magog, to gather them together for the war; the number of them is like the sand of the seashore. (Rev 20:7–8)

Similarly, Rev 11:7 and 13:7 attribute "the war" to the beast who comes from the sea.[17] That Satan empowers this beast (Rev 13:2) confirms that it is ultimately Satan and his minions that wage "the war." Finally, Rev 19:19 adds, "The beast and the kings of the earth and their armies assembled to make war." Thus, each of the occurrences of "the war" indicates that it is waged by Satan, the beast, and/or the nations/kings of the earth.

---

15. The NASB (as with most English versions) translates *polemos* as "battle" in Rev 9:7 and 9:9. In Rev 9:7, John notes, "The appearance of the locusts was like horses prepared for battle"; then in v. 9 he adds, "The sound of their wings was like the sound of chariots, of many horses rushing to battle."

16. It is conceivable that "the war" in Rev 12:7, which takes place in heaven, is an exception in that we have no statement as to who the instigator of that war is. However, since apocalypses often correlate events that occur in heaven with events on the earth, the war in Rev 12:7 likely corresponds to the other instances of "the war" where Satan is the mastermind.

17. In Rev 19:19, John indicates that "the kings of the earth and their armies" join the beast in waging this war.

A second feature of "the war" in Revelation is that Satan wages "the war" against Christ, the people of God, and/or the heavenly angels. This is evident in the first occurrence of "the war" (Rev 11:7), where it is explicitly waged against the two witnesses:[18]

> When they [the two witnesses] have finished their testimony, the beast that comes up out of the abyss will make war with them, and overcome them and kill them. (Rev 11:7)

In Rev 12:7, "the war" is waged in heaven against "Michael and his angels." Revelation 12:17 adds that Satan (the dragon) "went off to make war with the rest of her [the woman's] children," who are identified as those "who keep the commandments of God and hold to the testimony of Jesus."[19] Similarly, Rev 13:7 affirms that "the war" is waged against "the saints."[20] In addition, in Rev 19:19, "the war" is explicitly waged against Christ and his army. Finally, in Rev 20:8, Satan wages war against "the saints":

> [Satan and the nations] came up on the broad plain of the earth and surrounded the camp of the saints and the beloved city. (Rev 20:9)

In all six of these occurrences of "the war" in the book of Revelation, then, we see that it is a war waged by Satan and his minions against Christ, the people of God, and/or the angelic hosts. What, then, of the Armageddon passage?

"The War" in Revelation 16:12–16 (Armageddon)

It should not be surprising that the famed Armageddon passage (Rev 16:12–16) includes these same two features.

---

18. Regardless of how one identifies the two witnesses, they belong to the people of God. Some identify them as two individuals; others suggest they represent a portion of the church. Along with most interpreters, I contend that they represent all of God's people, and I argue for this view in my *Revelation and the Two Witnesses*, 34–36.

19. Some end-times pundits identify the offspring of the woman with the Jewish people. There is a basis for this reasoning in that earlier in Rev 12 the woman gave birth to the Messiah (Rev 12:5). However, those who "hold to the testimony of Jesus" (Rev 12:17) include more than ethnic Israelites. At the end of Rev 12, the woman represents the followers of Jesus, which includes Jews but cannot be restricted to Jews.

20. John uses "saints" thirteen times in the book of Revelation (5:8; 8:3, 4; 11:18; 13:7, 10; 14:12; 16:6; 17:6; 18:20, 24; 19:8; 20:9) either for the people of God or a subgroup within the people of God. In light of the parallels between Rev 11:7 and 13:7—in both instances, the war is explicitly waged by the beast—a strong case can be made that "saints" in Rev 13:7 refers to the people of God, as in Rev 11:7.

First, that Satan is the one who wages "the war" becomes evident in Rev 16:14, where we are told that "the war" is sparked by the "spirits of demons" that issue from the mouth of the dragon (Satan), the beast, and the false prophet (Rev 16:13–14).[21] This passage thus corresponds to the other six references to "the war" by naming Satan and his minions as its instigators.

Second, Rev 16:12–16 also matches the other six instances of "the war" by specifying that Satan wages it against the people of God. Although this theme may not be as apparent, a careful examination of Rev 16:12–16 confirms that the people of God are indeed the targets of Satan's war efforts.

The first indication that "the war" of Armageddon is waged against the people of God derives from literary parallels between "the war" in Rev 16:14 and "the war" in Rev 19:19 and 20:8.[22] That these three accounts of "the war" are linked is evident from John's repetition of the phrase "to gather them together for the war" (Rev 16:14; 19:19; 20:8).[23] In Rev 16:14 and 20:8, the identical phrase is used, and it appears with slight variation again in Rev 19:19.[24] The literary relationship between these three accounts is reinforced by the fact that the verb "to gather" (*sunagō*) occurs only five times in the book of Revelation (Rev 16:14, 16; 19:17, 19; 20:8) with all five appearing in just these three passages. Since we know that "the war" in the latter two accounts is waged against Christ, the people of God, and/or the heavenly angels, it stands to reason that they are Satan's targets in "the war" of Rev 16:12–16 as well.

Another indication that "the war" in Rev 16:12–16 is waged against the people of God is that John inserts a parenthetical exhortation to the people of God in Rev 16:15:

---

21. The use of "mouth" here is significant in that Jesus's sword proceeds from his mouth (Rev 1:16; 2:12, 16; 19:15, 21), and it is with this sword that Jesus wages war: "I will make war against them with the sword of My mouth" (Rev 2:16). See also Rev 19:15, "From His mouth comes a sharp sword, so that with it He may strike down the nations." Note that Rev 2:16 is not an additional reference to "the war" as the verbal form for "war" is used. The verbal form (*polemeō*) occurs six times in the book of Revelation (2:16; 12:7 [2x]; 13:4; 17:14; 19:11).

22. For a detailed discussion of the literary links between Rev 16:14, 19:19, and 20:8, see "Excursus: Armageddon part 2" in my *Revelation: A Love Story*, 356–58.

23. John's use of repetition is one of the key rhetorical features of the book of Revelation. John consistently links passages by repeating a key term or phrase. The strength of this connection is heightened when the term occurs in only two or three passages. For example, see the discussion of John's use of "strong angel" in my *Revelation: A Love Story*, 181–83.

24. Rev 16:14, "to gather (*sunagō*) them together for the war"; Rev 20:8, "to gather (*sunagō*) them together for the war"; Rev 19:19, "gathered together (*sunagō*) to make war" (NASB, modified).

"Behold, I am coming like a thief. Blessed is the one who stays awake and keeps his clothes, so that he will not walk about naked and men will not see his shame."[25]

That this is an exhortation to the people of God is abundantly evident. For one, Jesus[26] says, "I am coming." Though the verb "come" occurs thirty-six times in the book of Revelation,[27] the phrase "I am coming" occurs only seven times (Rev 2:5, 16; 3:11; 16:15; 22:7, 12, 20). The first three instances are found in the messages to the churches: Ephesus (Rev 2:5), Pergamum (Rev 2:16), and Philadelphia (Rev 3:11). The final three appear in the epilogue (Rev 22:7, 12, 20), addressing the readers of the Apocalypse. Since in these other instances "I am coming" is consistently addressed to the people of God, it stands to reason that "I am coming" in Rev 16:15 is directed at this audience as well.

Why would John insert an exhortation to the people of God in the midst of his description of the war of Armageddon? The only reasonable conclusion "is that the war directly pertains to them."[28] Why else would the people of God be exhorted to stay awake?

The book of Revelation does not depict an eschatological battle in which the nations of the world attack the Jewish State of Israel in the land of Palestine. Revelation uses "the war" (Armageddon) to describe the campaign Satan has been waging and continues to wage against Christ and the people of God.[29] Thus, the book of Revelation offers no basis for linking the attack of October 7 and the resultant war on Gaza directly to the war of Armageddon.

---

25. That Rev 16:15 is parenthetical is recognized by most English translations. The ESV, NASB, NET, NIV, NKJV, NLT, and NRSV all add parentheses around the verse. After the parenthetical remark, v. 16 resumes the narrative by repeating the verb "gather" found in v. 14.

26. That the speaker in Rev 16:15 is Jesus is indicated by the attribution of "I am coming." This statement occurs seven times in the book of Revelation (Rev 2:5, 16; 3:11; 16:15; 22:7, 12, 20); Christ is undoubtedly the speaker in the first three and likely the speaker in the last three. See below.

27. See Rev 1:4, 7, 8; 2:5, 16; 3:10, 11; 4:8; 5:7; 6:1, 3, 5, 7, 17; 7:13, 14; 8:3; 9:12; 11:14, 18; 14:7, 15; 16:15; 17:1, 10 (2x); 18:10; 19:7; 21:9; 22:7, 12, 17 (3x), 20 (2x).

28. Dalrymple, *Revelation: A Love Story*, 382.

29. Of course, the way in which the war is waged against Christ is by attacking His people. This is the essence of the Parable of the Sheep and the Goats: "To the extent that you did it to one of these brothers of Mine, *even the least of them*, you did it to Me" (Matt 25:40).

Armageddon: Satan's War Against the People of God

At this point, one might be tempted to conclude that "the war" Satan wages against the people of God is evident in the persecution of Christians around the world today (e.g., in North Korea, Nigeria, the Middle East, and many other parts of the world). But perhaps one of Satan's most effective wars is the one he is waging against the Western evangelical church. All too readily, we assume that "the war" of Armageddon refers solely to a physical war of persecution, imprisonment, and even death for Christians. I am not denying that Satan wages war against the people of God in these ways. The book of Revelation affirms that "in her [Babylon] was found the blood of prophets and of saints and of all who have been slain on the earth" (18:24). But should we assume that Satan's war is limited to inflicting physical suffering?

Satan's Use of Deception Against the People of God

What if Satan wages war against the people of God by deceiving them so that they believe what is false and thereby fail to proclaim the truth? What if the people of God come to endorse what is not only untrue but actually contrary to the very mission to which the people of God have been called?

That Satan uses deception as a means of waging war against the people of God explains John's parenthetical exhortation in the midst of his description of Armageddon:

> Blessed is the one who stays awake and keeps his clothes, so that he will not walk about naked and men will not see his shame.
> (Rev 16:15)

This exhortation corresponds to the message to the church in Sardis (Rev 3:1–6). For one, Rev 16:15 is linked with Rev 3:3 by the fact that references to a "thief" occur in only these two verses. John also connects the two accounts by means of the verb *grēgoreō*, translated "wake up" (Rev 3:2, 3) or "stay awake" (Rev 16:15).[30] This verb appears in Revelation only in these two passages.[31] A further link between Rev 16:15 and Rev 3:4 is John's use of the word *himatia*, "garments" or "clothing":

---

30. Although it is translated differently in Rev 3:2, 3 and 16:15, it is the same verb (*grēgoreō*) in both passages.

31. As noted earlier, John links passages by repeating certain words or phrases. The link is stronger when that word or phrase only occurs in two passages. See n23 above.

> But you have a few people in Sardis who have not soiled their garments; and they will walk with Me in white, for they are worthy. (Rev 3:4)

> Blessed is the one who stays awake and keeps his clothes, so that he will not walk about naked and men will not see his shame. (Rev 16:15)

That John refers to "garment(s)" seven times (see Rev 3:4, 5, 18; 4:4; 16:15; 19:13, 16) and that each of the other six occurrences refers to the clothing of either the people of God (Rev 3:4, 5, 18), the heavenly counterpart of the people of God (Rev 4:4), or Christ (Rev 19:13, 16), strongly suggests that 16:15 also depicts the clothing of the people of God.

The point in noting all of this is that the Armageddon passage brings us back to the message to the church in Sardis, which indicates that the people of God are in danger of falling asleep and failing to accomplish their missional task of following the Lamb in sacrificial love for the sake of the nations. Those who stay awake will not be ashamed. Those who fail to remain vigilant, however, will fall prey to the deceptive ways of the dragon, the beast, and the false prophet who wage war against them.

Conclusion

Nothing in the book of Revelation supports the notion that the present war on Gaza, or any future war that involves the nation of Israel or the Jewish people, signals the fulfillment of, or serves as a precursor to, the war of Armageddon. On the contrary, the book of Revelation explicitly affirms both that the agent of "the war" of Armageddon is Satan and his minions and that the ones targeted are Christ and the people of God.

Perhaps we can take this conclusion one step further. Can we not say that the popularity of this notion of Armageddon, which encourages the people of God to sit by idly, waiting for their Twitter feed to light up with news that Israel has been attacked, suggests that Satan has seduced much of the Western church? Could it be that the Western church's fervent support for militarism and the arming of Israel, leading to the destruction of Gaza to the point of rendering the region uninhabitable and effectively ethnically cleansed, is an example of Satan's deceptive war against God's people? Is not our failure to be a people known by our love (John 13:35), who live as if we are blessed when we pursue peace (Matt 5:9), who weep with those who weep (Rom 12:15), an indication that we have fallen prey to deception?

Armageddon is indeed upon us, and much of the Western evangelical church is losing the war. The irony is that those who support the war on Gaza believing that it heralds the unfolding of "biblical prophecy" are the very ones who have failed to "stay awake and keep [their] clothes" (Rev 16:15) in the time of crisis.

"The war" of Armageddon is not to be waged on the battlefields of Israel at the close of human history. It is waged every day in the diabolical propaganda of empires that deludes and deceives even the people of God so that they, too, condone war, violence, death, and destruction. We are called to be zealous advocates for peace, but we are condoning war. We are called to weep in the face of injustice, but we are rejoicing at genocide.

Bibliography

André, Fiona. "American Evangelicals Interpret Israel-Hamas War as a Prelude to End Times." *Religion News Service*, November 17, 2023. https://www.baptiststandard.com/news/faith-culture/evangelicals-see-israel-hamas-war-in-light-of-end-times/.

Bump, Philip. "Half of Evangelicals Support Israel Because They Believe It Is Important for Fulfilling End-Times Prophecy." *The Washington Post*, May 14, 2018. https://www.washingtonpost.com/news/politics/wp/2018/05/14/half-of-evangelicals-support-israel-because-they-believe-it-is-important-for-fulfilling-end-times-prophecy/.

Dalrymple, Rob. "My Thoughts on Biden's Speech Regarding the Tragic Events in Israel and Gaza." *Determinetruth*, October 8, 2023. https://www.patheos.com/blogs/determinetruth/2023/10/my-thoughts-on-bidens-speech-regarding-yesterdays-tragic-events-in-israel-and-gaza/.

———. *Revelation: A Love Story*. Eugene, OR: Cascade, 2024.

———. *Revelation and the Two Witnesses: The Implications for Understanding John's Depiction of the People of God and His Hortatory Intent*. Eugene, OR: Wipf & Stock, 2011.

———. *Understanding the New Testament and the End Times*. 2nd ed. Eugene, OR: Wipf & Stock, 2018.

Jaffe-Hoffman, Maayan. "Israel-Hamas Conflict: A Prophetic Window into End Times?" *The Jerusalem Post*, November 25, 2023. https://www.jpost.com/christianworld/article-775111.

Laurie, Greg. "What the Terror Attacks on Israel Mean for End Times Prophecy." October 9, 2023. https://www.youtube.com/watch?v=5495g3NT4VA.

McFadden, Robert D. "Harold Camping, Dogged Forecaster of the End of the World, Dies at 92." *The New York Times*, December 17, 2013. https://www.nytimes.com/2013/12/18/us/harold-camping-radio-entrepreneur-who-predicted-worlds-end-dies-at-92.html.

United Nations. "Gaza 'Unliveable,' Expert Tells Third Committee." UN Meetings Coverage and Press Releases. October 24, 2018. https://press.un.org/en/2018/gashc4242.doc.htm.

PART III

The Peoples of the Land
Taking Our Stand with the Vulnerable

CHAPTER THIRTEEN

Living the Future We Hope For

*Christians, Jews, and Muslims
at the Gaza Border*

MERCY AIKEN

On the Road to Gaza

IT IS A MID-AUGUST morning in 2024, as hot as you'd expect the Negev to be this time of year. After we stop at a gas station, Omar Haramy, our Palestinian Christian guide from Sabeel Jerusalem, remarks that we might be feeling homesick. If so, he will provide a symbol of America to make us feel better. Mischievously, he points to the golden arches of a McDonald's. We all groan.

  He likes to rub it in, this whole American empire thing.

  With locally made snacks in hand, our minibus heads south. The road signs indicate that we are close to the places that have become so familiar in the past year: Be'eri, Nahal Oz, Rafah.

  A week earlier, our coalition of twelve American Christian leaders and activists entered the Holy Land, determined to participate in a solidarity visit even as the threat of regional war was heightening. We spent the week visiting hotspots across the occupied West Bank and East Jerusalem. Our purpose was to observe what was happening in the Occupied Territories, to provide a protective presence for the vulnerable, to comfort those who mourn, to hear people's stories, and to share our experiences back home.

Our week in the Occupied Territories revealed a clear pattern. With all eyes on Gaza, Palestinians in the West Bank were more isolated and defenseless than ever. Whether forcibly evicted from their homes, facing the threat of expulsion, or experiencing home demolitions, arbitrary arrests, and settler/militia assaults, those who live under Occupation were enduring unprecedented levels of Israeli violence, with little to no accountability for the perpetrators.

To that point, about thirty Palestinian communities had been depopulated since October 7. We visited one of them, Umm Jamal, a small Bedouin community of about a hundred people. They were packing up to move after a week of unusually violent harassment from local settlers had rendered life unbearable. While world leaders still spoke of a two-state solution as the desired endgame of the conflict, settler militias—armed by Itamar Ben Gvir, Israel's National Minister of Security—were moving faster than ever across the West Bank, strategically undermining the last, thin hope of a viable Palestinian state.

In solidarity with prisoners and hostages, we had also prayed outside of Ofer prison, where thousands of Palestinians, including minors, were held in indefinite detention, in gruesome conditions made much worse after October 7—though not nearly as gruesome as those in Sde Tieman and other Israeli prison camps. We also visited the Hostage and Missing Families Forum in Tel Aviv, whose members were desperate to keep their loved ones in the consciousness of the Israeli public lest they be forgotten or de-prioritized in the expanding war.

Today is our final day, the culmination of an exhausting and extraordinary week. We will spend it at the Gaza border, starting with an interfaith prayer vigil with a coalition from Rabbis for Human Rights, where we will sing, lament, and pray together.

Omar waves toward the windows on the left. "We are now driving parallel to Gaza. It is just to the west. No more than five hundred meters from here."

This news makes us very quiet. People are dying, just over there, to our left. The dissonance is hard to bear.

Just to our left, how many Gazans lie trapped beneath the rubble of bombed buildings? How many hostages are still alive in tunnels beneath the earth? Gaza has become a subterranean sepulcher, a dungeon for the living. And for those above the earth, Gaza remains a catacomb, a darkness, a death camp, an isolation from which they rarely escape.

The bus driver interrupts my thoughts: "We are now passing the area where Gaza's churches are located." I draw a sharp breath, longing for a view of the place I've carried in my heart for ten months. A few months earlier, in Cairo, I'd met several families with whom I had spoken during the war. They had managed to exit Gaza after half a year holed up in the churches with other Christians. I knew their stories, their losses, their trauma, their narrow escapes, their anguish for the friends and family left behind—those killed in snipings and bombings or slowly dying through inadequate nutrition and lack of medicine.

"This area to the right"—the bus driver motions toward stark, white apartment buildings—"some Hamas fighters were hiding in this area for a few days before they found the last of them."

Occasionally, we pass discernible rows of old cactus fencing—all that remains of Palestinian ghost-villages depopulated in 1948, with most former residents displaced to Gaza. I wonder how many people who drive past the cacti have any idea of their history. "You can see that there is still plenty of space for Palestinians to return home—if space was the real issue," remarks Omar.

The whole land feels like one giant crime scene, scorched with history, haunted by events both recent and ancient.

The roads and land down here are empty. We pass several large dirt parking lots filled with dust-covered Israeli tanks and other military vehicles. We see a US and an Israeli flag planted together by the side of the road, and we groan again. That whole American empire thing.

Among the pale trees, I see a large banner with photos of the Israeli hostages and large block letters: "Bring them home now!" The bus driver confirms that this is the site of the Nova music festival, where Hamas militants killed several hundred young people and took about forty of them as hostages to Gaza. I stare as long as I can, till the place fades behind me.

A haunted area, indeed.

Prayer Meeting at the Gaza Border

We are late to the gathering. The GPS system is disrupted in this area, and we are having trouble finding the meeting place: the Maon Synagogue, a sixth-century archaeological site near Kibbutz Nirim and Kibbutz Nir Oz. When we finally pull into the parking lot, the rabbis are already there, laying out dates, grapes, cookies, fruit juice, and water on a picnic table. "Drink, eat up," they tell us. "You'll need sustenance for the heat of the day."

We are greeted by Rabbis for Human Rights director Avi Dabush. He's a survivor of October 7 at nearby Kibbutz Nirim. Along with his family, he spent over eight hours in the safe room of their house, hearing the voices of Hamas militants outside. Somehow, they were spared. They've not yet been able to return home, and his wife is too anguished to visit the area as he does today. Despite the trauma of October 7, or maybe because of it, he is more committed than ever to peacemaking—to ending the Occupation and its accompanying human rights abuses, to securing a better future based on mutual respect and legal equality for all people regardless of religion or ethnicity.

Together with his colleagues, Avi has prepared an interfaith worship service. One rabbi has a guitar. Some are women, one in orthodox attire. There is also a local imam, an African-descended citizen of Israel. He's elegantly attired in robes of white, gold, and black. He has many relatives in Gaza, he tells us. So far, they are all still alive.

They lead us to the Byzantine-era synagogue, where we gather under an awning that provides shade and allows us to view the mosaic floor decorated with plants, birds, and animals. "We chose this spot to pray," Avi tells us, "because not far from here is another ruin, a church, although it is not fully excavated. But it has a similar mosaic floor. It is unusual in Judaism to see such images in a synagogue, but these two mosaic floors are from the same era. This speaks to us of an amicable past and gives us hope for a better future."

We gather in an oblong circle beside the mosaic. "We must hold on to hope," Avi adds. "Hope stops hatred. Hatred happens in hopelessness." Omar nods his head.

"Religion can be used for hatred, but it can also be a powerful tool for justice and reconciliation. We want to partner with you to create a better future," our Palestinian guide says to the rabbis.

"We know that what is happening here is not normal. Life should be better. We can support a better reality in a logical way: knowing each other, loving and forgiving each other, being patient with each other—the things we do in a family—these are the things that make peace. When we see ourselves as family, we can walk the extra mile for the other. After October 7, we *must* speak together. This is our responsibility as religious leaders. We must live the future that we hope for."

We begin to pray and sing in three languages. Desert birds join us, twittering and squawking in their native tongues. I imagine a Jewish congregation worshiping here in times past alongside the nearby Christian congregation. Maybe the same desert birds joined in the songs as they are doing now. I recall that there are also churches and synagogues in Gaza from the same era—a recently excavated church and monastery in Jabalia; a synagogue in what is today the Rimal neighborhood of Gaza City—both with similar mosaic floors of plants and animals. I imagine, with hope, how the prayers from these ancient congregations might have harmonized on shared holy seasons, just as the floors complimented each other, and how Jews and Christians would have easily walked from here to the Mediterranean shoreline.

But today, the natural peace of the area is punctuated by the low hum of drones and the devastating thunder of bombs falling on Gaza, a few kilometers away. Some explosions are faint. Others are so loud that the shock takes our breath away.

Halfway through the service, an Israeli air raid siren goes off. We'd been warned about what to do. Part of the group runs to the nearby cement bomb shelter, and the other part drops to the platform beside the mosaic. I burrow my face into my arms, breathing in the scent of dusty wood, immersed in the sound of bombs and the distant wail of the siren. The noise subsides. We lay low for another minute or so before re-congregating, alternating between songs and prayers led by different people.

I offer my own prayer for Palestinian refugees. I'd penned it the night before on my iPhone, looking up the names of far-flung refugee camps across the region. I included the two camps we'd visited on our solidarity tour (Shuafat in Jerusalem and Balata in Nablus), as well as every single camp in Gaza.

> Dear God, source of being and light of life, it is to you that we lift our hearts here at the border of unspeakable suffering. Flowery words are not enough in this moment of anguish and measureless pain. Our comfort is knowing that all things are yours, and that those who suffer are not alone, for you are near to the brokenhearted and to those who are crushed in spirit, crushed in soul, and crushed in body. Lord, we remember the refugees today—from Aida in Bethlehem to Zarka in Jordan. From Balata in Nablus to Shuafat in Jerusalem. From Shatila in Lebanon to Yarmouk in Syria and all across Gaza: Rafah, Jabalia, Khan Younis, Al Shati, Nuseirat, Bureij, Maghazi, and Deir al Balah. None of these is outside your compassion. You know every infant, every little girl, every teenage boy, every hopeful mother, every tired father, every grandparent carrying the memories of home—its smells, shapes, plants, sounds, and history. You see those who bear the Nakba in their bones and cry a howling prayer, "How long, O Lord!?"
>
> We remember those who have been made refugees in the past few months, whose homes have been demolished, who have been evicted, or who are unable to safely return and are internally displaced.
>
> Jesus, you were also a refugee. We remember that your family rested in Gaza on the flight to Egypt. In Gaza you

also wept and giggled and perhaps took your first steps with death looming over your head. Lord, here at the Gaza border, we weep, we pray, we intercede for a just resolution for these refugees. We pray for your Holy Spirit, the spirit of wisdom and understanding, to move through the halls of earthly power and decision-makers. Let justice, mercy, healing, and restoration be for all the people of this land, and may fruitfulness and security be a shared gift for all its inhabitants.

Gather all humanity—refugees from our place of Origin—back to our true home in you, dear God.

Like the orthodox woman rabbi who wept as she prayed in Hebrew, I find myself weeping, even as I'd wept while writing the prayer.

In this land, it is the refugees that haunt me most. No matter where I go, I hear echoes of the past whispering—sometimes wailing—into the present. When I walk the romantic stone streets of Jaffa's old city, I seem to hear the ghosts of former Palestinian residents who were forced out in 1948 and whose descendants are rarely, if ever, allowed to visit. I feel their presence around every narrow corner, in the intricate hand-carvings on doors that are now gateways to art galleries. Some of those exiles and their descendants now live in Gaza.

Of Gaza's population of just over two million, over 80 percent are refugees. The Nakba tripled Gaza's population overnight and turned it into one of the most crowded places on earth. For the majority, their razed villages are within thirty to forty kilometers of the Gaza border. Other refugees came from cities as far away as Tiberias, Haifa, and Tantura.[1] Others came from Jerusalem and villages nearby, including Ein Karem (the traditional birthplace of John the Baptist) and Lifta (remnants of which are still standing in Jerusalem).

I think of "Hannah," with whom I'd communicated as she sheltered at the church in Gaza; a graduate of Bethlehem Bible College's distance learning program. After her eight-year-old daughter's pet turtle starved to death early in the war while they were sheltering in the church, she asked me to pray for her children. "My daughter is fading more every day, like a wilted flower. And my six-year-old son cannot control his bladder at night." She'd sent me videos of her children, speaking in halting English to the persistent hum of drones in the background, flinching as bombs went off, standing desolate in front of the rubble of their home. "My friend lived over there. She died," said the daughter, motioning in one direction. "And over there,

---

1. The story of the Tantura massacre is told in the 2022 documentary by the same name: https://www.tantura-film.com/.

my other friend died. Please pray for us, we want to live." Both "Hannah" and her husband descended from grandparents evicted from Jaffa in 1948. I'd met the whole family in person in Cairo just a few months earlier, on Orthodox Easter, where we celebrated Christ's resurrection for hours as only the Egyptians can do. They were staying in an extra room at a church with other refugees from Gaza, uncertain of the future, and in a state of shock. "If we could go back home, we would in a moment," said her husband. "It's a hard life, but it is home. It is where God called us. But there is nothing to return to. It will take decades to rebuild."

It was harder for Hannah to talk about her experiences during the genocide.

"Everything in Gaza is broken," she added. "Everyone is missing something, whether an eye or a leg, or a child or a parent, or a home. You see people rocking dead bodies by the side of the road. Everywhere you look, you see that no one is whole. Nothing is whole. Do you know what it means to be alive and dead at the same time? These are the people of Gaza."

A few weeks after arriving in Cairo, they flew to Sydney—creating a generational refugee trail beginning in Jaffa and ending in Australia; their exodus a harbinger of the final decimation of Gaza's tiny Christian community, one of the oldest in the world.

Such is the story of Palestinians. Global refugees, scattered families, and homeless even in their homeland.

For the tiny Christian community, further displacement and emigration is felt most acutely. A few days earlier, our delegation had visited the Armenian quarter in the Old City of Jerusalem, where Palestinian residents struggle to hold on to their property in the face of a powerful settler movement. We met with the Kisiya and Nassar families, both of whom lived just outside of Bethlehem. The Kisiyas had been forcibly expelled from their home by settlers on July 31. The nearby Nassar family has been struggling to hold on to their family farm for over thirty years, surrounded by ever-encroaching settlements and Israeli state harassment designed to wear them out.

Muslims were, of course, facing the same thing as Christians. We had dinner with Fakhri Abu Diab in Jerusalem's Silwan neighborhood under the jagged shadow of his multi-generational family home, which had been demolished by the Israeli military on February 14. We visited Shuafat camp in Jerusalem, where many residents are double refugees. After losing their homes in 1948, they resettled in the Mughrabi Quarter of the Old City, beside the Western Wall. After the quarter was demolished by the Israeli military in 1967, its residents were expelled to the outer edges of Jerusalem, near where Jeremiah the prophet once lived. Today their camp is an overcrowded slum, and the elementary schools are pockmarked with bullets from Israeli guns. Though they pay taxes to the city, Shuafat is cut off from the rest of Jerusalem and surrounded by the separation wall, its only entry and exit through a military checkpoint. This is the Jerusalem that most visitors never see, the Jerusalem that remains hidden from the eyes of shofar-blowing tourists.

Perhaps this area is the Jerusalem where Jeremiah might still feel most at home. One wonders what the prophet, who linked security with justice and saw injustice as idolatry, would have to say about all of this.

> For scoundrels are found among my people; they take over the goods of others. Like fowlers they set a trap; they catch human beings like a cage full of birds. (Jer 5:26 NRSV)

Finance Minister Bezalel Smotrich has repeated more than once that under his plan, Palestinians will essentially have three choices: they can choose to migrate from the Occupied Palestinian Territories; remain and live with permanent second-class status; or resist the Occupation, in which case "the Israel Defense Forces will know what to do."[2] The sentiment is reminiscent of ISIS, who famously offered Iraqi non-Muslims three choices: Leave this area, convert, or be killed.

Of course, all that we saw in the West Bank pales in comparison to Gaza, where large numbers have been killed or maimed and where the few that have escaped, like Hannah and her family, know that it most certainly means permanent exile from the land.

Palestinians in the West Bank watch the decimation of the Strip with a double dread, seeing it as a harbinger of things to come.

On the Outskirts of Hope

Our meeting with Rabbis for Human Rights ends, and Avi shares about his experience on October 7 and his vision for long-term peace. This is not about Jews against Arabs, or vice-versa. It's about the people who believe in the values of humanity and shared existence, versus those who do not," he explains.

> I believe that the best interest of my children is connected to the best interest of the children of Gaza. Only a better reality for their children will create a better reality for everyone. A lot of people in Israel still believe this, but they are afraid to say it now. Everyone is saying we need to use violence and force and beat them. They are all terrorists. I understand that. We suffered a

---

2. Mack, "Israel: Evidence of Bezalel Smotrich's Support for Genocide."

lot on October 7. In Nir Oz, over a hundred were kidnapped or killed. So, I understand—there is a voice of revenge and anger in each of us. But that is not the only voice we should listen to. I'm in the minority, but I am not afraid of that. Our purpose in this world is not to swim with the current. It is to do and convey the right thing. I fear that if we Jews give up our values, we'll collapse from inside. This is not only about Israel as a state, but also about our Jewish culture. I agree with Omar—this is the time to work harder for peace. We cannot change the past. We can only look to the future. We have a great history of flourishing together as Jews and Muslims across the Middle East. It is my dream that this can happen again.

Avi's ancestors came from Syria and Libya, and his own family lore is filled with memories of coexistence. He's not speaking naively, he tells us, but out of historical reality. Avi, like Omar and Jeremiah, carries the mark of another world within himself, a gateway into prophetic imagination, which is perhaps just common sense, or *logic*, as Omar called it.

The rabbis invite us to follow them to a nearby spot where we can see Khan Younis. We drive past bougainvillea growing next to citrus fields and more rows of cacti, indicating another depopulated Palestinian village. There are many trees here that I am told are Australian eucalyptus, planted in the 1930s by Jewish settlers to dry up the swampy areas. I recognize their long, pale green leaves from the videos of October 7.

Under those pale trees, some of the rabbis sing us an old kibbutz peacenik song written for Khan Younis in the 1950s:

> We will drag the watchtowers to the sea and drown them there.
> We will play together on the beach with the Palestinians.

We stand within walking distance of the dark corpse of Khan Younis, just a few kilometers away. It looks unreal, its blackened ruins like something from a dystopian science fiction movie, through shimmering heat waves. Right over there, the people we have been following for months on Instagram are surviving and dying beneath that burned and jagged skyline. We lift our hands over Khan Younis and pray again for Gaza.

Gaza has become a dark bruise upon the planet. She is the battered face of humanity. A place that future generations will excavate on their way down to those Byzantine mosaic floors. What will they say as they uncover the cement ruins; the tiny, crushed bones? Will they lament that international law was buried here among its mass graves and smashed hospitals and universities?

We part ways with the rabbis and make our way to the closed Kerem Shalom crossing that separates Egypt from Gaza before us. The land in every direction is flat and empty. We hold up our signs. "Stop the violence!" "Release all hostages!" "Arms embargo now!" "Let Gaza live!" "Ceasefire!" We link arms and sing old anti-war songs from the 1960s, lyrics courtesy of the Hebrew prophets. A few military vehicles circle us, but they decide we are not a threat and continue on their way. Wiping away our sweat, we decide to do the same.

We drive through Rehat, the largest Bedouin community in the Negev, down Palestine Street, a contested name with a court order against it. After an extravagant meal cooked for us by a talkative Bedouin woman—her son was arrested at age fifteen while passing by a demonstration; he was abused and tortured in prison and came out with psychological issues; he's in therapy now and doing much better, *alhamdillilah*—we make our way to a large awning in the center of town. Hundreds of Palestinian citizens of Israel along with a smaller contingent of Israeli Jews from the organization Standing Together are boxing pasta, rice, beans, lentils, and tins of tuna and vegetables, all destined for the hungry in Gaza.

Off to the side, I notice a mountain of donated items: za'atar, kitchen soap and sponges, bathroom soap, cooking oil, halva, tahini, cookies, and more. A Jewish woman from Standing Together tells me that these items are not allowed into Gaza. "Any soap that has alcohol in it is forbidden by the Israeli government," she tells me. "So is candy." I learn that these items will be distributed to the needy in the West Bank, where the economy is dead and people are more desperate than they were during COVID days.

With so much Israeli opposition and the crossings closed, how will the rest of the food get into Gaza? She tells me that they have a connection, who has a connection, who knows someone, and they are optimistic that this food will make it in.

"The previous campaign was stopped by extremist settlers. But we are hopeful that this food will enter Gaza in the next few weeks at the latest."

Almost everyone has a job, including sticky-fingered children who wander the crowd handing out pink and yellow popsicles. Having felt frustrated and helpless for so long, it is cathartic to channel our energy into something tangible. My job is taping up boxes. Many of them have messages written in Arabic from Palestinian citizens of Israel. "We love you, Gaza." "Stay strong." Most poignantly, "We are silent, but we are here."

Despite the joy and camaraderie, many people do not want to be photographed by the roaming Instagrammers. Ben Gvir has threatened that anyone who participates in this effort will have their citizenship revoked, a threat leveled at Palestinian citizens of Israel. Some people cover their faces every time a camera comes out. Others smile boldly, flashing victory signs. Such is the risk that people are willing to take when a "plausible genocide"[3] is occurring just a few miles away.

Where Do We Go from Here?

A few weeks later, I'm home. I'm still trying to discover if the food from Standing Together made it into Gaza. I hear conflicting reports. I never discover with any certainty what happened to it. Meanwhile, the war escalates across the region, and things look much worse than they did a few weeks before: War escalates with Lebanon, four Israeli hostages are found dead, Gaza continues to be obliterated as winter approaches. In the West Bank, the settlers continue to burn, steal, kill, and destroy with impunity.

In the middle of this ongoing genocide, I, like so many others, am looking for hope. What does hope look like when an entire people—their infrastructure and memories—is being wiped off of the map, and extended families are erased from the social registry?

Like so many Palestinians, my hope must remain in a God who is ultimately good and just; a God who sees and knows; a God who loves and takes into his dwelling place all who were denied justice on earth. For despite their deep and prolonged suffering, Palestinian faith in God remains as a marvel and a testimony to the rest of the world. If they can yet hold hope, how dare the rest of us give up?

"We do the right thing because it is the right thing to do, regardless of the outcome we see," a friend in Jerusalem told me once. Her simple and practical faith snapped me out of the despair that hovers over all who engage deeply in this issue.

Like so many Palestinians and Israelis, my hope also finds a resting place in the words spoken by God's prophets in this land so long ago. These prophets remind us by word and deed that God is present in every generation, even when it is so dark we cannot see to take the next step. Our faith in God is the light. We take the next step because we believe that he is still with us and will never abandon us.

I have seen this hope modeled over and over again by the likes of Omar, Avi, and the many others with whom I had the privilege to interact on this trip. I remember Omar's words as we came upon yet another Israeli roadblock on a Palestinian road:

---

3. *UN News*, "Rights Expert."

Someday these roadblocks will be part of the archaeological excavations of the ruins of another empire. Empires come and empires go, but the meek will inherit the earth. Every inch of it. This is why we remain optimistic, even when there is no hope left. We are people of the resurrection who trust a living God.

If the short view does not inspire hope, maybe the long one will. If the modern-day prophets of the land can yet hold on to hope, we must join them with actions that prove our hope. It is a moral imperative. We must live the future we hope for.

Bibliography

Mack, Eitay. "Israel: Evidence of Bezalel Smotrich's Support for Genocide Is Clear. The US Must Act." *Middle East Eye*, March 7, 2023. https://www.middleeasteye.net/opinion/israel-us-bezalel-smotrich-evidence-genocide-support.

Tantura: A Film by Alon Schwarz. Israel: Journeyman Pictures, 2022.

UN News. "Rights Expert Finds 'Reasonable Grounds' Genocide Is Being Committed in Gaza." March 26, 2024. https://news.un.org/en/story/2024/03/1147976.

CHAPTER FOURTEEN

Passing By on the Other Side
Christianity Today *Since October 7*[1]

BENJAMIN NORQUIST

AFTER OCTOBER 7, 2023, the Western media machine shifted into high gear. How did Hamas succeed in invading Israel? How did Israel fail to prevent this attack? Who are the hostages? What atrocities did Hamas (and other militant groups) commit? Christian media too, had plenty to say. *The Table Podcast* invited the president of Jews for Jesus to talk about Jewish longing for protection and justice.[2] The Billy Graham Evangelistic Association interviewed Joel Rosenberg about October 7 and end-times prophecy.[3] The *Catholic News Agency* actively covered the war in Gaza for months.[4] Christian media were paying attention.

Almost all of my go-to podcasts, secular and Christian alike, had episodes about October 7 and then about Gaza. There have been mountains of articles, social media posts, and public statements from organizations like the National Association of Evangelicals and the *National Catholic Register*.

---

1. Parts of this chapter are modified from Norquist, "Jesus' Comfort." Other parts draw on conversations with David Crump, Rob Dalrymple, and Scott Gustafson, with assistance from Hannah Hutton and Mackenzie Konjoyan.

2. In dialogue were Darrell Bock (Dallas Theological Seminary), David Brickner (Jews for Jesus), and Mitch Glaser (Chosen People Ministries).

3. Jerry Pierce interview with Joel Rosenberg, "'He's Calling People to Himself.'"

4. Marina, "What You Need to Know."

Christian Century published my article about how Israel turned water access into a weapon against Gaza.[5]

This chapter focuses on *Christianity Today* (hereafter, *CT*) and its coverage of the October 7 massacre and the ensuing genocide in Gaza. *CT* is a conservative-to-moderate Christian media organization founded by Billy Graham in 1956 to provide balanced coverage of matters within the church and beyond, from a Christian perspective.[6] *CT* describes itself as "a central nervous system for the global body of Christ" and a "voice for the church that shapes the evangelical conversation, brings important issues to the forefront, and challenges Christians to love and serve the overlooked."[7] Their mission is "to elevate the stories and ideas of the kingdom of God." Their vision: "A church more faithful to Christ and a world more drawn to him."[8] So many of these aspirations are deeply commendable.

I grew up with copies of the magazine on coffee tables at my church and in friends' homes. In recent years, when *CT* publicly criticized Christian Nationalism and the evangelical-MAGA alliance, I resubscribed. Historically structured around its print magazine, *CT* is increasingly active online with articles and podcasts, with a claimed monthly engagement of more than four million people worldwide.[9] Despite the global engagement, however, many see *CT* catering primarily to white evangelical Americans.

Moral Clarity and Moral Complexity

In the wake of October 7, Christian commentators were quick to weigh in, with *CT* providing one of the earliest responses. Editor-in-chief Russell Moore's article "American Christians Should Stand with Israel Under Attack" appeared on the day of the massacre.[10] Moore called on American Christians to unambiguously condemn Hamas and its attack, and to respond with "moral clarity" to this moral atrocity. He reiterated this theme in a follow-up article: "There are a lot of morally ambiguous questions . . . but this is not one."[11] His *un*ambiguous question was *Who is to blame for the atrocities?* His answer: *Hamas, full stop.* Since then, as far as I know, Moore has written little or nothing in *CT* about Gaza. Moore's clarity was shared

---

5. Norquist and Cannon, "In Gaza, Water Is Life."
6. *Christianity Today*, "Our History."
7. *Christianity Today*, "About."
8. *Christianity Today*, "About."
9. *Christianity Today*, "Advertising."
10. Moore, "American Christians."
11. Moore, "'Bothsidesism.'" See also Fisk, "Allure of Moral Clarity."

by *CT*'s Mike Cosper. "Evil wore no mask that day," said Cosper, standing among the burned out homes of Kfar Azah not far from Gaza. Clear-eyed and confident, Cosper saw a tidy binary between good people and pure evil.[12]

"Moral clarity" was not simply *CT*'s way of condemning Hamas's attack on civilians. As its editorializing would demonstrate, moral clarity proved to be essentializing: Israel was virtuous (imperfect, but essentially good), and Palestinian society (with exceptions) was fundamentally corrupt. In his March 2024 cover story for the magazine, Cosper went so far as to smear Palestinian Christian cultural values by attempting to link them to ideological hatred and extremism.[13]

What is true of Cosper's article is true of Moore and Cosper more generally. They neither see nor acknowledge the richness of Palestinian culture—the love for family and community, humor, longsuffering, hospitality, patient husbandry of the land—nor the commitments of many to peace and nonviolence, nor their longing for justice. For Moore and Cosper, Palestinians are two dimensional. They offer up malign caricatures rather than faithful characterizations, in contrast to the humane, nuanced portraits of Palestinians that we encounter in *CT* articles by Sophia Lee and Jayson Casper.[14] Why the dehumanizing portrayal from the most prominent voices at the organization?

When *CT* does acknowledge Palestinian virtue, it is limited to individual cases. Sophia Lee's March 2024 story, for example, about the Munayers, a Palestinian family known for peacemaking and nonviolence work, is substantive and nuanced.[15] But the way *CT* frames the story blunts its kingdom power. In my experience, the Munayers are *indicative* of Palestinian Christian commitments to peace, justice, and nonviolence. In *CT*'s framing, however, the Munayers are admirable, but scarcely relevant exceptions to the rule. By presenting this family as exceptional and irrelevant, *CT* implicitly casts aspersions on the rest of Palestinian society.

The flagship magazine could have called readers to stand with the Munayers and other peacemakers under attack. Instead, they turned a

---

12. Cosper made this statement on his podcast series *Promised Land*, which we discuss at length below. Many of us first encountered Mike Cosper in his 2021–2022 *CT* podcast *The Rise and Fall of Mars Hill*, which explored the darkness of immoral leadership and misogyny in the church.

13. Cosper, "Evil Ideas Behind October 7."

14. Casper, "Amid Israel-Hamas War"; and Casper, "Palestinian Evangelicals"; Lee, "Fractured Are the Peacemakers"; Surls, "He Fled His Gaza Home."

15. Lee, "Fractured Are the Peacemakers."

remarkable family into a curiosity and reinforced the falsehood that Palestinians committed to nonviolence are few, ineffective, and irrelevant.

CT's professedly clear vision, moreover, has another moral blind spot: Israeli oppression and injustice. Israel was founded in 1948 primarily on lands already home to Palestinians. In the months preceding and following the official declaration of statehood, Israel emptied 500 Palestinian villages and turned 750,000 Palestinians into lifelong refugees.[16] Still today Christians are leaving the Holy Land to escape Israeli state and settler brutality.[17] Israeli settler groups are pushing historic Christian communities out of the Old City of Jerusalem.[18] In recent years, some Jewish ideologues have been spitting on Jerusalem's Christian clergy.[19] Israel collects taxes from Palestinians but withholds distributions to Palestinian service providers as a way of exercising control over the Palestinian Authority.[20] Israel holds hundreds, sometimes thousands of Palestinians—many of them children—in military detention at any given time without charge or trial. Some remain imprisoned for years.[21] During the current war, Israeli guards have raped and tortured detainees.[22] Israel is using AI systems—one of which they've dubbed "The Gospel"—to generate lists of targets for bombing in Gaza.[23] Israeli snipers shoot non-combatants in the head.[24] Israeli units force Gazan civilians to serve as human shields.[25] Israeli settlers have attacked aid trucks and destroyed humanitarian supplies before they cross into Gaza.[26] A scan of their Palestine archives seems to suggest *CT* doesn't cover these stories.[27]

After decades of violent control and surging atrocities in Gaza and the West Bank, we search in vain for Moore's clarion call to stand with the Palestinians under attack. What we have here is not moral clarity; it is culpable partisanship.

---

16. Munayyer, "Nakba's Coming Stages."
17. Casper, "Why Many Christians Want to Leave."
18. Graham-Harrison and Kierszenbaum, "Jerusalem 'Land Grab.'"
19. US Department of State, "Custom Report." See also Cidor, "Why Do Jewish Extremists Spit on Christian Clergy?"
20. Filiu, "Benjamin Netanyahu's Financial War."
21. *Al Jazeera*, "Why Are There So Many."
22. United Nations, "Israel's Escalating Use of Torture."
23. See ch. 3 above, pp. 94–96. See also Abraham, "'Mass Assassination Factory.'"
24. Forensic Architecture, "Shireen Abu Akleh." See also Sidhwa, "65 Doctors, Nurses, and Paramedics."
25. Patta, "Israeli Soldier."
26. Morris, "Far-Right Israeli Settlers."
27. *Christianity Today*, "Palestine Archive."

If the plight of Palestinians en masse warrants attention, we might expect *CT* to show as much or more concern for Palestinian *Christians*. *CT* tells stories about the persecuted church around the world, including stories about Palestinian Christians. But when those Palestinian Christians name Israel as the main source of their trauma, *CT* generally falls silent. In his 2024 conversations with this community, Cosper argued as much as he listened.[28] *CT* seems reluctant to help us hear from Palestinians *on their own terms*. They've certainly had the chance—I know Palestinians who offered to share their experiences and perspectives in the pages of *CT* and have been turned down.

Part of the problem may be *CT*'s sources. The credits of Cosper's podcast acknowledge production help from the Philos Project, an organization that exists to equip Christians to "stand with Israel and the Jewish people," among other things.[29] Mike Cosper has hosted Philos's president and founder on a *CT* podcast.[30] Passages Israel is a Philos initiative to bring Christian college students on subsidized trips to show them the "ancient faith" and "modern miracle" of Israel.[31] Students of mine who joined these trips (I had a career in Christian higher education for years) returned with heads full of Israeli state narratives and Christian Zionist talking points. The Holy Land map Philos gave one of my students a few years ago gave little indication that the West Bank was Palestinian space, presenting it instead as a contiguous part of Israel. They had literally wiped Palestinians off the map.

Cosper and the Philos Project are concerned about antisemitism, as am I. But the notion that we battle antisemitism by erasing the rightful claims of Palestinians is doomed and, as Peter Beinart argues in his recent book,[32] it is dangerous for Israelis and Palestinians alike.

Complex Realities, Partisan Stories

As noted above, *CT* sent Mike Cosper to Israel shortly after October 7 on a trip that included a visit to Kfar Azah, a kibbutz that had endured some of the worst of Hamas's assault. Having interviewed Israelis from around the country, including a settler, along with a handful of Palestinians, Cosper produced *Promised Land*, a limited series podcast to help us reflect

---

28. See The Bulletin, "Part Three."
29. Philos Project: https://philosproject.org.
30. The Bulletin, "Making Sense of the Israel-Hamas War."
31. Passages Israel: https://www.passagesisrael.org.
32. Beinart, *Being Jewish*, 84–87.

PART III: The Peoples of the Land

on October 7 and its aftermath. Across six episodes, listeners are invited to consider the Jewish people's pursuit of a homeland, Palestinian ties to the land, double standards in the conflict, and contemporary Jewish settlement projects.

Cosper's team is good at what they do. *Promised Land* is richly produced with locally captured audio, including rocket sirens and air strikes. Its theme music is taken from Matthew Smith and Sandra McCracken's beautiful rendering of "On Jordan's Stormy Banks I Stand," a hymn written by English Baptist pastor Samuel Stennet (1727–1795). The lyrics have us standing on the far banks of the Jordan River looking across to the promised land, a metaphor for being close to death and anticipating heaven. Early Americans adopted it to imagine Kentucky and the trans-Appalachian lands that colonists wanted to settle. In the podcast, it pictures a world without antisemitism, woke ideology, and Jewish suffering. The suffering of Palestinians at the hands of Zionists, however, barely appears in this vision of redemption.

During the series Cosper interviews some nineteen people, including Israeli intellectuals, Jewish leaders, Israeli settlers, as well as four Palestinian academics and pastors. Despite Cosper's stated goal of listening to "both sides,"[33] *Promised Land* features disproportionately few Palestinian guests. Their voices occupy a tiny fraction of the soundtrack; all four are corralled into a single episode, with the other five episodes devoid of Palestinian perspectives. By focusing disproportionately on Israeli voices, Cosper minimizes the lived experiences of displaced Palestinians and those suffering under the systematic, hidden brutality of the occupation.

For the bulk of the series, when the subject is Palestinian culture, history, values, and desires, the voice we hear is Cosper's, or that of one of his Jewish Israeli guests. Characterizations derive from Cosper's limited experiences with Palestinians, from Israel's cultural, governmental, and military elites, and from Israeli fringe groups—in other words, from sources with skewed, pro-Israeli perspectives. This biased framing reduces Palestinians to stereotypes, minimizes their suffering, and erases their experiences.

In episode three, Cosper adopts an argumentative stance toward two of his Palestinian interviewees—a posture he does not adopt with any other interview subject. Despite claiming that his goal in conversation with one of these guests was "to hear his story, not so much to challenge it," he is argumentative and implicitly skeptical. Of his nineteen interviewees, Cosper argues only with Palestinians, both in the interview itself and in voiceover commentary. One of these Palestinians later described to me

---

33. Cosper states this goal in The Bulletin, "Part Six."

Cosper's unfriendliness: "What came through [in the interview] was a white Christian Zionist arrogance. He doesn't want to listen or understand, but he wants to cater to his backers and listeners while recycling Israeli state propaganda."[34]

In episode five, Cosper interviews an Israeli settler, Ari Abromowitz, to whom he gives a platform for airing his racism, anti-Arab hatred, and zeal for mass violence. We hear Abromowitz passionately cry out: "As much as I hate Hamas, and I want to slaughter every single one of them. And I would love the opportunity to do it."[35] Although Abromowitz finished by saying he couldn't carry out a slaughter, his Palestinian neighbors can readily imagine a day when it would be possible. Indeed, Abromowitz's settlement south of Bethlehem is in an area where Palestinians are being systematically and violently ripped from their land, a part of the story entirely missing from the podcast. Cosper provides air time for anti-Arab fanaticism but chooses not to challenge the racism and rhetoric of displacement. Nor does he include a single encounter with a Palestinian whose land Israel has taken in order to establish a settlement.

The podcast portrays Israel in an idealized light, normalizing settlements and platforming fringe Israelis who routinely violate the delicate status quo between religious groups in Jerusalem and want to build on al-Haram al-Sharif (the Temple Mount) a third Jewish temple. The host's warm approach to Israeli guests, contrasted with his adversarial tone toward Palestinians, showcases his bias. Cosper perpetuates myths that portray Israel as morally pure. Israel's decision in 1967 to leave Al-Aqsa (the Temple Mount) in Muslim hands is framed as singular wisdom and selflessness rather than as a political calculation. Jewish-only settlements are sanitized and described essentially as suburbs, obscuring their illegal status and unjust, exclusionary impact on Palestinians who are being driven from their homeland.

By presenting Palestinians as a monolithic group associated with radicalism and by filtering their perspectives through Israeli sources, the podcast traffics in stereotypes. Dehumanization makes it easy to dismiss Palestinian suffering and grievances. When Palestinian humanity is obscured, their lives and dignity are implicitly rendered less valuable, which can fuel apathy and hostility. As Rev. Dr. Munther Isaac recently said in a conference session hosted by the Network of Evangelicals for the Middle East, *our* dehumanizing words put *his* life in danger.[36]

---

34. Personal email to Ben Norquist.
35. The Bulletin, "Part Five."
36. "The Cost of Solidarity" breakout session at the Exiles in Babylon Conference,

Likewise, by normalizing settlements designated illegal in international courts, the podcast reinforces the narrative that Israeli actions—no matter how aggressive—are justified acts of self-defense, while Palestinian resistance is irrational and inherently violent. This framing legitimizes Israel's reliance on systemic violence, discrimination, and displacement, while silencing legitimate Palestinian grievances about such treatment.

By selectively using facts, reinforcing stereotypes, and failing to hold all sides morally accountable, the podcast further entrenches harmful narratives that hinder pathways to a just peace. This damages efforts by peacemakers—locally as well as globally—who are working toward mutual understanding and equitable solutions. All things considered, the *Promised Land* podcast demonizes and erases Palestinians while sanitizing and exonerating Israeli injustice. This imbalance not only distorts realities on the ground but also fails to call Christians to stand courageously with the oppressed and to seek peace.

Who Is My Neighbor?

A faithful Christian response would acknowledge moral complexity, foster theological maturity, and strengthen our resolve to listen to the voices of all who suffer. Jesus saw people his society rendered invisible. He went out of his way to invite them into his circle, be they children; people with leprosy, injuries, and disabilities; women working as prostitutes; or tax collectors. In John's Gospel, Jesus led his disciples through Samaria—to his disciples' surprise, for Jews and Samaritans hated one another. To their dismay, he spoke with a Samaritan woman, demonstrating that he *saw* her and recognized her as a human being.

In his day, Jesus encountered people who professed a moral clarity similar to what we find in the pages of *CT*. Some were "clear" that evil Rome should be resisted, with violence when necessary. Others were "clear" that guarding ritual purity might preclude caring for others. Some of Jesus' harshest rebukes targeted those who thought they had cornered the market on moral clarity, like some among the Pharisees whom Jesus called hypocrites and blind guides.

Confronted by a crowd of people ready to stone a woman for adultery, Jesus wrote in the dirt with his finger and said, "Let any one of you who is without sin be the first to throw a stone at her" (John 8:7 NRSV).[37]

April 3–5, 2025, in Minneapolis.

37. John 7:53—8:11, absent from the best Greek manuscripts, may not have appeared in the original Gospel of John. The story appears rooted in early oral tradition

Would-be executioners—ready to engage in "justified" violence—dropped their stones and drifted away. Clarity turned to complexity. Or perhaps to a deeper moral clarity, precisely what *CT* could—and should—be inviting its readers to enter into.

Luke's Gospel tells us that Jesus, when asked *who is my neighbor?* (i.e., who am I obliged to love?), told a story. A man is robbed and left for dead in the ditch. Two people with moral clarity and authority (a priest and a Levite) walk on past without lending aid. Only a despised Samaritan stops to care for the victim. In our day, the ditch is filled with Gaza's civilians, wounded, homeless, starving, and we are passing by on the other side of the road, whispering about just war or self-defense or Hamas terror or biblical covenants, while sending Israel weapons to bomb children in Gaza. Alas, *CT* has been helping us justify our decision to pass Palestinian victims by.

Christian media should be neither soothing the consciences nor defending the behavior of those who choose to ignore the needy during a crisis. Christian media, rather, should be calling us down into the ditch to join other peacemakers, to amplify the voices of victims, to deliver aid, and to resist the violence.

Palestinians are among those whom many American Christians have dehumanized. Marginalized. Rendered invisible. Essentialized to fill sinister roles within a cherished cultural myth. If we would follow Jesus, we must seek healing from this blindness and rediscover Palestinians' full humanity. We desperately need *Christianity Today* to help us in that quest.

Bibliography

Abraham, Yuval. "'A Mass Assassination Factory': Inside Israel's Calculated Bombing of Gaza." *+972 Magazine*, November 30, 2023. https://www.972mag.com/mass-assassination-factory-israel-calculated-bombing-gaza/.

Al Jazeera. "Why Are There So Many Palestinian Children in Israeli Prisons?" January 26, 2025. https://www.aljazeera.com/news/2025/1/26/why-are-there-so-many-palestinian-children-in-israeli-prisons?.

Beinart, Peter. *Being Jewish After the Destruction of Gaza: A Reckoning*. New York: Knopf, 2025.

Bock, Darrell, et al. *The Table Podcast*. November 7, 2023. https://voice.dts.edu/tablepodcast/reflections-hamas-attack-israel/.

The Bulletin. "Making Sense of the Israel-Hamas War." *Christianity Today*, October 9, 2023. https://www.christianitytoday.com/podcasts/the-bulletin/45-israel-hamas-war-palestine-attack-conflict-news/.

---

that may go back to Jesus's day.

———. "Part One: It's Complicated." *Promised Land. Christianity Today*, December 20, 2023. https://www.christianitytoday.com/podcasts/promised-land/60-promised-land-israel-hamas-kibbutz-kfar-aza/.

———. "Part Two: The Zionist Story." *Promised Land. Christianity Today*, February 9, 2024. https://www.christianitytoday.com/podcasts/promised-land/68-tb-promised-land/.

———. "Part Three: Rocks in Hard Places: From the Foundation Stone to Living Stones." *Promised Land. Christianity Today*, February 27, 2024. https://www.christianitytoday.com/podcasts/promised-land/rocks-in-hard-places/.

———. "Part Four: Empire of Refugees: Victims, Villains, and Settler Colonialism." *Promised Land. Christianity Today*, March 21, 2024. https://www.christianitytoday.com/podcasts/promised-land/empire-of-refugees-victims-villains-and-settler-colonialism/.

———. "Part Five: Settlers, Sacred Cows, and the Temple." *Promised Land. Christianity Today*, June 3, 2024. https://www.christianitytoday.com/podcasts/promised-land/5-settlers-sacred-cows-and-temple/.

———. "Part Six: Vote for Peace in a Time of War." *Promised Land. Christianity Today*, June 19, 2024. https://www.christianitytoday.com/podcasts/promised-land/vote-for-peace-in-time-of-war/.

Casper, Jayson. "Amid Israel-Hamas War, Local Christians Seek Righteous Anger and Gospel Hope." *Christianity Today*, October 11, 2023. https://www.christianitytoday.com/2023/10/israel-hamas-gaza-war-palestinian-evangelical-messianic-jew/.

———. "Palestinian Evangelicals Call Western Church to Repentance, Criticized in Return." *Christianity Today*, October 27, 2023. https://www.christianitytoday.com/2023/10/israel-hamas-war-palestinian-christian-mideast-statements/.

———. "Why Many Christians Want to Leave Palestine. And Why Most Won't." *Christianity Today*, August 4, 2020. https://www.christianitytoday.com/2020/08/palestinian-christians-survey-israel-emigration-one-state/.

Christianity Today. "About." https://www.christianitytoday.org/who-we-are/our-ministry/.

———. "Advertising." https://www.christianitytodayads.com/.

———. "Our History." https://www.christianitytoday.com/about/history/.

———. "Palestine Archive." https://www.christianitytoday.com/topics/palestine/.

Cidor, Peggy. "Why Do Jewish Extremists Spit on Christian Clergy in Jerusalem's Old City?" *The Jerusalem Post*, June 23, 2023. https://www.jpost.com/christianworld/article-747227.

Cosper, Mike. "The Evil Ideas Behind October 7." *Christianity Today*, March 2024. https://www.christianitytoday.com/2024/02/evil-ideas-behind-october-7/.

Filiu, Jean-Pierre. "Benjamin Netanyahu's Financial War Against the Palestinian Authority." *Le Monde*, July 15, 2024. https://www.lemonde.fr/en/international/article/2024/07/15/benjamin-netanyahu-s-financial-war-against-the-palestinian-authority_6684274_4.html.

Fisk, Bruce. "The Allure of Moral Clarity in a Time of War: A Response to Russell Moore." *Clarion Journal*, October 13, 2023. https://www.clarion-journal.com/clarion_journal_of_spirit/2023/10/the-allure-of-moral-clarity-in-a-time-of-war-a-response-to-russell-moore-by-bruce-fisk.html.

Forensic Architecture. "Shireen Abu Akleh: The Extrajudicial Killing of a Journalist." September 20, 2022. https://forensic-architecture.org/investigation/shireen-abu-akleh-the-targeted-killing-of-a-journalist?.

Graham-Harrison, Emma, and Quique Kierszenbaum. "Jerusalem 'Land Grab': Armenian Community Fear Eviction After Contentious Deal." *The Guardian*, March 3, 2024. https://www.theguardian.com/world/2024/mar/03/jerusalem-land-grab-armenian-community-fear-eviction-after-contentious-deal.

Gustafson, Scott. "Evangelical Leaders Challenge *Christianity Today* on Coverage of Gaza War." *Baptist News Global*, December 5, 2024. https://baptistnews.com/article/evangelical-leaders-challenge-christianity-today-on-coverage-of-gaza-war/.

Lee, Sophia. "Fractured Are the Peacemakers." *Christianity Today*, April 2024. https://www.christianitytoday.com/2024/03/israel-hamas-war-palestinian-peace-reconciliation-musalaha/.

Marina, Diego López. "What You Need to Know About the War Between Israel and Hamas." *Catholic News Agency*, October 17, 2023. https://www.catholicnewsagency.com/news/255721/what-you-need-to-know-about-the-war-between-israel-and-hamas.

Moore, Russell. "American Christians Should Stand with Israel Under Attack." *Christianity Today*, October 7, 2023. https://www.christianitytoday.com/2023/10/israel-hamas-middle-east-war-christians/.

———. "'Bothsidesism' About Hamas Is a Moral Failure." *Christianity Today*, October 12, 2023. https://www.christianitytoday.com/2023/10/israel-hamas-russell-moore-moral-terrorist/.

Morris, Loveday. "Far-Right Israeli Settlers Step Up Attacks on Aid Trucks Bound for Gaza." *The Washington Post*, May 26, 2024. https://www.washingtonpost.com/world/2024/05/26/west-bank-aid-trucks-gaza-settlers/.

Munayyer, Yousef. "The Nakba's Coming Stages." Arab Center, May 15, 2023. https://arabcenterdc.org/resource/the-nakbas-coming-stages-patterns-process-and-predictability/#.

Network of Evangelicals for the Middle East. https://www.youtube.com/@nemenetwork.

Norquist, Ben. "Jesus' Comfort Is for All Who Suffer: A Response to Mike Cosper and *Christianity Today*." *Religion News Service*, March 18, 2024. https://religionnews.com/2024/03/18/jesus-comfort-is-for-all-who-suffer-a-response-to-mike-cosper-and-christianity-today/.

Norquist, Ben, and Mae Elise Cannon. "In Gaza, Water Is Life." *Christian Century Magazine*, April 2024. https://www.christiancentury.org/features/gaza-water-life.

Patta, Deborah. "Israeli Soldier Tells CBS News He Was Ordered to Use Palestinians as Human Shields in Gaza." *CBS News*, March 26, 2025. https://www.cbsnews.com/news/israeli-soldier-palestinians-human-shields-gaza/.

Pierce, Jerry. "'He's Calling People to Himself': A Conversation on the Middle East with Joel Rosenberg." *Decision Magazine*, December 1, 2023. https://decisionmagazine.com/hes-calling-people-to-himself/.

Sidhwa, Feroze. "65 Doctors, Nurses, and Paramedics: What We Saw in Gaza." *The New York Times*, October 9, 2024. https://www.nytimes.com/interactive/2024/10/09/opinion/gaza-doctor-interviews.html.

Surls, Heather. "He Fled His Gaza Home. Now He Feeds His Fellow Displaced." *Christianity Today*, December 19, 2024. https://www.christianitytoday.com/2024/12/gaza-palestine-israel-christians-jabalia-aid-rafah/.

United Nations. "Israel's Escalating Use of Torture Against Palestinians in Custody a Preventable Crime Against Humanity: UN Experts." August 5, 2024. https://www.ohchr.org/en/press-releases/2024/08/israels-escalating-use-torture-against-palestinians-custody-preventable.

US Department of State, Office of International Religious Freedom. "Custom Report Excerpts: Israel, West Bank and Gaza." https://www.state.gov/report/custom/7dccc5dc7b/.

CHAPTER FIFTEEN

A Tale of Two Trips

Suzanne Watts Henderson

"Wait, what?" In July 2005, these two words became the simple, unsettling refrain my husband Bob and I exchanged at the close of each day.

That summer, we had received sabbatical grants that allowed our family to spend the month at Tantur Ecumenical Institute, a Catholic retreat center located on the border between Jerusalem and Bethlehem—that is, between Israel and the West Bank (Palestine). As we made plans and packed, we looked forward to following Jesus's itinerant path, encountering the place and its people not through the lens of religious tourism but through the lens of God's love. We wanted to meet the Holy Land's "living stones," to listen to their stories, to learn about their deep ties to the land, to bear witness to God's presence woven through this sacred place.

And that we did. We bought candy from shopkeepers at the Jerusalem market and swam at a kibbutz. (It was a hot summer!) We visited a Christian Peacemaker Team in the southern hills outside of Hebron, and Father Elias Chacour's Mar Elias school in the northern Arab Israeli town of Ibillin. We grocery shopped in a settlement and ate dinner in the home of our Palestinian taxi driver. Our days were marked by authentic, unfiltered conversation with Jews, Christians, and Muslims who call the land not just holy, but home.

Along the way, our daily encounters subtly and sometimes jarringly disrupted assumptions and stereotypes we did not realize we harbored—assumptions about the people and the place, yes, but also about our response to it all, as Christians first and as Americans second. It turned out we had a lot to unlearn. By the end of the stay, we came to see not just that "the truth will make you free" (John 8:32 NRSV) but also that the truth can be humbling, problematic, and deeply inconvenient.

You see, this was not our first visit to the Holy Land. In 1999, we toured Israel for eleven days with an interfaith coalition. This first visit underscored and normalized Zionist assumptions about Jewish superiority that are embedded in the American worldview across the political and theological spectrum. That meant that our return six years later left us bewildered and unsettled. "Wait, what?" became the question at the close of each day, as the threads of that carefully woven narrative were pulled out, one by one.

In this personal, biblical, and theological reflection, I hope to add my voice to other authors in this volume as together we call the American church to turn from falsehood toward the kind of truth that sets not only us, but all the people of the Holy Land—Jews, Christians, Muslims, and more—truly free.

Join Us for a Trip to Israel!

Let me begin with our first visit to the Holy Land. In the months before I entered a New Testament doctoral program, Bob and I had the great fortune of sharing a trip to Israel with an interfaith (Jewish and Christian) coalition led by the Greensboro Jewish Federation and subsidized by the United Jewish Appeal (UJA). For eleven dizzying days in the summer of 1999, we enjoyed a fast-paced, red-carpet encounter with the land alongside our Jewish neighbors. We floated in the Dead Sea and sailed the Sea of Galilee; we visited the Mount of the Beatitudes and Mount Tabor; we attended Shabbat services in Jerusalem and even stopped by the Bahai Temple in Haifa—a testimony to Israel's multifaith culture.

More than just holy sites, though, the trip included a drive to the northern border with Lebanon, where we heard about the dire and ongoing threat to Israel's existence and the bravery of Israelis daring to live within range of Hezbollah rockets. We watched sparks fly in a heated debate between a settler and a Palestinian. We visited the Shalom Hartman Institute, where we heard eminently reasonable calls for a two-state solution. We met Jewish immigrants who had escaped persecution and found a welcome in Israel. We walked alongside our Jewish companions at Yad Vashem, the Holocaust memorial museum, as they remembered relatives murdered in that conflagration.

Let me say how grateful we were (and remain) for the chance to spend this time with our Jewish neighbors from Greensboro. Back home we went to the same pool, played in the same park, shopped at the same grocery store, and cared about many of the same issues in our community. Yet it took a trip together, far from home, to transform acquaintance into friendship. Upon our return, we enjoyed a Shabbat meal in our friends' home and combined our efforts to address community issues from affordable housing to hunger. The shared time in the Holy Land had built a bridge of cooperation for the common good for which we were (and are) deeply grateful.

Yet as much as we value these relationships, I now recognize the ways in which this first trip subtly sharpened other divides—specifically, between us and a vaguely sinister group we simply called "the Palestinians." Our seminary experience had primed us to merge a biblical sense of Israel's chosenness with an unreflective acceptance of Israel's geopolitical claims to the land, without regard to those who had lived there for generations. In hindsight, our first trip built on that foundation of Jewish supremacy, shoring up assumptions and stereotypes that undergird widely held American ideas about the Holy Land and Gaza today—views that continue to shape media headlines and reporting from *Fox News* to the *New York Times*. Perhaps you recognize these claims.

"It's our land—God gave it to us."

Though our Old Testament classes in seminary were literary, historical, and theological—not explicitly political—they set us up to conflate the *biblical people* called Israel (Hebrews, Israelites, Judeans, Jews) with the *modern-day nation-state* of that name.[1] Together, the Torah's emphasis on the gift of land[2] and a Christian interest in the "covenant of grace" established in perpetuity

---

1. Even today, seminary professors (in the classroom or church settings) speak of "ancient Israel" in ways that can be misleading. Sometimes, of course, they refer to the nation or people who worshiped YHWH, but they often use the term in ways that suggest that "Israel" existed as a nation-state throughout much of the story of the Hebrew Bible (Old Testament) and even refer to Jesus's own homeland as "Israel." This inaccurate conflation of a people (oriented around a religious devotion to YHWH and to the Torah) with the geographic designation of the land is historically inaccurate and, in today's context, theologically problematic. As my friend Mitri Raheb says, "The US government may provide much of the hardware for the occupation, but it's the church—including seminary professors—that provides the software."

2. God first promises the land to Abram in Gen 12:7. Other passages that feature this promise include Gen 17:8, 26:3–4, and 28:13. Scholars trace the importance of this gift to the time of the Babylonian Exile (586–537 BCE), when many ancient Israelites had been taken into captivity and longed for a return to their homeland.

with David (2 Sam 7:16) suggested that the land called "Palestine" in Jesus's day had been the rightful Jewish homeland for around three millennia.

We were not at all surprised, then, to see our Jewish friends kiss the ground when we stepped off the plane in Tel Aviv. Many delighted in stories of family members who made *aliyah*, the Hebrew term for "going up" that Jews use to describe their "repatriation" to this God-given terrain. We joined them in planting trees, as if to say, "Israel is here to stay." And we lamented that the American Embassy was (at that time still) located in Tel Aviv, since the Jewish view was that it clearly belonged in Jerusalem.

In the wake of the Holocaust, of course, these claims were particularly compelling, especially to those of us carrying shame over Christian complicity with Hitler's regime. Who could balk at the notion that "Jews deserve a safe place to live" in light of the collective trauma of genocide? Who would not empathize with the sense of utter safety and belonging our friends enjoyed in this land? With Jews as an obvious target of persecution, we saw the gift of the land as part of God's care for this special if downtrodden people.

"Palestinians are a dirty, violent people who hate us and want to wipe Israel off the face of the earth."

Bob and I were both born in the 1960s, which means that we came of age after Israel had decisively defeated its neighbors and took control of the West Bank, the Sinai Peninsula, the Gaza Strip, and the Golan Heights in 1967—thus beginning a military occupation that persists to this day.[3] In adulthood, our only exposure to the word "Palestinian" came through news reports of violent acts such as hijackings, suicide bombings, and the PLO attack at the 1972 Munich Olympics. With scant understanding of the context for these atrocities, we easily absorbed the dominant narrative about unreasoning Palestinian hatred for Jews and Israel.

This story found sometimes subtle but all the more insidious confirmation throughout our trip, which mostly remained within Israel, as the danger and dirtiness associated with people and places called "Arab" or "Palestinian" was foremost in our Jewish friends' minds. Even the landscape we traveled etched a clear dividing line between sophisticated, well-resourced Jewish Israel and a more sinister Arab (Palestinian) presence. (Within

---

3. In the Camp David Accords peace deal signed in 1979, Israel agreed to withdraw from the Sinai Peninsula, a withdrawal completed in 1982. Since Israel's unilateral "withdrawal" from the Gaza Strip in 2005, the "occupation" entails direct control of Gaza's air and sea rights, most of its borders, and other facets of civil life. In effect, Gaza has been under a blockade ever since, as Israel limits the movement of goods and people into the territory, as well as the fishing rights of its residents.

Israel itself, Arab Israeli Palestinians[4] make up more than 20 percent of the population.) For instance, on our bus ride from Tel Aviv to Caesarea, our guide spoke in depth about Israel's critical water shortage even as he pointed to Jewish neighborhoods with green grass and swimming pools. Arab towns, on the other hand, were notably dusty, dilapidated, and lacking basic infrastructure.

One trip highlight was a tour of the tunnels underneath the Western Wall of what our Jewish friends called "the Temple Mount." (Palestinians know it as "Al Aqsa.") This underground passage takes tourists alongside the foundation of that platform, with a clear view of rubble from the Roman destruction of the last Jewish temple in 70 CE.[5] Exiting from the tunnel into the Muslim quarter, we were met by a young Israeli soldier who safeguarded our passage back to the Jewish quarter. It was a stark reminder that, for Jews, danger lurked around every corner.

Finally, what our trip leaders called a "conversation between extremists"—a Jewish settler and a Palestinian student activist—subtly reinforced this fear. Notably, we had met plenty of non-extremist, even peace-loving Israeli Jews. That meant that the settler's overt hatred for Palestinians struck us as an anomaly. But when the student—the only Palestinian voice we encountered—called stridently for freedom and displayed unvarnished resentment toward the settler, he confirmed and normalized our assumptions about Palestinian "hatred" of Jews.

"Israel is a virtuous and rare democracy in the Middle East, and a strategic military and economic ally that uses its formidable military power to protect this 'demonstration plot' of civility in a chaotic global neighborhood."

Our trip was marked by frequent reminders of the sense of safety, home, and joy that our Jewish neighbors carried throughout the stay. Their pride in Israel was visible and palpable, and the fact that Israel has no constitution was a detail mentioned only in passing, and with self-deprecating laughter.

---

4. Archbishop Elias Chacour was the first person I heard use this three-word phrase to introduce himself. It combines an ethnicity (Arab), a citizenship status (Israeli), and a cultural identity (Palestinian). Many Jews prefer to call Palestinians "Arabs," on the premise that there is no Palestinian state. Palestinians prefer "Palestinian" because it signals their rootedness in the land. The term "Palestine" was first used to describe this geographic area by the ancient historian Herodotus (fifth c. BCE).

5. Today, the platform supports two Muslim structures—the Dome of the Rock and Al Aqsa Mosque—and counts as Islam's third holiest site, after Mecca and Medina in Saudi Arabia.

We met refugees fleeing persecution in former Eastern Bloc and African countries and learned that, despite the challenges of integrating into a Western society, they were grateful to be among the majority.

As a result, we were neither surprised nor alarmed by the cloak of protection offered by our trip hosts. From interviews with IDF agents at the El Al gate in New York to our return to Tel Aviv's Ben Gurion airport at the close of our trip, we welcomed interrogation, checkpoints, armed guards, and other indicators of the "security industrial complex" woven into the fabric of Holy Land trips. After all, we were literally on the side of the virtuous and oppressed—the Jews—and could happily distance ourselves from all people and things Palestinian.

Part of Israeli pride extended to the IDF ("Israel Defense Forces"). Some of our neighbors had family members who had served in the IDF, and they regaled us with stories about the "most ethical army in the world," where officers lead soldiers into battle, and civilian casualties are painstakingly avoided. It was the Palestinian Authority (PA) that tortured its people, not the Israelis. (Our guide pointed out a "torture center" on our drive through PA-administered Jericho.)

Put simply, we walked away from our first trip with a clear sense that the Israelis were the good actors and the Palestinians were the violent ones; that it was too bad Israel did not yet control all the land, but that their divine rights to the land (and its resources) subsumed any conversation about human rights under the question of safety and security for Jews.

I do not blame my Jewish friends for their choices in planning the trip. We were invited (and our travel was subsidized) so that they could share their commitments, values, priorities, and dreams related to Israel. If, in hindsight, I came to feel somewhat duped, I owe that more to my own naiveté than to anything else. We did not know what we did not know and, frankly, little on the first trip (save the vague sense that Israel was green and "Arab towns" brown) stoked any curiosity or desire to learn more. But in a turn of events I attribute to God's spirit, we would come to have an experience not unlike the apostle Paul's, in which "something like scales" (Acts 9:18) would fall from our eyes.

"Living Stones"

Six years later, in 2005, we found ourselves back in the Holy Land. From border entry at Eilat to boarding gate at Tel Aviv, the month we spent outside of Jerusalem complicated and upended our previous assumptions and found us reimagining our calling as Christians—and Americans—in this landscape. By then we had grown vaguely aware of what some friends called "the plight of the Palestinians," but we knew little to nothing about their lived experience. We knew little to nothing, that is, about shifting borders, land confiscation, military detention, the impact of settlements on daily life, limited freedom of movement and access to water, or even codified laws of separation distinguishing Jews from non-Jewish citizens of Israel. Perhaps most importantly, we knew little about the "backstory" of Israel's establishment in 1948, the Palestinian dispossession they call the *Nakba* (Arabic for "catastrophe"), and the ongoing destruction of their lives and livelihoods ever since.

Here we were, then, in July 2005: a family of five (including three kids ages twelve, nine, and nine) at the crossing into Israel from Taba, Egypt—not the normal gate of entry for white Protestant Americans. In contrast to our first visit, we were stunned from the outset by the border soldiers' suspicious hostility toward us. (Remember, we thought we were aligned with the virtuous group.) Actual alarm bells and buzzers sounded when we naively mentioned we might visit friends in Ramallah (in the West Bank), as we had learned a group of Greensboro Quakers were leading a service trip there that month. After we reassured them that we did not have to go to Ramallah, the guards let us through, and we walked the hundred or so yards into Eilat, rollaboards in tow.

To get to Jerusalem, we boarded a bus for a two-hour ride that included a physical altercation over the sunshade and a detour on arrival, as protesters opposed to Israel's impending withdrawal from Gaza blocked our path. After we settled into a crowded hotel room for the night, our teenage daughter joined her dad on an ice cream outing, where they were lambasted by an angry shopkeeper who noticed the word "Presbyterian" on our daughter's youth group T-shirt. At that time, our Presbyterian denomination (PCUSA) was moving toward targeted divestment from companies profiting from the Israeli occupation, which led this woman to charge Presbyterians (like us!) with antisemitism.

And so it began. "Wait, what?" Our muffled pillow talk that night began to take stock of the radically different experience we were already having in the Holy Land. As we moved into our apartment in the Tantur community the next day, we took to heart our host's encouragement simply to go out and explore, to listen and to learn, to come to understanding based on first-hand experience. And that we did.

"Whose Land? Whose Promise?"[6]

Nuha Khoury was sharing exciting news with a group of visitors. (We had joined a Guilford College group for visits to Bethlehem, Hebron, and the Galilee.) We were in Bethlehem at Christmas Lutheran Church, where her brother-in-law Mitri Raheb was then pastor. Over the past decade the church had emerged as a shining example of the gospel by caring for the community through programs for children, youth, adults, and the aging population—all in the context of an increasingly challenging Israeli military occupation. Indeed, Raheb's book *Bethlehem Besieged* tells the story of the 2002 Israeli incursion into Bethlehem that shattered church windows, left bullet holes in walls, and saw his wife and daughter nearly killed by an Israeli sniper.

Just three years later, Raheb and his team were envisioning a new project that would expand their Christian witness in Palestine. Plans were underway to start a university that would be Palestine's first institution of higher learning devoted to arts and culture. The vision grew in part out of Raheb's astute observation about the curative power of the arts, after watching his young daughter turn to "crayon therapy" after her harrowing near miss. (Today, Dar al-Kalima flourishes as a fully accredited university located on a prime hilltop setting—even when under Israeli sniper attack, as it was as recently as September 2024.[7])

In the middle of Nuha's talk, a staff member interrupted her with what was clearly heart-breaking news. Her shoulders sunk as her face fell into her hands. We waited in silence until Nuha took a breath, sat straight up, and began to speak with tears brimming from her eyes. She explained that a hotel owned by her family had been recently seized by the IDF, and that the family had gone to court to demonstrate legal ownership. Even though courts had ruled in their favor, the news was that the soldiers were back, evicting the rightful owners and blocking the doors.

Americans cannot fathom that this kind of property seizure goes on virtually every day. We met dozens of Palestinians during our stay—mostly Christian, but some Muslims as well. To a person, they reported similar stories of land confiscation even when the family had resources enough to appeal in the courts.[8] Hearing these stories and sensing their deep rooted-

---

6. Title borrowed from Burge, *Whose Land? Whose Promise?*

7. Learn more about Dar Al-Kalima University at www.daralkalima.edu.ps/en. On the September 2024 attack, see Bright Stars of Bethlehem, "Dar al-Kalima University Under Attack."

8. Learn more about the Nassar family's decades-long struggle at the Tent of Nations website (https://tentofnations.com/). While writing this, I received news from

ness in the land, the seemingly benign claim that "God gave the Jews this land" unraveled.

Seizing land from the native population lies at the root of the Zionist vision of Israel and continues, unabated, to this day. In the late 1940s, after the United Nations sanctioned the establishment of two new nation states, over 750,000 Palestinians were either forcibly moved or lured into "temporarily" abandoning homes to which they would never be allowed return.[9] Such was the case with the Chacour family and other residents of the town of Biram.[10] When Jewish militants first arrived at the Christian town in the late 1940s, they were welcomed with open arms. After all, Chacour's family had heard of atrocities in Germany and wanted nothing more than to provide solace to their Abrahamic kin. Over the next few years, however, although the courts kept affirming the people's right to their homes, they were expelled. Ultimately their village was reduced to rubble.

We had just met Father Chacour, a priest who eventually started a school in the nearby village of Ibillin, and we were eager to visit the place where he grew up. As our bus pulled into a nicely maintained parking lot, we spied families at picnic tables and a sign that explained the historical significance of the site. Imagine our surprise when we read about the remains of an ancient synagogue—but nothing about the Arab village around the corner, behind a grove of trees. The not-so-subtle message of the sign: this land was, and always had been, Jewish land. Erased were all memories of other communities that had lived there for centuries.

"Come to my house for dinner tomorrow, four o'clock."

We live in North Carolina, a part of the American South that is known to lead with hospitality. Imagine our surprise, then, to find ourselves on the receiving end of a more gracious and authentic welcome from those we assumed would hold us in disdain. "Wait, what?"

---

another friend in the area whose family had had land confiscated that day by settlers, with the full support of the IDF.

9. This despite UN Resolution 194 (December 11, 1948), which resolves that "refugees wishing to return to their homes and live at peace with their neighbors should be permitted to do so at the earliest practicable date, and that compensation should be paid for the property of those choosing not to return and for loss of or damage to property which, under principles of international law or equity, should be made good by the Governments or authorities responsible." For the full text of the Resolution, see UN Digital Library, "Resolution 194 (III)."

10. Read the full story in Chacour, *Blood Brothers*.

Our second day at Tantur, we walked with our kids through the checkpoint (more on that below) into Bethlehem, where we enrolled them in the day camp started by Christmas Lutheran Church. On the hot walk home, we made an unplanned stop in a gift store. It looked dark, but when we entered, Mr. Canavati threw on the lights (and air conditioning) and welcomed us with open arms. He sent his son to get sodas for our kids, and we spent the next hour poking around his store and chatting with this aging shopkeeper. Any item that seemed even mildly interesting to our younger daughter quickly became a gift for her, since she so reminded him of his granddaughter who lives in the States. The Canavatis had encouraged their adult children not to settle in Bethlehem, since daily life under military occupation was so traumatizing for their grandchildren. What did Mr. Canavati want? Simply to live his life with the same freedoms experienced by Jews in the land. No more, no less.

It was our Palestinian Muslim taxi driver Assan who most challenged our assumptions about "Palestinians." We had met him at the taxi stand just inside the wall (he is not permitted to drive his car in Jerusalem) and had arranged for him to meet us there each day to drive our kids to their day camp. Along the way, Assan pointed out buildings destroyed by Israeli rockets (made in America), properties confiscated for settlement construction, roads he was not permitted to drive on, and water tanks atop Palestinian homes riddled with Israeli bullet holes. Sometimes, "flying checkpoints" popped up, clogging traffic; most of the time he turned around and found a different route.

After a few days, Assan invited us to his home—really, an intergenerational family compound—for dinner. At first, we balked. We knew he had a newborn—certainly not the stage of life when *we* would welcome strangers into *our* home. We also wondered if this was a Palestinian version of "Southern hospitality," which can reflect politeness more than genuine openheartedness. But Assan persisted, and we met him at the taxi stand the next day for what would prove to be the most sacramental meal of our stay.

At his home, we were greeted not just by Assan's wife and kids (including their one-week-old son), but also by his parents who lived upstairs, siblings, cousins, aunts, and uncles. Given our embarrassing inability to speak Arabic, we were glad to know that they all managed with some English. We held the new baby, shared a sumptuous feast, and mostly listened to their life stories, including the story of a cousin, commemorated as a martyr on the living room wall, who had been gunned down by an Israeli sniper. We learned more about settlements—Jewish neighborhoods built on Palestinian land in the West Bank—and settler access to water, roads, and other infrastructure that was denied to Palestinians. We also came to understand the settlements as a pretext of the military occupation, as the Israeli army is charged with "protecting" settlers. This protection entails strategies such as flying checkpoints to disrupt Palestinian movement within the West Bank, "night raids" of Palestinian homes designed to terrorize families and sometimes to arrest children and youth, and "administrative detention" consisting of months-long imprisonment without charges and, if and when charges are brought, a 99 percent conviction rate.[11]

"Wait, what?" We could not help but ask, "But why don't you hate us? America supports everything about this occupation that makes your life so hard." Assan looked puzzled as he replied. "Why would we hate you? You're people; that's the government. They're not the same." Then we asked about the Jews. "Horrible things happened to them in Germany, it's true. But why does that mean they get to steal our land? We'd rather live with them as we have for centuries before Israel existed, together sharing the same land."

Some Palestinians take matters into their own hands, and do so violently. But we came to see the context for that violence. As we sat with Elias Chacour in the board room of his Mar Elias School in northern Israel, we listened for over an hour to the life stories of suicide bombers. Each story was filled with trauma, dehumanization, and degradation. One told of a father dying in the parking lot of an Israeli hospital where he, as a Palestinian, could not be treated. One of a brother's death by Israeli sniper fire. One of a fiancé crushed in a home demolition. As we left the room, our nine-year-old son turned to me. "But Mom, I always thought the Israelis were the 'good guys' and the Palestinians were the 'bad guys.'" Wait, what? indeed.

"They treat us like animals."

Perhaps the most glaring and unsettling takeaway from our second trip was evidence at every turn of the Israeli government's intent to separate, subjugate, and ultimately eradicate the Palestinian people and their culture. We had unwittingly accepted a narrative about a virtuous, democratic Israel, focused on protecting Jews from imminent dangers posed by Palestinians. But once we encountered Palestinians as people, not as a vague "enemy," we witnessed first-hand Israeli strategies of degradation and provocation.

For one thing, riding Arab buses into Jerusalem meant being routinely interrupted by flying checkpoints, roadblocks set up in the name of

---

11. To learn more about the strategies of the occupation from current and former Israeli soldiers, see Breaking the Silence (www.breakingthesilence.org.il). Learn more about administrative detention, especially the treatment of children under this system, from Military Court Watch (https://militarycourtwatch.org).

"security." After soldiers boarded the bus and checked identity cards, they would often wait outside the bus in idle conversation for a few minutes or an hour before allowing us to proceed, and thus signaling a cavalier and deliberate delay of our departure. A twenty-minute ride could take an hour or more—inconvenient for a family on vacation but life-altering for people trying to get to work or home. Likewise, as we joined Palestinians returning to Bethlehem through Checkpoint 300 (the IDF monitors passage in both directions), it was a teenage soldier cradling an AR-15 who decided how long to detain us and when we could pass.

It was our visit to Hebron with Guilford College students that clarified for us the banality of the occupation. Our conversations with Community Peacemaker Teams[12] and with a former IDF (Jewish) soldier from Breaking the Silence revealed Israel's growing stranglehold on this once-flourishing Palestinian city deep in the West Bank. Settlers, having established a foothold, have attacked children on their way to school, uprooted olive trees (the villagers' livelihood), and even poisoned wells.[13] As our Jewish guide explained, the IDF is charged with protecting settlers, not with ensuring justice. Palestinian access to food, healthcare, commerce, school, and even to extended family members has been drastically limited by blockaded streets and checkpoints at every turn. The IDF policy, he shared, is meant to keep Palestinians on edge, demoralized, and hopeless. As our Palestinian bus driver put it, "they treat us like animals." Since October 7, what was already a suffocating situation has only grown more dire.[14]

Near the end of our stay, we toured the Holocaust Remembrance Center Yad Vashem. We wanted our children to understand the horrors of Nazi Germany to foster empathy with Jewish Israelis. On the walls of the memorial we read about specific German policies implemented in the 1930s designed first to identify and assign Jews second-class status, then to relocate them into ghettos, and then to curtail their freedom of movement through checkpoints and other means. It was our thirteen-year-old who pointed out that these stages of the Holocaust resembled policies in place today in the Holy Land. She was struck by Hitler's zeal to foment fear about the Other and to use that fear as the pretext for dehumanization and genocide. These new insights about antisemitism she had to absorb along with what she was learning about life as a Palestinian: identity cards, ghettos, restricted movement, night raids, administrative detention, all while

---

12. Formerly Christian Peacemaker Teams. Learn more here: https://cpt.org/.
13. Carr, "Letter from Tuwani."
14. Levy and Levac, "In Hebron, Palestinians Now Long for Apartheid."

she passed daily through the "security wall" that separates Jerusalem from Bethlehem.[15] It was her own "wait, what?" moment.

The Way of the Cross

In 2014, nine years after our second trip, I was leading a group of college students down Jerusalem's *Via Dolorosa*, which traces Jesus's way of the cross. One member of our group—not particularly religious himself—said this: "I get why Jesus died." He went on to connect his experience of the Israeli occupation of Palestine today with what he had learned about the Roman occupation of Palestine in Jesus's day. He recognized on a deep level that Jesus's unfettered devotion to God and to God's alternative "kingdom"— a kingdom that promotes human flourishing and recognizes God's image in all people—made him an "enemy of the people." So they arrested him at night, tried him in something of a kangaroo court, and hung him at a crossroads, to make a scapegoat and example of him.

At the historical level, scholars link Jesus's death to two episodes during the last week of his life. First, he staged his entry into Jerusalem in a way that heralded God's coming kingdom, which would rule not through military might but through humble service. People suffering under Roman rule hailed this new "king" with palm branches and cries of "hosanna" (literally, "save us"), a cry that some today might compare to "free Palestine!" But Jesus did not stop there. In a destructive display of rage, Jesus protested a temple economy in which subsistence-level farmers exchanged, at a markup, their local currency for temple coins needed to purchase sacrificial animals for Passover. Why did Jesus die? My student saw that he died at least in part because he challenged those who wielded religious and political power.[16]

As Christians, we celebrate the redemptive power of Jesus's death. But too often we forget the corollary: "If any wish to come after me, let them deny themselves and take up their cross and follow me. For those who want to save their life will lose it, and those who lose their life for my sake, and for the sake of the gospel, will save it" (Mark 8:34–35).[17] What does it mean to take up one's cross? On this point, our Palestinian friends have been our most helpful instructors.

---

15. One Jewish Israeli explained that "security wall" language is disingenuous, as thousands of Palestinians breach the wall each day to work in Israel. Palestinians refer to it as a "separation wall."

16. See Raheb and Watts Henderson, *Cross in Contexts*.

17. All citations of Scripture in this chapter are from the NRSV.

PART III: The Peoples of the Land

"What can we do to help?"

Over the last two decades, our relationships in the Holy Land have only grown deeper, as the plight of Palestinians has only grown more dire, even before the flare up in Gaza. What do our Palestinian friends want? Not the destruction of Israel, not the annihilation of the Jewish people. Simply this: freedom, equal access to infrastructure and opportunity, and basic human rights—the rights they and others insist are theirs according to international law.

Over the years, we have asked a consistent question: What can we do to help? Though we might expect requests for money or political advocacy (both of which they would welcome), our friends consistently make two simple requests: Come and be with us; go home and tell our story. This, it strikes me, is the gospel in a nutshell.

The plea to "come and be with us" resonates with Jesus's own ministry of presence. Throughout the Gospels, this itinerant Jewish-Palestinian rabbi sought out the least, the lost, the disregarded. From welcoming lepers to spending time with women and children, Jesus broke established protocols to signal the innate value of those suffering under palpably evil forces ranging from physical and mental illness to hunger and deprivation. To come alongside those who yearn for God's justice and cry for freedom is to follow the way of vulnerable solidarity that marked Jesus's life and death.

Too many American Christians tour the Holy Land without encountering the "least and the lost" who live there today. I know: I have taken a trip that not only insulated me from those realities but reinforced assumptions that I later found to be patently untrue. That is why we have committed to leading groups and sending people on trips that include, but go beyond, the kind of religious tourism that we first experienced. Our trips include a range of voices, from a range of perspectives—Jewish settlers and peace activists, religious leaders of all stripes, shopkeepers and people on the street. These "living stones" of the Holy Land all have important stories to tell; they are all created in God's image.

It was our friend and Muslim Palestinian tour guide who confirmed to us most powerfully the impact of our Christian presence in the Land. Several years ago, our group was delayed in getting through security at Tel Aviv, as my student (whose middle name is Mohammed) was detained and questioned at length about his Christian identity. As I finally reached our guide Sami, I blurted out, in jetlagged exhaustion and frustration, that this might be my last trip. Sami grabbed my shoulders and looked me squarely in the eye: "Don't say that, Suzanne. The chance to guide a trip of yours literally keeps me alive for the next two years. The whole world has forgotten us, but you remember us. You keep coming back."

For those who lack the means or opportunity to visit the Holy Land in person, the call to "come and be with us" can look, instead, like committing to learn and share the stories of all peoples in the Land. Churches can host Palestinian speakers. Adult classes can give space for discussion and discovery in ways that honor Palestinian voices. Clergy can forge relationships with local rabbis and Muslim community leaders.

This ministry of presence in all its forms can be costly, but it is the call to bear witness—"go home and tell our story"—that best resonates with our Christian calling on many levels. How does Jesus respond to the Gerasene man liberated from his demons? "Go home to your friends, and tell them how much the Lord has done for you" (Mark 5:19). In other words, help others to see God's work in the human condition to set us free from forces of evil. Again, just before his ascension, the risen Lord charges his followers this way: "you will be my witnesses . . . to the ends of the earth" (Acts 1:8).

Yet it's also true that bearing this kind of bold witness comes at a cost. Already, Jesus signals this in his call to discipleship: "if any want to become my followers, let them deny themselves and take up their cross and follow me" (Mark 8:34). After all, Christians are called to bear witness to more than just a story of *personal* salvation; "good news" in the New Testament entails the radical, cosmic claim that even when the forces of evil seem to prevail, the power of God works to bring life out of death and to engender hope in the midst of despair. As Jesus puts it in the Gospel of Luke (citing Isa 61:1–2):

> The Spirit of the Lord is upon me, because he has anointed me to bring good news to the poor. He has sent me to proclaim release to the captives and recovery of sight to the blind, to set free those who are oppressed, to proclaim the year of the Lord's favor.

In the American context, we encounter efforts to silence Palestinian voices across the land and in both major political parties. Those who try to tell the story in a political context are branded extremist or radical. Protesters calling for the liberation of Palestinians are dismissed as "naive," "coerced," or worse, "antisemitic" (even when they're Jewish). Preachers and church leaders who know the truth about Palestine sometimes hesitate to speak openly for fear of fallout or reprisal. With the Holocaust still casting a shadow over human history, these responses are understandable. Yet the horrific tragedy of one genocide does not mean that people of faith should turn a blind eye to atrocities against another ethnic group. Trauma-inspired fear is real. But as Christians, we follow a Lord who answers fear not with violence but with love. Indeed, as the writer of First John puts it, "perfect love casts out fear" (1 John 4:18). Can we trust that this divine gift of love ultimately sets us, and all people, free?

"What about Hamas?"

Friends and coworkers sometimes ask, "What do you think should happen in Gaza?" or "Why doesn't Hamas surrender?" These are understandable questions given the public focus on the events of October 7 in isolation from more than fifty years of Israel's military occupation. The massacres and kidnappings by Hamas are unconscionably horrific. As much as I yearn for freedom for my Palestinian brothers and sisters, I cannot sanction violence as a means to secure it.

But neither can I simply lament Israel's war on Gaza as something like a "necessary evil," an unfortunate but inescapable result of the October 7 attack. To endorse—explicitly or implicitly—Israel's wanton destruction of Gaza and its people, its arrest (kidnapping?) of thousands of Palestinians, most of whom neither live in Gaza nor identify with Hamas, and its aggression throughout the region only legitimizes the false myth of redemptive violence. It is this myth—the notion that our salvation requires the destruction of our enemies—that Jesus's death has turned on end.

As a Christian, I must go beyond lament to bear active witness to an alternative world order we call the kingdom of God—to a power structure marked not by force but by vulnerable solidarity with the weak; not by hatred but by love of God and neighbor; not by the self-concern of the powerful but by self-sacrifice for the good of others; not by ethnic or religious or social separation but by expansive, indiscriminate love. It is this kind of regime that brings release to all imprisoned in falsehood, violence, and fear. It is this kind of power that promises life, and life abundant, for all.

Bibliography

Bright Stars of Bethlehem. "Dar al-Kalima University Under Attack." September 16, 2024. https://www.brightstarsbethlehem.org/news/blog-post-title-one-m4372.

Burge, Gary M. *Whose Land? Whose Promise? What Christians Are Not Being Told About Israel and the Palestinians*. Cleveland: Pilgrim, 2003.

Carr, Joe. "Letter from Tuwani." *The Electronic Intifada*, October 15, 2004. https://electronicintifada.net/content/letter-tuwani/5270.

Chacour, Elias, with David Hazard. *Blood Brothers: The Unforgettable Story of a Palestinian Christian Working for Peace in Israel*. Grand Rapids: Chosen, 2003.

Levy, Gideon, and Alex Levac. "In Hebron, Palestinians Now Long for Apartheid as It Existed Before October 7." *Haaretz*, May 31, 2024. https://www.haaretz.com/israel-news/twilight-zone/2024-5-31/ty-article-magazine/.highlight/in-hebron-palestinians-now-long-for-apartheid-as-it-existed-before-october-7/0000018f-cfe6-d5bc-a1bf-dff672570000.

Raheb, Mitri. *Bethlehem Besieged: Stories of Hope in Times of Trouble*. Minneapolis: Fortress, 2004.

Raheb, Mitri, and Suzanne Watts Henderson. *The Cross in Contexts: Suffering and Redemption in Palestine*. Maryknoll, NY: Orbis, 2017.

United Nations Digital Library. "Resolution 194 (III). Palestine—Progress Report of the United Nations Mediator." December 11, 1948. https://digitallibrary.un.org/record/210025?ln=en&v=pdf.

CHAPTER SIXTEEN

Worshiping Jerusalem
Christian Colonizers and Colonized Christians[1]

DAVID M. CRUMP

Triumphant reports by the missions in fact tell us how deep the seeds of alienation have been sown among the colonized. . . . The Church in the colonies is a white man's Church, a foreigners' Church. It does not call the colonized to the ways of God, but to the ways of the white man, to the ways of the master, the ways of the oppressor.
—Frantz Fanon[2]

MY WIFE AND I stumbled into the Pentecost Sunday evening service at King of Kings, an evangelical megachurch in downtown Jerusalem, by accident. Or by providence. We were spending a month in 2023 (before October 7) living with friends in the West Bank while I was learning about contemporary inter-church relationships between Jewish Christians and Palestinian Christians in Palestine-Israel.

We had every intention of visiting a Jewish-Christian church that night, but had no idea that this particular gathering was one of the key

---

1. An earlier version of this chapter appeared as Crump, "Worshipping Jerusalem: Colonial Christianity Among Colonisers and the Colonised."
2. Fanon, *Wretched of the Earth*, 7.

congregations participating in "21 Days of Prayer for Jerusalem and the Nations," an initiative of American pastor Mike Bickle, leader of the International House of Prayer (IHOP) megachurch in Kansas City, Missouri.[3] On this night King of Kings would link arms via satellite with IHOP for a joint worship service to conclude the month of prayer and fasting. Looming over the auditorium stage was a large movie screen (the church meets in a renovated theatre) displaying the concurrent worship service in Kansas City, complete with satellite glitches and time delays.[4]

This was hardly what I expected when I set out to visit a Jewish Christian congregation in Jerusalem. Most of the service was conducted in English, with only two prayers and a few choruses offered in Hebrew. Most of the leadership spoke with American accents. Even though the church felt American evangelical, the focus throughout the service was on the people of Israel. We were repeatedly reminded that evangelizing the Jews would trigger the return of Messiah Jesus. Appealing to Rom 11:26, Bickle assured us that "when all Israel has been saved, then the Deliverer will come from Zion." By cobbling this passage from Romans together with Isa 62:6–7, and calling God's people to constant prayer for the glorious establishment of a "new Jerusalem" in the land of Israel, Bickle was telling us that this new Jerusalem was the lynchpin to the end of history as we know it. Israel's national repentance (Acts 3:19) and confession that Jesus is Messiah (Matt 23:39) is deeply connected to Jesus's second coming, the Great Commission, and "life from the dead" for the whole earth (Rom 11:15) that comes when God fulfills his promises to Israel. Jesus will not return until the leaders in Jerusalem, in accord with Ps 118:26, acknowledge him as Messiah.

According to Bickle and his Jerusalem compatriots, fasting and praying for massive Jewish conversion, around the world and especially in Jerusalem, should be the preoccupation of Christians everywhere. Pastor Bickle emphasized the importance of massive numbers for spiritual success, highlighting the tens of millions around the globe who, he claimed, had joined in this month of prayer and fasting for Israel's conversion. "Nothing like this has ever happened before in human history," he exclaimed repeatedly. He would later claim that "the trajectory of world history was shifted" because of these days of fasting and prayer.[5]

It was as if God needed satellite communication and mass media to mobilize global prayer. Not until Bickle's movement, live streamed on

---

3. See Isaiah62Fast.com. Others involved in shaping the project include Lou Engle and Jason Hubbard.

4. Bickle, "What Happens Now."

5. Bickle, "Why I Believe Human History Shifted."

YouTube, could Israel be redeemed. At one point, the song leaders had us singing about the virtues of Jerusalem. The ancient city had become an object of devotion in its own right. Worshiping Jesus had morphed into the adoration of an idealized Jerusalem. Over and over we were led to ask God (again, in English) to make Israel and Jerusalem "a praise in the earth" (Isa 62:7).

As my wife and I returned to our hotel room that night, she turned to me and said, "Well, I've never been asked to worship Jerusalem before." Neither had I. Nor had I ever encountered in person a theatrical, bright-lights, American-style production of colonizing Christianity.

Divided by the Walls We Build

Though the age of colonialism is generally thought to have ended by the mid-twentieth century, its aftershocks continue to reverberate throughout the world, not least in Israel-Palestine. Israel is a settler-colonial state. As anthropologist Patrick Wolfe has shown, *settler-colonialism is not an event; it is a structure*, a permanent structure controlling settler society until a decision is made to tear it down and build a new society in its place.[6] As I argue at length in *Like Birds in a Cage*, an adequate understanding of Israel's political and social life begins here.[7]

The Western church has long been a willing handmaiden to European colonial adventures, beginning with Columbus's (bloodthirsty) missionary efforts in the West Indies, continuing with Western evangelicalism's (more subtle) missionary efforts around the world, including in Israel. A colonizing church will support settler-colonial societies until it, too, confesses, repents, and begins to deconstruct its role in creating and maintaining the unjust disparities of settler-colonialism.[8]

---

6. Wolfe, *Settler Colonialism*, 163, also 2–3.

7. Crump, *Like Birds in a Cage*; Halper, *Decolonizing Israel*; Veracini, *Israel*. The distinguishing feature of settler-colonialism, as opposed to other forms of colonialism, is the replacement—indeed the erasure—of the indigenous people by the invading, immigrant population. The Israeli nation-state was founded by European immigrants whose leaders openly discussed the need to remove the native Palestinians from their land, whether by transfer or eradication. Since the creation of the Palestinian refugee crisis in the war of 1947–1949, Israel has continued a deliberate campaign of the steady, forced removal of as many Palestinians as possible from their historic homeland.

8. De las Casas, *Devastation of the Indies*. The entire book is shocking. "It would be hard to make anyone believe," writes de las Casas, "and harder still to narrate, the infamous deeds in all their details" (81). Also, Holt, *Indian Orphanages*, 49–52, 69, 74, on the loss of native culture, language, and traditions through the uniform imposition of the "common school agenda."

Over four weeks I met with Jewish Christian leaders in Israel and Palestinian Christian leaders in the West Bank. Only at King of Kings did I encounter a Palestinian pastor living and ministering in Israel. In all these encounters, I wanted to see if colonizer and colonized could gather and share in authentic Christian fellowship. I asked a number of people if they were involved in, or knew of, efforts to bring Palestinian and Jewish Christians together as one spiritual body for shared worship and fellowship as brothers and sisters in Christ. Was anyone working to overcome the disparate power dynamics at work in every relationship between a colonizing Zionist Jew and a colonized Palestinian Christian? If so, what were their experiences like? If not, what was preventing cross-cultural community from happening?

I was motivated to ask such questions by the powerful vision of church unity we find in the book of Eph 2:14–16:[9]

> For he [Jesus] himself is our peace, who has made the two groups [Jews and Gentiles] one and has destroyed the barrier, the dividing wall of hostility, by setting aside in his flesh the law with its commands and regulations. His purpose was to create in himself one new humanity out of the two, thus making peace, and in one body to reconcile both of them to God through the cross, by which he put to death their hostility.[10]

In 1960, speaking on *Meet the Press* about the racial divide in the United States, Martin Luther King Jr. said, "It is appalling that the most segregated hour of Christian America is 11 o'clock on Sunday morning."[11] The sad ecclesiastical reality King described subverted the picture Paul paints in Ephesians. I suspected, based on experience and study, that ethnic segregation was even more pronounced among Israeli and Palestinian churches. I knew of US congregations working to overcome the racial divide. Would I find similar efforts in Israel?

My informal research and my experience at King of Kings suggested that in most faith communities in Israel, the colonizers and the colonized inhabited different worlds, even in worship. The leaders I met were consistently discouraged. Some had given up hope for reconciliation and multiethnic community. Past efforts at integrating the two communities have currently been put on hold.

Palestinian leaders spoke with one voice. Yes, occasional prayer meetings occurred where Jews and Palestinians shared a few songs and said their

---

9. Crump, *Like Birds in a Cage*, 120–29.
10. All citations of Scripture in this chapter are from the NIV.
11. King, "Most Segregated Hour."

hellos, but meaningful, long-term "body life" together where people carry each other's burdens, weeping with those who weep and rejoicing with those who rejoice, was yet unrealized.

The problem, as it was described to me, was that the Jewish church in Israel has expanded its circle of doctrinal essentials well beyond the historic Christian faith as represented by the Nicene Creed, with its focus on Jesus Christ and his redemptive work. This wider theological circle now includes political Zionist elements, especially the right of Jews as God's chosen people to all the land of Israel. As Salim Munayer, founder of *Musalaha*, a Palestinian reconciliation organization, explained to me,

> They [Jewish Christians] are highly nationalistic and promote Jewish supremacy. We [Palestinian Christians] are told that we must accept their end times theology about the Jewish claim to the land before we can have real fellowship.

Christ may have taken down first-century religious barriers separating Jews from gentiles, but Israeli Jewish Christians have erected their own ethnic, nationalistic, territorial "walls of hostility."

I heard this complaint time and again from the Palestinian church leaders I spoke with. *Musalaha* (Arabic for "Reconciliation") was originally created to achieve exactly these cross-cultural, ecumenical goals. Their organizational priorities, however, have moved away from Jewish-Palestinian Christian reconciliation toward Christian-Muslim religious dialogue, since they discovered that Jewish and Muslim circles outside of the church are more open to biblical principles of reconciliation.[12] Palestinian Christian engagement with their Islamic neighbors is proving more productive than parallel efforts with their Israeli brothers and sisters in Christ.

Perhaps most disheartening was my conversation with Lisa Loden, a respected leader in the Jewish Christian community who, it turns out, has contributed a chapter to this book. Long engaged in bridging the chasm between Jewish and Palestinian Christians in Israel, Loden calls herself an ecumenical Jewish disciple of Jesus.[13] But even she exudes defeat when asked about the state of Jewish-Palestinian Christian communion. "The interest and the energy simply aren't there," she told me. Jewish Christians were sometimes put off, she said, by the fact that Palestinians seem unwilling to move beyond their own stories of historic suffering and reluctant to leave the past in the past in order to focus on the future. But in terms of obstacles in the way of Jewish-Palestinian reconciliation, this was the smallest.

---

12. Musalaha's website describes the initiative: https://musalaha.org/.

13. Munayer and Loden, *Land Cries Out*; Munayer and Loden, *Through My Enemy's Eyes*. See also Loden's contribution to this volume (ch. 8).

Greater by far were Jewish Christian apathy toward inter-ethnic fellowship; their inability to understand the lived experience of Palestinian brothers and sisters; and their laser-like focus on the Jewish state as fulfillment of end times hopes.

I do not fault Palestinian leaders for insisting that Jewish brothers and sisters acknowledge the ravaging consequences of colonization, from the 1948 Nakba to fifty-eight years and counting of brutal Israeli military occupation in the West Bank and Gaza. If they weren't asked to embrace, as a prerequisite to Christian unity, a Zionist nationalism that oppresses them daily, they could engage as equals rather than as victims of Jewish colonial dominance.

As I left the Loden residence north of Tel Aviv and returned to my lodgings in the West Bank, my perspective on these issues began to shift. Surely there are spiritual and theological dimensions to this cross-cultural stalemate. But I could not ignore the asymmetrical power relationships in present day Israel. Israeli Jewish Zionists, Christian or not, hold all the power as victorious colonizers over local Palestinians. Palestinians languish as the disempowered, colonized subjects, relegated to second-class citizenship in their own land. Rarely do the powerful choose to relinquish power, much less share it with the disempowered who have been forced to submit to colonial control.

Palestinians want Jewish brothers and sisters—who enjoy ethnic, national privileges they have not known since the founding of the modern, Jewish ethnocracy—to acknowledge the causes of Palestinian suffering and repent of their complicity. Humanly speaking, it is little wonder that Zionist Jews refuse to reckon with their colonial sins. Hardcore Zionists defend their nationalistic version of Israel's history and fight to maintain the status quo. Others refuse or seem unable to view themselves as conquerors of the land and its native inhabitants. Zionist Christians seem to believe that Jewish hegemony over Palestine and its indigenous people is a reality resulting from an act of God. According to their theology, a victorious military history grants them the right to demand fealty to the Zionist cause as a precondition to inter-ethnic Christian fellowship. How this posture squares with the call to be followers of the crucified, suffering messiah who loves all people equally, or Paul's vision in Ephesians that the work of Christ makes one new humanity, not one part of humanity holding ruthless power over another, is far from apparent.

Yes, one would hope for more, much more, from people who call themselves Christians. Renouncing personal power and privilege is what Jesus expected from his disciples. On one occasion, when Jesus's disciples were jockeying for position among themselves, Jesus corrected them by saying, "You know that the rulers of the Gentiles lord it over them. . . . Not so with you. Instead, whoever wants to become great among you must be your servant, and whoever wants to be first must be your slave" (Matt 20:25–27).

Sadly, church history demonstrates how naïve Christians can be in mistaking their own culture and its vices for the faithful embodiment of the gospel. Extending the abuse of others hardens human hearts to the Holy Spirit's promptings that would tear down these walls of hostility. Christians have often been asleep and have needed awakening to begin to correct the abuses of their forebears. We live in such a time with regard to Christian Zionism and its blindness to the suffering at their gates.

The Pieces Fall into Place

I was becoming impatient with a three-hour service focused on the adoration of Jerusalem and on modern, secular Israel's centrality to the return of Christ. Mike Bickle's effusive self-promotion did little to soothe my nerves. Several lines from their songs professed ignorance or perhaps hypocrisy. Again and again we sang about the promised watchers on the walls (Isa 62:6) and joined in asking the Lord to save his people.

Imagine how "watchers on the wall" would strike a Palestinian Christian used to seeing military ramparts along the Separation Wall that snakes around their home—walled-in and under constant threat of military crackdown. Palestinians are experts at watching the wall. Imagine the situational blindness of song leaders who encourage oppressors to call God "to save his people" within earshot of oppressed people crying out to this same God for rescue?

Repeating ourselves, we sang a prayer to feel what God feels, see what God sees, love what God loves, forgetting that the Lord had already told us what he loves, what he sees, and what we must do: "Learn to do right; seek justice. Defend the oppressed. Take up the cause of the fatherless; plead the case of the widow" (Isa 1:17). "Maintain justice and do what is right" (Isa 56:1). "He has shown you, O mortal, what is good. And what does the Lord require of you? To act justly and to love mercy and to walk humbly with your God" (Mic 6:8).

This service was staged at the epicenter of one of history's most protracted human-rights disasters. Some three million Palestinians live in East Jerusalem and the West Bank. Two and one half million live in the Gaza Strip. Approximately 1.8 million Palestinians live inside Israel proper where they are legally registered as second-class citizens.[14] All of them face

---

14. Crump, *Like Birds in a Cage*, 191–97.

insuperable hardships imposed by a Zionist nation-state. Yet speaker after speaker mounted the platform to plead for God's mighty hand to work miracles. Not one plea for God to relieve Palestinian suffering, lift oppression, and end Gaza's blockade and the West Bank's military occupation.

Two years later, the questions I posed then have become all the more pressing. Israeli bombing has turned Gaza into an uninhabitable, chaotic, rubble-strewn moonscape pockmarked with bomb craters from horizon to horizon. Crushed high-rise apartments contain the decaying corpses of tens of thousands of innocent human beings whose only crime was being a Palestinian. Jagged concrete and twisted rebar form tombstones for families killed *en masse* by Israeli missiles.

Have the Jewish Christians who gathered that night at King of Kings ever joined a demonstration—not just anti-Netanyahu but anti-war—and demanded justice for all? Have any of them written to Knesset members to condemn Israel's excessive force in Gaza? Has King of Kings held prayer vigils not only for Israeli hostages held by Hamas, but also for Palestinian prisoners tortured in Israeli prisons while held under military detention without prospect of release? Have other Jewish-Christian churches in Israel held services of collective repentance or called their government to account for the ongoing genocide in Gaza?

If this is too much to expect of Israeli Christian Zionists, might we ask them at least to acknowledge the suffering of their Palestinian neighbors? Or challenge their leaders to treat all Israeli citizens equitably? I counted three prayers that night that mentioned "blessing our Arab brothers and sisters." The remarks were brief. Almost an afterthought. In that 2023 Jewish Christian worship service in Israel, a large crowd of white, middle-class worshipers remained blind to the injustice and pain their Zionism imposed on the native people. The scene reminded me of Albert Memmi's description in *The Colonizer and the Colonized* of the colonizer's psychological state:

> Accepting the reality of being a colonizer means agreeing to be a nonlegitimate privileged person, that is, a usurper . . . . To possess victory completely he needs to absolve himself of it and the conditions under which it was attained . . . . He attempts to falsify history, he rewrites laws, he would extinguish memories—anything to succeed in transforming his usurpation into legitimacy.[15]

It is this quest for legitimacy that prevents Jewish Zionist churches from recognizing the inhumanity of their colonial mentality. If King of Kings is

---

15. Memmi, *Colonizer*, 52.

typical of Jewish Christian thinking across Israel, we should not be surprised that Jewish-Palestinian Christian relations are unhealthy, even moribund.

The service concluded with the Lord's Supper led by Palestinian pastor Sayid (not his real name). He was accompanied on stage by the leader of *Tikkun Global*, a Jewish Christian organization whose website (tikkunglobal.org) says it is "a global family, contending for *revival* and *restoration* from Jerusalem, Judea, Samaria to the ends of the earth and back again." "Judea and Samaria" are the Israeli terms of reference for the occupied West Bank. I suspect that Tikkun Global's efforts at revival and restoration pass by the impoverished Palestinian villages, Bedouin encampments, and seventy-six-year-old refugee camps scattered throughout this occupied territory.

With his arm firmly across Pastor Sayid's shoulder, the Tikkun leader introduced the Palestinian pastor as evidence of Christian unity between Jewish and Palestinian congregations in Israel. Pastor Sayid's congregation was described as mixed, composed of both Jewish and Palestinian Christians. (I have been unable to visit this church, much to my disappointment.)

In Pastor Sayid's prayer for the communion elements, he included brief words for the people of Gaza, East Jerusalem, and the West Bank. Like a falcon seizing its prey, the leader from Tikkun Global accosted the pastor, mid-prayer, to explain to the congregation that:

> the people of Gaza and the West Bank display so much hate; there is so much hatred there. But we want to show them Jesus and replace that hate with love. We want to show them love.

Not a hint that occupied Palestinians might have legitimate grounds for their anger and "hatred." This was not a moment for humane, informed reflection but for Zionist exhortation. One wonders how much Palestinian hatred Tikkun Global has replaced with Christian love, given their tacit support of Israel's rampage in Gaza and the eviction of over 40,000 Palestinians from West Bank homes between January and March of 2025. Are there signs of repentance for harnessing the gospel of Jesus Christ to the ideology of political Zionism?

The acceptable contours having been delineated by his Zionist companion, Pastor Sayid was allowed to resume his prayer for unity as the bread and wine were distributed. I have never seen a more blatant example of public stage management. Pastor Sayid had a specific role to play, and a stage director was there to ensure that he stuck to the script.

As the service ended and the crowd began to mill about, I searched for Pastor Sayid. When I found him, I introduced myself and asked if he had time for a few questions. Not the ideal setting for an interview, but my only opportunity. Our conversation included the following exchange:

Me: "Pastor, as an Arab national in Israel, do you feel that you have equal rights and privileges with the Jewish nationals you worship with?"

Sayid: "No, I do not."

Me: "You are treated as a second-class citizen?"

Sayid: "Yes, I am."

Me: "Do you feel that your Jewish brothers and sisters speak out on your behalf, defending your right to equal treatment and equal citizenship under the law?"

Sayid: "No, they do not. But I don't expect them to."

At this point his American wife explained to me that her husband did not get involved with politics. He did not seek political solutions to worldly problems. I wondered if an American Bible college or seminary had encouraged him to turn a blind eye to worldly injustice. In any case, my question concerned not his political inactivity, but the political apathy of his Jewish brothers and sisters, the power brokers in their relationship.

I turned to Israel's military occupation of Gaza and the West Bank: "Aren't you bothered by the suffering of your fellow Palestinians who live under Israel's military occupation just next door? Wouldn't you like to help them?" Sayid repeatedly evaded this question, no matter how I reframed it, always with the same arguments of distraction that echoed familiar Zionist talking-points:

- Gaza has turned into a nest for terrorism.
- Palestinian communities in Israel have the highest crime rates in the country.
- Palestinians in the West Bank wish they could live in Israel; none wants to move to the surrounding Arab countries.
- Israeli soldiers are humane. They only shoot back after being attacked.

I was stunned. Nothing he said addressed my questions about the occupation. He echoed instead the Zionist defense of Israel's militaristic status quo, which I had encountered often, though never on the lips of a Palestinian.

I had never met anyone who had so completely assimilated to his colonizer's perspective on the colonized—an inferior, inherently violent, unruly, primitive people. He appeared accustomed to being stage-managed by his Jewish brothers. He did not seem troubled by the interruption of his prayer. Over decades Pastor Sayid's mind had become as colonized as was his homeland, a condition Frantz Fanon described in his classic, *The Wretched of the Earth*, as internal colonization:

[In colonial societies] the teaching of moral reflexes handed down from father to son, the exemplary integrity of workers decorated after fifty years of loyal and faithful service, the fostering of love for harmony and wisdom, those aesthetic forms of respect for the status quo, instill in the exploited a mood of submission and inhibition which considerably eases the task of the agents of law and order.[16]

Singing for the exaltation of Jerusalem had not elevated my spirits. Speaking with Pastor Sayid made me wonder how many Palestinian Christians in Israel were similarly colonized, having replaced moral outrage toward settler-colonial violence with impotent quietism.

Christian discipleship does not require me to submit silently to an unjust, illegitimate authority that systematically oppresses my neighbors. Neither does Christian discipleship allow others to accept a system that confers on them superior status. To his followers Jesus said, "it will not be this way among you" (Mark 10:42–45). He told his disciples to deny themselves and take up their cross (Mark 8:34). He challenged them to become like little children, to count themselves among the least (Luke 9:46–48), and to find the lowliest seat at the table (Luke 14:7–11). The true church will never stop contending for Christ's new creation, and will ever celebrate that God's purpose was "to create in himself one new humanity out of the two, making peace," so that all God's people will live equally together as one (Eph 2:15).

Bibliography

Bickle, Mike. "What Happens Now That the Isaiah 62 Global Fast Is Over (May 28)." May 31, 2023. https://www.youtube.com/watch?v=sgs6RadtPe4.

———. "Why I Believe Human History Shifted in May 2023." June 5, 2023. https://www.youtube.com/watch?v=l4mvL_Npw9M.

Crump, David. *Like Birds in a Cage: Christian Zionism's Collusion in Israel's Oppression of the Palestinian People.* Eugene, OR: Cascade, 2021.

———. "Worshipping Jerusalem: Colonial Christianity Among Colonisers and the Colonised." *Journal of Holy Land and Palestine Studies* 24 (2025) 37–48.

de las Casas, Bartolomé. *The Devastation of the Indies: A Brief Account.* 1542. Repr., Baltimore: Johns Hopkins University Press, 1992.

Fanon, Frantz. *The Wretched of the Earth.* New York: Grove, 1963.

Halper, Jeff. *Decolonizing Israel, Liberating Palestine: Zionism, Settler Colonialism, and the Case for One Democratic State.* London: Pluto, 2021.

Holt, Marilyn Irvin. *Indian Orphanages.* Lawrence: University Press of Kansas, 2001.

King, Martin Luther, Jr. "The Most Segregated Hour in America." https://www.youtube.com/watch?v=1q881g1L_d8.

---

16. Fanon, *Wretched*, 3–4.

Memmi, Albert. *The Colonizer and the Colonized.* Boston: Beacon, 1965.
Munayer, Salim, and Lisa Loden, eds. *The Land Cries Out: Theology of the Land in the Israeli-Palestinian Context.* Eugene, OR: Cascade, 2012.
———. *Through My Enemy's Eyes: Envisioning Reconciliation in Israel-Palestine.* London: Paternoster, 2013.
Veracini, Lorenzo. *Israel and Settler Society.* London: Pluto, 2006.
Wolfe, Patrick. *Settler Colonialism and the Transformation of Anthropology: The Politics and Poetics of an Ethnographic Event.* London: Cassell, 1999.

CHAPTER SEVENTEEN

A Great Awakening

Mennonite Action and Palestinian Liberation

Amy Yoder McGloughlin

In the days and weeks following October 7, Christians were silent about what they saw unfolding in Gaza and Israel. In my interfaith circles, the Jewish community was in pain and outrage, and the Muslim community withdrew from interfaith conversations. And Christians? We were mute. There were no apparent organizing efforts to respond to the bombing of Gaza.

As a Christian and a religious leader, I felt ill equipped for this moment, at a time when speaking out about Palestine risked charges of antisemitism. It seemed that the only things Christians were permitted to do was to condemn Hamas and grieve the Israeli lives lost. To lament the loss of Palestinian life felt like a betrayal of the Jewish community with whom I had been working for so long to build bridges. I longed for a way for Mennonites and other Peace Church traditions to organize for the peace and safety of Palestinians, understanding that safety for Palestinians would benefit everyone.

The Spark of Mennonite Action

When Hamas attacked Israel on October 7, 2023, I was in Palestine leading a delegation of Jews and Christians organized by Community Peacemaker

Teams. We were forty-six miles from Gaza, in an area of the West Bank that is heavily occupied by the Israel Defense Forces (IDF). Within an hour of learning about the Hamas attacks, I was guiding the delegation out of the city of Hebron and negotiating with angry Israeli soldiers for access to public transportation in the main city square.

Our goal was to get to Jerusalem, where we would be closer to the airport. We tried to pass through the checkpoints between the West Bank and Israel but made it only as far as Bethlehem. For two days this little interfaith delegation was stuck behind the Israeli checkpoints, stranded in Bethlehem with other tourists and local Palestinians. There, we received the kindest hospitality. The Al Aqleh family hosted us in their hostel. We were supported by local shopkeepers who were concerned for our welfare. Taxi drivers promised to keep an eye on the checkpoints to help us get through. Palestinian friends reached out to me to help plan our next steps for exiting the West Bank.

On October 9, our hosts made plans to get us out of the West Bank. They tried to get us through the checkpoints with a bus full of tourists that had been given permission by the military to exit the area. When that didn't work, they brought us to the main checkpoint in Bethlehem, Checkpoint 300, to see if we could appeal to the soldiers there, but that checkpoint was locked and abandoned. We headed to a flying checkpoint nearby—a four-foot-tall pile of rubble that had been bulldozed across a street. Beyond the rubble, we could see the butts of soldiers' guns. Our host was ready to try another checkpoint, but I insisted we stop so I could try to get us across.

I walked up to the checkpoint, my US passport held high, and insisted that my delegation be let across. Much to my surprise, the soldiers allowed us to pass. We escaped the West Bank—clearly because of the privilege that comes with American citizenship.

After arriving safely in Jerusalem, we spent the next day and a half figuring out how to get home. An amazing network of Palestinian friends let me know when the Jordanian border was open and called a cab for us. Friends in the US helped us navigate the airlines to get a flight out of Amman.

Palestine has ignited my desire for justice in the world. But it is a place I am free to leave, while dear friends who live there cannot even pass through checkpoints. My friends are facing increasing violence in the West Bank, including violence from settlers who have been deputized by the military to "keep the peace," an arrangement that has resulted instead in increased attacks on Palestinian homes and livestock. I have never been to Gaza—it was nearly impossible for most internationals to enter before the war, and it's even harder now—but the genocide there feels personal to me because I know so many Palestinians. I have worked alongside them for the last decade, believing that they can and should be free. That close to twelve hundred Israelis were killed on October 7 and roughly two hundred and fifty abducted that day, more than fifty of whom continue to be held hostage in Gaza,[1] also feels personal to me, in part because the people with whom I began this work for Palestine belonged to the Jewish community in Philadelphia. As a Mennonite Christian, I believe that all of God's beloved people should be able to live in peace and wholeness.

When I arrived in the US on October 13, nearly a week after the crisis began, I was an emotional wreck. I had just spent six days struggling to hold it together, leading and caring for stressed-out delegates, one of whom was a seventeen-year-old member of my congregation. I was in survival mode.

A couple of days later, I left Philadelphia and drove twelve hours to the Midwest just to hug my kids. I spent a lot of quiet time with my spouse, relieved to be with him again. I didn't sleep. I read the news. I messaged friends in Palestine to make sure they were okay. I cried . . . a lot.

A few weeks later, Nick Martin, a community organizer in Lancaster, Pennsylvania, messaged me and posed the idea of Mennonite Action, an organization combining Mennonite theology and traditions with public action for Palestine. "Do you think this could work?" he asked. I was immediately on board. Nick and his co-founder, Adam Ramer, sought to ground this organization in the values instilled in them as children. A decade ago they had left the Mennonite Church, frustrated by the disparity they saw between teaching and practice. But the horrors unfolding in Gaza brought them back to their faith tradition. In the same way, Mennonite Action brought me back to myself and to what I knew: working together with other Mennonites was an antidote to the tears, anxiety, and isolation I felt watching a genocide and feeling powerless to stop it.

Principles and Purpose of Mennonite Action

The initial purpose statement for this still-evolving organization read:

> Mennonite Action is a movement of Mennonites bonded by a common belief that we have a responsibility to use our voices as powerfully as possible for the cause of peace and justice. We are mobilizing fellow Mennonites and Anabaptists across the United States and Canada to use creative nonviolent actions to demand a ceasefire, end the US and western funded occupation of Palestine, and build for a lasting peace.

---

1. Bisset et al., "Hamas Took 251 Hostages."

> We are Mennonites and Anabaptists, rooted in values that our cultural or spiritual ancestors passed down: peace, justice, community, mutual aid, and service. We know that these shared values fly higher than any nation's flag. We refuse to turn a blind eye to violence and oppression no matter who is perpetrating it—even, and especially, our own governments.
>
> We know that what's happening right now in Israel and Palestine is unprecedented and tragic. We draw on our Mennonite history of opposing war, and in providing aid and relief to Palestine and to the Middle East. We are making a choice to act together, publicly, as Mennonites in this critical moment.[2]

The idea of Mennonite Action made sense to me. It would use the tools we Mennonites had at our disposal to make our voices heard—traditions of song, art, and quilt-making, all firmly rooted in deep theological and ethical commitments to peace. In this way, Mennonite Action was designed to emulate other direct-action groups like Jewish Voice for Peace, Rabbis for Ceasefire, and IfNotNow, who protest the occupation of Palestine from the standpoint of their Jewish identity, faith, rituals, songs, and traditions. These movements inspired Mennonite Action to use our own songs, traditions, theology in similar, yet distinctly Anabaptist, ways.

It took no convincing for me to agree to become active in this movement. Here I could bring together my Anabaptist values, my desire for community, and my urge to respond publicly to what I was seeing in Gaza and what I had witnessed personally in the West Bank.

The early coordinating committee for Mennonite Action created guiding principles for our work, drawing on Nick's and Adam's experience as organizers, our collective Anabaptist values, and the input of other Mennonites already working for Palestinian liberation:

> **People**
> We take action that invites our neighbors in. Our actions are made possible by all of us together—a congregation of purpose spanning country lines. We are Mennonites and interfaith allies acting together in our peacemaking.
>
> **Peace**
> We believe in peace. We believe all people deserve to live full lives of dignity and prosperity. We believe that our actions must not cause harm to other people. True peace is not conflict-aversion. To be effective peacemakers in today's world requires us

---

2. Mennonite Action, "Who We Are."

to step into a public, peaceful confrontation with the powerful forces that are making war.

Public
We take action that brings our faith and our values forward into the public sphere. When we are citizens and taxpayers in powerful nations that wage war in our name, our voices are needed in public. This moment calls for Mennonites to engage in visible and vocal nonviolent action for peace and justice.

Power
We must take responsibility for the power that we have by virtue of being Anabaptist citizens of western nations. It's not right—but it is reality—that westerners have significantly more political power than most people living in Palestine. That means we also have a responsibility to use our voice and our influence as effectively as possible, especially as our governments play such a large role in this situation.

Liberation
We believe in taking action that supports and uplifts the people of Palestine to live with peace and dignity. We believe in an end to the occupation of Palestine. We believe in a future where Palestinians, Israelis, Jews, Muslims, Christians and everyone else can live peacefully together. And more broadly, we believe in taking action for peace—and in opposition to all war and occupation.

Prayer
Our actions are prayers for peace. Our actions mourn the loss of life and celebrate the joy of living. We work to stop war and violence through prayerful action.[3]

These principles reflect a new generation of Mennonite theological and ethical discourse. Our commitment to peace now includes a healthy understanding of conflict; we have an analysis of power and understand the nature of privilege; we are committed to centering the experiences and insights of oppressed communities; our collective witness brings our traditionally quiet values into the public square by integrating our spiritual practices with the work of social justice; and we are focused on the good news of God's liberating love.

Mennonite Action has been a movement of spiritual transformation and awakening for me and for many others. This movement has brought young people who had left the church back into religious circles by offering

---

3. Mennonite Action, "Our Movement Principles."

them a space where they can connect the values they were taught and the rituals that ground them with concrete actions toward building justice and peace. It has also been a way for folks inside the church who have longed to act communally on things we care about to do public theology together.

In December 2023, Mennonite Action organized people across the US and Canada to visit their political leaders and call for action. Forty-three groups totaling seventeen hundred people met with their representatives to deliver petitions signed by Mennonites from around the country demanding a ceasefire. These actions shared common themes, but each had its own unique regional style. Some group members had a lot of experience with public action; their engagements, like those organized by Mennonites in Philadelphia and Raleigh, were well organized, public, and impossible to ignore. My Frazer Mennonite Church congregation, most of whom were new to public action, started out more gently. Since we are folks that love to eat, and because we wanted to stress hospitality in our visit, we brought pie for everyone in Representative Chrissy Houlihan's West Chester, Pennsylvania, office. It's hard to turn away a conversation with your constituents if they are offering pie!

In January 2024, Mennonite Action gathered in Washington, DC, for an arrestable event. One hundred and thirty-five people between the ages of eighteen and eighty sang together peacefully in the Capitol Rotunda, demanding a ceasefire from our elected officials and refusing to leave when instructed by police. While the singers were being arrested inside, over one hundred more stood outside singing, praying, and encouraging those being led away in handcuffs.

Local Chapters Set on Fire

It seemed that a new Pentecost was happening in the Mennonite Church.

In March 2024, Mennonite Action organized another week of events, with one thousand people participating in twenty-five actions calling our representatives to "send aid, not bombs." During this week, Mennonite Action Philadelphia brought care kits for Gaza to their city council representatives and asked them to support a ceasefire resolution. Most were turned away, but security allowed a few children from the group to come in and talk to a representative—a moment of empowerment for these youth.

In Chicago, Mennonite Action demonstrators spread fourteen hundred shoes across the city's Federal Plaza, each pair representing around twenty-five lives lost in Gaza. Chicago area Mennonites and interfaith allies gathered to sing together, to share stories, and to demand that Illinois representatives take action to support a ceasefire and send aid to Gaza. Thanks to one of the local supporting organizations, all of the shoes displayed were sent to Gaza on the Freedom Flotilla.[4]

Something wonderful and exciting happened in many of these actions: local chapters began doing their own coalition building, independent of the organizational work of Mennonite Action. In these events, Mennonites often partnered with other organizations like American Muslims for Palestine, Jewish Voice for Peace, and IfNotNow. While speaking out for justice, these local Mennonite Action chapters were building friendships across religious and theological lines. This is how community works.

Just as Mennonite Action intentionally borrowed its design from already-existing organizations, so it has inspired the formation of another organization, Christians for a Free Palestine, an ecumenical movement that seeks to bring together all Christians to struggle for an end to Israel's occupation of Palestine using shared rituals, songs, theology, and other practices.[5]

In April 2024, Christians for a Free Palestine gathered in Washington, DC, to call for a ceasefire. They began with an outdoor communion service, using common Christian rituals and songs to root participants in their faith as they prepared for their work. Afterward, they moved inside to the Senate cafeteria, where they sang and chanted demands that our elected officials take action to stop the genocide in Gaza.

Mennonite Action and the Next Great Awakening

Movements like Mennonite Action are spiritual movements rooted in our historical traditions and practices and grounded in our desire to see God's kingdom on earth as it is in heaven. I believe these movements are the vanguard of the next great spiritual awakening in this country.

In *Christianity After Religion*, Diana Butler Bass outlines the ways in which conventional churches are dying. She names what so many of us have been seeing—particularly after the COVID-19 pandemic. The significant decline in attendance over the last decade worries many of us who love

---

4. The Freedom Flotilla Coalition, "Who We Are." On May 2, 2025, while anchored in international waters off the coast of Malta (1,200 miles from Israel), the *Conscience*, carrying tons of aid for Gaza, was struck by two missiles that ignited fires and disabled the ship. See *The New Arab*, "Turkey Blocks Flotilla"; Freedom Flotilla Coalition, "Freedom Flotilla Coalition Meets"; Freedom Flotilla Coalition, "Airstrike on 'Conscience' Confirmed."

5. Christians for a Free Palestine, "About."

the church and believe in the power of the church to transform lives and communities.

While the decline of the church might be scary to those among us who don't like change, the loss of numbers and influence is shaking things loose and creating new opportunities. We now have the occasion—or perhaps the divine imperative—to rebuild with the essentials of Christianity. What are the most important things on which the church of the twenty-first century will be built?

Butler Bass looks hopefully toward the future of the church. Retelling the history of great awakenings in the North American church, she predicts what might revive and renew the church today.

According to Butler Bass, the first Great Awakening in the US occurred in the 1700s. Jonathan Edwards led the way, believing that the transformation of the church was only possible through prayer. All the faithful could do was pray, and God would take care of everything else.

During the second Great Awakening, fifty years later, it was preaching that fostered revival. Pastors and revivalists emphasized the power of the sermon, full of emotion and vivid imagery, to propel people to experience God's embrace once again.

The third Great Awakening, beginning in the last decade of the nineteenth century, was a complex intertwining of two spiritual impulses: evangelicalism and liberalism. For some in the evangelical movement, it meant receiving Pentecostal gifts like speaking in tongues and miraculous healing. And for liberal Christianity, science, history, psychology, sociology, theology, and biblical criticism became pathways to participation in the reign of God. These two awakenings were often hostile to one another, but they each led to new visions of faith and faithfulness.

Butler Bass describes the next great awakening, the one I believe we are experiencing now, as one of performance. She writes:

> This awakening is being performed in the networked world, where the border between the sacred and the secular has eroded and where the love of God and neighbor—and the new vision of belonging, behaving and believing—is being staged far beyond conventional religious communities.
>
> Although churches seem to be the most natural space to perform spiritual awakening, the disconcerting reality is that many people in Western society see churches more as museums of religion than sacred stages that dramatize the movement of God's spirit.

> Perform faith. Display the kingdom of God in all you do. Anticipate the reign of God in spiritual practices. Act up and out for God's love.[6]

This great awakening began, I believe, during the civil rights movement of the 1960s, when the Rev. Dr. Martin Luther King Jr. led black people of faith out of the sanctuary and into the streets. At the time, white communities showed only limited solidarity for justice. Today we see white churches beginning to understand systemic racism and work in solidarity with oppressed communities to make God's justice known more fully. The spark that began in the 1960s is spreading into churches of all races.

According to Butler Bass, performing faith involves four important actions:

1. Preparing by learning the story,
2. Practicing, or rehearsing a new way of life,
3. Playing or having fun in community, and
4. Participating or joining with others towards the work of God's liberating love.[7]

I believe Mennonite Action and movements like it are demonstrating these characteristics of spiritual awakening.

Mennonite Action is "preparing" for our actions in a couple of key ways. We have monthly mass calls where we hear stories about what is happening in Gaza and the West Bank and learn how other chapters are organizing themselves. Moreover, this learning happens in the context of our faith stories. The Good News Jesus announced is crucial grounding for this work. Jesus inaugurated his public ministry in the synagogue of Nazareth by reading from the book of Isaiah:

> The Spirit of the Lord is upon me, because he has anointed me to bring good news to the poor. He has sent me to proclaim release to the captives and recovery of sight to the blind, to let the oppressed go free, to proclaim the year of the Lord's favor.[8]

If liberation for all God's beloved is the good news of Jesus's ministry, and if we are called to the way of discipleship, then it follows that this is our work: to be good news for the poor, freedom for prisoners, recovery of sight for the blind, freedom for the oppressed, and economic liberation for all.

---

6. Butler Bass, *Christianity After Religion*, 258.
7. Butler Bass, *Christianity After Religion*, 259–61.
8. Luke 4:18–19 NRSV.

Mennonite Action is firmly committed to this mission. We are listening to Palestinian stories and learning to tell our own stories, and these narratives are preparing us for the work of solidarity and activism.

"Practicing a new way of life" is manifested when Mennonite Action chapters gather to plan public demonstrations and to learn about effective strategies for change. Adam and Nick have traveled to many communities to train them in grassroots organizing, and local chapters have gathered to plan and strategize—actions that are only possible because we are rooted in our biblical stories and the stories of our beloved Palestinian friends.

Another way we rehearse a new way of life is practicing the spiritual disciplines. In order to be strong for this work, we must be rooted deeply in spiritual practices that keep us focused on loving God and neighbor. This is why our monthly calls begin with practices like silence or contemplative prayer. This is why our public activities involve singing songs that remind us of who we are and why we gather. We rehearse this way of life devoted to liberation by participating in and drawing from our deep faith traditions.

I cannot take part in these public actions without prayer and spiritual preparation both beforehand and afterward. Since I am transgressing social boundaries in these actions, I can only step over those lines and bring worship into the public square when I have fully rooted myself in who I am, the purpose of the act, and the power of the Spirit. Even so, after public acts I find myself unmoored and need to return to spiritual practices of prayer and silence so that I can reconnect my spirit with God's Spirit.

The next action Butler Bass outlines is "play." To perform faith, we must have fun together:

> Performance involves the hard work of practice, but it also entails *play*. Sometimes movements of change bog down because those involved become so serious about the work that they forget about the basic human need for fun, delight, and joy. Awakening cannot happen without laughter and lightness. ... Making a difference in the world, worshiping God, embracing new friends, feasting together, celebrating small successes, doing meaningful work—these are all things that make people happy.[9]

It is refreshing when the discipline, rehearsal, and work of justice also involves play. Justice movements that are inattentive to this need sputter and burn out. To play means to build deep friendships that allow us to support one another in the joys and difficulties of life.

---

9. Butler Bass, *Christianity After Religion*, 260.

After we've prepared, practiced, and played, we "participate" together in the work of the reign of God. That is why organizations like Mennonite Action are working toward a ceasefire in Gaza—to contribute to the justice of God, which seeks freedom for the oppressed.

In many ways, these four principles are all things churches have been practicing within their walls. What's different now is that we're carrying them onto the street. When we practice our faith beyond the boundaries of the church building, we declare the streets sacred; when we march for justice, we proclaim that our cries for justice are acts of prayer and announcements of Jesus' good news. The Mennonite church of the past has often been insular. In recent decades we find ourselves becoming more comfortable practicing our faith in the open, combining worship with justice-seeking in the public square.

For many Christians, including me, integrating worship and public action is a challenging departure from traditional ways of doing church. It makes worship—conventionally a curated set of songs, prayers, and sermons inside a private building—somewhat wild and out of control. In the movement represented by Mennonite Action, worship feels a little dangerous, and that's exactly as it should be. This new awakening is reminiscent of the first Pentecost in Acts 2, which was itself wild, unpredictable, uncontrollable, and public. It caused a stir in the community and provoked many to ask curious questions. To bring worship into the street guarantees unpredictable responses from onlookers, but it also affords an opportunity to invite others into this new awakening of the Spirit.

Our struggle for justice is the most holy work we can do, the most in-the-spirit-of-Jesus thing we can practice. These actions flow most naturally from my Anabaptist theology, from my discipleship, and from my love for God and my neighbors. The love of justice rooted in Anabaptist theology is the reason Nick and Adam began a conversation about how their faith tradition demanded that they respond to Gaza. It's why I responded so readily to Nick's call. It's why I return to Palestine every year. It's why I write about Palestine, and it's why I march in the streets and risk arrest. The work of justice is holy work. And participating in this work is an act of faith and a cry for God's justice to be awakened and revealed in the world.

Mennonite Action isn't perfect. But it gives me hope to work with other Mennonites for the sake of Palestinian liberation. It gives me hope to tap into our spiritual practices, traditions, and faith in order to raise our voices in the public square. It gives me hope that my Palestinian friends are seeing our work and feeling encouraged and supported. And it gives me hope to watch a generation of Mennonites who had lost the fire of their faith be reignited in a practice of discipleship that activates their spiritual traditions in the struggle for the liberation Jesus announced for all of God's beloved.

Bibliography

Bisset, Victoria, et al. "Hamas Took 251 Hostages from Israel into Gaza. Where Are They?" *The Washington Post*, updated May 13, 2025. https://www.washingtonpost.com/world/interactive/hamas-hostages-israel-war-gaza/.

Butler Bass, Diana. *Christianity After Religion: The End of Church and the Birth of a New Spiritual Awakening*. New York: HarperCollins, 2012.

Christians for a Free Palestine. "About." https://christiansforafreepalestine.com/about.

Freedom Flotilla Coalition. "Airstrike on 'Conscience' Confirmed; Crew Evacuated; FFC Still Denied Investigation." May 20, 2025. https://freedomflotilla.org/2025/05/21/airstrike-confirmed/.

———. "Freedom Flotilla Coalition Meets to Support Its Turkish Member and Stand for the People in Gaza." December 13, 2024. https://freedomflotilla.org/2024/12/13/9263/.

———. "Who We Are." https://freedomflotilla.org/who-we-are/.

Mennonite Action. "Our Movement Principles." https://www.mennoniteaction.org/principles.

———. "Who We Are." https://www.mennoniteaction.org/about.

The New Arab. "Turkey Blocks Flotilla Holding 5,000 Tonnes of Aid to Famine-Threatened Gaza." September 5, 2024. https://www.newarab.com/news/turkey-blocks-gaza-bound-flotilla-carrying-5000-tonnes-aid.

CHAPTER EIGHTEEN

Being Christian After the Desolation of Gaza

J. Ross Wagner

TOGETHER WITH MY COLLEAGUES whose work appears in this volume, I believe something is tragically wrong with a Christian community that is silent in the face of Israel's unrelenting war on the people of Gaza—if not actively complicit in it. Inspired by Peter Beinart's forthright reckoning with *Being Jewish After the Destruction of Gaza*, this essay is my attempt, as an American Christian, to reckon with what it means to bear truthful witness to the good news of Jesus Christ in such a time as this.

We Need a New Story

Nothing is more human than telling stories to make sense of the world and our place in it. But the stories we tell do not only grant us vision; they also have the power to occlude our sight.

In his recent book, Peter Beinart takes an unflinching look at the story his community tells to justify the horror Israelis have inflicted on Gaza—"the story Jews tell ourselves to block out the screams . . . the story that convinces even Jews who are genuinely pained by Gaza's agony that there is no other way to keep us safe"—and asks what that story may be hiding from their eyes.[1]

---

1. Beinart, *Being Jewish*, 9.

Beinart minces no words: "Jews have been victims of some of the worst atrocities in history."[2] Nevertheless, he finds it lamentable that generations of "Jews in Israel and the diaspora have built our identity around [a] story of collective victimhood and moral infallibility."[3]

> The problem with our communal story is not that it acknowledges the crimes we have suffered. The problem is that it ignores the crimes we commit. We are forever Esther and our detractors are forever Haman, even when a nuclear-armed Jewish state subjugates millions of Palestinians who lack citizenship in the country they've inhabited for their entire lives. By seeing a Jewish state as forever abused, never the abuser, we deny its capacity for evil.[4]

This communal story blinds its tellers to the truth and "camouflages domination as self-defense."[5] What is more, by "offer[ing] infinite license to fallible human beings,"[6] it "confers on mortals a level of veneration that we do not deserve and will always abuse."[7]

Such unconditional devotion to the State of Israel, Beinart charges, amounts to a form of "idolatry" that "suffuses contemporary Jewish life."[8]

> Worshipping a country that elevates Jews over Palestinians replaces Judaism's universal God—who makes special demands on Jews but cherishes all people—with a tribal deity that considers Jewish life precious and Palestinian life cheap.[9]

His frank conclusion: "we need a new story."[10]

---

2. Beinart, *Being Jewish*, 30. Many of these, of course, at the hands of those who professed to be Jesus's followers.

3. Beinart, *Being Jewish*, 107.

4. Beinart, *Being Jewish*, 31.

5. Beinart, *Being Jewish*, 10.

6. Beinart, *Being Jewish*, 10.

7. Beinart, *Being Jewish*, 103.

8. Beinart, *Being Jewish*, 102. "In most of the Jewish world today, rejecting Jewish statehood is a greater heresy than rejecting Judaism itself" (102). Beinart acknowledges the intimate connection many feel between Jewish statehood and their own sense of Jewish identity. "For many of us, questioning Jewish statehood means questioning Jewishness. . . . Remove Jewish statehood from Jewish identity and, for many Jews around the world, it's not clear what is left" (107).

9. Beinart, *Being Jewish*, 103. For evidence that some Christians are likewise guilty of this sort of idolatry, see David Crump's essay "Worshiping Jerusalem" (ch. 16 in this volume) and the discussion of American civil religion below.

10. This is the title Beinart gives to his "Prologue" (*Being Jewish*, 7).

Beinart addresses his jeremiad to fellow Jews. But as a Christian in America, I cannot help seeing myself and my own community reflected in the mirror he so courageously holds up to his own. As Beinart recognizes, the story his people tells about itself is but one "version of a story told in many variations by many peoples in many places who decide that protecting themselves requires subjugating others, that equality is tantamount to death."[11]

A clear-eyed glance at America reveals that many Christians in this country believe that the only path to peace and safety lies in the application of overwhelming force against our enemies, foreign and domestic. That for the sake of "freedom," each of us must be willing to offer the state "the last full measure of devotion" that scripture tells us belongs to God alone.[12] American civil religion has long sought, often with spectacular success, to co-opt the stories and symbols of Christianity for its own project of nation-building. As Harry Stout observes,

> American civil religion borrows so heavily from the language and cadences of traditional faiths, many Americans see no conflict or distinction between the two. Many Americans equate dying for their country with dying for their faith. In America's civil religion, serving country can be coequal with serving God.[13]

As a baptized Christian raised in the Midwest, I was catechized in American civil religion in public schools during the 1970s and 1980s and confirmed in a mainline church whose Boy Scout troop trained me "to do my duty to God and my country." As an adult striving to follow Jesus, however, I have learned that "country" is never content to take second place.[14]

This became crystal clear to me on the first anniversary of 9/11. Tuning in to the national broadcast on my car radio, I listened with dismay as President Bush justified the "war on terror" as a crusade to "extend the blessings of freedom" to all humankind. He concluded by draping America in the garb of divinity:

---

11. Beinart, *Being Jewish*, 9.

12. The quoted words come from Abraham Lincoln's Gettysburg Address, which, like many Americans of my generation, I memorized as a child. According to Stout, the speech became "in American memory . . . the sacred scripture of the Civil War's innermost spiritual meaning" (*On the Altar of the Nation*, 270).

13. Stout, *On the Altar of the Nation*, xviii.

14. "American civil religion is religious *and* ideological, cultural *and* theological. For that reason it exerts enormous power on the loyalties and perceptions of its citizens: a power that can be even greater than traditional theistic beliefs and rituals" (Stout, *On the Altar of the Nation*, xx).

Ours is the cause of human dignity; freedom guided by conscience and guarded by peace. This ideal of America is the hope of all mankind. That hope drew millions to this harbor. That hope still lights our way. *And the light shines in the darkness. And the darkness will not overcome it.*[15]

The United States is a country where national holidays are integrated seamlessly into the liturgical calendar of many churches and where Sunday school children pledge undivided allegiance to both American and Christian flags. Who could be surprised, then, to find our president venerating America as the incarnate Word of God or to see the scriptures of our national religion slipped in between the covers of the Holy Bible?[16]

The tales Americans tell about ourselves have long been entangled with stories about Israel.[17] Puritan settlers imagined North America to be a new promised land, with indigenous peoples who resisted colonization cast in the role of Amalek.[18] Over time, Americans came to view themselves as

---

15. Bush, "President's Remarks to the Nation" (emphasis mine). Stanley Hauerwas notes that "democracy has been a particularly subtle temptation to Christianity. Christians have never killed as willingly as when they have been asked to do so for 'freedom'" (*Dispatches*, 134). What is more, "democracies by their very nature seem to require that wars be fought in the name of ideals, which makes war self-justifying" (Hauerwas, *War*, 34). This is convenient, since it is impossible to legitimize campaigns such as the "war on terror" using traditional just war criteria. "If a war is to be just, your enemy must know before the war begins what specifiable political purpose the war is to serve. . . . But a 'war on terrorism' is a war without limit. Americans want to wipe this enemy off the face of the earth. Moreover, America even gets to decide who counts and does not count as a terrorist, which means Americans get to have it any way they want it. For example, some are captured as prisoners of war; some are detainees. No problem. When you are the biggest kid on the block, you can say whatever you want to say, even if what you say is nonsense. . . . We all know the first casualty in war is truth" (Hauerwas, *Performing*, 207).

16. According to the official website (https://godblesstheusabible.com), the *God Bless the USA Bible* "features copies of the handwritten chorus to 'God Bless The USA,' The US Constitution, The Bill of Rights, The Declaration of Independence, and The Pledge of Allegiance." Multiple editions are for sale, including a *Golden Age Edition*, "custom embossed to commemorate the Golden Age of America and the 45th & 47th President of the United States, Donald J. Trump," and *The Day God Intervened Edition*, issued "in remembrance of the day that God intervened during President Donald J. Trump's assassination attempt." A cool $1000 will get you the *President Donald J. Trump Signature Edition* (Only 1000 Available! While Supplies Last!) with "President Donald J. Trump's Hand-Signed Signature" inside the front cover.

17. The literature on this topic is voluminous and growing. Lewis (*Short History*) offers an accessible survey of the development of Christian Zionism from the sixteenth century to the present, along with copious suggestions for further reading.

18. Lewis, *Short History*, 86–91. The period is examined in greater detail in Robert O. Smith, *More Desired*, 117–40. Bruce Fisk critiques the weaponization of biblical Amalek by Zionists and Christian Zionists in ch. 2 of this volume.

the nation appointed by God to restore the chosen people, Israel, to their ancestral land.[19] Ties between the United States and the State of Israel drew tighter during the Cold War years, as the two nations joined forces to defend democracy and "the Judeo-Christian tradition" against the onslaught of "godless communism" and resurgent Islam.[20] After 9/11, Israel became a key ally in the "war on terror." Successive US administrations have continued to pledge "ironclad" support for the Jewish state, regarding it as a vital bulwark against the Iranian "axis of resistance."

Christian Zionism has been a driving force in white evangelical politics in America since the mid-1970s; as such, it has often exerted an outsized influence on US foreign policy in the Middle East.[21] Speaking in 2017 to a meeting of Christians United for Israel (CUFI), a Christian Zionist organization led by Texas pastor John Hagee claiming over ten million members, Israeli Prime Minister Benjamin Netanyahu hardly exaggerated in saying, "Israel has no better friend than America. And Israel has no better friend in America than you."[22] CUFI's website trumpets its numerous lobbying accomplishments "for Zion's sake," including its role in persuading the first Trump administration to transfer the US Embassy to Jerusalem (2018), to cut off all aid provided to Palestinians through UNRWA (2018), and to recognize Israeli sovereignty over the Golan Heights (2019).[23] With Trump back in the White House, white evangelical leaders—many of them ardent Christian Zionists—are enjoying unprecedented access to the halls of power.[24]

---

19. On the crucial role played in this development by Blackstone, "America's first quintessential Christian Zionist," see Smith, *More Desired*, 163–84; Lewis, *Short History*, 153–59. Yaakov Ariel comments, "Blackstone devised a theory that has become a cornerstone of American Christian Zionists ever since. The American evangelist asserted that the United States had a special role and mission in God's plans for humanity: that of a modern Cyrus, to help restore the Jews to Zion. God has chosen America for that mission on account of its moral superiority over other nations, and America is judged according to the way it carries out its mission" ("Unexpected Alliance," 77–78).

20. Amy Kaplan's *Our American Israel* untangles the varied ways Americans and Israelis have inscribed themselves into one another's national mythologies.

21. See ch. 2 in this volume; Ariel, *Unusual Relationship*, 171–213; Goldman, *Zeal for Zion*, 270–308.

22. Stoli, "Netanyahu."

23. Christians United for Israel, "Policy Accomplishments."

24. White evangelicals have been Donald Trump's most consistent and consequential supporters for three election cycles. In 2024, they favored Trump by sixty-five points, while Trump lost the rest of the electorate by eighteen points (Guskin et al., "Exit Polls"). See further Dias and Graham, "White House of Worship." On the influence of Christian Zionists in Trump's second administration, see the introduction to this volume by Bruce Fisk.

Increasingly, support for Israel among American evangelicals is driven less by end-times speculations than by "a type of nation-based prosperity theology."[25] Central to this belief-system are biblical texts, such as Gen 12:3, that are understood to promise "blessing" to peoples and nations that "bless" the State of Israel.[26] Mike Huckabee, a Southern Baptist pastor, staunch Christian Zionist, and newly confirmed US ambassador to Israel, is a vocal proponent of this viewpoint: "Without any apology, I believe those who bless Israel will be blessed; those who curse Israel will be cursed. I want to be on the blessing side."[27] Christian Zionism and Christian Nationalism have proven to be an intoxicating mix for many.[28] Who could be surprised, then, to find white American evangelicals among the most fervent supporters[29] of Israel's genocidal war on the population of Gaza?[30]

Blinded to the manifold ways we have allowed ourselves to be co-opted by forms of American civil religion, held captive to the story that our security depends on dominating others, many Christians in the United States find ourselves incapable of imagining a world in which God's kingdom comes not through "the terrible swift sword" of the nation-state but through the loving, courageous, peaceful, and persevering witness of the church.[31] Prioritizing allegiance to nation over membership in the body of Christ and denying our own diaspora identity as the people of God who

---

25. Hummel notes, "In its most activist circles today, Christian Zionism is less about apocalyptic theology or evangelism than it is a range of political, historical, and theological arguments in favor of the state of Israel based on mutual and covenantal solidarity. In recent years, a type of nation-based prosperity theology, promising material blessings to those who bless Israel, has played a prominent role" (Hummel, *Covenant Brothers*, 3; cited in Lewis, *Short History*, 314).

26. As Lewis demonstrates (*Short History*, 316–43), over the past three decades this version of Christian Zionism has been "glocalized" as "Christian Zionists throughout the world conceive of their own nation in relationship to Israel. . . . These nations become in some sense 'Christian nations'—that is, individually they become 'elect/chosen' nations through their support and blessing of Israel, the uniquely elect nation" (318–19).

27. Boorstein, "Huckabee." For an illuminating debate on the meaning of Gen 12:3 and the role it should play in shaping a Christian stance toward the State of Israel, see Bruce Fisk, "Genesis 12:3," with a response by Darrell Bock ("Response") and a rejoinder by Fisk ("Response").

28. See Cannon and Fisk, "Christian Nationalism and Christian Zionism."

29. For evidence, see chs. 2 and 14 in this volume.

30. On the terminology, see University Network for Human Rights et al., "Genocide in Gaza"; Blatman and Goldberg, "There's No Auschwitz in Gaza. But It's Still Genocide."

31. For notable exceptions to this generalization, see the chapters in Part 3 of this volume.

"have here no lasting city,"[32] we cannot fathom God's good future for the Jewish people apart from nationalistic narratives of blood and soil, conquest and settlement.[33] Rightly deploring the war crimes committed by Hamas on October 7, we seem unable to acknowledge, let alone condemn, the horrors Israel has been inflicting on Gaza for decades.[34] Thus we show ourselves to be partisans rather than peacemakers, warriors for "Western civilization" rather than witnesses to Jesus Christ.

We, too, need a new story.

Recovering the Christian Story

Though it is not his aim, Beinart suggests a way forward for Christians seeking a story powerful enough to challenge the interlaced narratives of American exceptionalism and Christian Zionism. Searching through the vast trove of Jewish tradition, he discovers a better story: one that "speaks about God liberating us from being masters."[35]

According to the Law of Moses, every fiftieth year was to be a Jubilee: a holy year of rest from labor, release from bondage, and return to home and family. "You shall hallow the fiftieth year and you shall proclaim liberty throughout the land to all its inhabitants" (Lev 25:10). Beinart finds contemporary promise in this ancient statute:

> A commentary attributed (perhaps incorrectly) to the eighteenth-century German rabbi Yaakov Yehoshua Falk notes that the last three words [of Lev 25:10] are oddly expansive. Since only slaves are being freed, why doesn't the verse say, "Proclaim release throughout the land for all its slaves?" The commentary finds the answer in the Talmud, which declares, "One who acquires a Hebrew slave is like one who acquires a master." Slaveholding makes you a kind of slave. That's why the Jubilee year brings liberty to "all the inhabitants" of the land. By freeing the oppressed, it frees oppressors too.[36]

Just as Beinart turns to tradition and finds a new old story, so we American Christians must return to Scripture to discover the old story

---

32. Heb 13:14; cf. Heb 11:8–16.

33. For alternative ways Jews have imagined this future, see, e.g., Boyarin, *No-State Solution*; Halper, *Decolonizing Israel*; Manekin, *End of Days*.

34. See ch. 1 and the "Gaza Timeline" included as an appendix to this volume.

35. Beinart, *Being Jewish*, 118.

36. Beinart, *Being Jewish*, 118.

anew: the story of the God who liberates us from our misplaced loyalties and empowers us to live the gospel of Jesus Christ, who is our peace.[37] Fittingly, the Jubilee will be our starting point as well.[38]

Jesus and the Eschatological Jubilee

According to Luke, Jesus returns to Nazareth after his baptism in the Jordan and temptation in the wilderness, filled with the Holy Spirit (Luke 4:14–16). Standing in the synagogue on the Sabbath day and reading from the scroll of Isaiah, he claims to be the Lord's anointed, the one graced with the divine Spirit and sent "to proclaim the year of the Lord's favor" (Luke 4:19/Isa 61:2, echoing Lev 25:10). "Today, in your hearing," Jesus declares, the promise of the eschatological Jubilee "is fulfilled" (4:21).

In the Spirit-filled person of the beloved Son and chosen Servant (3:22), God's reign has broken into a world whose kingdoms had been given into the hand of the adversary (4:5–6).[39] God has sent Jesus to a people chafing under the Roman yoke with the commission "to bring good news to the poor ... to announce release to the captives and recovery of sight to the blind, to set the oppressed free" (Luke 4:18/Isa 61:1). And so, empowered by the Spirit, Jesus "plunders the strong man" (11:20–23), proclaiming liberty throughout the land by "doing good and healing all who were oppressed by the devil" (Acts 10:38).

In the "little flock" gathered around Jesus (Luke 12:32; cf. Acts 20:28) the politics of God's kingdom are made manifest. Here the proud are debased and the humble receive grace; the powerful are dethroned and the lowly raised up; the rich are sent away empty and the hungry fed.[40] Through

---

37. I offer the following retelling of the Christian story in the conviction that the interpretation of scripture is integral to the task of theology: that is, to the church's critical reflection on what is required to speak and embody the gospel truly in its present context. Cf. Barth (*Dogmatics in Outline*, 9–14) and Gutiérrez (*Theology of Liberation*, 11), who defines "theology as a critical reflection on praxis in light of the Word." As Hauerwas recognizes, "The most orthodox Christological or Trinitarian affirmations are essentially false when they are embedded in lives and social practices which make it clear that it makes no difference whether Jesus lived, died, or was resurrected" (*Dispatches*, 23). Scripture citations are from the NRSV unless otherwise noted.

38. Trocmé, *Jesus*, 13–68; Yoder, *Politics of Jesus*, 28–33, 60–75. Given the significance of the Zionist imaginary for American national self-definition, it is not surprising to find one of the iconic symbols of the Revolution bearing a reference to the Jubilee. But like the cracked "Liberty Bell" on which it is engraved, the proclamation of Lev 25:10 remains mute when sounded apart from the one true story that gives it meaning.

39. See Raheb, *Faith in the Face of Empire*.

40. As Mary sings in Luke 1:46–55.

Jesus's ministry, broken bodies are restored, ruptured relationships are repaired, and strangers are received into God's family. The lost are found and the dead brought back to life, sinners find redemption, and the unjust learn to practice justice.

Luke provides a paradigmatic example of what liberation looks like in the person of Zacchaeus. Welcoming God's kingdom leads this wealthy tax farmer not only to make restitution for wrongs done—"if I have defrauded anyone of anything, I will pay back four times as much"—but to embrace the radical sharing of resources that is the hallmark of Jesus's true disciples: "half of my possessions, Lord, I will give to the poor" (19:8). Thus Zacchaeus finds himself mercifully restored to right standing in the family of God: "Today salvation has come to this house," Jesus affirms, "because he too is a son of Abraham" (19:9).[41]

As children of God, Jesus's followers are called to grow into the likeness of their heavenly Father.

> Love your enemies, do good to those who hate you, bless those who curse you, pray for those who abuse you. . . . Your reward will be great, and you will be children of the Most High; for he is kind to the ungrateful and the wicked. Be merciful, just as your Father is merciful. (6:35–36)

Jesus himself, the beloved Son, models this way of life to the very last. Unwavering in his proclamation of the just and peaceable reign of God, the kingdom that is already present "in your midst" (17:21), he boldly confronts the religious and political elites whose willing—and profitable—collaboration with Rome immiserates his people. Yet Jesus rejects the path of armed resistance, refusing to betray the character of God's kingdom through recourse to violence. Committing himself into the hands of the One who judges justly, he gives himself up as an innocent victim to state-sanctioned terror—with a prayer for his executioners on his lips: "Father, forgive them; for they do not know what they are doing" (23:34). His disciples must be prepared to walk the same path: "If any want to become my followers, let them deny themselves and take up their cross daily and follow me."[42]

---

41. On "salvation" in Luke's Gospel, see further Acosta, "From What Do We Need to Be Saved?"

42. Luke 9:23. Trocmé cautions would-be disciples: "Jesus stated, 'Blessed are those who are persecuted because of righteousness,' without promising any earthly success other than the final coming of God's kingdom." His call to take up the cross "is a preparation for the possible failure of their attempts [to resist evil nonviolently] and for physical death, when the enemy will think he is the victor. God alone will change the cross into a victory" (*Jesus*, 156).

To the surprise and consternation of his hearers in Nazareth, Jesus declares that God's mercy includes even gentiles within its wide embrace (4:22–30). In this respect as well, the Jubilee he heralds fulfills the words of the prophets. From the very start of his narrative, Luke makes it clear that the good news is for everyone. Full of the Spirit, Simeon stands in the temple courts; taking the infant Jesus in his arms, he recognizes him to be the promised servant of the Lord, commissioned to be "a light for revelation to the Gentiles and for glory to your people Israel" (Luke 2:32, echoing Isa 49:6). Through Jesus, "all flesh shall see the salvation of God" (Luke 3:6, quoting Isa 40:5 LXX). So too, at the end of Luke's narrative, the risen Jesus stands among his bewildered disciples; embracing them in his peace, he opens their minds to understand the prophetic scriptures, and he sends them to bear the good news of this salvation to all peoples.

> Thus it is written, that the Messiah is to suffer and to rise from the dead on the third day, and that repentance and forgiveness of sins is to be proclaimed in his name to all nations, beginning from Jerusalem. (24:46–47)

"Of these things," Jesus tells his followers, "you are witnesses" (24:48).

Spirit-Empowered Witness

As Luke's second volume opens, the risen Jesus appears to his apostles over a period of forty days, "speaking about the kingdom of God" (Acts 1:3). When his followers wonder if sovereignty is going to be restored to Israel, Jesus offers them a far more expansive vision of God's reign: "You will receive power when the Holy Spirit has come upon you; and you will be my witnesses in Jerusalem, in all Judea and Samaria, and to the ends of the earth" (Acts 1:8).[43] As Peter Walker explains,

> The hopes of restoration *have* been fulfilled, but not in the expected way. Hence when [Luke] records Jesus' answer to the disciples' agitated question in Acts 1, he almost certainly intends us to hear this as meaning: "Your understanding of restoration is wrong; Israel has been restored in my resurrection, and you will be witnesses of this fact from Jerusalem to the ends of the earth. The restored kingdom of Israel is the world coming under the rule of Israel's true king." The throne of David is no longer empty, but in accordance with God's promise it has now been

---

43. Jesus's sending of the apostles "to the ends of the earth" recalls Isa 49:6, echoed earlier in Simeon's song (Luke 2:32).

occupied by the risen Jesus (Acts 2:30–31). Israel's kingdom has therefore been restored through the resurrection of her king—the one whom God has made both Lord and Messiah (2:36).[44]

The kingdom is both "now"—for the risen and enthroned Jesus is present and active in the world through the Spirit—and "not-yet." In this time between Jesus's ascension and his return in glory (1:9–11), the apostles' witness will find social embodiment in particular communities of disciples, as diverse as the human family itself, whose Spirit-filled manner of life testifies, however imperfectly, to the character of the kingdom inaugurated by Jesus.[45]

> The political novelty that God brings into the world is a community of those who serve instead of ruling, who suffer instead of inflicting suffering, whose fellowship crosses social lines instead of reinforcing them. The new Christian community in which walls are broken down not by human idealism or democratic legalism but by the work of Christ is not only a vehicle of the gospel or a fruit of the gospel; it is the good news. It is not merely the agent of mission or the constituency of a mission agency. It is the mission.[46]

Through the outpouring of the Spirit at Pentecost, the discord of Babel is finally harmonized. But God does not restore community by reimposing a colorless uniformity. Quite the contrary. The fullness of salvation comes to light only as the gospel takes root in all the rich variety of human languages and cultures. Through the church's Spirit-empowered witness "to the ends of the earth," each and every language becomes an instrument for proclaiming the good news of what God has done; each and every culture contributes resources for furthering God's reconciling work among all peoples. Thus, Jesus's followers not only display the character of God's kingdom in their common life (Acts 2:42–47); through their ongoing witness they discover ever new dimensions of the manifold grace of God.[47]

---

44. Walker, "Land in the New Testament," 108; I owe this reference to Chapman, *Christian Zionism*, 39.

45. "Luke narrates the salvation that attends the Christian mission as something that entails necessarily the formation of a community, a public pattern of life that witnesses to the present dominion of the resurrected Lord of all" (Rowe, *World Upside Down*, 154).

46. Hauerwas, *War*, 167.

47. Andrew Walls remarks, "As Paul and his fellow missionaries explain and translate the significance of the Christ in a world that is Gentile and Hellenistic, that significance is seen to be greater than anyone had realized before.... As [Christ] enters new areas of thought and life, he fills the picture.... It is surely right to see the process as

The early chapters of Acts trace the progress of the gospel as the Spirit leads the way, through persecution, from Jerusalem to Judea and Samaria (8:1–25) and out into the diaspora (11:19–21). A watershed moment occurs in Acts 10. Jesus Christ, the beloved Son in whom God "proclaims the good news of peace," is revealed to be not simply Israel's Messiah but "Lord of all people" (10:36).[48] Through Peter's boundary-crossing witness, the Spirit falls upon a Roman centurion and his household, and the church in Jerusalem learns that "God shows no partiality" (10:34). For "God has granted even to the Gentiles the repentance that leads to life" (11:18). This discovery compels the community in Jerusalem to search the Scriptures for a pattern of communal life consonant with their new social and political reality—the differentiated unity of Jew and gentile in Christ that God has brought into being through the Spirit.[49] For as Peter recognizes, "God . . . testified to [the gentiles] by giving them the Holy Spirit, just as he did to us [Jews]; and in cleansing their hearts by faith he has made no distinction between them and us" (15:8–9).

In the second half of Acts, the apostles' witness to the good news of God's reign spreads ever wider among both Jews and gentiles. As it does, the church takes on new social forms with new particularities. Yet the singular basis for its unity remains God's proclamation of peace through Jesus Christ (10:36). Gradually, Luke's focus shifts to Paul, who resolutely carries out the commission of the risen Lord. In his hearing before Agrippa, Paul avers:

> I was not disobedient to the heavenly vision, but declared first to those in Damascus, then in Jerusalem and throughout the countryside of Judea, and also to the Gentiles, that they should repent and turn to God and do deeds consistent with repentance. . . . To this day I have had help from God, and so I stand here, testifying to both small and great, saying nothing but what the prophets and Moses said would take place: that the Messiah must suffer, and that, by being the first to rise from the dead, he would proclaim light both to our people and to the Gentiles. (Acts 26:19–23)

Paul and the communities he founds bear witness to the gospel of peace by their words and in their bodies. "Through many afflictions we

---

being repeated in subsequent transmission of the faith across cultural lines. . . . The full-grown humanity of Christ [cf. Eph 4:13] requires all the Christian generations, just as it embodies all the cultural variety that six continents can bring" (*Missionary Movement*, xvii).

48. Note the echo of Isa 52:7, where the proclamation of peace consists in the good news, "Your God reigns."

49. On the Jerusalem Council (Acts 15), see Bauckham, "James and the Gentiles."

must enter the kingdom of heaven," Paul and Barnabas remind the new believers (14:22). Like Jesus, they refuse violence as a means to accomplish God's ends. The pattern is established in the fearless testimony of the Jerusalem apostles, beaten but not silenced by the Sanhedrin (5:40–42), and it is sealed in the witness of Stephen, whose dying words echo the prayer of Jesus: "Lord, do not hold this sin against them" (Acts 7:60; cf. Luke 23:34).

Luke's narrative closes with Paul lodged in the heart of the Empire: a prisoner of Caesar freely "welcoming all who came to him, proclaiming the kingdom of God and teaching about the Lord Jesus Christ with all boldness and without hindrance" (28:31). But the story continues beyond the bounds of the narrative as communities of Spirit-empowered witnesses spread ever further and, by faithfully following the way of Jesus, manifest the just and peaceful reign of God in all the world.

Reconciliation and New Creation

Jesus's announcement of the eschatological Jubilee (Luke 4:16–21) reverberates in Paul's plea to his converts in Corinth "not to receive the grace of God in vain" (2 Cor 6:1).

> For God says, "At an acceptable time I have listened to you, and on a day of salvation I have helped you." (2 Cor 6:2, citing Isa 49:8)

The acceptable time, the day of salvation, is now! For "in Christ, God was reconciling the world to himself" (5:19).

The deepest truth about the world, Paul maintains, is that the world has been reconciled to God in Christ. While this truth remains to be revealed in all its glorious fullness,[50] it is no less an eschatological reality to be inhabited in the here and now. "If anyone is in Christ—new creation! Everything old has passed away; see, everything has become new!" (5:17). Reconciled to God, those who belong to Christ are commissioned as ambassadors of the Messiah, bearers of the message of reconciliation. Through them, as though through Christ himself, the divine appeal rings out wider and wider: "Be reconciled to God!" (5:18–20).

> The love of Christ urges us on, because we are convinced that one has died for all; therefore all have died. And he died for all, so that those who live might live no longer for themselves, but for him who died and was raised for them. (2 Cor 5:14–15)

---

50. See 2 Cor 4:16—5:10; cf. 1 Cor 15:20–58; Rom 8:18–39.

To be united to Christ is thus to live simultaneously in the "already" and in the "not-yet" of the new creation. Already, the creator "has shone in our hearts to give the light of the knowledge of the glory of God in the face of Jesus Christ" (4:6). In this "acceptable time," the liberating Spirit is transforming those who turn to the Lord into the image of Christ, "from one degree of glory to another" (3:18).

Nonetheless, Christ's glory is "not yet" fully revealed; for now, it remains hidden in clay jars (4:7). Failing to recognize this, the Corinthians run the risk of "receiving the grace of God in vain" (6:1). Fascinated by pedigree and status, hungering for power and prestige, clinging to wealth and privilege, they are easy prey for self-promoting "super-apostles" peddling "another Jesus" (11:4).[51] For Paul, in contrast, following Jesus means not passive acquiescence to the way things are—let alone cashing in on the status quo—but bold and costly witness to the just peace that is God's kingdom. It is only as Jesus's followers lay down their lives in Christlike service to others, bearing his death in their own bodies, that Jesus's resurrection life becomes visible in their mortal flesh (4:7–12). Paul's apostleship is thus characterized by "weaknesses, insults, hardships, persecutions, and calamities for the sake of Christ" (12:10).[52] But he is content. Such afflictions are the very means by which God is conforming him to the glorious likeness of Christ, who is the image of God (cf. 4:4, 16–18). And God, the reconciler of all creation, is near at hand with a word of promise: "My grace is sufficient for you, for my power is made perfect in weakness" (12:9).

This promise is for the Corinthians, too. The apostle longs for them to be reconciled that they might join him in his Christ-bearing mission of reconciliation.[53] He invites them to share their possessions generously in obedience to their "confession of the gospel of Christ" (9:13). As they participate in the generosity of Jesus (8:8–9), the grace of God that is at work among them will become evident to all.[54] "Our hope is that, as your faith increases, our sphere of action among you may be greatly enlarged, so that we may proclaim the good news in lands beyond you" (10:15–16).

Throughout his long and tumultuous relationship with the church in Corinth, Paul remains stubbornly confident that they, too, will learn to live as God's reconciled people, even in this time of "not-yet." For the apostle

---

51. *Plus ça change* . . . . See French, "Donald Trump Leap of Faith."

52. Terry Eagleton comments, "The New Testament is a brutal destroyer of human illusions. If you follow Jesus and don't end up dead, it appears you have some explaining to do. The stark signifier of the human condition is one who spoke up for love and justice and was done to death for his pains" (*Reason, Faith, and Revolution*, 27).

53. Wagner, "*Missio Dei*," 20–23.

54. See Barclay, "Manna," 419–26.

recognizes the magnitude of the "interchange" God has already accomplished on their behalf: "For our sake God made him to be sin who knew no sin, so that in him we might become the righteousness of God" (5:21).[55]

Conformed to the Image of God's Son

The letter to the Romans represents the most complete telling of the gospel story we have from Paul's own pen.[56] In Jesus Christ, the apostle proclaims, God has revealed his righteousness—God's saving power for everyone who trusts—for the Jew first and also for the Greek (1:16–17).[57] There is no distinction, since all have sinned and fall short of the glory of God (3:22–23). Through Adam's transgression sin first entered the world, and all Adam's descendants are captive to—and complicit in—death's cruel dominion over creation (5:12–14). But now, the Creator has come in person to vindicate the divine righteousness, setting things right by restoring to right standing all who trust in Jesus's righteous act (3:21–26; cf. 5:18).

In the sovereign freedom of love, the one God of Jews and gentiles has determined to justify the circumcised on the ground of faith and the uncircumcised through that same faith (3:29–30). Once and for all, God has shown that he is God for all. Like Abraham, who received the divine promise that he would inherit the world and become the father of many nations, so also his descendants, circumcised and uncircumcised alike, are justified by sharing Abraham's trust in God, who justifies the ungodly (4:5, 9–24)—the God who raised from the dead Jesus our Lord, who was handed over to death for our trespasses and was raised for our justification (4:25).

As Paul surveys the scope of God's saving work in Romans 5–8, his discourse crackles with the tension between the now and the not-yet. In the center stands the faithful Lord Jesus Christ, through whom we have now obtained right standing with God: peace and reconciliation and access to God's gracious presence. The love of God, demonstrated in Christ's death for us, has been poured into our hearts through the Holy Spirit given to us. And yet we live in hope. For we have not yet received the fullness of our

---

55. See Hooker, "Interchange in Christ."

56. My synopsis of Romans draws heavily on the language of the NRSV, though I largely forego quotation marks to make for easier reading.

57. Christians believe that God's saving purposes for all humankind find their focus in the particular history of Jesus of Nazareth, who is true son of Adam (Luke 3:23–38) only as he is the singular son of David, son of Abraham (Matt 1:1–17). The story of God's saving actions in Christ through the Spirit can no more be told apart from Israel's story than it can be narrated apart from the story of all humanity, indeed of all creation.

salvation, the share in the glory of God secured for us by the life of our risen Lord (5:1–11).

As Paul recounts in Romans 6, all who have been baptized into Christ Jesus have been baptized into his death and buried with him. Our "old human being" has been crucified with Christ so that, freed from sin, we might walk in newness of life even now. And because we have been united with Christ in his death, we trust that one day we will also share in his resurrection (6:1–10). In the not-yet of our present time, we enact the freedom that is already ours by rejecting sin's empty claims on us; turning from the false gods of comfort and security, privilege and wealth, power and prestige and predominance, we willingly offer ourselves to God as slaves of righteousness (6:11–23). As Paul will show in Romans 12, this service of God, which is perfect freedom, is nothing other than our own joyful embodiment of the pattern of Jesus's life (cf. 6:17).

Paul's celebration of redemption's "now" reaches a crescendo in Rom 8. For those who are in Christ Jesus, there is now no condemnation. Emancipated from the law of sin and of death, we are at liberty to walk in step with the Spirit of Christ who dwells in us. Setting our minds on the things of the Spirit, we find ourselves free to experience the life and peace and pleasure of the Father. For God has given us the Spirit of adoption, who testifies within us that we are God's children: heirs of God and joint-heirs with Christ (8:1–17a).

Nevertheless, the inheritance is not yet fully ours. In the present time we also share Christ's sufferings, bearing witness to God's righteous reign in creative, courageous resistance to the injustice, violence, and oppression that still ravage God's good creation. Indeed, creation itself groans with the pangs of labor as it eagerly anticipates the unveiling of the children of God. For when we who have the first-fruits of the Spirit at last receive our promised adoption—the resurrection of our bodies—all creation will be liberated from its bondage to decay to share in the glorious freedom of God's children. Meanwhile, the Spirit helps us in our weakness, interceding for the saints according to the will of God (8:17b–27).

In the end, the apostle attests, God's good purposes will not be frustrated.

> Those whom God foreknew he also predestined to be conformed to the image of his Son, in order that he might be the firstborn within a large family. And those whom he predestined he also called; and those whom he called he also justified; and those whom he justified he also glorified. (8:29–30)

Once again, Paul grounds hope for the "not-yet" in the presence of the "already." God's righteousness—God's faithfulness to deliver creation from the nothingness of sin and death and decay—has been definitively displayed in the Father's mighty acts in Jesus Christ, through the Spirit, for us.

> He who did not withhold his own Son, but gave him up for all of us, will he not with him also give us everything else? Who will bring any charge against God's elect? It is God who justifies. Who is to condemn? It is Christ Jesus, who died, yes, who was raised, who is at the right hand of God, who indeed intercedes for us. (8:32–34)

"Who will separate us from the love of Christ?" Paul asks. The answer is unequivocal: no suffering in the present time, no calamity yet to come, no power on earth or under the earth or in the heavens, "nor anything else in all creation, will be able to separate us from the love of God in Christ Jesus our Lord" (8:35–39).

This very same divine love grounds Paul's confidence that God has not forsaken the apostle's kindred according to the flesh who are presently cut off from Christ. For though these "Israelites" (9:4) are now "enemies with respect to the gospel," they remain, "with respect to election, beloved of God on account of their ancestors" (11:29). For this reason, Paul is certain that their part in the story is not yet finished.[58] In the present time, God has preserved "a remnant, chosen by grace" (11:5) as the downpayment on Israel's future: "If the part of the dough offered as first fruits is holy, then the whole batch is holy; and if the root is holy, then the branches also are holy" (11:16). Though "the rest" have been "hardened" (11:8), they have not "stumbled so as to fall" (11:11). Rather, in the mystery of God's mercy, their "misstep" and their "loss" will one day end with their "full inclusion" (11:12); their "estrangement" will give way to their "acceptance" (11:15); and "all Israel will be saved" (11:26).[59] In unsearchable wisdom, God has determined to deliver all humanity from complicity in the reign of sin and

---

58. See further Wagner, "'Enemies' Yet 'Beloved' Still."

59. Paul is speaking in Rom 9–11 of "Israel" as the people descended from Abraham through the line of Isaac and Jacob (9:6–13). As Beinart observes, to confuse this Israel with the modern nation-state of that name is not only deeply anachronistic, it is pernicious. "In Jewish tradition, states have no inherent value. States are not created in the image of God; human beings are. States are mere instruments. They can protect human flourishing, or they can destroy it. If they do the latter, they should be reconstituted to make them more respectful of human life. The legitimacy of a Jewish state—like the holiness of the Jewish people—is conditional on how it behaves" (*Being Jewish*, 100).

death by imprisoning all under disobedience—that God may have mercy on all (11:30–36).[60]

This divine mercy is disclosed in the gospel Paul proclaims. God has acted to redeem Jew and gentile alike from the reign of sin and death by uniting us through faith to Christ, who died and rose again on our behalf. And the glorious fullness of redemption will be our participation in the life of God as those who have been conformed to the image of God's Son.

Now, in this tensive time between Jesus's resurrection and our own, God's Spirit is at work in the community of Jesus's followers, refashioning us, as a body, into the likeness of Christ. And so, recalling God's mercies, Paul makes this appeal:

> Present your bodies as a living sacrifice, holy and acceptable to God, which is your spiritual worship. Do not be conformed to this world, but be transformed by the renewing of your minds. (Rom 12:1–2)

The pattern of life toward which redeemed humans are being transformed is that of Jesus's own glad self-giving to God in service to others.[61] The Spirit empowers us to be a people who, like Jesus, bless when cursed; a people who refuse to take revenge into our own hands; a people who work steadfastly and courageously to overcome evil with good, confident that God will judge the world with justice and impartiality (12:14–21).[62] Sharing our possessions, opening our homes, our one law is the law of love.

> Owe no one anything, except to love one another; for the one who loves another has fulfilled the law. The commandments . . . are summed up in this word, "Love your neighbor as yourself." (Rom 13:8–10)

Such love is tireless in its opposition to all that dehumanizes, oppresses, and exploits the neighbor. It is likewise unshakable in its commitment to

---

60. Notably, Paul does not speak of Israel's salvation in terms of a return to the Land. Harper concludes his careful sifting of the evidence as follows: "Paul began to see the promise of the Land from a new perspective in light of the Messiah's coming" (*Paul and Philo*, 82); that is to say, "for Paul, the 'inheritance' of God's people was the this-worldly renewal of all things, sometimes expressed as 'the kingdom of God' (1 Cor 15:24)" (235). As Gary Burge puts it, "An ethnocentric territoriality anchored to ancestral theological claims cannot survive Paul's fresh rearrangement of God's saving purposes in Christ" (*Jesus and the Land*, 90–91).

61. It is no accident that Paul's language in this section of Romans is particularly dense with allusions to early traditions about Jesus's own manner of life. See Thompson, *Clothed with Christ*.

62. See Kairos Palestine et al., "Call for Repentance," 3.

fostering the neighbor's flourishing, recognizing every human being as a fellow bearer of the divine image.

God-graced diversity is essential to the healthy functioning of the one body of Christ (12:3–8). Thus, despite significant differences of conviction and practice, Jesus's followers are to strive together in love to embody "the righteousness and peace and joy in the Holy Spirit" that is God's kingdom (14:17).[63] Paul prays that God will grant the believers in Rome "the same attitude of mind toward each other"—the mindset that is "in accordance with Christ Jesus" (15:5; cf. NIV).[64]

> Welcome one another, therefore, just as Christ has welcomed you, for the glory of God. For I tell you that Christ has become a servant of the circumcised on behalf of the truth of God in order that he might confirm the promises given to the patriarchs, and in order that the Gentiles might glorify God for his mercy. (15:7–9a)

Through Christ's gracious self-giving on their behalf, Jew and gentile alike are released from bondage to sin and death and freed to recognize one another as co-recipients of divine mercy. Together they find themselves liberated for joyful worship[65] and sacrificial witness to the kingdom of God,[66] whose advent is visible in their midst even now.

Christ Is Our Peace

For Christians, peace is not a utopian dream but "an eschatological reality," the very end for which God has destined the world.[67] Writing from a prison

---

63. "The weak in faith" of whom Paul speaks (Rom 14:1) are most likely Jewish Christ-followers or perhaps gentiles who have been strongly influenced by the practices of the former. See Reasoner, *Strong and the Weak*. Whatever the precise reasons for the tensions within the house-churches in Rome, Paul responds with a clear call to accept one another in Christ without demanding uniformity in non-essential matters. The apostle's vision of the unity of Jew and gentile in Christ thus embraces a robust diversity within the one community.

64. The apostle epitomizes this mindset in the so-called "Christ hymn" in Phil 2:1–11. See further Wagner, "*Missio Dei*," 25–26.

65. "No matter what the sociological significance or number of its members may be, the church becomes for the world what the world is meant to be, that is, one people united by the worship of God" (Hauerwas, *War*, 139, summarizing the view of Karl Rahner).

66. Note Paul's expectation that unity among the believers in Rome will lead them to partner with him in proclaiming the good news of Christ in Spain (15:14–33).

67. Hauerwas, *War*, 45.

cell,[68] Paul shares his insight into "the mystery of Christ" that "has now been revealed to his holy apostles and prophets by the Spirit" (Eph 3:4–5), "the plan . . . hidden for ages in God who created all things" (3:9).

> With all wisdom and insight God has made known to us the mystery of his will, according to his good pleasure that he set forth in Christ, as a plan for the fullness of time, to gather up all things in Christ, things in heaven and things on earth. (Eph 1:8–10)

In Jesus Christ, God has revealed his eternal design for the cosmos.[69] And God's purpose is peace. Not merely the absence of conflict, but the condition of well-being the Scriptures call *shalom*: wholeness and health and human flourishing in harmony with God and with all of creation. Chosen in love from before the foundation of the world to be adopted as God's children, human beings have now, through the death of the beloved Son, received redemption, forgiveness, and the promised Holy Spirit, the pledge of their full inheritance as members of God's own family (1:3–14). The principalities and powers of the cosmos have been brought back into order under Christ, who sits enthroned at God's right hand (1:20–22).[70]

In Christ, the deepest enmities among human beings have likewise been overcome. Nothing was more fundamental to the social, religious, and political worlds inhabited by Jesus's earliest followers than the separation between Jew and gentile. Even this division, Paul maintains, God has now transcended in Jesus Christ. For "he is our peace" (2:14).

As in Romans, here too the apostle writes gentiles into the story of Israel even as he contextualizes Israel's story within the larger narrative of God's redemption of the cosmos. Thus Paul both acknowledges the salvation-historical priority of the Jews in God's redemptive plan and insists on

---

68. Whatever one thinks about the authorship of Ephesians—and the question is not so easily settled as is often maintained (cf. Campbell, *Framing Paul*, 309–38)—the letter gives voice to the "canonical Paul," whose writings serve to shape the theological reasoning of the church (see further Childs, *Church's Guide*, 79–81, 92–94).

69. "If revelation is to be taken seriously as the revelation of God, and not just as an emphatic expression for a discovery which man has made in himself or in his cosmos by his own powers, then in any doctrine of revelation we must deal expressly with the point that constitutes the mystery of revelation, the starting-point of all thought and language about it. At all costs we must make it clear that an ultimate mystery is involved here. It can be contemplated, acknowledged, worshipped and confessed as such, but it cannot be solved, or transformed into a non-mystery" (Barth, *Church Dogmatics* I/2, 126).

70. In ascending to heaven after descending to the lower parts of the earth, Christ the king has set to right every part of his dominion (Eph 4:8–10).

the equal status of Jew and gentile in Christ.[71] As the first witnesses to the risen Jesus and as those who received the gift of God's Spirit at Pentecost, Jews were "the first to have put [their] hope in the Messiah" (1:12); now, through their trusting response to the gospel, gentiles also have received the Spirit of promise (1:13), who guarantees the common inheritance of Jew and gentile in Christ (1:14).

As in Romans, here too Paul contends that Jews and gentiles share a parallel plight and that God rescues both on precisely the same basis. Those who were once "dead in trespasses and sins," enslaved to "the ruler of the power of the air" (2:1-3), God has now made alive with Christ. "In Christ Jesus," Jew and gentile alike have been created anew "for good works, which God prepared beforehand to be our way of life" (2:4-10).

In Eph 2:11, for the first time, Paul addresses his audience not as "saints" but as "you Gentiles." Yet he adds here a crucial qualifying phrase: "in the flesh." For as he goes on to show, the fleshly basis on which their status as outsiders was once determined has now been superseded by God's action "in Christ." As uncircumcised gentiles, they had been excluded from the *politeia* of Israel—the manner of life constituted by keeping the commandments of God enjoined in the Law.[72] Living outside this *politeia*, they had been "strangers to the covenants of promise." As those who did not know the true God (cf. Gal 4:8), they had been "without hope" (2:12).

"But now, in Christ Jesus," all has changed. Those once "far away" have now been "brought near" by the blood of Christ (2:13). "He himself is our peace," for by his death he has demolished the "separation wall" between Jew and gentile, the "hostility" that divides us (2:14). In his "flesh," nailed to the cross, Jesus has put that hostility to death: "creating in himself one new humanity in place of the two, thus making peace, and . . . reconciling both groups to God in one body" (2:15-16).[73]

The creation of "one new human" in Christ overcomes enmity without eliminating human diversity. For even as he celebrates the unity of the one body of Christ, Paul continues to differentiate gentile from Jew:

---

71. The impartiality of God is a recurrent theme in Paul's letters (Rom 2:11; 3:22; 10:12; Eph 6:9; Col 3:25), as elsewhere in the apostolic writings (e.g., Acts 10:34; 11:12; 15:9; 1 Pet 1:17; cf. Matt 22:16; Mark 12:14).

72. Hellenistic Jewish writers use the term *politeia* when speaking of the ancestral Laws that distinguish Israel's particular form of communal life from that of the gentiles around them: e.g., 2 Macc 4:11; 8:17; 4 Macc 4:19; 8:7; 17:9; Jos. *Ant.* 3.213; 4.45-46, 194, 302; 5.132-33; Philo, *Spec. Leg.* 1.63; 2:73; *Vit. Mos.* 2.49. On the importance of this political term in Philo's discussions of proselytism (e.g., Spec. Leg. 1.51 Virt. 175-86, 219, cf. 102-4), see Borgen, *Early Christianity*, 56-59, 62-63.

73. Cf. David Crump's discussion of this passage in ch. 16 above.

> So he came and proclaimed peace to you who were far off and peace to those who were near; for through him both of us have access in one Spirit to the Father. (Eph 2:17–18)

On the one hand, Paul echoes the language of Isa 52:7 and 57:19 to depict Christ's peacemaking as the fulfillment of Israel's own ancient hopes for redemption.[74] On the other hand, gentiles are "no longer strangers and aliens"—not because they have joined (or replaced) the *politeia* of Israel, but because they are now "fellow citizens *with the saints* [i.e., Jews and gentiles who belong to Christ]." By God's grace, gentiles, too, are now

> members of [God's] household, built on the foundation of the apostles and prophets, with Christ Jesus himself as the chief cornerstone. In him the whole building is joined together and rises to become a holy temple in the Lord. And in him you too are being built together to become a dwelling in which God lives by his Spirit. (2:19–22 NIV)[75]

In the present time, the body of Christ is called to embody in its common life the just and peaceful humanity of Jesus Christ. In this way, they are "the anticipation of the peace God wills for all people."[76] Hence, Paul urges his hearers to

> lead a life worthy of the calling to which you have been called, with all humility and gentleness, with patience, bearing with one another in love, making every effort to maintain the unity of the Spirit in the bond of peace. (Eph 4:1–3)

The victorious Christ has granted the members of his body a variety of gifts that together they may grow "to maturity, to the measure of the full stature of Christ" (4:7–13). The apostle stretches metaphor to the breaking point: as head, Christ is both the goal of the body's growth—"grow up in every way into him who is the head, into Christ" (4:15)—and the source "from whom the whole body . . . grows and builds itself up in love" (4:16).

As those "learning" Christ, believers must put away the pattern of the "old human" and "be renewed in the spirit of their minds" (4:20–23).

---

74. The Old Greek version of Isa 52:7 reads, "I am here as springtime upon the mountains, like the feet of the one who proclaims the good news of a message of peace." Isaiah 57:19 runs, "Peace upon peace to those who are far off and to those who are near. And the Lord said, 'I will heal them.'" See further Moritz, *Profound Mystery*, 31–55; Burge, *Galatians and Ephesians*, 195–202.

75. Cf. Eph 3:6: ". . . the Gentiles have become fellow heirs, members of the same body, and sharers in the promise in Christ Jesus through the gospel."

76. Hauerwas, *War*, 131.

Putting on the "new human, created according to the likeness of God in true righteousness and holiness" (4:24), they find they are enabled to live truthfully (25), to renounce bitterness and anger (26), and to eschew violence and injustice (28–31). As "beloved children," they are to embrace the way of forgiveness and peace and so become "imitators of God" (5:1; cf. Luke 6:36; Matt 5:9) by being conformed to the pattern of Christ.

> Live in love, as Christ loved us and gave himself up for us, a fragrant offering and sacrifice to God. (Eph 5:2)

If peace is now given to the world in Christ, it is nevertheless, in this time of not-yet, a peace for which Christ's followers must actively contend (6:10–20).[77] They struggle "not against enemies of blood and flesh, but against the rulers, against the authorities, against the cosmic powers of this present darkness, against the spiritual forces of evil in the heavenly places" (6:12). They have been fitted with "the whole armor of God"—truth, righteousness, faith, salvation—that they may "stand firm." Yet, as befits those commissioned by Christ as heralds of his "gospel of peace" (6:15), they carry no weapon but the word of God.[78]

Living the Christian Story: A *Kairos* Moment for the Church in America

Christians in America stand at a moment of crisis. The gospel tells us that Jesus has inaugurated God's Jubilee, the year of the Lord's favor, and that the Spirit has sent us to bear witness to the advent of God's kingdom. Once and for all, the righteousness of God has been revealed in the life, death, resurrection, and ascension of Jesus Christ, the one through whom God has reconciled the world. As those created anew in Christ, who is our peace, we are called to bear the gospel of peace to the world.

And yet—as the essays in this volume show in painful detail—many American Christians are betraying this very gospel: when we shut our eyes to war crimes committed in the name of God and country; when we stop our ears to the cries of Gaza's displaced and destitute; when we refrain from protesting our own nation's support for Israeli policies of apartheid, ethnic cleansing, and annexation of occupied territories.

---

77. I echo here the motto of the Matthew 25 Initiative of the Anglican Church in North America: "Contending for Shalom" (https://www.anglicanjusticeandmercy.org). See further the essay by Ruth Padilla DeBorst (ch. 10) in this volume.

78. The enemies to whom Christ proclaimed peace (Eph 2:17, echoing Isa 52:7) are themselves transformed into heralds of peace (cf. 2 Cor 5:18–20).

In this time of crisis, our Palestinian brothers and sisters in Christ dare to speak the truth to us in love.[79] Out of the desolation of Gaza, they have issued an urgent call to repentance, summoning us to a radical reorientation of mind that will bring our lives into alignment with the truth of the gospel.

> Words fail to express our shock and horror with regard to the on-going war in our land. We deeply mourn the death and suffering of all people because it is our firm conviction that all humans are made in God's image. We are also profoundly troubled when the name of God is invoked to promote violence and religious-national ideologies. Further, we watch with horror the way many western Christians are offering unwavering support to Israel's war against the people of Palestine. While we recognize the numerous voices that have spoken and continue to speak for the cause of truth and justice in our land, we write to challenge western theologians and church leaders who have voiced uncritical support for Israel and to call them to repent and change. . . .
>
> Regrettably, many western Christians across wide denominational and theological spectra adopt Zionist theologies and interpretations that justify war, making them complicit in Israel's violence and oppression. . . .
>
> Crucially, we reject all theologies and interpretations that legitimize the wars of the powerful. We strongly urge western Christians to come alongside us in this. . . .
>
> Finally, and we say it with a broken heart, we hold western church leaders and theologians who rally behind Israel's wars accountable for their theological and political complicity in the Israeli crimes against the Palestinians, which have been committed over the last 75 years. We call upon them to reexamine their positions and to change their direction, remembering that God "will judge the world in justice" (Acts 17:31).[80]

---

79. See the essays in this volume by Lamma Mansour (ch. 6), Yousef AlKhouri (ch. 9), and Anton Deik (ch. 11) as well as Daniel Bannoura's "A Palestinian Christian Response" in ch. 5, pp. 136–38.

80. Kairos Palestine et al., "Call for Repentance." Kairos Palestine (www.kairospalestine.ps) is an ecumenical, nonviolent movement of Palestinian Christians seeking justice and peace for all the inhabitants of the land. It traces its roots to the 2009 document "A Moment of Truth," which took inspiration from the 1985 *Kairos Document* issued by Christians in South Africa during the era of apartheid. The Greek word *kairos* denotes "a moment of truth," a crisis that is at the same time "the moment of grace and opportunity, the favourable time in which God issues a challenge to decisive action" (The KAIROS Theologians, *Kairos Document*, 1).

What would it look like for American Christians to heed this call?

Repentance requires truthful speech and truthful action. Only by telling anew the true story of the gospel, only by living as witnesses to the truth that Christ is our peace, can we resist the lie from which the politics of domination derives its power.[81]

Telling the true story begins in worship. As John Webster explains, "The definitive act of the church is faithful hearing of the gospel of salvation announced by the risen Christ in the Spirit's power through the service of Holy Scripture."[82] This is God's gracious work within us and among us:

> Through the incarnate Word, crucified and risen, we are made capable of hearing the gospel, but only as we are at one and the same time put to death and raised to new life. Through the Spirit of the crucified and risen Christ we are given the capacity to set mind and will on the truth of the gospel and so read [Scripture] as those who have been reconciled to God.[83]

In its worship, the church gathers to celebrate and re-present the scriptural story of redemption that we might live truthfully in the midst of this already-and-not-yet redeemed world.[84] Wielded by the Spirit, God's word is

---

81. Aleksandr Solzhenitsyn's words, spoken out of his bitter experience of life under a totalitarian regime, ring no less true today: "Let us not forget that violence does not and cannot exist by itself: It is invariably intertwined with *the lie*. They are linked in the most intimate, most organic and profound fashion: Violence cannot conceal itself behind anything except lies, and lies have nothing to maintain them save violence. Anyone who has once proclaimed violence as his *method* must inexorably choose the lie as his *principle*. At birth, violence acts openly and even takes pride in itself. But as soon as it gains strength and becomes firmly established, it begins to sense the air around it growing thinner; it can no longer exist without veiling itself in a mist of lies, without concealing itself behind the sugary words of falsehood. No longer does violence always and necessarily lunge straight for your throat; more often than not it demands of its subjects only that they pledge allegiance to lies, that they participate in falsehood. The simple act of an ordinary brave man is not to participate in lies, not to support false actions!" (Solzhenitsyn, "Nobel Lecture," part seven; emphasis original).

82. Webster, *Holy Scripture*, 44. Scripture's authority in the church thus consists in "its Spirit-bestowed capacity to quicken the church to truthful speech and righteous action" (Webster, *Holy Scripture*, 52; cf. Jenson, "Religious Power of Scripture").

83. Webster, *Holy Scripture*, 89.

84. According to the Orthodox theologian Alexander Schmemann, "The Church is the sacrament of the Kingdom—not because she possesses divinely instituted acts called 'sacraments,' but because first of all she is the possibility given to man to see in and through this world the 'world to come,' to see and to 'live' it in Christ. It is only when in the darkness of *this world* we discern that Christ has *already* 'filled all things with himself' [cf. Eph 1:23; 4:10] that these *things*, whatever they may be, are revealed and given to us full of meaning and beauty." (Schmemann, *For the Life of the World*, 138; emphasis original). This is as true of the church's life as it is of the eucharistic

a powerful weapon. "Living and active, sharper than any two-edged sword . . . it is able to judge the thoughts and intentions of the heart" (Heb 4:12). Through the word, God unmasks our complicity in the lie that peace is to be purchased at the cost of endless warfare, that safety can be secured only by subjugating others. Through the word, God's Spirit liberates us from falsehood by "taking every thought captive to obey Christ" (2 Cor 10:5).[85]

Living the true story consists in following Jesus. The risen Lord left clear instructions for his church: not to stand around speculating idly about "times or periods that the Father has set by his own authority" but to bear witness, in the power of the Spirit, to God's reign among all the kingdoms of the earth (Acts 1:7–8). We are to "make disciples of all nations, baptizing them in the name of the Father and of the Son and of the Holy Spirit." According to Jesus, the *sine qua non* of discipleship is "obey[ing] everything that I have commanded you" (Matt 28:20) for the kingdom that is coming is present even now in communities conformed to the pattern of Jesus's own joyful self-giving to God in loving service to others.

To such communities, Jesus promises his presence "to the end of the age" (Matt 28:20). Jesus is among them not only as they gather together in his name (Matt 18:20). He is also present in those to whom they are sent. As they feed the hungry and give water to those who thirst, as they clothe the naked and shelter the stranger, as they care for the sick and accompany the incarcerated, they encounter Jesus afresh (Matt 25:31–46).[86]

Faced with the desolation of Gaza, the challenge before American Christians is this. Dare we open our eyes and see Jesus in the faces of Palestinians: those who are starved by Israel's blockade on food entering Gaza;[87]

---

liturgy. "The Church is itself a *leitourgia*, a ministry, a calling to act in this world after the fashion of Christ, to bear testimony to him and his kingdom" (34).

85. In a joint open letter, Kairos Southern Africa and Kairos Palestine admonish Western Christians: "Most of the churches in Europe and the USA seem not to have repudiated their colonial and racist history. Because of this, the lens through which our lives are being viewed is still colored by their sins of colonialism and racism. Now and once again, we need to hold this before you and make you aware of this. This is a projection of the worst kind and is inconsistent with the Jesus we know from our Scriptures. We therefore call you to deep repentance. . . . We put our trust in the Jesus who proclaimed Good News to the poor and oppressed. Jesus reminds us all that God is not a tribal God, but a God who cares deeply for all peoples. This same Jesus fills us with hope and joy, and we pray deeply that you too will meet this Jesus and be liberated by him." See Kairos Southern Africa and Kairos Palestine, "Joint Open Letter."

86. An insight Ramone Romero captures powerfully in the painting that appears on the cover of this volume.

87. "Nearly half a million Palestinians are facing possible starvation, living in 'catastrophic' levels of hunger, and 1 million others can barely get enough food, according to findings by the Integrated Food Security Phase Classification, a leading international

those who hunger because they have been deprived of their land or cut off from their fields by separation barriers and settlements;[88] those who thirst due to the ruin of Gaza's infrastructure or to the systematic expropriation of West Bank water sources by settlers?[89] Will we recognize Jesus in the two million Gazans bombed out of house and home by months of indiscriminate airstrikes—men, women, and children driven from place to place, crowded into ever narrower "safe zones" that provide no sure protection against further attacks;[90] in the multitudes deprived of shelter through years of relentless home demolitions and unjust seizures of property in East Jerusalem and the West Bank?[91] Will we meet Jesus in the throngs of sick and wounded forced to go without the most basic medical care due to Israel's decimation of Gaza's health system;[92] in the thousands of Palestinians incarcerated in Israeli prisons, subjected to degrading and inhumane treatment as they are held without charges for months on end?[93]

Do we have ears to hear our Lord's promise?

> Truly I tell you, whatever you did for one of the least of these brothers and sisters of mine, you did for me. (Matt 25:40)

---

authority on the severity of hunger crises" (Mednick, "Food Security Experts"). See Carroll, "This Is the Moment"; Hasson, "Gates of Hell"; and ch. 1 above.

88. See the UN Office for the Coordination of Humanitarian Affairs, "Humanitarian Situation Update #279"; Kristof, "Why Palestinian Christians Feel Betrayed"; B'Tselem, "2024 West Bank Olive Harvest"; Buxbaum, "World Heritage Site Under Threat."

89. In February 2025, the World Bank Group reported that over 89 percent of Gaza's infrastructure in the water, sanitation, and hygiene sector is "either destroyed or partially damaged" (World Bank Group, "Gaza," 37). See also Samad et al., "Water War Crimes"; Lonsdorf, "In the Occupied West Bank"; B'Tselem, "Parched."

90. According to the UN Office for the Coordination of Humanitarian Affairs, as of April 3, 2025, 92 percent of the housing units in Gaza have been destroyed or damaged, and 1,875,000 people are in need of emergency shelter and essential household items ("Reported Impact Snapshot"). See the UN Office of the High Commissioner for Human Rights, "Gaza"; Mordechai, "Bearing Witness"; and ch. 3 above, "Bombing in the Name of the Gospel."

91. See Human Rights Watch, *Threshold Crossed*; Tan, "After Decades Fighting Demolitions"; UN Office for the Coordination of Humanitarian Affairs, "Humanitarian Situation Update #279"; Scheindlin, "Analysis"; Levy and Levac, "Israel Is Gazafiying the West Bank."

92. As of February 2025, the World Bank Group reports "significant damage to hospitals (95 percent of all hospitals), private health facilities (91 percent), and public health centers (88 percent), alongside critical facilities such as pharmacies, dental practices, and maternity clinics" (World Bank Group, "Gaza," 28).

93. See the devastating exposé by B'Tselem, "Welcome to Hell"; David Crump, "Prisoner Abuse and Evangelical Indifference," ch. 4 in this volume.

According to Stanley Hauerwas, "Just as the lie lives parasitically off the truth, so violence cannot be named or identified unless our lives are constituted by more determinative practices of peace."[94] Thus, "Christian nonviolence . . . does not begin with a theory or conception about violence, war, 'the state of society,' and so on, but rather with practices such as forgiveness and reconciliation."[95] For American Christians, the question comes down to this: will we respond to Jesus's call to take up our cross daily and, by patiently engaging in the practices of peace, come to know and inhabit the fullness of the peace that is Jesus?

Our Christian brothers and sisters in Palestine have long been following Jesus on this path, daring to imagine a future of *shalom* for Jews, Muslims, and Christians alike based on recognition of one another as beloved children of God.

> We have studied our vocation and have come to know it better in the midst of suffering and pain: today, we bear the strength of love rather than that of revenge, a culture of life rather than a culture of death. This is a source of hope for us, for the Church, and for the world.[96]

In their steadfast commitment to "creative resistance grounded in the radical logic of Christ's love" that seeks "the liberation of both the oppressed and the oppressor," Palestinian Christians embody the peace of Christ that is the deepest truth of the world and the only genuine alternative to enmity, strife,

---

94. Hauerwas, *Performing*, 170–71.

95. Hauerwas, *Dispatches*, 130.

96. Kairos Palestine, "Moment of Truth," 3.4.5. "The Resurrection is the source of our hope. Just as Christ rose in victory over death and evil, so too we are able . . . to vanquish the evil of war. We will remain a witnessing, steadfast and active Church in the land of the Resurrection" (3.5). Christians commit themselves to nonviolence not as a pragmatic strategy to bring God's peace on earth but because to live otherwise would be to deny the truth that God has reconciled the world in Christ. This politics of peace is simply unintelligible if God has not raised Jesus from the dead and exalted the crucified one as Lord of all.

and wars without end.⁹⁷ In faith, hope, and love, they invite us to walk this path in solidarity with them.⁹⁸

Such solidarity in Christ will take as many forms as the Spirit inspires. Let me close by mentioning three: prayer, prophetic witness, and presence.⁹⁹ Jesus taught his followers "to pray always and not to lose heart," for the Lord is the just judge who will not long delay in granting justice to God's own people who cry to him day and night (Luke 18:1–8).¹⁰⁰

Prayer like this will propel us to prophetic speech and prophetic action. Within the church, this means speaking the truth in love, challenging flawed theologies that would justify the oppression of Palestinians and summoning our brothers and sisters to right thinking and right action consistent with the truth of the gospel (Gal 2:14). In the wider body politic, this entails engaging in creative, nonviolent advocacy and direct action, calling on our elected leaders to seek a just peace in Palestine by defending human rights and upholding international law for all who live in the Land.¹⁰¹ On the international stage, this involves partnering with people of good will who are working toward a common future for Israelis and Palestinians based on dignity and equality for all.¹⁰²

Finally, we can offer the solidarity of presence. Our brothers and sisters invite us to come and stand alongside them:

---

97. Kairos Palestine, "Declaration to the World," 3. Lesslie Newbigin asks, "How is it possible that the gospel should be credible, that people should come to believe that the power which has the last word in human affairs is represented by a man hanging on a cross? I am suggesting that the only answer, the only hermeneutic of the gospel, is a congregation of men and women who believe it and live by it" (Newbigin, *Gospel*, 227). A promising secular analogue to this vision of the Christian community as embodied witness to the reality of God's kingdom is found in the notion of prefigurative politics, "a political orientation based on the premise that the ends a social movement achieves are fundamentally shaped by the means it employs, and that movements should therefore do their best to choose means that embody or 'prefigure' the kind of society they want to bring about" (Leach, "Prefigurative Politics," 1004).

98. Kairos Palestine, "Moment of Truth."

99. See further Kairos Palestine, "Cry for Hope."

100. See the prayers of lament and hope offered by Lisa Loden (ch. 8) and Mercy Aiken (ch. 13).

101. The 5 Calls app (https://5calls.org/) makes it easy for Americans to exercise their right to lobby their elected officials. For creative examples of nonviolent direct action, see Amy Yoder McGloughlin's story of Mennonite Action in ch. 17.

102. The Network of Evangelicals for the Middle East (https://www.neme.network) and Churches for Middle East Peace (https://cmep.org/) provide educational resources and practical opportunities for Christians in America seeking faithful ways to partner with others in the work of peace-building.

Come and see the reality in the Holy Land with compassionate eyes for the suffering of Palestinians, and stand in solidarity with grassroots initiatives on the part of all faiths and secular groups who challenge the occupation and who work for a just peace.[103]

By the grace of God, this moment of crisis is simultaneously a *kairos*—a moment of opportunity—for Christians in America. This very day, Paul's call to the Corinthians rings out anew:

> God says, "At an acceptable time [*kairos dektos*] I have listened to you, and on a day of salvation I have helped you." See, now is the acceptable time; see, now is the day of salvation!
>
> We entreat you on behalf of Christ: be reconciled to God![104]

Let us not be found to have received the grace of God in vain.[105]

Bibliography

Acosta, Milton. "From What Do We Need to Be Saved? Reflections on God's Justice and Material Salvation." In *So Great a Salvation: Soteriology in the Majority World*, edited by Gene L. Green et al., 93–115. Grand Rapids: Eerdmans, 2017.

Ariel, Yaakov. "An Unexpected Alliance: Christian Zionism and Its Historical Significance." *Modern Judaism* 26 (2006) 74–100.

———. *An Unusual Relationship: Evangelical Christians and Jews*. New York: New York University Press, 2013.

Barclay, John M. G. "Manna and the Circulation of Grace: A Study of 2 Corinthians 8:1–15." In *The Word Leaps the Gap: Essays on Scripture and Theology in Honor of Richard B. Hays*, edited by J. Ross Wagner et al., 409–26. Grand Rapids: Eerdmans, 2008.

Barth, Karl. *Church Dogmatics I/2: The Doctrine of the Word of God*. Translated by G. T. Thomson and Harold Knight. Edited by G. W. Bromiley and T. F. Torrance. Edinburgh: T. & T. Clark, 1956.

---

103. Kairos Palestine, "Cry for Hope," 3. Recall the plea of Suzanne Watts Henderson's friend and guide Sami not to stop visiting Palestine (ch. 15 above).

104. 2 Cor 6:2; 5:20.

105. The word of warning issued by South African Christians in 1985 is no less urgent in our present *kairos* moment: "It is a dangerous time because, if this opportunity is missed, and allowed to pass by, the loss for the Church, for the Gospel and for all the people of South Africa [read: Palestine, Israel, and America], will be immeasurable. Jesus wept over Jerusalem. He wept over the tragedy of the destruction of the city and the massacre of the people that was imminent, 'and all because you did not recognise your opportunity (KAIROS) when God offered it' (Lk 19:44)" (The KAIROS Theologians, *Kairos Document*, 1).

———. *Dogmatics in Outline*. Translated by G. T. Thomson. New York: Philosophical Library, 1949.

Bauckham, Richard. "James and the Gentiles (Acts 15.13–21)." In *History, Literature, and Society in the Book of Acts*, edited by Ben Witherington III, 154–84. Cambridge: Cambridge University Press, 1996.

Beinart, Peter. *Being Jewish After the Destruction of Gaza: A Reckoning*. New York: Knopf, 2025.

Blatman, Daniel, and Amos Goldberg. "There's No Auschwitz in Gaza. But It's Still Genocide." *Haaretz*, January 30, 2025. https://www.haaretz.com/israel-news/2025-1-30/ty-article-magazine/.highlight/theres-no-auschwitz-in-gaza-but-its-still-genocide/00000194-b8af-dee1-a5dc-fcff384b0000?utm_source=.

Bock, Darrell L. "A Response to 'Genesis 12:3, Christian Zionism, and Blessing Israel.'" *Bibliotheca Sacra* 180 (2023) 164–75.

Boorstein, Rebecca. "Huckabee Pick as Israel Ambassador Reflects Long Evangelical Alliance." *The Washington Post*, December 2, 2024. https://www.washingtonpost.com/politics/2024/12/02/evangelicals-israel-trump-huckabee/.

Borgen, Peder. *Early Christianity and Hellenistic Judaism*. Edinburgh: T. & T. Clark, 1996.

Boyarin, Daniel. *The No-State Solution: A Jewish Manifesto*. New Haven, CT: Yale University Press, 2023.

B'Tselem. "2024 West Bank Olive Harvest: Israel Furthers Land Grab Through Tighter Restrictions on Palestinians and Extreme State Violence." January 22, 2025. https://www.btselem.org/video/20250122_2024_west_bank_olive_harvest_israel_furthers_land_grab_through_tighter_restrictions_on_palestinians_and_extreme_state_violence#full.

———. "Parched: Israel's Policy of Water Deprivation in the West Bank." May 2023. https://www.btselem.org/publications/202305_parched.

———. "Welcome to Hell: The Israeli Prison System as a Network of Torture Camps." August 2024. https://www.btselem.org/publications/202408_welcome_to_hell.

Burge, Gary. *Galatians and Ephesians*. Grand Rapids: Kregel, 2025.

———. *Jesus and the Land: The New Testament Challenge to "Holy Land" Theology*. Grand Rapids: Baker, 2010.

Bush, George W. "President's Remarks to the Nation." The White House, September 11, 2002. https://georgewbush-whitehouse.archives.gov/news/releases/2002/09/20020911-3.html.

Buxbaum, Jessica. "A World Heritage Site Under Threat: Palestinian Christians Fight to Reclaim UNESCO Land Seized by Israeli Settlers." *The New Arab*, August 15, 2024. https://www.newarab.com/features/palestinian-christians-demand-settler-stolen-unesco-land-back.

Campbell, Douglas. *Framing Paul: An Epistolary Biography*. Grand Rapids: Eerdmans, 2014.

Cannon, Mae Elise, and Bruce N. Fisk. "Christian Nationalism and Christian Zionism: Two Sides of the Same Coin?" *Christians for Social Action*, July 28, 2021. https://christiansforsocialaction.org/resource/christian-nationalism-and-christian-zionism-two-sides-of-the-same-coin/.

Carroll, Sean. "This Is the Moment of Moral Reckoning in Gaza." *The New York Times*, May 6, 2025. https://www.nytimes.com/2025/05/06/opinion/gaza-israel-aid-starvation.html.

Chapman, Colin. *Christian Zionism and the Restoration of Israel: How Should We Interpret the Scriptures?* Eugene, OR: Cascade, 2021.

Childs, Brevard S. *The Church's Guide for Reading Paul: The Canonical Shaping of the Pauline Corpus.* Grand Rapids: Eerdmans, 2008.

Christians United for Israel. "Policy Accomplishments." https://cufi.org/about/policy/policy-accomplishments/.

Dias, Elizabeth, and Ruth Graham. "White House of Worship: Trump Elevates Christian Prayer and Power." *The New York Times*, April 18, 2025. https://www.nytimes.com/2025/04/18/us/politics/white-house-prayers.html?.

Eagleton, Terry. *Reason, Faith, and Revolution: Reflections on the God Debate.* New Haven, CT: Yale University Press, 2009.

Fisk, Bruce N. "Genesis 12:3, Christian Zionism, and Blessing Israel." *Bibliotheca Sacra* 180 (2023) 144–63.

———. "A Response to Darrell Bock." *Bibliotheca Sacra* 180 (2023) 176–78.

French, David. "The Donald Trump Leap of Faith." *The New York Times*, April 3, 2025. https://www.nytimes.com/2025/04/03/opinion/trump-evangelicals-easter.html.

Goldman, Shalom. *Zeal for Zion: Christians, Jews and the Idea of the Promised Land.* Chapel Hill, NC: University of North Carolina Press, 2014.

Guskin, Emily, et al. "Exit Polls from the 2024 Presidential Election." *The Washington Post*, December 2, 2024. https://www.washingtonpost.com/elections/interactive/2024/exit-polls-2024-election/.

Gutiérrez, Gustavo. *A Theology of Liberation: History, Politics and Salvation.* Edited by Sister Caridad Inda and John Eagleson. Maryknoll, NY: Orbis, 1973.

Halper, Jeff. *Decolonizing Israel, Liberating Palestine: Zionism, Settler Colonialism, and the Case for One Democratic State.* London: Pluto, 2021.

Harper, John-Paul. *Paul and Philo on the Politics of the Land, Jerusalem, and Temple.* Wissenschaftliche Untersuchungen zum Neuen Testament 2.562. Tübingen: Mohr-Siebeck, 2021.

Hasson, Nir. "'The Gates of Hell Are Open Night and Day': Malnutrition, Illness and Lack of Drinking Water Plague Gaza." *Haaretz*, April 9, 2025. https://www.haaretz.com/middle-east-news/palestinians/2025-4-09/ty-article-magazine/.premium/the-gates-of-hell-are-open-malnutrition-illness-and-lack-of-drinking-water-plague-gaza/.

Hauerwas, Stanley. *Dispatches from the Front: Theological Engagements with the Secular.* Durham, NC: Duke University Press, 1994.

———. *Performing the Faith.* Grand Rapids: Brazos, 2004.

———. *War and the American Difference: Theological Reflections on Violence and National Identity.* Grand Rapids: Baker, 2011.

Hooker, Morna D. "Interchange in Christ." *Journal of Theological Studies* n.s. 22 (1971) 349–61.

Human Rights Watch. *A Threshold Crossed: Israeli Authorities and the Crimes of Apartheid and Persecution.* April 27, 2021. https://www.hrw.org/report/2021/04/27/threshold-crossed/israeli-authorities-and-crimes-apartheid-and-persecution.

Hummel, Daniel G. *Covenant Brothers: Evangelicals, Jews, and U.S.-Israeli Relations.* Philadelphia: University of Pennsylvania Press, 2019.

Jenson, Robert. "The Religious Power of Scripture." *Scottish Journal of Theology* 52 (1999) 89–105.

Kairos Palestine. "Cry for Hope: A Call to Decisive Action." July 1, 2020. https://cryforhope.org/.

———. "A Declaration to the World." Beit Sahour, November 18–19, 2022. https://www.kairospalestine.ps/images/KP_GKJ_Conference_Statement_2022.pdf.

———. "A Moment of Truth: A Word of Faith, Hope and Love from the Heart of Palestinian Suffering." December 15, 2009. https://www.kairospalestine.ps/index.php/about-kairos/kairos-palestine-document.

Kairos Palestine, et al. "A Call for Repentance: An Open Letter from Palestinian Christians to Western Church Leaders and Theologians." October 20, 2023. https://www.change.org/p/an-open-letter-from-palestinian-christians-to-western-church-leaders-and-theologians.

Kairos Southern Africa and Kairos Palestine. "Joint Kairos Southern Africa and Kairos Palestine Open Letter to Church Leaders and Christians in the USA, Europe and the Ecumenical Family." November 1, 2023. https://www.kairospalestine.ps/images/Joint_open_letter_Kairos_SA_and_Kairos_Palestine_-_final.pdf.

The KAIROS Theologians. *The Kairos Document: A Theological Comment on the Political Crisis in South Africa*. First published 1985. 2nd rev. ed. Braamfontein, South Africa: Skotaville, 1986. https://www.sahistory.org.za/sites/default/files/archive-files3/b0019860000.026.009.354.pdf.

Kaplan, Amy. *Our American Israel: The Story of an Entangled Alliance*. Cambridge, MA: Harvard University Press, 2018.

Kristof, Nicholas. "Why Palestinian Christians Feel Betrayed by American Christians." *The New York Times*, April 9, 2025. https://www.nytimes.com/2025/04/09/opinion/palestinian-christian-us-evangelicals-gaza.html.

Leach, Darcy K. "Prefigurative Politics." In *The Wiley-Blackwell Encyclopedia of Social and Political Movements*, edited by D. A. Snow et al., 3:1004–6. Oxford: Wiley-Blackwell, 2022.

Levy, Gideon, and Alex Levac. "Israel Is Gazafiying the West Bank, and Turning These Palestinians Into Refugees Yet Again." *Haaretz*, March 1, 2025. https://www.haaretz.com/israel-news/twilight-zone/2025-3-01/ty-article-magazine/.highlight/israel-is-gazafiying-the-west-bank-and-turning-these-palestinians-into-refugees-yet-again/00000195-4839-df18-a1fd-c8f906a60000.

Lewis, Donald M. *A Short History of Christian Zionism: From the Reformation to the Twenty-First Century*. Downers Grove, IL: IVP Academic, 2021.

Lincoln, Abraham. "The Gettysburg Address." Delivered November 19, 1863. https://www.abrahamlincolnonline.org/lincoln/speeches/gettysburg.htm.

Lonsdorf, Kat. "In the Occupied West Bank, Palestinians Struggle to Access Water." NPR, September 25, 2024. https://www.npr.org/2024/09/25/g-s1-24207/palestinians-west-bank-water-israel.

Manekin, Mikhael. *End of Days: Ethics, Tradition, and Power in Israel*. Translated by Maya Rosen. Boston: Academic Studies, 2023.

Mednick, Sam. "Food Security Experts Warn Gaza Is at Critical Risk of Famine If Israel Doesn't End Its Blockade." Associated Press News, May 12, 2025. https://apnews.com/article/gaza-famine-war-israel-1360c6d16902c163234b0eb1e96e694b.

Mordechai, Lee. "Bearing Witness to the Israel-Gaza War." Version 6.6.0. March 9, 2025. https://witnessing-the-gaza-war.com/wp-content/uploads/2025/03/Gaza_English-v6.6.0-9.3.25.pdf.

Moritz, Thorsten. *A Profound Mystery: The Use of the Old Testament in Ephesians.* Leiden: Brill, 1996.

Newbigin, Lesslie. *The Gospel in a Pluralist Society.* Grand Rapids: Eerdmans, 1989.

Raheb, Mitri. *Faith in the Face of Empire: The Bible Through Palestinian Eyes.* Maryknoll, NY: Orbis, 2014.

Reasoner, Mark. *The Strong and the Weak: Romans 14.1–15.13 in Context.* Cambridge: Cambridge University Press, 1999.

Rowe, C. Kavin. *World Upside Down: Reading Acts in the Graeco-Roman Age.* Oxford: Oxford University Press, 2009.

Samad, Lama Abdul, et al. "Water War Crimes: How Israel Has Weaponised Water in Its Military Campaign in Gaza." *Oxfam International,* July 18, 2024. https://policy-practice.oxfam.org/resources/water-war-crimes-how-israel-has-weaponised-water-in-its-military-campaign-in-ga-621609/.

Scheindlin, Dahlia. "Analysis: How Israel Is Bringing West Bank-Style Annexation to Gaza." *Haaretz,* April 10, 2025. https://www.haaretz.com/israel-news/2025-4-10/ty-article/.premium/how-israel-is-bringing-west-bank-style-annexation-to-gaza/.

Schmemann, Alexander. *For the Life of the World.* Yonkers, NY: St. Vladimir's Seminary Press, 2018.

Smith, Robert O. *More Desired Than Our Owne Salvation: The Roots of Christian Zionism.* New York: Oxford University Press, 2013.

Solzhenitsyn, Aleksandr. "Nobel Lecture (1970)." Translated by Alexis Klimoff. https://www.solzhenitsyncenter.org/nobel-lecture.

Stoli, Rebecca Shimoni. "Netanyahu: Evangelical Christians Are Israel's Best Friends." *The Times of Israel,* July 18, 2017. https://www.timesofisrael.com/netanyahu-evangelical-christians-are-israels-best-friends/.

Stout, Harry S. *Upon the Altar of the Nation: A Moral History of the Civil War.* New York: Penguin, 2007.

Tan, Rebecca. "After Decades Fighting Demolitions, Palestinian Sees Own Home Wrecked." *The Washington Post,* December 24, 2024. https://www.washingtonpost.com/world/2024/12/24/israel-demolitions-palestinians-east-jerusalem/.

Thompson, Michael. *Clothed with Christ: The Example and Teaching of Jesus in Romans 12.1–15.13.* Sheffield: JSOT Press, 1991.

Trocmé, André. *Jesus and the Nonviolent Revolution.* Walden, NY: Plough, 2003.

United Nations Office for the Coordination of Humanitarian Affairs. "Humanitarian Situation Update #279: West Bank." April 10, 2025. https://www.ochaopt.org/content/humanitarian-situation-update-279-west-bank.

———. "Reported Impact Snapshot: Gaza Strip (3 April 2025)." https://www.ochaopt.org/content/reported-impact-snapshot-gaza-strip-3-april-2025.

United Nations Office of the High Commissioner for Human Rights. "End Unfolding Genocide or Watch It End Life in Gaza: UN Experts Say States Face Defining Choice." May 7, 2025. https://www.ohchr.org/en/press-releases/2025/05/end-unfolding-genocide-or-watch-it-end-life-gaza-un-experts-say-states-face.

———. "Gaza: Increasing Israeli 'Evacuation Orders' Lead to Forcible Transfer of Palestinians." April 11, 2025. https://www.ohchr.org/en/press-briefing-notes/2025/04/gaza-increasing-israeli-evacuation-orders-lead-forcible-transfer.

University Network for Human Rights, et al. "Genocide in Gaza: Analysis of International Law and Its Application to Israel's Military Actions Since October 7, 2023." May 15, 2024. https://static1.squarespace.com/static/66a134337e960f229da81434/

t/66fb05bb0497da4726e125d8/1727727037094/Genocide+in+Gaza+-+Final+version+051524.pdf.

Wagner, J. Ross. "'Enemies' Yet 'Beloved' Still: Election and the Love of God in Romans 9–11." In *God and Israel: Providence and Purpose in Romans 9–11*, edited by Todd D. Still, 95–113. Waco, TX: Baylor University Press, 2017.

———. "*Missio Dei*: Envisioning an Apostolic Reading of Scripture." *Missiology: An International Review* 37 (2009) 19–32.

Walker, Peter W. L. "The Land in the New Testament: The Land and Jesus Himself." In *The Land of Promise: Biblical, Theological and Contemporary Perspectives*, edited by Philip Johnston and Peter Walker, 100–120. Downers Grove, IL: InterVarsity, 2000.

Walls, Andrew F. *The Missionary Movement in Christian History: Studies in the Transmission of Faith*. Edinburgh: T. & T. Clark, 1996.

Webster, John. *Holy Scripture: A Dogmatic Sketch*. Cambridge: Cambridge University Press, 2003.

World Bank Group. "Gaza and West Bank Interim Rapid Damage and Needs Assessment (February 2025)." February 21, 2025. https://thedocs.worldbank.org/en/doc/133c3304e29086819c1119fe8e85366b-0280012025/original/Gaza-RDNA-final-med.pdf.

Yoder, John Howard. *The Politics of Jesus: Vicit Agnus Noster*. Grand Rapids: Eerdmans, 1972.

APPENDIX

A Gaza Timeline

Bruce N. Fisk

Given that this timeline focuses on Gaza, we might be fairly accused of artificially separating the tiny territory from the larger region of which it is an integral part and committing numerous sins of omission. As a partial remedy, we would point to works in the bibliography, some of which also include timelines, and to the historical resources collated by Ben Norquist and posted to NEME's website (https://www.neme.network/resources). We include Gaza's appearances in the Bible but disavow efforts to weaponize such texts in a campaign to dispossess the Land's inhabitants.

    Gaza's importance in antiquity is tied to its location along the coastal trade route between Egypt and Syria. The area we call Gaza today was thus successively occupied by Canaanites/Phoenicians, Egyptians, and Philistines, who developed its economy, trade routes, seaports, and urban centers and conducted international trade.

Josh 10:41	The Israelites conquer "from Kadesh Barnea to Gaza."
Josh 13:3	Gaza is one of several Philistine cities resistant to Israelite conquest.
Judg 1:18	Though the city is predominantly Avvite and/or Canaanite, the tribe of "Judah took Gaza with its territory."
Judg 16	Samson goes to Philistine-controlled Gaza, destroys city gate and temple.

Appendix

The "land of the Philistines" mentioned in Judges and Samuel includes Gaza but may have been fifteen to twenty times larger than today's Gaza Strip.

11th/10th c. BCE	Israelites rule over Gaza under David and Solomon (1 Kgs 4:24).
8th c.	Amos (1:6–7) pronounces judgment on Philistine Gaza.
734	Assyria/Tiglath-Pileser III conquers Gaza.
720	Assyria conquers and (probably) destroys Gaza. Philistia becomes a de facto province of Assyria.
7th c.	Oracles against the nations (Jer 25:20 and Zeph 2:4) include Gaza and Judah.
609	Egypt/Pharaoh Neco II captures Gaza from the Babylonians.
6th c.	Zechariah (9:5) foresees judgment on coastal cities including Gaza.
587	Babylon captures Jerusalem and destroys the Temple.
529	Persia/Cambyses conquers Gaza; the city becomes a Persian fortress.
332	**Alexander the Great** besieges Gaza for 5 months and destroys it. Nabateans use the port for exporting spices. Gaza is ruled by Ptolemies and then Seleucids.
2nd c.	Jonathan, brother of Judas Maccabeus, subjugates Gaza.
57	Roman general **Pompey** "frees" the city. Gaza is rebuilt, fortified.
30	Octavian grants Gaza to **Herod the Great**.
6–4 BCE	According to ancient tradition, when **Joseph, Mary, and Jesus** fled Herod the Great, their path to Egypt passed through Gaza.
1st c. CE	**Philip**, en route to Gaza, baptizes Ethiopian eunuch (Acts 8:26–28).
4th c.	**Hilarion** establishes Palestinian monasticism in Gaza.
5th c.	Bishop **Porphyrius** converts pagan Gaza to Christianity. Pagan temples are destroyed. There is a Christian center of learning and monasticism, a famous Rhetorical School, and a Jewish minority.

425	A church is built on the site of today's **Church of Saint Porphyrius** in Gaza City. (It becomes a mosque in the seventh century.)
7th c. to 15th c.	Much of Gaza converts to Islam. Churches are turned into mosques.
1100	King Baldwin I of Jerusalem captures Gaza from the Fatimids during the Crusades.
1149/1152	Gaza is refortified under **King Baldwin III** of Jerusalem.
1150s	The **Crusaders** build and dedicate the current Church of Saint Porphyrius.
1170	Ayyubid Sultan **Saladin** pillages what had been built up around the fortress.
1187	Crusaders surrender the city to Saladin. Fortifications are destroyed.
1193	**King Richard the Lionheart** retakes the city but the walls are dismantled.
1260	The **Mongols** destroy Gaza. Mamelukes renovate the Great Mosque.
1277	**Mamelukes** based in Gaza attack the crusaders.
1290	Mameluke rule. Jewish community revived in the fourteenth century.
1516	Under the rule of the **Ottoman Turks** Gaza is a state in the Palestinian territory (along with Jerusalem and Nablus) within the province of Damascus. Gaza prospers. Small Jewish community expands, home to the messianic Shabbatean movement (**Shabbtai Tzvi**).
1516–1918	Ottoman rule over Palestine.
1799	**Napoleon Bonaparte**, after capturing Egypt, briefly occupies the city before moving on to Ramla, Jaffa, and beyond.
1832	**Muhammad Ali**, Ottoman governor of Egypt, conquers Gaza.
1834	Palestinian Arabs across the region revolt against Egypt.
1856	The Church of Saint Porphyrius is renovated.
1880s	As part of a wave of 25,000 immigrants arriving to Palestine from eastern Europe (the "**First Aliyah**"), supported by Zionist groups like *Hovevei Zion*, Jews establish a community in Gaza.

Appendix

1896	**Theodor Herzl** publishes *Der Judenstaat*, a call to establish a Jewish state. Plans to colonize Palestine are underway.
1897	The **World Zionist Organization** is founded in Switzerland.
1904–1914	The "**Second Aliyah**" sees 40,000 European Jews migrate to Palestine. Zionists view the indigenous Arab population as a "problem."
1914–1918	**World War I**
1915–1916	**Husayn-McMahon** correspondence: letters between the British government and the Sharif of Mecca, promising Arab independence in exchange for support in defeating the Ottoman Empire.
1916	The secret **Sykes-Picot** agreement between Britain and France proposed an international regime to govern much of the Holy Land, including Jerusalem and Gaza.
1917	During World War I, the British lose two battles in Gaza. General **Edmund Allenby** wins the third, after which the British advance on Jerusalem.
	November 2 — The **Balfour Declaration** expresses British support for a "national home for the Jewish people" in Palestine and intention not to "prejudice the civil and religious rights of existing non-Jewish communities in Palestine."
1919–1933	The "**Third Aliyah**" describes another wave of 35,000 Jewish immigrants.
1920–1948	Gaza is part of Mandatory Palestine under **British** control.
1928	The **Muslim Brotherhood** is established in Egypt.
1929	Palestinians demonstrate and riot against the British and Zionists across the Land. The British evacuate Gaza's Jewish community to Tel Aviv.
1936	**Arab Revolt** begins.
1939–1945	**World War II**
1946	October — Zionists establish Kfar Darom, a religious kibbutz, near Deir al-Balah, to ensure the region would be part of a future Jewish state. (The Egyptian army drives out the residents in the summer of 1948.)

1947		The **UN General Assembly** approves **Resolution 181**, a plan to partition Palestine and make Gaza part of the Arab state.
1947–1949		The **Nakba**: Zionist forces displace 200,000 Palestinians to Gaza (about one-quarter of the total number of refugees from the war) and prevent their return. They join 60,000 Palestinians already living in Gaza, which comprises only 2 percent of historical Palestine by area.
1948	May 14	**Israel** declares statehood. War ensues.
	July	Egyptian forces prevent the expulsion of Palestinians from the Gaza Strip.
		Yasser Arafat fights in Gaza alongside members of the Muslim Brotherhood.
	October–December	Israel expels a number of Bedouin tribes to Gaza: Jubarat, Tarabin, Tayaha (half to Gaza), al-Hajajre.
	November	Israel expels the population of Isdud and Majdal to Gaza.
		Yigal Alon wants Israel to occupy Gaza and part of the Sinai, but **David Ben-Gurion** prevents it.
	December 11	The UN General Assembly passes **Resolution 194,** which urges that Palestinian refugees wishing to return to their homes and live at peace with their neighbors should be allowed to do so at the earliest practicable date, and that those who choose not to return should be compensated for their property.
1949	February 24	**Armistice** (ceasefire) agreement between Israel and Egypt sets the border of the Gaza Strip.
1949–1967		Gaza under **Egyptian** military control, at first officially under the All-Palestine Government, then in 1959 under the United Arab Republic. Gazans are neither made citizens of Egypt nor allowed to return to homes in Israel. Egypt restricts travel and employment.

Appendix

1950	March	Israel passes the **Absentee Properties Law**, which legalizes Israel's expropriation of land, homes, businesses, and assets belonging to Palestinians who fled or were expelled during the 1948 War.
1955	February	Israel strikes an Egyptian base in Gaza, retaliating against Palestinian guerrilla infiltration and undermining Nasser's prestige.
1956	November	Israel captures Gaza during Sinai conflict and holds it until March 1957.
	November 3	IDF soldiers massacre more than 200 Palestinians in Khan Yunis.
	November 12	IDF soldiers massacre more than 100 Palestinians in Rafah.
1963		Professionals begin to plan for Israeli rule of Gaza and the West Bank.
1967	June	During the **Six-Day War** (or **the June War**), Israel takes control of Gaza's 450,000 Palestinians, of whom 315,000 are refugees.
	June 18	Israeli ministers discuss how to reduce Gaza's population, perhaps by transferring them to Egypt, the West Bank, or Jordan.
	June 23	Prime Minister **Levi Eshkol** announces that Gaza (and the West Bank) will remain under Israeli control.
		Israel's archaeological authority takes over all sites in Gaza and the West Bank.
	July	Officer **Mordechai Gur** proposes to transfer Gaza's refugees to the West Bank.
	November	UN Security Council **Resolution 242** declares "the inadmissibility of the acquisition of territory by war."
1968	May	Israel begins allowing Palestinians from Israel to visit the occupied territories, after 19 years of separation.

		Rabin and Alon begin to establish Jewish colonies (later known as **Gush Katif**) between Gaza City and the southern end of the Strip. (Between 1967 and 1993, Israel builds more than 20 settlements in Gaza.)
1970	December	**Kfar Darom**, Israel's first settlement in Gaza, is established.
1971		Israel begins building a fence on the perimeter of Gaza and carves roads through crowded refugee camps after demolishing houses.
	July	Israel invades Jabaliya and al-Shati refugee camps, destroys more than 6,000 homes, and forces more than 15,000 to move to Gaza City, El-Arish, and the West Bank.
		Moshe Dayan makes Gaza economically dependent as a source of cheap labor and a captive market for Israeli goods.
1975	September	**Menachem Begin** (Likud) promises that, if elected, Israel will never return territories occupied in 1967.
1978	September 1	**Camp David Accords** brokered by **Jimmy Carter** between **Menachem Begin** (Israel) and **Anwar Sadat** (Egypt).
1979	March 26	**Egypt-Israel peace treaty**. Israel agrees to withdraw from Sinai; Egypt promises diplomatic relations and opens Suez Canal to Israeli ships. Egypt renounces claims on the Gaza Strip. Israel is to end its occupation of Palestinian territories.
1981		Israel establishes the **Civil Administration**, part of the Defense Ministry, to oversee civil matters in the Occupied Palestinian Territories, including Gaza until 2005.
1987		**First Intifada** begins in the Gaza Strip. First year death toll in Gaza: 142 Palestinians, 0 Israelis.

	December 8	A truck kills 4 in Jabaliya refugee camp. Local reactions include stone throwing, demonstrations, roadblocks, strikes, and civil disobedience. Israeli retaliation kills 6 Palestinians in the first week, followed by mass arrests, closures of schools, shops, and businesses, and excessive brutality.
	December 10	**Sheikh Ahmed Ismail Hassan Yassin** co-founds **Hamas**, affiliates with the **Muslim Brotherhood**.
	December 22	UN Security Council **Resolution 605** condemns Israeli open fire on Palestinian civilians and violations of the Geneva Convention.
1988	March 23	**Mahmoud Zahar** (co-founder of Hamas) proposes to **Shimon Peres** (then minister of Foreign Affairs) tacit recognition of Israel in exchange for its withdrawal from the territories occupied in 1967.
	July 31	**Jordan** relinquishes claims on East Jerusalem and the West Bank.
	August	**Yassin** authors Hamas's first **charter** (not a binding manifesto), declaring Palestine an Islamic *waqf* (inalienable bequest).
	November 15	The **PLO** proclaims an independent State of Palestine.
	December	**Yasser Arafat** addresses the UN General Assembly, recognizes Israel, concedes the partition of Palestine (with an Arab state in the West Bank and Gaza), and advocates diplomacy. Hamas sees PLO concessions as defeat and insists that armed struggle is still required.
1989	April 2	Arafat is elected president of the proclaimed State of Palestine.
1993	The PLO recognizes the State of Israel and the right of its citizens to live in peace. Gaza Strip comes under **Palestinian Authority** jurisdiction and is to be the first territory to gain autonomy.	

	April 16	First suicide bombing claimed by Hamas strikes Mehola Junction in the West Bank; 1 killed, 10 injured.
	September	The **Declaration of Principles** (the "Oslo Accords") is signed by Peres, Abbas, and Clinton. (Arafat and Rabin attend.) This effectively reduces "Palestine" to the West Bank and Gaza.
1994	May 4	The Gaza-Jericho Agreement marks the dawn of the Oslo Accords.
		Yasser Arafat (whose father is from Gaza) moves to Gaza City.
1994–1995		Under the **Oslo Accords**, the Palestinian Authority gains nominal control of Gaza. Settlement building continues, and settlers control most water resources. Gaza is cut off from the West Bank.
1994–1996		Israel builds a barrier along the 37-mile perimeter of Gaza.
1997		Israel releases **Ahmed Yassin** from prison. **Ismail Haniyeh** becomes his personal assistant.
2000–2005	**Second Intifada**	
2000	September	Gazans destroy much of Israel's perimeter barrier.
		Muhammad al-Durrah, Palestinian boy shot dead hiding behind his father, becomes an iconic image of IDF violence against children.
	December	Israel rebuilds the perimeter barrier and adds a 1-kilometer buffer zone.
2004		IDF begins building a mock city in the Negev to train soldiers for attacks on Gaza.
	February	**Ariel Sharon** announces plan to remove settlements from Gaza.
	March 14	Two Gazans infiltrate Ashdod port and detonate explosive belts, killing 10 and injuring 16. Hamas and Fatah claim responsibility.
	March 22	Israeli helicopter gunship kills Hamas leader **Sheikh Yassin**.

Appendix

	May 12–24	IDF launches operation *Rainbow in Cloud* against Rafah and smuggling tunnels after 11 Israeli soldiers from the Givati Brigade and the Engineering Corps' tunnels unit were killed in attacks on aging M113 Armored Personnel Carriers.
	September	Qassam rocket kills 2 Israeli children in **Sderot**.
	September 29–October 16	IDF launches operation *Days of Penitence* with heavy bombardment of Beit Hanoun and the Beit Lahia and Jabaliya refugee camps; 130 Palestinians and 1 Israeli are killed.
	October 5	The US vetoes a UN Security Council resolution condemning the assault.
	November 11	**Yasser Arafat** dies; **Mahmoud Abbas** becomes president of the PA.
2005		Gaza's population reaches 1.4 million Palestinians; 8,500 Jews in 21 settlements (17 recognized, 4 unauthorized) cover 25 percent of territory, using 40 percent of fertile land and most water resources.
	February	Hamas and Islamic Jihad reject truce between Israel and the PA.
	August	**Disengagement**: Under **Ariel Sharon**, Israel unilaterally withdraws army, 21 settlements, and about 9,000 settlers from Gaza to freeze the political process, ceding control to the Palestinian Authority. Hamas claims this vindicates the strategy of armed resistance. The international community sees the occupation continuing under different conditions.
	September	Hamas fires about 40 Qassam rockets at Israel, killing 6, said to be retaliating for mass arrests and an explosion that killed 15 Gazans and injured many. IDF launches operation *First Rain* with heavy bombardment of vast areas from the land, sea, and air.
2005–2006		Israel enhances its perimeter barrier and widens the buffer zone.

2006	Summer	After Israel suffers defeat by Hezbollah in southern Lebanon, it intensifies bombing of Gaza.
2005–2008		More than 1,200 Palestinians are killed (as many as half are civilians and one-quarter children). Israel's punitive Gaza policy contrasts sharply with the West Bank, where settlements, settler roads, army bases, and slow population transfer are steps toward annexation. The siege of Gaza intensifies; 80 percent of population is dependent on aid.
2006	January	Hamas defeats Fatah, winning a majority in the PA legislative council.
		Haniyeh is sworn in as prime minister.
		International community rejects a Hamas-led government; US/EU cut off funding. Attempted coup against Hamas. US pledges assistance to Fatah. The parties fail to reach a power-sharing agreement.
	June	Seven members of the **Ghalia family** are killed on a Gaza beach.
		Hamas retracts its commitment to the 2005 ceasefire.
	June 25	Entering Israel via an 800-meter tunnel under the perimeter barrier, Hamas kills 2 Israeli soldiers and captures **Gilad Shalit**. Israel responds with operation *Summer Rains*, including a destructive ground invasion.
	November	Israel's operation *Autumn Clouds* kills 70 Gazans in 48 hours and, by the end of November, almost 200, half of them children and women.
2007		*Battle of Gaza*: Hamas seizes control of Gaza, creating a separate Palestinian government. Israel imposes a blockade on Gaza.
2008	January	Hamas militants blow a hole in the barrier; thousands of Gazans enter the Sinai to purchase food and supplies but return within a week.

Appendix

	June	Six-month ceasefire, followed by targeted assassinations by Israel and Hamas rockets. Hamas wants the ceasefire to continue.
	October	*Haaretz* refers for the first time to Israel's "**Dahiya Doctrine**" of total, punitive destruction, applied in Lebanon in 2006, and now in Gaza.
	November 4	Israeli army attacks a Hamas tunnel, kills 6. Hamas fires 30 rockets.
	November 18	Declaring the end of the ceasefire, Hamas resumes rocket fire, damaging houses.
	December 27	Israel launches operation *Cast Lead*, including aerial bombing and ground assault. Death toll: 1,400 Palestinians (two-thirds of them non-combatants) and 12 Israelis. Thousands are wounded. UN finds Israel and Palestinian militants guilty of war crimes.
2009	January 3	Ground invasion of Gaza begins.
	January 16	Israeli tank shells kill 3 daughters and niece of **Dr. Izzeldin Abuelaish**.
	January 17	Israel announces a ceasefire. Hamas follows a day later.
	January 20	**Barack Obama** is inaugurated US president.
	September 15	The **Goldstone Report**, commissioned by the UNHRC to investigate military operations in Gaza from December 27, 2008, to January 18, 2009, is released. Both Israel and Palestinian militants are condemned. Israel is singled out for breaches of the 4th Geneva Convention.
2010	May	"Peace Flotilla" including the **Mavi Marmara** approaches Gaza. Israeli commandos board in international waters, kill 9 Turkish citizens.
2011	February	"Arab Spring" overthrows Egypt's **President Mubarak**.
	April	Israel's **Iron Dome** defense system intercepts a missile from Gaza for the first time.

	October	Hamas exchanges **Gilad Shalit** for 1,027 Palestinian prisoners, including future Hamas leader **Yahya Sinwar**.
2012		Hamas fires rockets (reaching Tel Aviv for the first time). Eight days of Israeli airstrikes. The head of Hamas's military wing is killed.
		Operation *Pillar of Defense* kills almost 180 people, mostly civilians. UN finds both sides guilty of war crimes. Egypt brokers short-lived ceasefire.
2014		Hamas members kidnap and kill 3 Israeli teens in the West Bank. Operation *Brother's Keeper*: Israel arrests 350 Palestinians in the hunt, knowing the teens are already dead.
	July	Operation *Protective Edge*: 7 weeks of airstrikes, ground operations, naval blockades. Most Hamas rockets are intercepted by Iron Dome. At least 2,200 Gazans die (mostly civilians, more than 500 children). Many injured/displaced. Major damage to infrastructure. Israeli blockade produces shortages of basic necessities.
2016		**Ismail Haniyeh** becomes Hamas leader, replacing **Khaled Mashaal**.
2017		**Hamas charter** is revised.
2017–2021		Israel builds an underground border wall around Gaza to block tunnels.
2018	March 30	**The Great March of Return** begins on *Land Day*. Weekly demonstrations along the perimeter fence demand the right of return and oppose the blockade and US recognition of Jerusalem as Israel's capital. Tens of thousands participate (both independents and Hamas). Tactics include stone throwing, Molotov cocktails, and tire burning. IDF sees the protests as armed conflict and claims Hamas is using human shields, kills 223 Palestinians and wounds thousands.
	May	Palestinians begin using incendiary balloons and kites.

Appendix

2019	December 27	**Great March of Return** ends.
2020	August	After two weeks of balloons and rockets launched from Gaza, Israel bans imports to the enclave except food and medical supplies.
2021	March 21	First two cases of COVID-19 reported in Gaza City.
	May	Palestinians demonstrate at **Al Aqsa** for 11 days. Hamas fires rockets from Gaza. Israel kills 261 Palestinians and injures more than 2,000. During the same period: 10 Israeli deaths and 710 injuries.
2022		Israel strikes senior Islamic Jihad commander; Islamic Jihad fires 1,000 rockets; 44 Palestinians killed (15 children) over 3 days of violence.
	August	Operation *Breaking Dawn*: Israeli airstrikes on Gaza; 49 Palestinians killed (17 children).
	November	**Benjamin Netanyahu** becomes prime minister again, forming the most right-wing, nationalist government in Israel's history.
2023	January	Israeli troops raid a refugee camp and kill 7 Palestinian gunmen and 2 civilians. Islamic Jihad responds with rockets. No casualties. Israeli air strikes on Gaza.
	May	Multiple Israeli airstrikes kill 33, including members of PIJ and PFLP and civilians. Palestinian militants fire several hundred rockets. Most are intercepted by the Iron Dome; one kills 1 and wounds 5.
	September	Hamas organizes demonstrations near the barrier.

In 2023, prior to October 7, Israeli forces kill 234 West Bank Palestinians. Jewish settlers kill 9.

October 7	Launching operation *Al-Aqsa Flood* around 6:30 a.m., Hamas breaches barrier, attacks bases, kibbutzim, and Nova music festival. First wave (the initial half-hour): 1,200 Hamas commandos. Second wave (7 a.m. to 9 a.m.): 2,000 commandos and gunmen from other organizations. Third wave: mostly civilians. In the first 3 hours militants kill 157 soldiers in border outposts. The Israeli Air Force fires 11,000 shells, drops more than 500 one-ton bombs, launches 180 missiles, and reportedly kills 1,000 fighters. Ultimately, Gaza militants abduct 251 people (including 44 from the festival and 74 from kibbutz Nir Oz) and kill as many as 1,139, though an unknown but substantial number of these are killed by Israel's own forces.
October 10	Israeli army declares full control of all Israeli territory.
October 11	President **Joe Biden** repeats the false claims of Israeli government and media about Hamas beheading babies.
October 13	Israel instructs 1.1 million Gazans to evacuate south within 24 hours.
	Within a week of October 7 Israel has conducted 6,000 airstrikes.
October 17	Explosion at the **Al-Ahli Arab Hospital** in Gaza City kills and wounds hundreds. Israel immediately blames a failed **Palestinian Islamic Jihad** rocket for the carnage. The US, France, the UK, Canada, and many media outlets share Israel's assessment, but evidence assessed by Forensic Architecture, Earshot, and other investigators points to an Israeli airstrike.
October 19	Israeli airstrike damages part of the **Church of Saint Porphyrius** in Gaza City (dating to the Crusader period, built on the site of a fifth-century church) where 500 Muslims and Christians are sheltering. At least 18 killed.

Appendix

October 22	Israeli bomb destroys the house of Palestinian journalist and co-founder of *We Are Not Numbers* **Ahmed Alnaouq** in Deir Al-Balah, central Gaza, killing 21 members of his family (including 14 children).
October 27	*Battle of Hanoun* begins, lasting until May 31, 2024.
October 28	Second phase of Israel's assault begins with ground incursions.
October 31	Israel bombs **Jabaliya refugee camp** with at least 2 2,000-pound bombs, killing 106 (including 54 children). More than 1.4 million are internally displaced. Jordan, Chile, Colombia recall ambassadors from Israel; Bolivia, Bahrain sever diplomatic ties.
November 2	Siege of **Gaza City** begins.
November 4	Israeli airstrike on **Al-Fakhoora school** in Jabaliya kills 15, injures 70.
	Oxfam reports only 2 percent of Gaza's usual food supply has entered from Egypt. Israeli airstrike kills 47 in **al-Maghazi refugee camp** (to which Israel had advised north Gazans to evacuate).
November 11	Siege of **Al-Shifa hospital** begins in Gaza City. Present were 1,500 patients, 1,500 medical workers, and about 15,000 people seeking shelter.
	Israel's Ministry of Foreign Affairs posts a fake video of a nurse at Al-Shifa claiming it was overrun with Hamas militants.
November 24–30	**Temporary ceasefire**. Hamas releases 69 hostages. Israel releases 180 prisoners, mostly women and teenagers, including Ahed Tamimi.
December	**Bethlehem** cancels public celebrations of Christmas.

	December 6	Israeli forces in northern Gaza shoot and kill 6 members of the Abu Salah family waving white flags.
	December 7	Israeli airstrike on the Shejaiya refugee camp kills **Dr. Refaat al-Areer**, Palestinian writer and professor at the Islamic University of Gaza.
	December 15	IDF shoots, kills 3 escaped **Israeli hostages** in Gaza City who were shirtless, waving a white flag, and calling for help in Hebrew.
	December 22	UN Security Council resolution demands unhindered, expanded humanitarian access. The US abstains from the vote.
		Death toll milestone: 20,000 (1 percent of population).
	December 23	At Christmas Lutheran Church in Bethlehem, **Munther Isaac** preaches "Christ in the Rubble: A Liturgy of Lament."
	December 24	At the Christmas Eve mass in St. Peter's Basilica, **Pope Francis** says, "Tonight, our hearts are in Bethlehem, where the Prince of Peace is once more rejected by the futile logic of war, by the clash of arms that even today prevents him from finding room in the world."
	December 24–25	Israeli airstrike kills 106 in the **al-Maghazi refugee camp**.
	December 29	**South Africa** files a case with the **International Court of Justice (ICJ)**, alleging that Israel's conduct in Gaza amounted to genocide.
2024	January 24	Explosion and building collapse in **Khan Yunis** kills 21 Israeli soldiers. Deadliest day for the IDF since October 7, 2023.
	January 26	ICJ delivers interim judgment, concluding that Palestinians have plausible rights to be protected from genocide, and ordering Israel to act to prevent acts of genocide; stops short of calling for an immediate ceasefire.

	On the same day Israel alleges that 12 UN employees participated in the October 7 attack. US pauses additional funding of **UNRWA**.
January 28	5,000 Israelis attend a conference calling for Jewish settlements in Gaza, titled *Conference for the Victory of Israel—Settlement Brings Security: Returning to the Gaza Strip and Northern Samaria* in Jerusalem. Speakers include **Bezalel Smotrich** and **Itamar Ben Gvir**.
January 29	Five year-old **Hind Rajab** flees Gaza City with her family, 6 of whom are shot by an Israeli tank. Hind and cousin Layan Hamadeh call the Red Crescent Society. Both are shot dead, as are 2 ambulance workers.
February 20	The US is the only country to veto a **UN Security Council** draft resolution, blocking a demand for immediate ceasefire.
February 29	**Flour Massacre** in Gaza City: IDF opens fire on Palestinians seeking food from humanitarian aid trucks, killing 119, injuring 760. IDF claims the dead were trampled by fellow Palestinians.
March 2	Three US military planes (C-130s) air-drop more than 38,000 meals into Gaza (at a time when UNOCHA says 576,000 people are a step away from famine).
March 6	The IDF's **Netzarim Corridor** road reaches the Mediterranean coast, splitting Gaza in two.
March 7	Biden directs the US military to construct a temporary pier for humanitarian aid.
March 18	Second raid of **Al-Shifa hospital** begins, ending on April 1 with most buildings damaged or destroyed. Mass casualties, mass graves, arrests, displacement, destruction by tank and bulldozer, interrogations.
April 1	Drones strike **World Central Kitchen** aid convoy, killing 7 workers.

April 17	Gaza Solidarity Encampment at **Columbia University**. Student and faculty protesters demand university divestment from Israel.
April 22	Student protests spread in the US. Several thousand protesters are arrested in the US across 60 campuses.
May 7	Campus protests spread to Europe. Arrests in the Netherlands, UK, Germany, Belgium, Australia, Canada.
May 17	The US-built **floating pier** ("JLOTS maritime corridor") sees its first shipment of humanitarian aid.
May 26	The **Rafah tent massacre**: Israel drops two 250-pound bombs on a civilian encampment in the Tel al-Sultan refugee camp, Rafah, killing about 50, many of whom burn to death, and injuring 249.
May 31	**Joe Biden** presents a 3-phase **ceasefire proposal** that includes return of hostages, release of hundreds of Palestinian prisoners, Israeli troop withdrawal, entrance of 600 aid trucks daily.
May–July	**JLOTS floating pier** intended for humanitarian aid operates for only 20 days before closing on July 17. USAID says it delivered enough to feed 450,000 people for one month.
June 4	The US House of Representatives votes to pass legislation sanctioning the ICJ after its prosecutor applies for arrest warrants against Israeli officials.
June 8	IDF operation (aided by US intelligence) rescues 4 hostages in the **Nuseirat** refugee camp in central Gaza, killing 276 and injuring 698 Palestinians. (IDF acknowledges fewer than 100 deaths.) Hamas claims the IDF raid killed 3 other hostages.
July 7	**Al-Ahli Arab hospital** is evacuated and forced out of service.

Appendix

July 9	IDF attacks in Gaza City and **Deir al-Balah** kill at least 50 and injure 80.
July 13	Israel assassinates **Mohammed Deif** in an airstrike in al-Mawasi, an area the IDF had declared a humanitarian "safe zone."
July 29	Nine IDF soldiers are detained for allegedly abusing Palestinians at **Sde Teiman prison**. Far-right activists and government officials storm 2 military facilities and demonstrate against the detainment.
July 31	Israel assassinates **Ismail Haniyeh** in Tehran.
August 10	The IDF drops 3 JDAM/Mark 84 (2,000 pound) bombs at once on **al-Tabin elementary school** in Gaza City's Daraj district packed with refugees seeking shelter.
October	Israel considers the **Generals' Plan**: empty northern Gaza and declare any Palestinians who remain combatants.
October 16	IDF kills Hamas leader **Yahya Sinwar** in Rafah.
October 19	IDF attacks on **Beit Lahia** in northern Gaza kill 92, injure more than 100.
October 28	The Israeli Knesset passes a bill prohibiting **UNRWA** from operating "within Israel's sovereign territory," which is meant to apply to the West Bank and Gaza.
October 29	IDF airstrike on a five-story residence in **Beit Lahia** kills between 55 and 93.
November 16	**Armed gangs** raid a convoy of 109 UN aid trucks near the Kerem Shalom border crossing. The perpetrators may have been protected by the IDF.
November 21	ICC issues arrest warrants for **Benjamin Netanyahu**, former Minister of Defense **Yoav Gallant**, and the (deceased) head of Hamas's military wing, **Mohammed Deif**, alleging war crimes and crimes against humanity.

	December	**Bethlehem** cancels public Christmas celebrations again.
2025	January 15	**Ceasefire proposal** in 3 stages: 6-week ceasefire with the release of Israeli hostages in exchange for some Palestinians being held by Israel; a permanent ceasefire including Israel's withdrawal from Gaza; and a 3–5 year reconstruction process.
	January 19	**Ceasefire** begins. First exchange of hostages: 3 Israelis; 90 Palestinian women and children. Hundreds of aid trucks enter Gaza. Breaches: between January 19 and February 12, the IDF killed 118 Gazans. **Itamar Ben-Gvir** (*Jewish Power* party) resigns from Netanyahu's Cabinet to protest the ceasefire, weakening the governing coalition.
	January 21	IDF begins operation *Iron Wall* in the West Bank. Troops invade the **Jenin refugee camp** with drones, planes, armored vehicles, and bulldozers; evict inhabitants; begin destroying homes and infrastructure. Chief of General Staff **Herzl Halevi** and Major General **Yaron Finkelman** announce their resignations from the IDF due to their roles in the military's failure on October 7.
	January 25	Second exchange: 4 Israelis; 200 Palestinians.
	January 27	IDF troops invade the **Tul Karm refugee camp**.
	January 30	Third exchange: 3 Israelis, 5 Thai; 110 Palestinians.
	February 1	Fourth exchange: 3 Israeli-mixed nationals; 183 Palestinians.
	February 4	At a White House news conference with Netanyahu, President **Donald Trump** announces the US will take over the Gaza Strip, displace its population, and turn it into "the Riviera of the Middle East."

February 7	IDF troops invade the **Nur Shams refugee camp**.
February 8	Fifth exchange: 3 Israelis; 183 Palestinians.
February 15	Sixth exchange: 3 Israelis; 369 Palestinians.
February 22	Seventh exchange: 6 Israelis; Israel delays release of Palestinians.
February 23	Defense Minister Israel Katz announces that 40,000 Palestinians displaced from the Jenin, Tul Karm, and Nur Shams refugee camps will not be allowed to return home for a year.
February 27	Israel releases 642 Palestinians. Israeli military releases findings from internal investigations of October 7 security failures.
March 1	First (6-week) phase of Israel/Hamas **ceasefire deal expires**. Israel proposes to extend the first-phase ceasefire to receive more hostages. Hamas wants to proceed with the original second phase plan. First full day of **Ramadan**.
March 2	Abandoning the terms of the second phase, Israel proposes to extend the first-phase ceasefire for 7 more weeks and demands Hamas release half the remaining living hostages and half the deceased. (Of the 59 Israeli hostages remaining in Gaza, 24 are thought to be alive.) Netanyahu closes all crossings into Gaza and blocks entry of humanitarian aid.
March 4	Arab leaders meet in Cairo and endorse Egypt's $53 billion plan to restore Gaza. The plan has 3 components: interim measures, reconstruction, and governance. Israel continues to back Trump's plan to displace Gazans.

March 8	ICE detains **Mahmoud Khalil** (Palestinian/Syrian/Algerian, born to Palestinian refugees from Tiberias; US green card holder; Columbia U. graduate) but does not charge him. Campus protests he led against the Gaza assault are alleged to be antisemitic and to foster a hostile environment for Jewish students at Columbia.
March 10	Jesse Furman, district judge of New York, halts attempts to deport Khalil.
March 13	On behalf of Khalil and other students, the Council on American–Islamic Relations sues Columbia and Barnard College for disclosing student records to the Education and Workforce Committee of the U.S. House of Representatives, allegedly to avoid losing federal funding. At a Jewish Voice for Peace sit-in at Trump Tower in New York protesting Khalil's detention, about 100 are arrested.
March 15	Israeli drone attack kills 9 journalists and volunteers with UK charity Al-Khair Foundation setting up tents for displaced Palestinians. During the 2 months of "ceasefire" that began on Jan. 19, Israel has killed 170.
March 17	UNOCHA releases a report on casualties since Israel launched its assault on Gaza. Palestinians: 48,577 fatalities, 112,041 injuries. Israelis: 407 fatalities, 2,584 injuries.
March 18	Netanyahu announces that Israel is abandoning phase 2 of the ceasefire negotiations and resuming their full assault. With White House approval, Israel conducts major airstrikes across Gaza, by far the largest since the ceasefire began. The Gaza Health Ministry reports more than 400 killed (including entire families and 5 senior Hamas officials) and 500 wounded. Itamar Ben-Gvir announces his return to Netanyahu's governing coalition. Deadly Israeli strikes continue daily.

March 19   Tanks and infantry enter central Gaza at the **Netzarim Corridor**.

March 21   Defense Minister **Israel Katz** announces the IDF will seize and retain parts of the Gaza Strip if hostages are not released.

March 23   Israel's security cabinet approves a directorate that will help Gazans "voluntarily" depart to a third state. Golani brigade soldiers attack humanitarian vehicles (marked and illuminated) in southern Rafah, shooting occupants at close range, killing 10 Red Crescent workers, 6 Civil Defense emergency responders, and a UN worker. They bury the dead in mass graves and bulldoze and crush ambulances, a fire truck, and a UN vehicle. The missing bodies are not found for 8 days. (A later Israeli military report will say the killings were caused by "several professional failures, breaches of orders, and a failure to fully report the incident.")

Israel strikes the Nasser Hospital, destroying a surgery department and killing Ismail Barhoum, a Hamas political bureau member, and others.

March 25   Hundreds of Gazans protest Hamas, calling for its overthrow.

March 27   Physicians for Human Rights report that 24 medical workers in Israeli detention are facing extreme violence and humiliation.

April 3   The Gaza Health Ministry's official death toll in Gaza reaches 50,523.

Select Bibliography on Israel/Palestine History

Adwan, Sami, Dan Bar-On, and Eyal Naveh, eds. *Side by Side: Parallel Histories of Israel-Palestine*. New York: The New Press, 2012.

Dowty, Alan. *Israel/Palestine*. 5th ed. Cambridge: Polity, 2023.

Filiu, Jean-Pierre. *Gaza: A History*. New York: Oxford University Press, 2014.

Gilbert, Martin. *Israel: A History*. New York: Harper, 1998, 2008.

Khalidi, Rashid. *The Hundred Years' War on Palestine: A History of Settler Colonialism and Resistance, 1917–2017*. New York: Metropolitan, 2020.

Kramer, Gudrun. *A History of Palestine: From the Ottoman Conquest to the Founding of the State of Israel*. Princeton, NJ: Princeton University Press, 2008.

Masalha, Nur. *Palestine: A Four Thousand Year History*. London: Zed Books, 1999.

Morris, Benny. *Righteous Victims: A History of the Zionist-Arab Conflict, 1881–2001*. New York: Vintage, 2001.

Pappé, Ilan. *The Biggest Prison on Earth: A History of Gaza and the Occupied Territories*. London: One World, 2017.

———. *The Ethnic Cleansing of Palestine*. Oxford: One World, 2006.

———. *A Very Short History of the Israel-Palestine Conflict*. London: One World, 2024.

Slater, Jerome. *Mythologies Without End: The US, Israel, and the Arab-Israeli Conflict, 1917–2020*. New York: Oxford University Press, 2020.

Smith, Charles D. *Palestine and the Arab-Israeli Conflict: A History with Documents*. 10th ed. New York: Bedford/St. Martin's, 2020.

www.ingramcontent.com/pod-product-compliance
Lightning Source LLC
Chambersburg PA
CBHW031416230426
43668CB00007B/322